MW00659030

Diane

Joe Montalbano

Guilherme Motta

REGISTERED

NO. 120 OF 500

AUTOGRAPHED COPY

AGILE *Almanac*

BOOK 2: PROGRAMS WITH MULTI- AND VIRTUAL-TEAM ENVIRONMENTS

AGILE *Almanac*

BOOK 2: PROGRAMS WITH MULTI- AND VIRTUAL-TEAM ENVIRONMENTS

JOHN G. STENBECK, LEAD AUTHOR, AND
JOE MONTALBANO, MARK PHILLIPY, DIANE BRADY,
JAMES SPERRY, STEVEN M. McGEE, SR., MICHAEL WILLIAMS,
GUILHERME MOTTA, DOUG MARTIN, NICHOLE TUBIOLO,
DIANE McCANN, AND RICK A. MORRIS, CO-AUTHORS

First Edition

GR8 PM

Traditional. Agile. Hybrid.

Spokane, WA

Agile Almanac

Book 2: PROGRAMS WITH MULTI- AND VIRTUAL-TEAM ENVIRONMENTS

John G. Stenbeck, Lead Author, and Joe Montalbano, Mark Phillipy, Diane Brady, James Sperry, Steven M. McGee, Sr., Michael Williams, Guilherme Motta, Doug Martin, Nichole Tubiolo, Diane McCann, and Rick A. Morris, Co-Authors.

Published by:

GR8PM, Inc.
1818 W. Francis Ave. #228, Spokane, WA 99205 USA
(619) 890-5807
custserv@gr8pm.com; http://www.gr8pm.com/

ISBN-13: 978-0-9846693-7-0

This book includes material based on the Project Management Institute, *A Guide to the Project Management Body of Knowledge, (PMBOK® Guide) – Fifth Edition, Project Management Institute, Inc. 2012.*

The book also contains many references to other registered terms such as PMP®, PgMP®, CAPM®, PMI-SP®, PMI-RMP®, or PMI-ACP®, which are registered marks of the Project Management Institute, Inc.

TABLE OF
CONTENTS

Table of Contents

FOREWORD

James R. Snyder | *PMI Founder*

If you are looking for the elusive, and probably non-existent, silver bullet for all your project, Program, and Portfolio management issues, this is not the right book for you! However, if you want a practical approach to the management of complex project problems, and some insights into the integration of your projects across your whole enterprise, then please read on. This exciting approach to using the Agile processes offers new and well thought out ideas and best practices that will go a long way to making sense out of the ever-changing, chaotic, project management environment in which we all live and work. This high-speed, high-risk environment is the world of managing project oriented work, is a part of every profession, and impacts every part of our working life.

The author of this book, John Stenbeck, has made significant contributions to the project management profession as a major supporter of the understanding and application of Agile processes and practices across a number of industries and disciplines. His relaxed, pragmatic application of Agile techniques to complex project management problems has been well received in many major corporations, and has contributed significantly to project completion success rates. He calls it the way he sees it and is not tied to the blind application of any one set of tools and methods.

The *Agile Almanac – Book 1* brought together the science behind the best Agile practices helping to define the choices for implementation of these tools to appropriate projects in appropriate ways. By gathering all the best practices of both historic project management and the newer, emerging methods for managing project oriented work; John developed a guide for application in the field, not just in the minds of developers and consultants. Now, with help from a distinguished, international group of co-authors, including Rick Morris, an evangelist for project management who is a practitioner, consultant, author, mentor and expert, they have assembled a vast collection of knowledge and practical experience to show us the next steps in using Agile methods in the bigger world of multi-project Programs. Their work builds on the use of Agile and classic technology to solve the problems of large multi-projects environments of today.

This book takes the next step up in the hierarchy of project management by moving from the management of smaller, unrelated, single projects to the much more complex, chaotic, and inter-related planning and management of large integrated projects, Programs, and Portfolios. This book provides a well-documented look at the inter-relationships between projects and Programs, and examines the existing Frameworks for project/Program integration. It also unveils the development, design, and implementation of the emerging Agile Integration Framework for large, inter-related, multi-project Programs as a new tool to deal with the complex project mix that represents the business environment we live in today.

This new approach scales Agile to encompass the broad, complex, and inter-dependent nature of the environment found in most major businesses, and uses some very basic project management processes to do so by using PMI's *PMBOK® Guide.* The new Agile Integrated Framework developed here suggests that Critical Path Method (CPM) analysis be used to identify and clarify projects and their specific activities, which will be key in improving enterprise-wide total project performance. While the new immerging Framework for scaling Agile for large projects, Programs, and Portfolios relies heavily on both Traditional project management tools as well as the newer Agile processes and techniques, it retains the flexibility of the Agile process. It strongly supports and empowers teams to optimize project performance throughout the entire enterprise.

As Project Managers of today, we are well beyond the notion that all projects are alike and can be managed in the same way. Those of us with more than the early signs of gray hair know that just the opposite is true in the real project world. No two projects are ever the same, and no two projects can be managed using the same tools, in the same way, every time. Just as projects are unique and dynamic so must be the approach to their management. Over the last fifty years, we have seen the rise and fall of a number of "right and only" ways to manage project work. The failure of these approaches can be laid at the feet of the very nature of a project – all are unique and dynamic, and so must be their management. In the Agile Integrated Framework we see an approach, which recognizes the need for integrated, flexible solutions to project and Program management. What we have needed is a Framework that not only integrates the large and inter-connected projects in a business venture, but also the tools, processes and techniques available to manage them. This book takes us a long way towards meeting that need.

I think that you will find one of the most engaging aspects of this work is that it is not just an academic adventure into a new approach to solving a major project management issue, but also a practical guide to making the solution work. You will find some excellent examples of how to make these new ideas for the scaling of Agile approaches to the integrated management of larger, and more complex, projects and Programs accompanied with the research-backed reasoning for making it all work.

You will learn a lot that will be immediately applicable to your business and enjoy the style and no nonsense approach of the writing! Have fun and prepare to scale your Agile processes to handle all your project work.

FOREWORD

Troy Hazard | *Serial Entrepreneur, Best Selling Author*

For 25 years, I have bought and sold companies, in different industries, in different countries, for different opportunities. Key to that process is to understand how to add enterprise value to the business, and manage the project from zero to hero, leaving the business in a better place than when we arrived. Sound familiar?

Along this journey the core to our commercial intelligence has been our ability recognize perception over reality, truth over fear, and commerciality over confidence. To do that, we've learned we need to be both practitioner and philosopher; and there is a fine line between the two.

The practitioner actually practices what they preach. The philosophizer muses over what could be.

The *Agile Almanac – Book 2* is a classic representation of how to merge practice with philosophy, and turn what could be into what should be.

John Stenbeck helps you look beyond the practical message to the philosophical, personal application in your business and life, to enlighten you on a path to be the unicorn amongst peers.

If you are seeking to drive your business or career from what could be to what should be, then this book is a personal program management Roadmap. It will challenge your thought process and approach, and redefine the way you add enterprise value to every Program on the path to the outcome you seek.

FOREWORD

John Gates, Ph.D. | *Partner, Avion Consulting*

As a management consultant, I regularly work with leaders, teams, and organizations striving to succeed in an ever more complex and challenging environment. Specific challenges that the clients I serve face on a daily basis include increasingly lofty customer demands, pressure to continuously improve products and services, and in many cases, an expectation on the part of both internal and external stakeholders that excellent results be achieved with fewer resources.

These challenges are evident and pronounced in every industry in which we work – for-profit, not-for-profit, and everything in between. Of course, successful organizations, and those who lead them, understand that every challenge represents an opportunity. Those that lean into such challenges, and find ways to turn them to their advantage, are the ones that thrive. There are many keys to successfully navigating these turbulent waters, including having the right vision and strategy, effective leadership, and employee engagement.

But, in our experience, a key differentiator between the winners and losers in today's turbulent business environment is effective program and project management. One of the true thought leaders in this field today is John Stenbeck, author of the best-selling *"Agile Almanac – Book 1,"* and now lead-author of the new *"Agile Almanac – Book 2."* In this second volume in the Agile Almanac Series, Stenbeck and his co-authors, all Agile luminaries, expertly guide practitioners through Agile Program Management best practices that have been widely used and proven to be reliable. Beyond that, the authors challenge common wisdom and provide, in essence, a graduate-level education to anyone interested in the field of Program and project management.

The first volume in this Agile Almanac Series deals with single-team projects, whereas Book 2 addresses challenges associated with projects and programs being executed in environments that include the use of multiple teams with virtual, remote, and distributed elements. Written in a very practical way, such that the reader can focus on content that is most specific to one's own environment and specific concerns, this book is an essential resource for virtually anybody in any organization with responsibility for ensuring that Agile Program Management best practices are being used to get the best possible results from projects, programs, and portfolios.

PART ONE

INTRODUCTION

CHAPTER

1

Critical Foundation

Overview

Over the last 5 years I have been privileged to speak at more than 250 events and engage in focused discussions with more than 3,000 active Agile practitioners. Their collective wisdom has allowed me to combine a rarely-seen, cogent assessment of Agile factors. The elite team of co-authors, who have invested extensive amounts of time putting together this second book in the Agile Almanac, likewise endorsed this assessment then leveraged it to maximize the value of every chapter in this field guide and desk reference.

The vision of this book is to act like a Rosetta stone for Program Managers to help stakeholders, executives, and technical development professionals by providing a common lexicon to use to speak with one another in understandable terms.

Agile has been part of the technical and technology world in the past. Simply recall RAD, RUP, and Spiral and your mind will begin to fill with the many other fads and flavors-of-the-month that briefly held sway. But there is something quantifiably different about Scrum and the many variants that have come forth since the *Agile Manifesto* was published in 2001. Some unseen force seems to have been at work to foster the broad adoption, acceptance, and undeniable success of Agile. This same force also seems to have moved beyond the current body of knowledge shared and published in Scrum-aligned circles.

Agile has operated with a hero-centric organizational model, which is part of the reason many practitioners and teams love it – because being a hero is intoxicating! However, hero-centric models are self-limiting and organizationally unsustainable. Scaling Agile will require a post-heroic organizational model that empowers and enables teams and individuals to be their best while also optimizing the throughput of the whole enterprise.

A required foundation for successfully implementing, then scaling, Agile is an understanding of the factor or factors driving organizations of every size, shape, and variety to use – or at least attempt to use – Agile.

This chapter will help set a foundation for success using and scaling Agile. It will also lay out the structure of this book and suggest how to use it. Mastering this content will benefit everyone in the organization in many ways.

Technology as an Enabler of Chaotic Expectations

Between approximately 1980 and 2015 the transistors on integrated circuits (IC) increased in density from roughly 50 thousand to nearly 10 billion. The

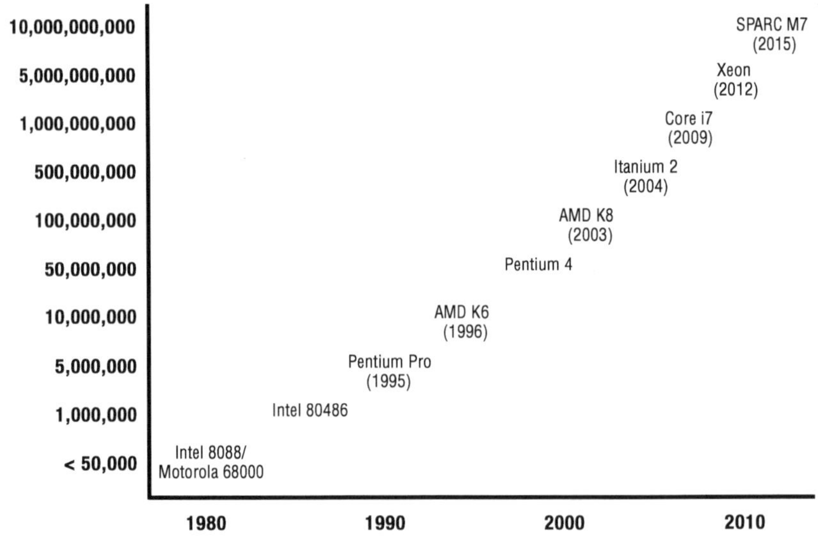

Figure 1.01 | Transistors per Integrated Circuit (IC)

trajectory, which resembled the "Moore's Law" forecast made by Gordon Moore in 1965, has unlocked profound and nearly unimaginable improvements in the capabilities, miniaturization, and integration of devices of all kinds. *(See Figure 1.01.)*

The increased density on ICs expanded approximately 1,000 rough orders of magnitude (ROM), where a ROM is defined as 10 times greater than the base. *(See Figure 1.02.)* This expansion in processing capacity has had an impact comparable to humans harnessing fire and developing the steam engine. Both fire and steam engines unlocked profound eras of opportunity while simultaneously triggering avalanches of increased societal complexity.

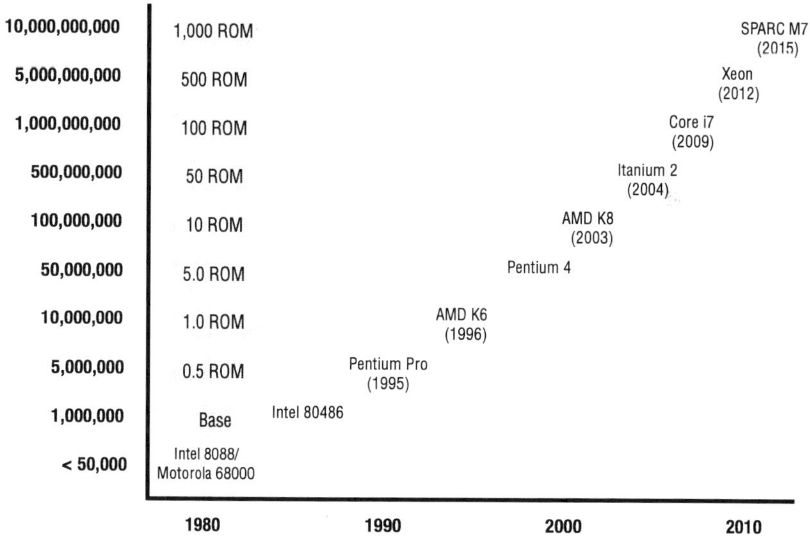

Figure 1.02 | Transistors per Integrated Circuit (IC)

The improvement of ICs has unleashed an era of profound opportunity while triggering a tsunami of technical complexity.

That technical power and complexity can be seen in the growth of the Internet during the same timeframe. The number of hosts grew from 213 with ARPANET to 1 billion a few years ago, as shown in *Figure 1.03*. Users grew from a small cadre of technically-gifted geeks to approximately one-third of the global population while content grew from isolated, esoteric topics to every imaginable category, in every language used by humankind.

The growth of the Internet made it the most universal platform for communication in the history of humanity. It also induced a non-linear

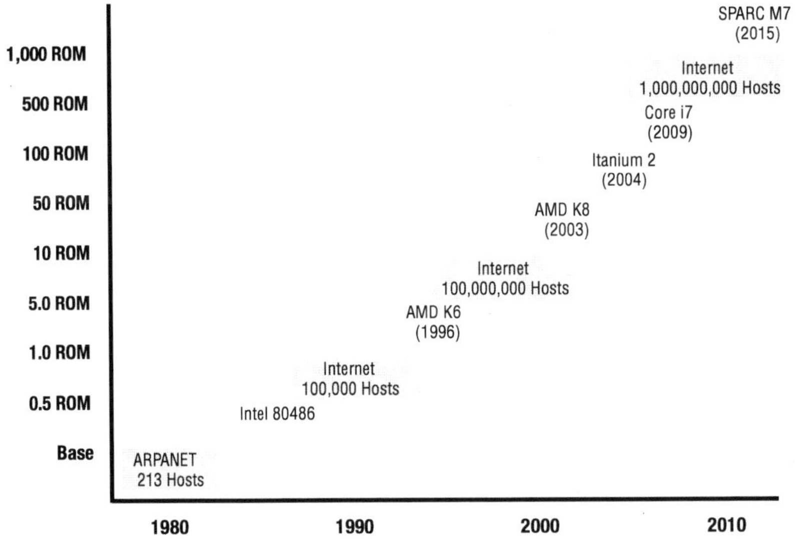

Figure 1.03 | Internet Growth

increase in communication complexity. The amount of information available is increasing at such a rapid rate, exceeding the ability of anyone to comprehensively organize, assess, or consume it.

The communication complexity has been amplified by the number of ways the Internet can be accessed, manipulated, and leveraged to, for example, create derivatives or services based on the information. *(See Figure 1.04.)*

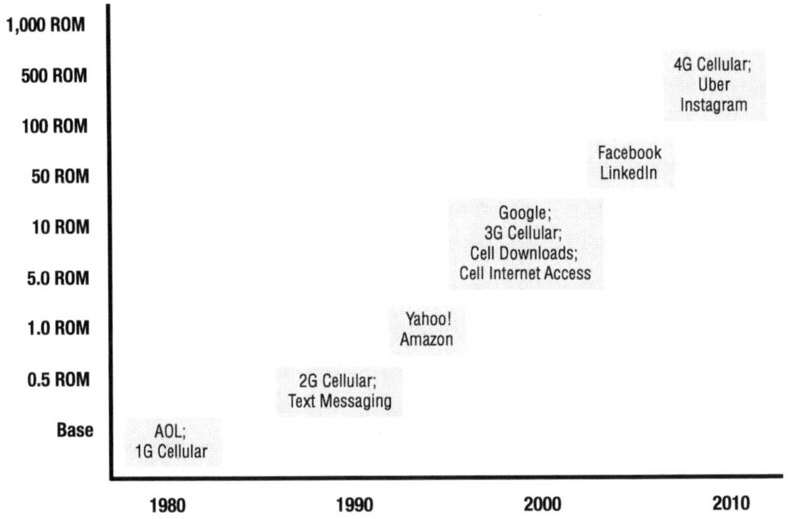

Figure 1.04 | Customer Expectation Complexity

One critical outcome of this unbridled growth in sources of information, channels for accessing it, and tools for manipulating it has been a correlated growth in the complexity of customer expectations.

Organizations can now reach customers or constituents anywhere, anytime on the globe. Consequently, those same customers and constituents are suffering from information overload greater than any other time in history. Conversely, they can also find sources for anything imaginable, from anywhere on the globe, but the volume of choices has become a bewildering array of indecipherable confusion. Simultaneously, this group has learned, between Amazon, Google, and Facebook, that they can have anything they want almost immediately, for near-zero cost.

The result is a business environment of chaotic, unrealistic expectations enabled by seemingly unlimited technological advancements colliding with the proverbial laws of physics.

Project Management as an Antidote to Chaotic Expectations

Seeking a way to manage, or even benefit from, these chaotic, unrealistic expectations, businesses and organizations of every type turned to project management as the solution. One measure of this interest can be seen in the growth of the Project Management Institute (PMI) from 10,000 members in 1994 to over 750,000 certified Project Management Professionals (PMP®) in January 2017. *(Figure 1.05.)*

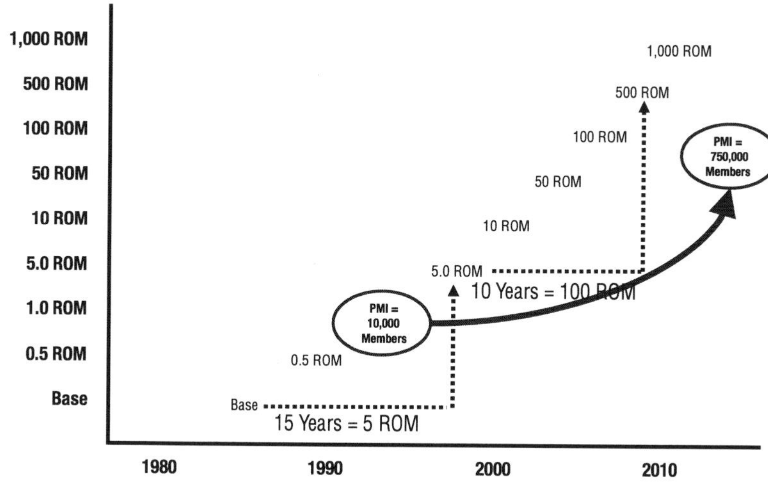

Figure 1.05 | Project Management Complexity

PMI's approach, commonly called the Traditional or Waterfall methodology, is cataloged in various editions of *A Guide to the Project Management Body of Knowledge, (PMBOK® Guide).* Amongst the generally accepted principles the *PMBOK® Guide* offers are guidelines that correlate levels of estimation with percentage of design completion and expected accuracy ranges for forecasts. The Rough Order of Magnitude (ROM) level of estimates are used when the Design Completion is less than ten (10%) percent and have an expected range of accuracy of +100% to – 50%. The Budgetary level of estimates are used when the Design Completion is approximately 15% to 25% complete and have an expected range of accuracy of +30% to – 15%. The Definitive level of estimates are used when the Design Completion is approximately 45% to 100% complete and have an expected range of accuracy of +15% to – 5%. *(See Figure 1.06.)*

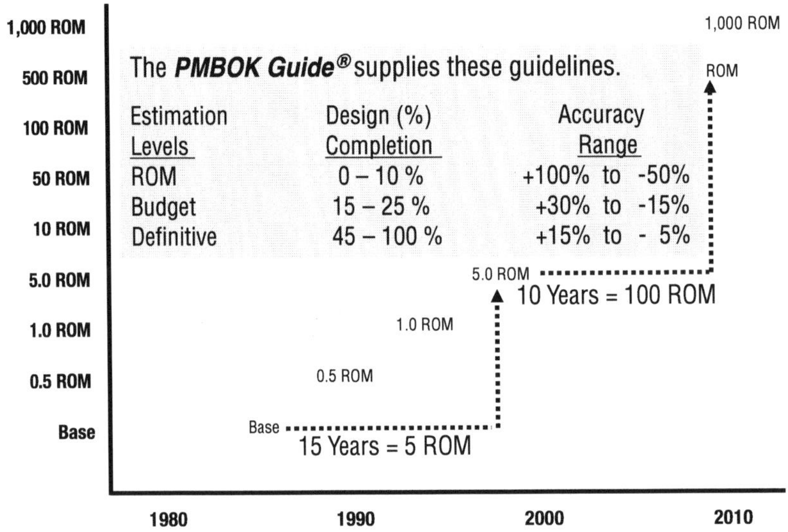

Figure 1.06 | Project Management Complexity

The PMBOK® Guide approach was apparently adequate during the years prior to 1990. But as the acceleration of environmental complexity became non-linear, growing evidence emerged that the estimating standards were inadequate. The biennial Chaos Report (from the Standish Group) became known as the seminal authority on the topic. When the first report was published in 1994 it created an awareness of a critical problem and fueled the perception of PMI as the source of the solution and certified PMP®s as the practitioners delivering it. In the years since, the Chaos Reports have shown the reality that project outcomes have remained mostly static. The results show that only about one third of projects are in the category defined as "Success", one third are "Challenged", and one third are "Failed."

It became clear that something more needed to be done. In a variety of places, people and organizations began using ideas from product development best practices and Lean Principles to create a better solution. And unlike the environment years before when RAD, RUP, Spiral, and a host of other iterative methods emerged but failed to gain widespread traction, a fertile environment, driven by the collision of technical capability, communication complexity, and customer demand, arose. *(See Figure 1.07.)*

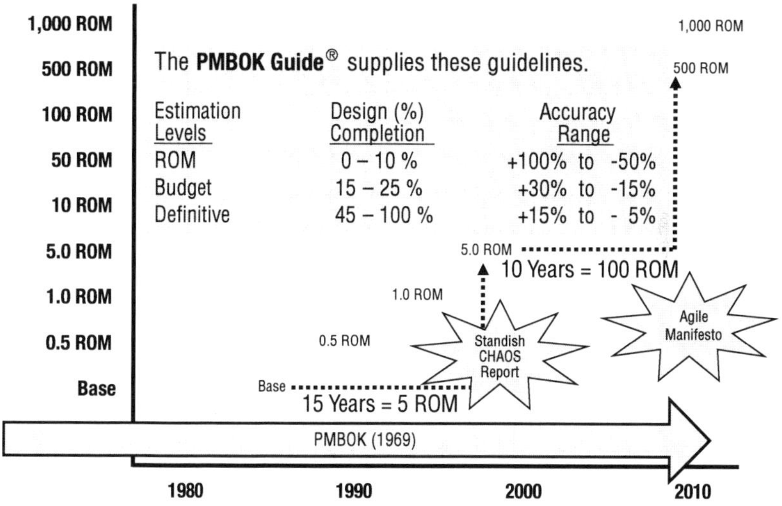

Figure 1.07 | Project Management Complexity

Scrum as an Antidote to Chaotic Expectations

In 2001, seventeen software development thought leaders met at the Snowbird Ski Resort in Utah and wrote the *Agile Manifesto,* launching the Scrum Alliance into this fertile environment. The conditions were excellent and their thinking was clearly articulated, allowing the Scrum Framework to gain widespread traction.

In particular, the focus on iterative development, anchored by customer involvement, proved to be a powerful application of Lean Principles to the non-linear complexity of the environment. That non-linear complexity came to be expressed by the concept of a Cone of Uncertainty where a difficult problem was overcome by incremental steps towards the solution. Each step forward eliminated one or more of the unknown factors or challenges. It also helped the intended beneficiary – referred to as the Customer, but included any key stakeholders – to clarify what the solution needed to accomplish in order to create value. *(See Figure 1.08.)*

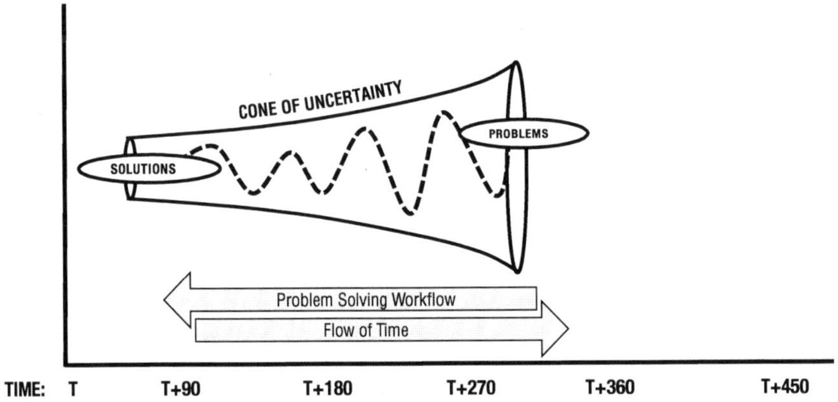

Figure 1.08 | Project Management and Non-Linear Complexity

The combination of continuous Product improvement and continuous Process improvement produced desirable, even amazing, results for many challenging projects dealing with the non-linear distortion of time and size. It did so by leveraging Test-Driven Development (TDD) to deal with distortion caused by size. Additionally, it drastically lowered the cost of producing forecasts with an appropriate planning-level of accuracy to deal with the time distortion.

It turned out to be 'synthesized genius' that integrated project management and Lean Principles to solve near-term issues as the path to an overall solution. Even though the principles behind this breakthrough were not specifically identified in the Scrum Guide, the Scrum Framework worked for its many adherents. It provided a path forward to good results in a chaotic environment, but on a limited scale.

Today's situation benefits from the 15 years of experimentation and adaptation that has occurred using Scrum and its variants. However, the situation now fits the adage often ascribed to Einstein that 'the level of thinking that got us here is not the level of thinking needed to solve the problems that face us here.' To solve the problems we face now, we must ask, "What is the intelligent way forward from here?"

Proven Principles as a Solution to Competitive Complexity and Uncertainty

Responding to market forces and customer demand, in 2011, PMI committed itself to developing a certification program and called it the PMI Agile Certified Practitioner (PMI-ACP®). The program was launched in 2012 and became the fastest growing certification in PMI history, even outpacing the Project Management Professionals (PMP®) standard bearer, exceeding 15,000 certification holders by the end of 2016. Because of that indisputable evidence, PMI's leadership decided that an almost unprecedented update to the *PMBOK® Guide* was required.

The *PMBOK® Guide Sixth Edition* was released in 2017. It included Agile content in every single Knowledge Area, a change so fundamental, the *PMBOK® Guide* was released, in unprecedented fashion, in English and 10 other languages simultaneously.

The *PMBOK® Guide Sixth Edition* is an important milestone in the drive to find the most intelligent way forward, but it is not the solution. *(See Figure 1.09.)* It will play a significant role in developing the solution, but is not the sole source of it. Because the solution must effectively respond to changes far larger than those currently being managed using Scrum or one of the other "Big 5" Agile Frameworks – Scrum, XP, Lean Software Development, Kanban, or Hybrid – none of them is the sole source of the solution either. Agile will also play a significant role in developing the solution, but it, alone, is not the sole source of it.

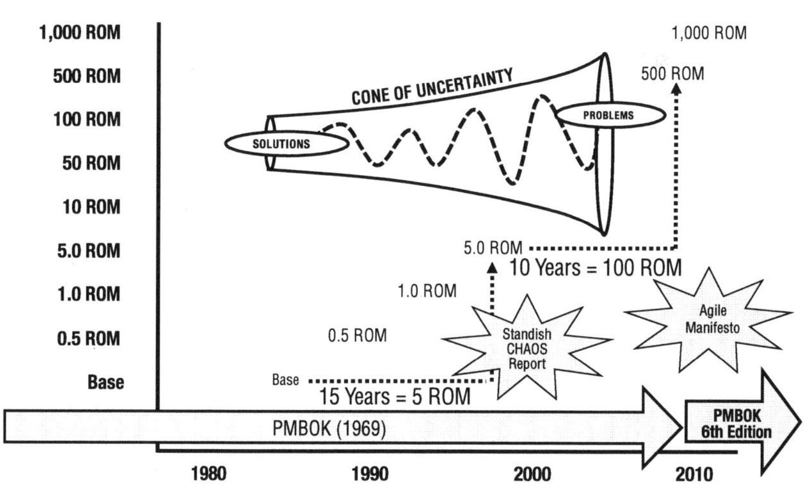

Figure 1.09 | Project Management and Non-Linear Complexity

The solution will be found using integrative thinking – a "both/and" not an "either/or" model. The solution must employ principles proven to be effective across many industries and not limited to just one, such as software. It must have a comprehensive understanding of the marketplace challenges caused by non-linear complexity and uncertainty and apply proven principles supported by a set of tools that can cope with the demands of iterative, interactive planning, and development while also complying with rigorous Generally Accepted Accounting Principles (GAAP). It must accomplish all of that while integrating the important differences in planning and implementing responsive changes to customer demands in an environment where the ROM levels of change are historically unprecedented.

The *PMBOK® Guide Sixth Edition,* while important, lacks the required expertise to progressively elaborate from strategic long-term planning with, perhaps, 15 or more ROM levels of change in order to feed subsequent levels of planning down to operational planning with a far more manageable 1 ROM level of change. Conversely, the existing "Big 5" Agile Frameworks, while important, are well adapted only to operational planning with 1 ROM level of variation and lack tools for handling budgets or scaling planning and scheduling to the long-term with 15+ ROM levels of variation. *(See Figure 1.10.)*

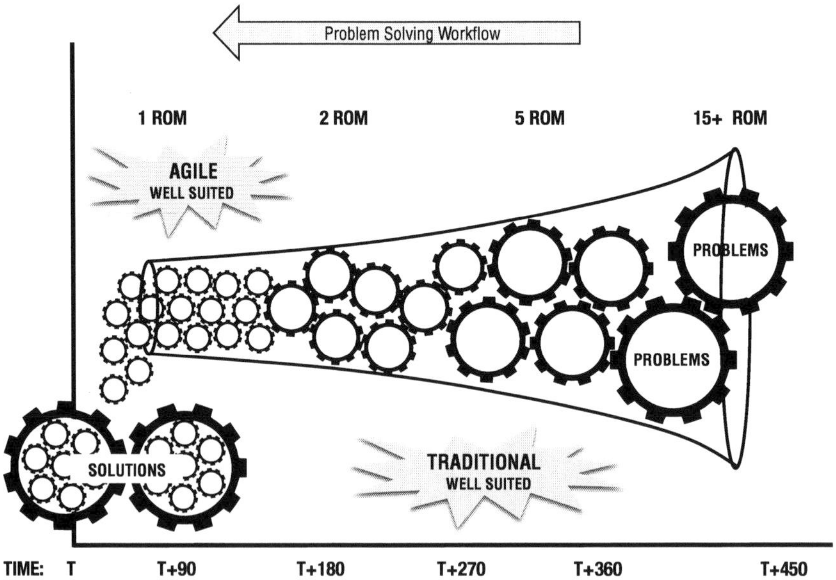

Figure 1.10 | Business Management: Non-Linear Complexity and Uncertainty

Therefore, the solution to this must employ integrative "both/and" thinking where proven principles offer a comprehensive model that supports robust, reliable decision-making in spite of non-linear distortion caused by long timeframes and massive sizes of the desired outcomes.

The solution can be found at the overlapping intersection of the *PMBOK® Guide*, the "Big 5", and traditional business schools, all of which have developed planning principles acknowledging various aspects of the problem while using different lexicons to describe it. *(See Figure 1.11.)*

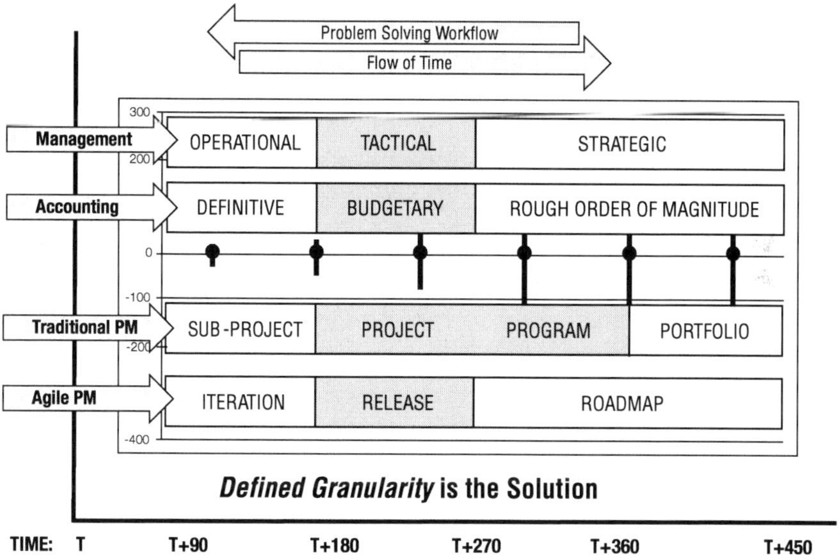

Figure 1.11 | **Business Management: Non-Linear Complexity and Uncertainty**

They all share the unarticulated understanding of the Cone of Uncertainty and the non-linear nature of time and size distortion causing it. They all also lack a full response to the technical, communication, and customer expectation complexity and uncertainty facing organizations today, as shown previously.

The vision of Book 2 of the Agile Almanac series is to provide an all-encompassing assessment of scaling Agile in the mid-term, tactical environment preceding operational planning, which was covered in Book 1.

Part One begins with a highly insightful discussion of the interrelationships between Project, Program, and Portfolio Management with an eye to supporting Program Managers, Project Management Offices (PMO), directors, and business unit leaders. It also includes a highly practical discussion of Agile Myths, Misconceptions, and Anti-Patterns.

Part Two provides a comprehensive evaluation of the existing and emerging Frameworks – including Scrum of Scrums (SoS), Scaled Agile Framework (SAFe), Large Scale Scrum (LeSS), Disciplined Agile Delivery (DAD), Kanban, DevOps, and the *PMBOK® Guide Sixth Edition.* It then moves beyond the current Frameworks, introducing the ***Agile Integration Framework***, a true "Graduate School" approach to scaling Agile across enterprises in private, public, and non-profit domains.

The ***Agile Integration Framework*** will address how to optimize the whole organizational process from "Ideation" to delivery of "Customer Delight". It will demonstrate how to minimize the sub-optimization of development teams while maximizing enterprise throughput so the organization thrives in its battles to acquire the dollar-denoted votes of constituents and consumers.

Part Three delivers a comprehensive discussion of how to deal with environments complicated by Multiple-Teams and Virtual/Remote resources, a need for robust Estimating, Scheduling, and Scope and Integration management, and the intractable challenges of Risk, Quality, and Budget management.

Part Four closes out the book with two Appendices. The first Appendix provides an incomparable set of Academic Resources to support corporate trainers, university professors, and business researchers. The second Appendix is an unparalleled, top-to-bottom, roadmap and walk-through of how to organize and implement the toolset needed to cope with the demands of iterative, interactive planning and development while also complying with rigorous Generally Accepted Accounting Principles (GAAP). It details how to accomplish all of that while integrating responsive changes to customer demands in an environment where the ROM levels of change are historically unprecedented.

For any Program Manager to be a true professional, they must have proven tools and techniques that meet the needs of programs across every domain. They must also be able to effectively share and apply them in ways that empower program performance. That means they must host lunch and learns, speak convincingly to key stakeholders, and unlock important, yet intangible customer loyalty. These resources equip them to do exactly that!

Henry Ford once said, "Thinking is the hardest work there is, which is probably the reason so few engage in it!" The co-authors of the Agile Almanac - Book 2 have joined the "few" in order to provide a "short cut" to accelerate careers and save years of research and study. It is our solemn belief that this work will enable an organization, its vision, and the stakeholders it serves to reach the leading edge of market leadership.

Understanding Almanac - Book 2

The goal of this book is to serve the global community by offering only best practices that have been widely used and proven reliable. It presents recognized principles wherever they have been found and brings a unique perspective to the divergent, often conflicting and accusatory, viewpoints expressed by various "evangelists" who have created a "battlefield" with an absence of thought leadership.

Experience in delivering projects encompassing an immense number of industries and institutions has convinced us that Agile can, and must, be scaled as an extension of Lean Principles using integrative thinking at the overlapping intersection of the *PMBOK® Guide,* "Big 5" Agile Frameworks, and traditional business schools.

This book is going to increase Agile Program Management expertise and move an organization from playing checkers to playing chess when designing and executing programs!

How the Almanac Helps Practitioners and Organizations

The Agile Almanac book series allows practitioners and organizations to select precisely the content they need and zero in on applying it in the ways best suited to the context of their environments. We often remind students that the organization does not care whether they use Traditional methods, Agile techniques, or Aunt Suzy's recipe. The organization only cares about results! In fact, they demand results as the validation that the Program Manager is a professional.

At the highest level, the Agile domain can be divided into three sub-domains - Single-team Projects and Exam Prep, Programs with Multi- and Virtual-Team Environments, and Portfolio Management and Enterprise Scaling. Each sub-domain is covered in its own book.

Book 1: Single-Team Projects & Exam Prep (*Amazon #1 Best Seller* upon release, 12/2015) Covers Agile Project Management, Lean Principles, and the "Big 5" Agile Frameworks:

- Scrum
- eXtreme Programming (XP)
- Lean Software Development (LSD)
- Kanban Basic Practices
- Hybrid Project Management

Book 1 focuses on the needs of individual practitioners, whether highly experienced or new to Agile Project Management, and provides detailed insight and analysis regarding if, when, and how to use the "Big 5" Frameworks. It also includes solid preparation for PMI's Agile Certified Practitioner (PMI-ACP®) exam.

It has been extended with an On-Demand training course (which also became an *Amazon #1 Best Seller* just 5 hours after release, 09/2016).

Book 2: Programs with Multi- and Virtual-Team Environments *(this book)* Co-authored by Agile luminaries with a focus on the needs of Program Managers and organizations dealing with the challenges of large programs being executed in environments that include the use of multiple and/or virtual, remote, and distributed teams.

It provides insight and help for organizations whether they are a public agency, department or command competing for tax dollars in budget battles, or a commercial entity battling for consumer dollars.

Book 3: Portfolios and Enterprise Scaling (planned release in Q2, 2018)

- Agile Portfolio Management
- Agile Maturity Matrix Instrument (AMMI Assessment)
- Scaling Agile to the Enterprise

Book Three will be focused on the needs of organizational leaders and senior practitioners supporting Project Management Offices (PMOs), portfolios, and strategic decision-making. It will include an assessment instrument, analysis tools, and planning techniques that optimize total throughput within overall resource limits. It will provide insight that increases the top and bottom line as well as employee engagement.

Important Structural Highlights and Conventions of Book 2

PART ONE - INTRODUCTION

Part One covers the interrelationships between Project, Program, and Portfolio Management. These chapters are written with an eye to supporting Program Managers, Project Management Offices (PMO), directors, and business unit leaders. It also includes a highly practical discussion of Agile Myths, Misconceptions, and Anti-Patterns.

PART TWO - FRAMEWORKS

Part Two covers Scrum of Scrums (SoS), Kanban, DevOps, Scaled Agile Framework (SAFe), Disciplined Agile Delivery (DAD), Large Scale Scrum (LeSS), the *PMBOK® Guide Sixth Edition,* and the Agile Integration Framework (AIF).

The structure of each chapter in Part Two will follow a shared format in order to aid the reader with making cross-comparisons. The structure is:

Overview

Benefits / Challenges

Description of Program-level Attributes for:

- Roles
- Workflow
- Ceremonies
- Artifacts

How to Make it Work Effectively

Tools and Practices Recommendations

PART THREE - APPLIED SCALED AGILE

Part Three, with a perspective focused on program-level execution, covers Agile with Multi-Team Environments, Estimating and Scope Management, Integration and Scheduling, and Risk, Quality, and Budget Management.

The structure of each chapter in Part Three will share the same format as Part Two.

PART FOUR - APPENDICES

Each Appendix in Part Four will be an unparalleled, top-to-bottom, resource that is historically unprecedented. Appendix A – Academic Resources provides an immense cache of specific resources to support professors and trainers. Appendix B – Advanced Toolset provides specific, detailed information for configuring the tools teams, Program Managers, and PMOs need.

PART FIVE - ABOUT THE AUTHORS & RESOURCES

Part Five includes sections for About the Authors, Editor, and Graphic Designer, and Glossary and Index.

CHAPTER

2

Agile Myths, Misconceptions, and Anti-Patterns

Overview

This chapter shares, explores, analyzes, and debunks the most common myths, misconceptions, and anti-patterns plaguing serious Agile practitioners and the organizations they serve. The information and fact-based arguments presented will assist readers in becoming effective change agents by empowering them to overcome the typical resistance encountered when stakeholders have heard or experienced the negative repercussions caused by these myths, misconceptions, and anti-patterns. It is critical to the success of any Agile leader shouldering the responsibility of leading a journey toward Agile transformation, or even a limited Agile adoption, that they be forewarned because as the old saying goes, "Fore-warned is fore-armed!" Anti-patterns will be explored in a role-based examination of common dysfunctions. It will be followed by an exploration of common Agile myths and misconceptions. The final section will address myths and misconceptions specific to scaled Agile environments.

Before beginning, here's a note about dogma. Agile is a values and principles based philosophy complete with its own "Manifesto." Most popular Agile Frameworks even have their own corresponding set of values and principles. Because these Frameworks and Agile thinking are based on values, many "dogmatic" wars develop among colleagues, especially in the early stages of an Agile adoption. "That's not Scrum!" is often heard with its sibling, "That's not even Agile!" usually following not far behind. Many such battles are waged between, and among, people who have just returned from their first Agile training and notice that what is being implemented, especially if it is at scale, is not exactly the Agile they were taught. Further, only a small portion of projects are done with a pure Agile approach, with many using a hybrid approach. Readers are urged to view Agility as a continuum and the journey to Agility as one that is never complete.

When implementing Agile in an organization, the question that should be asked isn't necessarily, "Is this pure Agile?" The answer will usually be "No" because it is the wrong question. Asking better questions leads to better answers. Some questions to consider include the following. If their answers are yes, they are probably a good starting point.

- "Is this method more in line with Agile values and principles than what was being used before?"
- "Does this approach provide transparency along with opportunities for inspection and adaptation?"
- "Does this method move the organization closer to building an environment that embraces the four Agile values and the 12 Agile principles?"
- "Is this method the best method for this project and this team?"

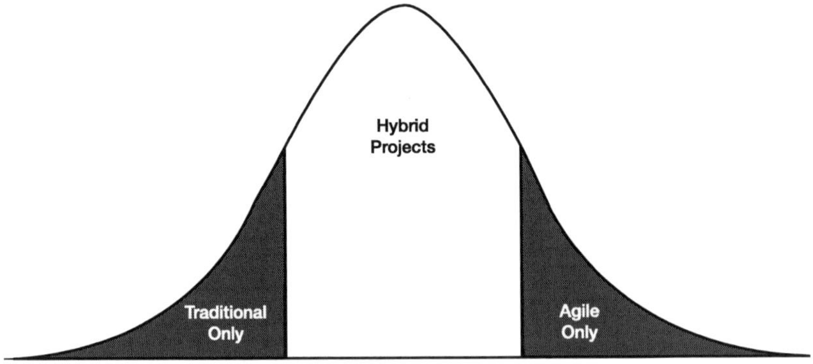

Figure 2.01 | Total Projects by Framework

When evaluating Framework choices many organizations and practitioners find the real consideration is not whether it is ideologically pure, but rather, whether it will enhance customer value and business results better than the current method.

An experienced Agile Coach can look at an organization and predict the success or failure of an Agile transformation effort with much greater accuracy than your local meteorologist can predict rain. The red flags that Coaches use to perform that assessment are discussed in the following section. They are the same red flags a Program Manager must use to assess and re-assess team needs. With that understanding, here are proven content and suggestions to help guide this process.

Anti-Patterns

Dysfunctions in the Product Owner Role

The Product Owner role has the highest correlation to the success or failure of most Agile implementations because it is the role responsible for maximizing value and being the "voice of the Customer" and primary source for setting the team's direction. This makes it vitally important that the Program Manager and the Product Manager be closely involved with selecting, grooming, and coaching the Product Owners. *The Agile Almanac - Book 1* covers the Product Owner role in detail.

Story from the Trenches

"I was running an internal Introduction to Scrum course, where departments that were interested in adopting or were about to start a project using this approach, would come and learn about the topic. We would talk about tools, techniques, new language, what it meant, and what would change. During the introductions, one of the younger men in the room sat at the back "suited and booted," looking very formal. He said it was likely he would be a Product Owner as he was currently a Team Leader.

As the day progressed, we started on the topic of culture change and how the Scrum culture differs from the waterfall (Traditional) project world. This gentleman said he didn't think the culture was an issue as this was just a project, everything else remained the same. So, I asked him, 'do you wear the suit, shirt, tie, polished shoes on a Saturday?' He said 'no'. I asked, 'why not'. 'Because it is not as comfortable as jeans, trainers, and a T-shirt,' came the response. 'Oh,' I said, 'so this company is now empowering you to make application decisions that will have a material impact on customers and therefore share price, profits, and reputation. But you don't feel empowered enough to dress yourself?' A week later he walked in wearing a polo shirt and chinos."

Rick Allan
Southampton, UK

Common mistakes the Program Manager needs to be aware of when assigning the Product Owner role include:

Picking the Wrong Person to be Product Owner
Finding the right person to be the Product Owner is as difficult as it is important. Poor choices are, perhaps, the most common mistake in Agile, including:

- *Picking an Executive to be the Product Owner.* At first it might seem logical for a department manager or executive to be the Product Owner. Experience has shown that this is seldom the best decision and is, in many cases, the worst. Product Owners must dedicate intense, almost exclusive, focus because they are the person closest to the intersection of customer aspirations and product functionality. The Product Owner is the voice of the customer, users, and key stakeholders so they must be available to work with the development team daily.

Availability is a 'luxury' an executive rarely has. Most executives and department managers are too busy with other day-to-day responsibilities to honor the commitment of a Product Owner to be available to interact with the team every day. The importance of this daily interaction, and of the Product Owner's availability to engage with the team, cannot be overstated.

Fig 2.02 | Executive as Product Owner

- *Picking a Project Manager to be the Product Owner.* Sometimes people who were Project Managers before an Agile adoption are in-tune enough with the product and its user base to become a good Product Owner, but this is an exception rather than a rule. This role demands someone who knows enough about the needs of the product and users that they can make good decisions, while also being internally motivated to want to fill this role. Many Project Managers see the Product Owner role as a step down, so they resent it instead of embrace it.

- *Picking a Business Analyst to be the Product Owner.* Senior Business Analysts have the required technical skills to fulfill the role, which they perceive as a promotion and are motivated to take it. The challenge is that this role demands someone who not only knows enough about the needs of the organization and the users, but someone who can, and will, make the tough, sometimes on-the spot, decisions needed by the Development Team without having to consult others. Many Business Analysts act as a "Product Owner by Proxy" because it is not in the nature of the Business Analyst role, and perhaps their make-up, to make decisions and accept responsibility for them, which becomes a fatal flaw for a Product Owner.

Product Owner Not Present or Not Engaged
The Product Owner must choose to prioritize fulfillment of their obligations to the team. They must make time as needed to sit with the team and answer questions. An example of how they might spend that time includes studying the results of Spikes then discussing their impact on Backlog items. Regardless of how much the Product Owner knows about the product and the needs of its users and the organization, if they are unavailable or disengaged, it is a recipe for disaster. The Product Owner's number one responsibility is to the team.

Fig 2.03 | Product Owner Not Engaged

More Than One Product Owner Per Team
One of the core values that a Product Owner provides is clarity and consistency. Because of the high level of complexity and uncertainty in the development environment, the team must have a single voice to articulate the vision and make decisions about the incremental steps that will be used to fulfill it. When a second Product Owner gets involved, under the

mistaken assumption that it will help the primary Product Owner, a chaotic phenomenon ensues called "diffusion of responsibility," characterized by a diminished degree of responsibility, ownership, and engagement of the Product Owner. The Program Manager must recognize this situation and cure it by redefining roles such that there is only one Product Owner for any given unit of functionality.

Fig 2.04 | More Than One Product Owner Per Team

There is a Portuguese saying that, "A dog with two owners dies hungry." This is because each owner assumes the dog will be taken care of by the other. This is also one of the key reasons for the Product Owner being a single individual and not a committee. The Product Owner increases the speed of the team by providing timely, reliable decision-making. If the Program is producing a deliverable simply too large or complex for a single Product Owner to handle, it is necessary, and far wiser, to decompose the deliverable into independent, de-coupled units of functionality, each with their own Product Owner and Program Roadmap defining the integration points where the final deliverable will be reviewed, tested, and assembled. Chapter 4 will cover this in more depth.

Dysfunctions in the Scrum Master Role

Second only to the Product Owner role, the impacts of the Scrum Master, both positive and negative, have a major effect on Agile organizations. This is one of the reasons consulting with a good Agile Coach is discussed at length in Chapter 3.

Dysfunctions that can be traced to the Scrum Master role include:

Sprints Extending Beyond Timebox
This is commonly seen in organizations as they first start with Agile. This occurs when the Development Team includes too much work into their Sprint Backlog and cannot finish within the agreed upon timebox. If the Sprint Goal is not achieved at the end of the Sprint, the Product Owner may extend the timebox until the work is finished. This breaks the development cadence and impedes the learning curve leading to more reliable sizing

of future Sprint Backlogs. The Program Manager should not allow this to happen because it undermines the process for building a planning process that produces robust, reliable forecasts used to influence stakeholder expectations.

Daily Stand-ups Not Effective or Happening Consistently

One of the clearest warning signs that the Program is at risk is when Daily Stand-up meetings are not consistently held or are ineffective. The Daily Stand-up meeting serves as the team's cornerstone for synchronization and is the primary opportunity for inspection and adaptation. It also serves as an "alert mechanism" to bring obstacles to the surface. When the Daily Stand-up does not happen, impediments are allowed to grow unrecognized until they become blockers like the iceberg that sunk the Titanic.

Dysfunctional Behaviors Not Addressed

Because Agile programs operate in an environment of high complexity and uncertainty, the team dynamic plays a vital role in producing progress amid the Cone of Uncertainty. That means the Program Manager must cultivate an environment of personal safety so crucial conversations happen as needed to enable the Development Team to be fully functional. That sometimes means doing a constructive intervention focused on the behaviors needed to fulfill the team's obligations to the Program. When this doesn't happen, multiple dysfunctions can arise.

The Program Manager must provide a set of transparent guidelines for Scrum Masters seeking direction from Project Managers or the Program Manager. Those guidelines must explain when it is the right time to escalate to the Program Manager, such as defining a reasonable timeframe for the team to resolve the dysfunction themselves or a threshold for how many teams are affected by the dysfunction. The guidelines should be developed in collaboration with the Project Managers and Scrum Masters across the Program so they reflect the good judgment and perspectives of each viewpoint.

Fig 2.05 | Dysfunctions in Leadership

When dysfunctions cannot be resolved by the Program Manager,

Program risk increases substantially and should be escalated to the Sponsor level.

Dysfunctions in Leadership

Leading the transformation to a Lean-Agile organization is no small feat and is difficult even when the Program Manager is knowledgeable, experienced, and engaged. The Program Manager is responsible for cultivating leadership at all levels. They not only understand Lean-Agile principles, but actively apply them to support the organizational change the Program needs to succeed. Here are some common leadership dysfunctions.

Not Actively Supporting and Embracing the Change
This is a big one! An Agile Program will drive a transformation that cannot happen without leadership. Simply signing off and moving on is the lip service that will induce failure. The Program Manager must actively work to incrementally, and where required, dramatically change the mindset across every level of the Program in word and deed, every day.

Story Points Misunderstood
This is one of the biggest challenges for business leadership. The Program Manager, aided by the Project Managers, must consistently and accurately portray the use of Story Points in order for the Agile adoption supporting the Program to succeed. There are two commonly misunderstood facets of Story Points. One is that they are non-linear so a Fibonacci sequence or similar scale is used to assign them. The other is that they are unique to each team. For example, in a four-week Iteration, if one team completes 35 Story Points writing simple reports while another team completes 35 Story Points writing difficult algorithms, it doesn't make sense to assume they had the same perspective on the difficulty of a Story Point.

Convincing executive management that Story Points are valid for planning purposes and useful as a performance or progress metric, and they cannot, and should not, be normalized across teams is a challenge for the Program Manager to own.

Inadequate Training
This surprisingly common dysfunction occurs despite mountains of evidence demonstrating a powerful, positive ROI and the very real, very steep cost for failure. The conundrum is that leadership often requires training for their

staff, but fails to invest in themselves. The logic that "The Scrum Guide is only 16 pages long, so perhaps only the Development Team needs two days of training on it" is deeply flawed. For Programs to succeed, Program Managers must invest in themselves and be persuasive in arranging the correct type of training for senior stakeholders.

This dysfunction presents itself when leadership lacks the ability to effectively embrace change by cultivating an environment of personal safety where teams can exercise the Agile mindset of "Fail fast to succeed sooner" without fear of career suicide. Leadership must reward the team for taking risks and enduring setbacks because these make the Agile Program succeed.

Myths and Misconceptions

Agile attracts myths and misconceptions like a picnic attracts ants. Some of the most common ones make Agile about as welcome as the ants too. Program Managers are encouraged to use this section to prepare for effective dialogues with stakeholders and teams. This chapter provides insights that will resonate with them and increase the Program Manager's ability to influence, persuade, and lead them.

Agile is Only for Software

The fact that the visionaries who gathered in Snowbird, Utah in 2001 to write the Agile Manifesto were software development professionals frustrated with the failings of Traditional Project Management does not mean Agile is for software only. Many of the practices that have grown out of the Agile Manifesto can be directly traced to Lean Manufacturing, the Toyota Production System, and W. Edwards Deming in the 1950s.

Here are two good examples of Agile in non-software environments.

- The SAAB JAS 39 Gripen fighter jet *(shown in Figure 2.06)*, was built using Agile methods and has the lowest cost of any Western fighter jet according to a study published by IHS Jane's in 2012.[1] The Gripen operating costs are just 65% of the F-16E![2] An analysis of the Agile application to this project concluded,

Fig 2.06 | SAAB JAS 39 Gripen Jet Fighter

"Through Agile practices Saab…[achieved] an aircraft delivered for lower cost, with higher speed, and greater quality."[3]

- In 2012, an all-volunteer Seattle team entered the Progressive Insurance X $10 Million Prize competition with the goal of building a 100 MPG street legal car (shown in Figure 2 – 07). The self-funded team used Agile methods and, in three months, tied for 10th place against many other, well-funded teams using Traditional methods with more time. The final product was built entirely with off-the-shelf parts, got 100 MPG, did 0 – 60 in less than 5 seconds, and had a top speed of 149 MPH.[4]

Fig 2.07 | Wikispeed Car

The important take-away is that Program Managers now have a vast array of new Agile tools in their toolbox and should use them to guide, help and influence executives, Portfolio Managers, Product Managers, and other stakeholders wherever those tools add value, regardless of the industry, product, or service.

Too Many Meetings

A common complaint Program Managers will hear is, "I am too busy to participate in so many meetings. I won't have time to work." Program Managers must be persuasive in explaining that meetings reduce risk and rework, which is waste, by ensuring that vital communication happens in the large, complex, and uncertain environment of the Program. Agile is a big culture shift and Program Managers have to own the responsibility of leading the change. Regular meetings are an essential feature of Agile. It is critical for team members to communicate consistently in order to succeed. Properly managed Agile meetings are productive collaborations in which critical work synchronization, alignment, and integration is actually accomplished.

Two Weeks is Too Short

The most common timebox for Iteration length is two weeks. Many companies mistakenly think they must use two-week Iterations, which are too short for their industry. However, Agile does not specify one Iteration length as good and another as bad. The key is to understand that the shorter the timebox, the faster feedback is received, teams learn, and processes improve. However, shorter Iterations increase the number of Iterations and, thus, the number of meetings. Meetings increase overhead or, in Lean terms, increase waste. Therefore, the only reason to shorten Iterations is when the increased learning and process improvement provide a positive ROI.

In recent years, some Agile consulting firms have been training teams by initially using daily Iterations to speed up acquisition of all the needed Agile skills. Basically, by going through all the Agile ceremonies - working with Product and Iteration Backlogs, and holding review and Retrospective meetings - with each daily Iteration, the team hyper-accelerates through the learning curve. While it is not sustainable in the long term, it is great for teaching, getting to know team members, and sharing the importance of Agile values and principles.

With a little discipline, proper training, and good engineering practices, it is possible to have a sustainable and healthy work environment with timeboxes that are the appropriate length, even in two-week Iterations!

Every Iteration Must Deploy into Production

The Scrum Guide, on page 8, states, "The heart of Scrum is a Sprint, a timebox of one month or less during which a "Done", a useable and potentially releasable Product Increment, is created."

Every Sprint needs a high-level Sprint Goal or Sprint Objective. The set of User Stories promoted from the Product Backlog to the Sprint Backlog needs to be the set providing the highest value for the end-user and organization. However, the idea that each Sprint will deliver value does not mean that every Sprint will deploy in production. Many times, Agile teams deliver fully shippable code at the end of their Sprint, but the Product Owner decides to release it at a later date.

Depending on the system, adding or changing a feature may require training users and support activities, which might be too costly to do with every Sprint (regardless of the length). On the other hand, many teams who work with XP and Agile perform multiple deployments into production each day. The difference here is the kind of system and confidence provided by automation and good practices that lead to the right amount of quality, security, and performance.

Amazon provides an insightful case study of the interface between Iterations, releasing into production, and having Program level standards. Amazon releases into production from as many as 1,000 development teams per day. That's right, ***per day!*** But the vast majority of those Releases impact simple user preferences or fixes to the appearance or operation of non-core functions. Conversely, any Iteration where the deliverable will impact core functions, such as security, credit card processing, or the personally-identifiable-data of customers, sellers or advertisers, absolutely may not be released until it has been approved by a predefined set of stakeholders along a prescribed escalation path.

Program practices such as source control management and continuous integration will play a big role in defining the mandatory quality and security of the Program's Potentially Shippable Increments (PSI) and will, therefore, directly influence the frequency of those deliverables being released into production. Be careful not to mix up continuous deployment with continuous delivery.

Agile Projects are Difficult to Budget

Agile provides the most value for Programs where there is unavoidable high complexity and uncertainty. Agile embraces the perspective that scope will change as learning and discovery happen in the midst of high complexity and uncertainty. By aligning budget and schedule expectations with appropriate planning-levels of granularity, Agile Programs can develop robust, useful project and financial plans where the greatest risk of unpredictable and unmanageable variances has occurred for most organizations. In other words, Agile Program Management improves budgeting accuracy on the projects that have historically been the toughest to get right.

A Program with a fixed budget will deliver as many high priority Features as possible from the Minimum Viable Product (MVP) and when the budget is spent, the Sponsor or key stakeholders will decide if further work should occur.

Likewise, a Program with a fixed timeframe will work to deliver as many high priority Features as possible from the MVP until the predetermined deadline is reached. The Sponsor or key stakeholders will then decide if further work should occur.

For Program Managers, the brilliance behind this model is that the remaining Backlog items will be judged on their own merits. If the value of the remaining Backlog items does not exceed the cost of producing them, the Program ends.

Budgeting is Difficult Because There is no End

Some Programs support Products, tangible or intangible, that have their own Product Lifecycle based on the ongoing financial viability of the Product or Product Suite. The challenge for Program Managers is that, by definition, Programs and Projects have a beginning and an end. But when the Program supports a Product that does not have a predefined end, then neither does the Program. In such cases the Program and Program Manager must accept that the Product Lifecycle will cause a continual need to develop and improve the Product. In such circumstances, the Program adds great value because, rather than disband and reform teams over and over, it keeps the Development Team together. This avoids the waste of repeatedly forcing teams to go through the forming, norming, and storming phases[5] of team development. It allows the Product to benefit from unbroken periods of robust deliverables from high performing teams.

It also means the Program can provide known, dependable development with a consistent cost that can be reliably forecasted and budgeted. Release Plans can be developed to aid financial planning for platform and infrastructure improvements supporting the planned, additional Features.

Accounting Cannot Capitalize Development Done with Agile

Generally speaking, using a scaled Agile Framework implies the organization has made a commitment to create competitive advantage. However, many organizations feel that once the decision to use Agile methodologies has been made, the ability to capitalize the development work is lost. This is due to the flawed thinking that it too difficult to quantify or track Development Team work and split it between work that qualifies under capitalization rules and work that must be expensed. The concept of Story Points also tends to create a "translation issue" for accounting. Luckily, going Agile does not mean sacrificing the ability to capitalize work as long as the correct focus is established between accounting and the Development Teams. With some simple configurations of the right development tool (as discussed in

Appendix B) the information can flow freely to accomplish both accounting and development reporting tasks.

There are three main ways that organizations have been capitalizing work in Agile environments.

- Normalize Story Points using a formula, such as capitalize 80% of completed Story Points per Release and expense the other 20%, after the formula is approved by accounting and the auditing firm.
- Use an integrated timesheet in a hybrid project management environment. Since many organizations are still tracking time to capitalize development efforts, an integrated timesheet, using line items for each Agile Feature, Function or Capability being developed, can report a value for capitalization and another for expense.
- Breakdown the Tasks under a User Story to create the percentage of effort that is capital and expense per release. Then the tool records who is on the team, the team cost, and the capital and expense transactions in a fully automated way.

Creating these solutions requires collaboration between the accounting, audit, management, and development teams. The right tool, properly configured, can easily automate these functions so the organization maintains the key advantage of capitalizing development efforts.

Agile is Faster and Cheaper than Other Methods

Agile Frameworks are often adopted because of a desire to bring products to market faster with the expectation that they will also be cheaper than if other methods were used. No one can fault that logic. It is important, however, for Program Managers to understand exactly what Agile can and cannot do before making the decision to use an Agile Framework.

While it is true that Agile methods will, in the right circumstances, help organizations prioritize product Features by value and teams develop small, fully functioning units of value in short timeframes, the idea should be clarified. The catch is that the value will be delivered incrementally and iteratively. Smart organizations will find ways to monetize their products at the lowest possible level and use those early revenues to improve ROI or fund development of further Features. That does not mean that Agile methods will "auto-magically" help organizations iterate towards a completed product faster than Traditional methods. What it does mean is that when the Agile Product Owner or Program Manager sees that the point of diminishing marginal returns has been reached, they will choose to assign the team to other work with a higher ROI. Because of this, comparing products developed using Agile versus Traditional methods is not an apples-to-apples comparison.

It's Okay to Tell the Executives (or Stakeholders) to Wait and See

Some Agile aficionados seem to think Agile empowers them to tell executives and stakeholders, "You'll just have to wait and see what turns out because Agile means no long-term planning." Perhaps they work in places where the boss says, "Take all the time and money you need to complete the project!" For the rest of us, that is just a dream.

Fig 2.08 | It's Okay to say, "Wait and See!"

Agile thrives in environments where frequent changes and technological uncertainty are common. Remember, Principle #2 of the *Agile Manifesto* says, "Welcome changing requirements, even late in development. Agile processes harness change for the customer's competitive advantage." This does not mean, however, that there is no long-term planning in Agile or that Agile Program Managers are unable to give their stakeholders a Product Roadmap or Release Plan.

In Scrum, for example, planning is done at five, increasingly granular levels – Product Vision, Product Roadmap, Release Plan, Sprint Plan, and Daily Stand-up. Unlike a Release Plan in a Traditional project, a Scrum Release Plan has scope, not date or quality, as its variable.[6] For example, a Product Owner can tell executives and stakeholders that the Release Plan for the next two months calls for Features E, F, G, and H to be released. The only variable is how much of each Feature will be released. The Development Team may be able to complete all of Features E, F, and G, but possibly only half of the planned functionality for Feature H. Since Feature H is the lowest priority Feature, the team will build the MVP first, adding other, lower priority functionality later. In this way Agile Program Managers can communicate to their stakeholders a high-level Release Plan that they can work with so long as they accept that scope is variable.

Agile Uses "Generalizing Specialists"

While the origin of the term "generalizing specialists" cannot be definitively assessed, it is commonly interpreted to mean a person with deep expertise in a particular area who also has experience within an array of other, usually related, areas. The hypothesis would appear to be that the type of person able to master multiple skills has a strong ability to learn new skills quickly. The idea seems to have emanated from the software industry referring to programmers who also do other development-related tasks, such as testing.

Generalizing specialists may be a good idea, but is a misconception in the sense of being a less-than-robust response to the central challenge. In this case, the central challenge is how to avoid the risk of dependency on sole-source providers of particular skills because they can leave the organization, creating a major operational deficit. Let's look at this in analogies from different viewpoints.

From an accounting perspective, each member of the team is a resource paid in proportion to the tacit knowledge they can supply. An increase in tacit knowledge, also known as experience or battle scars, is why a typical engineer with 10 years of experience gets paid more than a recent college graduate in the same field. If the more experienced engineer leaves an organization, it is likely harder, and more expensive, to fill the void.

An alternate, and, perhaps, stronger solution for this problem is tribal knowledge. It is not uncommon during Olympic track and field relay races for the team with the fastest runners to fail to win the race. But 100 percent of the time, the winning team is a team that did not drop the baton. The baton is the symbol of tribal knowledge and the runners are the sole-source providers of skill.

One of the powerful factors common to Agile approaches is cross-functional teams. Each member of the cross-functional team contributes tacit knowledge while the system of Iteration Planning and Stand-up Meetings, plus other tools and activities, such as User Stories and Planning Poker, creates tribal knowledge. This is so because over the course of time, for example in software development, the programmer explains to the quality assurance team member that if they changed the interface of their activities in a certain way it would aid the programmer, and vice versa. This continuous process improvement creates tribal knowledge reducing the impact of a highly paid, sole-source skill provider leaving the organization because it reduces the transition cost and learning curve for the new hire. That is so because when the new programmer arrives, the quality assurance team member explains how the interface works and high-speed productivity resumes without the risk of the baton being dropped.

This approach also compensates for a nearly-fatal flaw in the assumptions underpinning the "generalizing specialists" solution. In a great many environments, sole-source skill providers are as different as zebras and giraffes. Asking them to be generalizing specialists is like hoping for a striped giraffe. Agile offers a much more reliable solution with a systemic approach, creating easy-to-hold batons of tribal knowledge.

Agile Opposes "Big Design Up Front (BDUF)"

Perhaps the root of this misconception can be traced back to the Scrum Guide published in November 2009 by Scrum.org, owned and shared by Jeff Sutherland and Ken Schwaber. On page 8 it said, "Release planning is entirely optional. If Scrum team(s) start work without the meeting, the absence of its artifacts will become apparent as impediments that need to be resolved. Work to resolve the impediments will become items in the Product Backlog."

Apparently, somehow, somewhere, someone saw and started parroting only, "Release Planning is entirely optional," missing the critical warning that followed stating that if teams started work without the Release Plan artifacts it would become an impediment to resolve. Implementing single-team Agile, much less scaling it, with an Iteration-plus-Backlog-only mindset is a simple recipe for creating disasters. The lack of good Release Planning is rampant in parts of the Agile community, rejecting it as unnecessary, which contributes to discrediting Agile.

The idea that anything but the smallest, most inconsequential development could be done with no Big Design Up Front (BDUF) is even more dangerous and ludicrous than heavy-weight planning done under the banner of Release Planning. Two examples add insight. First, XP uses the principle of Incremental Architectural Planning as its version of a BDUF. Second, Lean Software Development applies the principle of Optimize the Whole, which implies the assumption of a BDUF of the whole.

To succeed in scaling Agile, professional practitioners must be prepared to respond to this canard whenever they see it raise its ugly head! The solution is to cultivate an understanding of how to align planning granularity with decision-making granularity, which will be covered in depth in Chapter 11.

As Agile Scales... So Do the Myths

Agile Doesn't Work with Distributed Teams

The annual *State of Agile Development* report, funded by VersionOne, and the *State of Scrum* report issued by the Scrum Alliance are both generally accepted as reliable sources of information regarding Agile.

According to the 2017 *State of Agile Development* report, "86% of respondents had at least some distributed teams practicing Agile" while "51% reported using Agile to manage outsourced IT projects."[7] The 2017 State of Scrum report stated that 54% of respondents said Scrum teams had members who were "...distributed across different sites and/or geographic areas".[8] While it is generally accepted that collocated teams provide many benefits in Agile development, in practice it is not mandatory. To be clear, collocation is still preferred, but distributed teams have become far more common.

Driven by industry trends toward distributed workforces, and remote and offshore workers, Agile practices have adapted. Most companies decided that the benefits of Agile outweigh any challenges remote teams or workers introduce. A variety of technologies and software has been introduced to help these distributed Agile teams communicate. Some of the scaled Agile Frameworks, such as SAFe®, make provisions for including remote and vendor teams in planning.

Impossible to Integrate Agile and Non-Agile Teams

Integrating Traditional and Agile teams in a Program is unavoidable. Therefore, Program Managers are required to lead the planning and implement carefully crafted communication-by-design instead of communication-by-accident in order to ensure success.

In practice, the most important principle is to map out the integration points using the old school approach of building a logic network then enhancing it with the Agile techniques for low-tech, high-touch methods and a focus on being effective before being efficient. Being effective in delivering Customer Value must have priority over being efficient in the development how-to approach.

A complete presentation of how to do this is included in Chapter 11.

Conclusion

This chapter has covered the most common and highest-value risks and anti-patterns in Agile. The tools provided to avoid them, or at least begin a dialogue about them with stakeholders, will be of great value to many Program Managers. For more Agile Myths, Misconceptions, Anti-Patterns, some interesting Horror Stories, or to contribute your own, please join the GR8PM Tribe at GR8PM.com.

CHAPTER

3

Agile Program Management

Overview

This chapter examines the interrelationships between Project, Program, and Portfolio Management with an eye to supporting Program Managers, Project Management Office (PMO) directors, and business unit leaders. It also includes a highly practical discussion of things to consider, avoid or watch closely when scaling Agile, and when Agile Program Management (APM) is needed in addition to an Agile Framework such as Scrum, eXtreme Programming (XP), and Kanban. There is no perfect Framework for scaling Agile so a careful assessment of the pros and cons of each option's viability within particular environments is required to determine the best choice.

In *Lean Software Development: An Agile Toolkit* by Mary and Tom Poppendeick, the seven Lean Principles are summarized into six essential guidelines for scaling Agile. They define the Lean approach as:

1) Optimize the Whole
2) Defer Commitment
3) Deliver Fast
4) Eliminate Waste
5) Build Quality in
6) Empower Team Learning

The main purpose of a Program starts with the principle "Optimize the Whole." This is a guiding principle because a

Program orchestrates the overall delivery of a complex product or service, tangible or intangible, in an environment that is uncertain. *(See Figure 3.01.)*

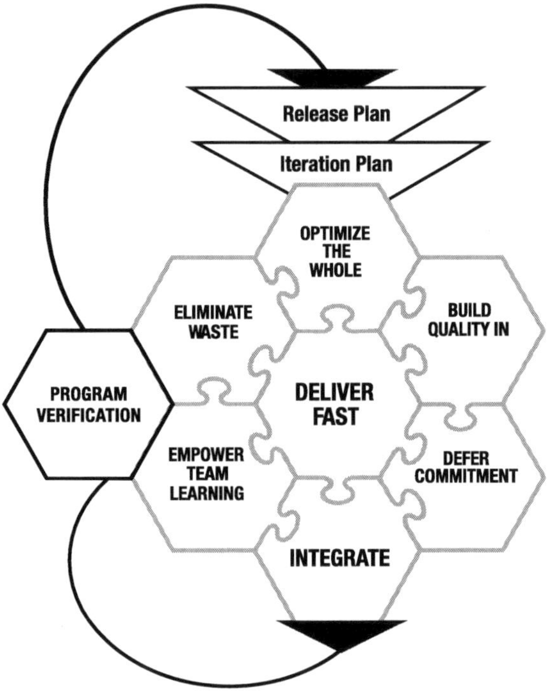

Fig 3.01 | Lean Principles for Agile Programs

With optimizing the whole as the main purpose, important environmental considerations include the following.

If the deliverable is intangible, such as software, ask:

- Will continuous integration and deployment be required to test successful deployment across multiple projects?
- Will an automated deployment process be used by all projects? Should it be the only way to deploy? This level of discipline supports potential future needs for rapid adaptation by ensuring that "deployment scripts" to fix bugs are present, disaster recovery actions are implemented or major marketplace changes are responded to.
- Will there be requirements that all Features, Functions, Capabilities (FFCs), and components follow a specific deployment pipeline across multiple projects?

If the deliverable is tangible, such as constructing a shopping center, ask:

- Will there be requirements that FFCs and components from multiple projects align to integration points for inspections or approvals within the implementation pipeline?
- Will there be regulatory-mandated testing procedures, underwriting requirements, or funding phase gates that must be complied with across multiple projects?

The obvious insight is that feedback loops across the Program are critical and complex so they cannot be left to chance. They must be purposefully designed into the Program.

Delivering fast allows for verification that all FFCs and components align with the standards defined by the Program to ensure full utility for the Customer, thereby producing Customer Delight. Feedback loops must confirm the right level of quality has been met and that the deliverable is "fit for purpose" as defined by the Customer. They also allow time for adjustments before the cost to adapt becomes prohibitive. Feedback loops minimize cycle time (from Ideation to Customer Delight, as noted in Chapter 1), which eliminates waste, leading to significant financial benefits.

At a Program level, some questions to ask to define feedback criteria include:

- Are all changes required to follow the same feedback process?
- How quickly must feedback be received?
- What is the process each project should follow to incorporate feedback? How quickly must the feedback be applied?

If the deliverable is intangible, such as developing software, should the feedback process include:

- Testing every piece of code?
- Confirming unit testing has a specific percentage of coverage with all tests passing?
- Validating a specific percentage of quality measures or acceptance criteria are met?
- Demonstrating Features using actual or sample sets of data at specific, scheduled intervals?
- Verifying nonfunctional requirements for performance, portability, maintainability, interoperability, or security pass appropriate testing on a defined, periodic basis?

If the deliverable is tangible, such as aerospace hardware, should the feedback process require:

- Peer-reviews of a prototype or mock-up?

- Non-destructive and destructive performance testing measured against designated thresholds?
- Incremental demonstrations of the product that precede the final deliverable?
- Performance of pilot tests by selected key stakeholders or groups?
- An implementation plan review to assess the probability of a successful go-live and to define appropriate support contingencies in the event of partial or complete failure?

A certain amount of overhead is required to ensure all projects remain synchronized and that value is being delivered. Lean thinking helps keep over-engineering under control at the Program level without surrendering an effective focus on quality and speed at the Project level.

Agile Program Activities

Planning activities for Agile Programs include:

- Creating a Program Charter that clearly and concisely articulates the over-arching strategic vision to provide actionable insights for the team.
- Defining the Minimal Viable Outcomes (MVO) governing the Minimal Marketable Features (MMF) to be included in the Program Roadmap and its Backlog.
- Collaborating with Subject Matter Experts (SME) to determine how to decompose the work across projects while assessing and balancing the potential risks of different combinations of inter-project dependencies.
- Creating a robust communication plan that contains standards for the various stakeholder groups with thresholds for escalation and resource commitments to ensure its implementation.

Executing activities for Agile Programs include:

- Continuous review and improvement of the Roadmap.
- Communicating changes to Release and Iteration plans.
- Tracking Program progress and communicating work issues and risks.
- Managing inter-project and inter-team escalations to optimize the whole.

- Fostering cross-project collaboration and coordination to ensure alignment and integration for Program success.
- Using early opportunities to inspect and adapt to optimize results and minimize cost.
- Communicating integration points, timing for data roll-ups, and overarching process requirements so that project-level work metrics are clearly understood.
- Guiding decisions to optimize Program direction and delivery, Customer business value, and Program trade-offs.
- Fully engaging in project-level ceremonies where product, progress, and quality are demonstrated or reviewed.
- Providing appropriate coaching and demonstrating servant leadership every day.

Benefits / Challenges

Business Value is True North

When there is clarity about the enterprise's direction and how its purpose ties to the work being done, navigating marketplace uncertainty and Program complexity becomes much easier. "True North" is a Lean term originating from the Toyota Production System (TPS). It describes the ideal that will create the most customer value and therefore the highest level of organizational success. Agile Program Management (APM) is a process that advances the enterprise towards this state of perfection. The big benefit of properly implementing APM is the creation of an environment where every project and team understands how its work aligns with True North and finds itself motivated to continually strive towards attaining it.

Achieving a culture focused on True North is not easy, but neither is marketplace leadership! As noted business and technical guru Rick Morris has said, "Culture eats Vision for lunch!" If enterprise leaders shy away from concretely supporting the culture change required to achieve a True North culture, its Vision will be devoured by the competitor who does exercise the discipline to do so.

APM benefits the organization by valuing projects and self-directed teams operating with a commitment to work together to achieve better alignment to the enterprise Vision and optimize the whole Value Stream from Ideation to

Customer Delight. The outcome will be marketplace leadership that translates into increasing financial results at both the top and bottom line.

Impact of Culture Change

Enterprise leaders must commit to making, the sometimes significant, changes required to support APM as a strategic marketplace competency. The big challenge, and the area they most often fail to confront, is the consequences of their own, inaccurate assumptions and expectations regarding planning and decision-making. Three examples include leaders who:

- ***Set a tone of "Everything is #1 Priority."*** This error is indicative of a likely failure to define overall metrics for success and funding gates that are coupled with honest evaluations and accountability at the senior level.
- ***Believe every aspect of product or service development is compressible.*** This error shows itself in unrealistic demands for impossible delivery dates usually coupled with a failure to understand the compounding of risk that is driven by frenzied, chaotic attempts to fulfill their fantasy.
- ***Set business or Program goals without a disciplined, iterative analysis of the real constraints impacting probable risks and success.*** This error is seen in examples like the 2013 launch of HealthCare.gov[1] and Boeing Dreamliner 787 batteries[2].

Agile Program Management requires a disciplined focus on strategic-level planning so that proper information from the macro-dynamic level can feed subsequent levels of the micro-dynamic process in both effective and efficient ways. Several areas where executive support – from Program Managers to Project Management Office directors and business unit leaders – is required to create a culture that can leverage and support APM include:

- Subjecting their expectations to an appropriate process of rolling wave planning and progressive elaboration to cultivate a high-trust relationship with the experts responsible for developing market-leading results that please constituents and customers.
- Removing limits imposed by organizational silos as well as opposition to a "fail fast to succeed sooner" mindset. Such opposition impedes using the Lean principle of delivering fast.
- Supporting continuous improvement, which means allowing experimentation that may fail. Experimentation is the only way to find

sustainable processes that deliver high-quality products and services at reasonable cost. Sharing these experiments across the Program as they become good practices will also increase efficiencies.

Ultimately, choosing APM as part of a strategic business commitment to marketplace leadership will lead to an unassailable competitive advantage if executed correctly.

Program-level Attributes

An over-arching Program is only needed when projects are operating interdependently. When that is the case, utilizing a Framework, as a basic process to report status and risks in a consistent manner, becomes advisable. Here are some considerations.

An over-arching Program is needed when:

- There is one strategic objective across multiple teams.
- Cross-dependencies are embedded in the teams' work-streams and coordination of several projects is required.
- Collaboration across teams and projects is needed because integration points on FFCs and components must have the same look and feel.
- Multiple projects touch a client or key stakeholder group and efficiencies can be gained by coordinating a joint release of products or services.

If an over-arching Program is needed, key Agile elements to consider are:

- Thinking through everything strategically, rather than tactically, with an Agile perspective using Lean principles.
- Articulating the Program Vision and business value across all channels and communicating how each project integrates into that Vision.
- Determining which benefits, dependencies, and risks are better shared across projects.
- Keeping projects loosely coupled, using embedded feedback loops and transparency across the Program, to keep them synchronized.
- Creating an ecosystem that promotes both high performance and high trust.

Servant Leadership
Giving the team space to be creative and innovative is essential because it fosters the best outcomes. Servant leadership is proven to greatly enhance the probability of creating the desired environment. Agile Programs often find it is necessary to educate and influence stakeholders to embrace this leadership style by sharing why it works. Servant leadership enables teams to do things in a collaborative way that is extremely powerful. Servant leaders are unusually talented facilitators, coordinators, partners, and coalition-builders.

In Kent M. Keith's, *The Case of the Servant Leadership*, he describes the best servant leaders by stating that they:

- Are self-aware.
- Listen.
- Serve the people who work "for" them.
- Coach people.
- Help other people.
- Unleash the energy and intelligence of others.
- Work to develop their foresight so they can act, not react.

Learning to work in this state of mind is often a transformation effort for those who choose it. It takes practice and having an Agile Coach greatly increases the chances of mastering servant leadership. *The Case of the Servant Leadership* is a succinct book that should be on every Agile leader's bookshelf.

Roles

How an Agile Program team is defined is highly dependent upon the type of Program involved, such as operational equipment, capital improvements, or tangible or intangible products or services. It is also dependent on the number of teams and the coordination they require, as well as the expected duration of the Program. Two common elements are a Core Program Team and a Technical Program Team.

Core Program Team
A Core Program Team is responsible for successful delivery of the Program

and their focus is cross-project collaboration and coordination. Membership includes whoever is needed to successfully scale Agile for the Program, but is dependent on how tightly the projects are coupled and complex the work is, and what type of cross-project collaboration and communication is necessary.

Other things to consider when deciding on the Core Program Team configuration are the timing of demonstrations, review meetings and Retrospectives because the Core Program Team attends all demonstrations in order to ensure the right level of collaboration and integration occurs. When work is less tightly coupled, perhaps different Core Program Team members can cover different projects, but still maintain the overall synchronization needed. It is best to start with the minimum Core Program Team members expected then scale as needed at the Last Responsible Moment. Core Program Team members can include the following roles.

Program Manager – manages the overall Program budget, has authority to make budgetary decisions, hires and manages the Core Team resources, sets and manages high-level Program Vision and expectations, reports Program status at the executive and leadership levels, creates the Program Charter, Roadmap, and Backlog, and is responsible for delivering the Program outcome successfully.

Program Product Owner – balances the Backlogs across the Program. A key role of APM is monitoring individual products and project teams to validate they are delivering priority User Stories. For example, if one team is ready to work on their #1 Backlog item, but it integrates to a #20 priority for a different team, an adjustment may be required.

Program Coordinator – manages day-to-day budget tracking, progress reporting, and Backlog synchronization as directed by the Program Manager. Program Coordinators also follow-up on cross-project reporting of risks and impediments to ensure it is updated and accurate.

Program Specialist – manages specific Program elements, such as cross-program architecture, engineering, and quality practices, or feature driven components, as directed by the Program Manager. Typically, the Program Specialist ensures cross-dependency risks are transparent and being worked so the Program can deliver successfully. If the Program is very large, this role may be part of a Technical Program Team and include several different roles.

Agile Change\Transition Manager – supports Program and project teams by advising on change management considerations, especially when the significant change is being introduced to the customer base. This role often works closely with the Program Coach to promote and support organizational culture change needed for the Program success.

Communication Specialist – supports program and project teams by advising on enterprise and executive level and external communication needs.

Program Coach – supports project teams by coaching them as a group, as well as individually, to increase their mastery of Agile and Lean principles and skills, by providing training, advice, and guidance. The Program Coach helps teams understand critical skills and behaviors, such as transparency, collaboration, accountability, retrospection, and adaption. This creates a culture where all members take responsibility for the consequences of team decisions.

Workflow

Program agility requires looking at the Program's entire Value Stream from inception to delivery of business value. *(See Figure 3.02.)*

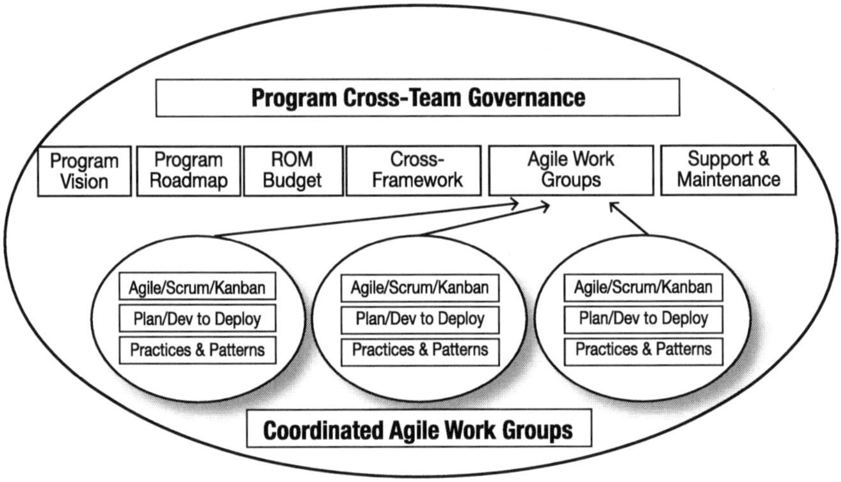

Figure 3.02 | Lean Program Value Stream Map

Program agility will look different depending on the organizational environment, product or service being delivered, and the size and complexity of the Program. Visualizing and documenting the workflow showing how the Program delivers customer value from ideation to actual product or service is a valuable exercise. An approach for Value Stream Mapping will be described in the Organizational Culture Change for Agile Programs section.

Continuous Improvement (Kaizen)

The Japanese word "Kaizen" refers to incremental, continuous improvement of a process and originates in Lean Manufacturing. Kaizen, the Toyota Way, and the Plan-Do-Check-Act (PDCA) cycle carried over from Lean Manufacturing to the Agile way of thinking about continuous Project and Program improvement.

The Agile journey is one of continuous improvement. It is required to successfully scale Agile for Programs. There are important questions that need to be answered when scaling, such as:

- What practices should be across all projects?
- Which of those practices are guidelines or suggestions?
- Which ones need to be mandated for all projects?

This is where an Agile PMO must help provide answers and direction. More detailed coverage of continuous improvement will be given in the section on making scaled Agile work effectively.

Programs and Agile Governance Structures

Agile Programs require different governance because planning, estimating, developing, and testing with Agile projects is very different from how Traditional projects are managed and executed. Therefore, the Program practices used for coordinating and reporting progress done in short cycles by the projects must be designed to integrate all the information and guide the iterative, incremental development process. Without proper practices working in concert, Program completion could be delayed or even fail.

There is a vital partnership between the PMO and the Program Manager that must be developed to create an environment that fully supports scaled Agile practices. The PMO must provide guidance regarding the right practices for the Program Manager to use and also provide coaching if needed. Key elements that must be in place for this partnership to function properly are listed below. The PMO must:

- Understand Agile processes, the benefits of Agile practices, and how to determine if, and when, an Agile Framework is the right choice.
- Provide the help needed to adopt the right Agile practices for the Program.
- Play an active role and advocate for lightweight practices that serve the Program.
- Work directly with the Program Manager to determine the best Agile configuration for the Program and standardization with adequate and appropriate flexibility.
- Model, cultivate, and support servant leadership across all Programs.
- Be represented at product demonstration meetings and able to provide competent facilitators for Release retrospectives, if requested.
- Be a source for Agile Coaches, consultants, and mentors, when requested.
- Play an active role in forming, supporting, and facilitating the development of Communities of Practices (CoP) and Centers of Excellence (CoE).
- Ensure regulatory compliance, alignment with industry standards, and application of organizational standards using a Barely Sufficient best practice approach for lightweight oversight.

Setting expectations with critical stakeholders is the combined responsibility of the PMO and the Program Manager. Together they must successfully manage customers, senior managers, and development teams that all have different perspectives on the process changes the Program requires in order to achieve the benefits of an Agile delivery model!

Ceremonies

In addition to the ceremonies used by teams for Agile development or Agile projects, there are additional ceremonies at the Program level.

Daily Stand-up for Core Program Team

This typically includes representatives from each project team reporting progress and receiving information applicable to all teams on a daily basis.

Executive Roadshows
Programs evoke and require additional, specific communication with executives, internal and external stakeholders, and key sponsors of the change management. This communication must be designed and have a regular, periodic cadence. Different stakeholders may need, or prefer, different levels of detail so having several different Roadshows may be necessary across the lifecycle of the Program.

Agile Governance Meetings
The Core Program Team needs to have regular check-in meetings, typically weekly at the beginning of the Program, to review inter-project dependencies, risks, impediments, and development activities to confirm proper synchronization. The meetings need to have a regular, periodic cadence in order to properly prepare upcoming communication about change management issues and development activities.

Impediment and Escalation Forums
When impediments cannot be resolved with inter-project team communications, a defined escalation process must exist to support them and the success of the Program. To be effective, an Impediment and Escalation Forum must have a set of transparent guidelines that can be actively worked by the Project Managers seeking guidance from the Program Manager. Those guidelines must explain when it is the right time to escalate to the Program Manager, such as defining a reasonable timeframe for the team to resolve the impediment themselves or a threshold for how many teams are affected by an obstacle. The guidelines should be developed in collaboration with key people throughout the Program so they reflect the good judgment and perspectives from each viewpoint.

When impediments cannot be resolved by the Program Manager, program risk increases substantially and should be escalated to the Sponsor level.

Artifacts

There are several key artifacts needed to manage a Lean/Agile program (see the Tools and Practices section for artifact samples and templates). Additional artifacts may be needed (think Lean), but this list should always be part of the Program artifacts.

1. Program Charter
2. Program Roadmap

3. Program Executive Status Report
4. Program Backlog or Story Board
5. Program Schedule
6. Communication and Escalation Forum
7. Dependencies Mapping
8. Program Risks and Impediments Plan

How to Make it Work Effectively

It is a given that at some point in scaling Agile, more Traditional project management practices and tools will be needed at the Program or Project roll-up level. Lean thinking provides an excellent umbrella in which to make these Agile Program Management decisions. Lean thinking has its root in Lean Manufacturing, which requires fast delivery, high quality, and waste removal all while reducing costs. This has been proven to work on a large scale. The key to remaining Agile and applying Traditional project management tools is also applying Lean principles and thinking to everything.

Focus on the big picture and follow these Lean Thinking concepts at the Program level:

- Delegate work and methods to individual projects while still retaining responsibility for the outcomes.
- Set the outcomes or goals expected of the teams.
- Use Value Stream Mapping to understand the value chain and where there is waste.
- Use visual controls and walking around to evaluate progress.
- Be involved in problem solving and Kaizen events.
- Help teams avoid waste they cannot see (optimize the whole).

At the Project level, focus is on Agile practices and tools needed in the environment to get the work done. At the Program level, the focus is on integration, optimizing the whole Program for best results and reducing waste. The idea is to ensure cross-coupling and develop and increase cross-collaboration, awareness of decreasing cross-dependencies and cross-risks, while looking for opportunities where volume or scale, not as strong at the individual project level, can be exploited at the Program level (e.g. cross-learning, cross-tools) for greater efficiency.

Enterprise Support - Attitudes That Support Agile

Many Agile adoption efforts operate from the bottom up, in a grassroots fashion. As great results are achieved, they spread out. But, often as they scale up, their performance goes down and the Agile advantage is lost. This has caused some to say that Agile does not scale well and only works with small teams. The issue is of a different variety all together. The sluggishness comes with lack of alignment and collaboration at the Program or Executive level. The teams get mired in "non-value added" processes and requirements due to the lack of alignment and collaboration. Non-value added is a Lean term for any work that does not add value as defined by the customer, which is a type of waste and slows the delivery of business value. This is why executive sponsorship, with a healthy understanding of Agile concepts, is so valuable, as it can foster the right level of "non-value added" work. Balancing business value, agility, and operational efficiency is a critical concept to scale teams, and enterprise support is needed to navigate this and get to the minimum "non-value added" requirements.

Collaboration, Respect, and Trust

Due to Agile's adaptive nature, collaboration is very important to create successful teams. As you begin to scale, this becomes even more crucial. Every opportunity to promote collaboration and respect within the teams should be taken and advanced.

Nurturing a collaborative and respectful environment is essential to getting full team interaction. It gets the artistic juices flowing, works through conflict, and develops trust. Collaboration, by itself, can lead to over-enthusiastic individuals running over their teammates, which prevents full participation. Respect places the boundaries on behaviors. Be self-aware. Pay attention to team members and their needs by listening and encouraging participation. Every team should spend time understanding what collaboration and respect represent within the team. Leaders can foster this internally with the team and externally with stakeholders and customers. This allows for healthy growth and is the cornerstone of trust, which enables cooperative behavior without the need for monitoring. With trust, there is comfort in the relationship, commitment to one another, and the willingness to be vulnerable and take some risks because the expectation is that the team will be there as backup and provide support.

Agile Coaching

Coaching is a required element of transformation if results better than mediocre are desired. A Coach supports coachees in reaching Agile/Lean skills and the culture and mindset required for the Agile transformation by providing training, advice, and guidance.

Teams need Coaches that help them understand what it means to be Agile. Coaching supports skills and behaviors that promote good Agile health (transparency, collaboration, accountability, retrospect, and adaption). Agile coaching matters because it helps produce better products and services, and adds value and purpose to people's work lives. (This is part of creating that culture where people take responsibility for consequences referenced above.)

Agile is easy to get started, but hard to sustain over time. This is mainly because Agile is transparent, exposing inefficiencies, broken processes, and "sludge" that has been in the organization and systems for years. Everyone needs ongoing coaching to get through the rough patches on the way to being a great Agilest!

Here are some examples of the responsibilities of a Coach.

- Stands-up Agile teams
- Introduces and inspires Agile/Lean values and principles
- Coaches one-on-one as well as whole teams
- Coaches teams and others through conflict and change
- Helps the team achieve higher performance
- Coaches Product Owners, managers, and those outside of the Agile/Lean environment on the skills and processes of Agile
- Coaches up the management structure on Agile principles
- Masters their own emotions and puts the needs of others ahead of them

The stage in which the coachee and/or team are in their Agile journey determines the techniques the Coach uses with them. Initially, this is providing strong guidance, but later it is asking powerful questions to elicit deeper thinking and guide the team to focus on their commitments, other agreements, and Agile principles. Once the teams are well formed and knowledgeable in the practices, the Coach can help them make decisions with new techniques, engineering, and other improvements for even greater performance.

Anyone who takes multiple teams beyond getting Agile practices up and running and moves on to pursuing high performance is an Agile Coach. But there are definitely different levels! The Coach for the teams may be an experienced internal resource, but the Coach for the managers and executives might need to be an external resource capable of talking about the organizational benefits for high performing Agile teams (cost efficiency of faster delivery, higher quality outcomes, less technical debt, and cost reduction due to lower maintenance cost, organizational impediments).

Coaching sponsors and the C-suite is an area often forgotten (see the bullet points in "Culture Change Needed for Agile Programs"). Managers also need a greater understanding of their influence on the teams and how they must help set the stage for good Agile performance.

If the following warning signs show up in the organization, it is time to bring in an Agile Coach.

- Teams are consistently not making their commitments.
- Teams are showing signs of escalating discord.
- Team agreements are not being honored.
- The Definition of Done is not sufficient or is not being followed by the teams.
- The Scrum Masters are telling the team what to do.
- Team members are not working on activities committed to in planning.
- Stories are being split into waterfall form (design, development, test, deploy).
- Product Owners are not present in ceremonies and the Backlog is not groomed in preparation for planning.
- Sponsors, managers, and others outside the teams are requesting work not on the Backlog.
- The managers or Product Owners are telling the team how to do their work.
- Impediments, which the teams cannot solve, are not getting resolved by management.

There are pros and cons to using outsourcing, in-house, peer organizations, and professional Coaches. It depends a lot on the environment and circumstance. Outsourcing can be more expensive but worth it if the skills can be confirmed. Less skilled Coaches can be very costly when you calculate the cost of product delay and the loss of momentum in the Agile transformation itself. Use of in-house Coaches can be cost efficient if good, skilled Coaches are available. Use of a peer organization is great if it is available and the skills of these Coaches confirmed. A professional Coach is usually a good choice and can quickly get things working well because of their broad experience. They can be a significant investment so vetting is essential to obtaining the right resource. Skilled Coaches will be able to walk you through their process.

Vetting a Coach can include asking:

- What area they consider to be their best coaching (transformation, high performance, technical).
- What servant leadership qualities they value.
- For references and following-up with each one.
- About their certification and verifying it with the source.
- About recent engagements and listening for the level of confidence in their voice.
- About recent training they have conducted and to review their materials.
- How they measure their coaching success with clients.
- How they would go about solving a current problem.

How to engage a Coach is, again, dependent upon the environment and circumstance. When first launching an Agile transformation, offsite training and practice makes great sense as everyone's full attention for an extended period of time will be needed. A shorter time for interaction is needed once things are moving, making onsite a better choice. When any of the aforementioned warning signs are present, regular coaching is a must until things improve. When only occasional problems surface, moving to an on-call model, via phone or in-person engagement, at regularly scheduled intervals, is more appropriate. Inspect and adapt as needed.

Communicating Agile to Management

Agile and the Stakeholders

The process of gathering stakeholder needs may be a lighter touch in an Agile Program and/or large projects, but it is still crucial. This typically includes talking about how an Agile Framework is different from Traditional methodology and educating stakeholders on ceremonies, radiators, and Agile principles. Make sure to address their reporting needs too, as stakeholders are unlikely to be attending Stand-ups or demonstrations!

Agile and the CFO

A CFO is primarily concerned with cost, delivery dates, and overall ROI of the Program/Project. Be prepared to talk about cost per cycle, the Roadmap and Minimal Marketing Features (MMFs), building highest priority Features first to allow for reduced scope, interpretation of the Release Burn-up chart, Feature reporting (red, green, yellow), and the schedule bubble chart. Confirm the use of artifacts and cadence of reporting to the CFO, and add this to the communication plan.

Agile and the Executive Team

Executives are focused on very high-level status. They want a dashboard of planned to actual (budget, schedule, and Feature scope). Review options for the dashboard, determine reporting vehicle, and cadence, and add this to the communication plan. Escalation parameters for impediments and risk/issue reporting should also be discussed so everyone gets the level of detail needed and understands their involvement expectations.

Agile Program Responsibilities

As stated previously, the key responsibilities of the Program are to facilitate and coordinate the work across projects. This requires collaboration with the teams at a level that allows enough understanding that risks can be identified and reduced. The Program is responsible for removing obstacles that cannot be removed at the individual project level to achieve the required results. It is also responsible for identifying lessons learned and improvements, as early as possible, that can benefit other teams and projects so everyone can fail fast and learn quickly. With the Agile/Lean Program management approach, always work to ensure collaboration is maximized and waste eliminated! The symbiotic relationship between Program and Projects requires two important things to work well. First, the Program must be seen as adding value. Second, the Feature and/or component project teams must be committed to the Program vision.

Using Agile and Lean thinking at the Program level will allow effective engagement with the project teams to drive the work forward quickly. However, driving the work forward is not meant to be done in a command-

and-control style. It is driving forward with the focus on Customer Value. This is a big shift for many. By focusing on what value is being delivered and in what order, the desired outcome, and what product is to be delivered next, the team drives the work towards the prioritization to correctly build the greatest value first throughout all projects.

Coordinating of Projects

At the Project level, teams may be using various Agile Frameworks (Scrum, Kanban, Lean, etc.). It is the Program's responsibility to make sure reporting progress, adaption, and synchronization happen across projects. *(See Figure 3.03.)*

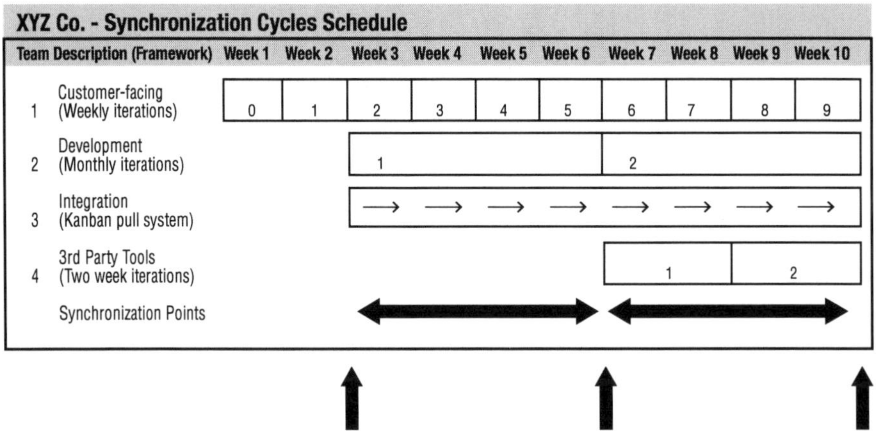

Figure 3.03 | Synchronization Across Teams

The short feedback loop from each Iteration can be applied at the Program level for a holistic view of progress and quick learning, which allows for early adjustments, when costs to make changes are the lowest, and the schedule can accommodate these adjustments easily without compromising quality. The goal at the Program level is allowing the teams to focus on creating and delivering great products (services, features, components) and ensure integration across those products, so the Program is able to deliver on the Vision and objectives for the over-arching Program.

With this understanding of Program-focus versus Project-focus responsibilities, the Program can work to promote solid principles and technical practices, and foster cross-team collaboration and optimization. This allows the Program to show its value to the individual project teams it serves and gives teams full rein to create and work fast.

As covered earlier, Lean thinking focuses on eliminating waste and optimizing the whole. Agile thinking is focused on delivery of complete and fully tested segments of customer-valued products, with early adjustments via regular inspection. The blending of these principles for a Program approach works well regardless of what systems/tools are chosen. It is the mindset drawn from, and thinking applied, that makes the Program successful (see Culture and Mindset Change in the next section). Likewise, it is not which Framework is chosen; it is how it is applied across the Program.

A key aspect of the Program, regardless of the context, is that it needs to allow for agility. Not everything can realistically be planned for in a complex environment at the start of the Program. It is necessary to create a Roadmap, set the direction, plan a little and continue to learn and adapt. Over the life of the Program, plan in detail for things on the near horizon and continue to adapt and be flexible, as well as less precise, for items further out on the horizon. Maintain the original vision, but allow the individual projects to change direction or even how they work. Be prepared to embrace change for the good of the whole!

There is no rule for mixing and matching Frameworks and tools except to choose what works the best for the environment. The key is to experiment, learn, and adapt. But, regardless of the Framework or tools used, the teams must deliver completed Features and/or components on a regular, coordinating cadence in order to track progress and assess overall program progress.

Culture and Mindset Change

"An agile mindset is the set of attitudes supporting an agile working environment. These include respect, collaboration, improvement and learning cycles, pride in ownership, focus on delivering value, and the ability to adapt to change. This mindset is necessary to cultivate high-performing teams, who in turn deliver amazing value for their customers."[3]

- Susan McIntosh

Many enterprises launching an Agile transformation believe that they are doing well when they can recite the *Agile Manifesto*, the 12 principles, and/or the 7 Lean Principles, follow the ceremonies, read a Burn-down chart, and understand the processes they should follow. In fact, this is only the starting point on the Agile journey! You must understand the why behind the various ceremonies, and the reason to use one tool or process over another, or even when to do a combination! Some people do Agile for years and never realize the full benefits because they just follow the process.

The Agile journey is one of continuous improvement and experimentation, failures, and successes. Learn and adapt, then do it all over again. Always keep the antenna up, assessing and transmitting, looking back and looking forward, focusing on reducing risk and delivering value, balancing the *Agile Manifesto* and Agile/Lean principles with alignment of the Program, the organization, and the stakeholders in order to maximize the whole system.

People may say, "I won't do that…it isn't Agile", or, "I can't do that…it isn't Scrum". But Agile is not done, it is felt. The Agile mindset is about adapting to your environment and working with others, with laser focus, on delivering business value. To serve the Program well, some trade-offs are necessary in order to coordinate between teams, collaborate across projects, and scale teams. Be flexible and adapt to change!

Support An Environment of Safety

The path to high performance is scattered with failures along the way. The process of learning means trying new things, taking some risks, figuring out what works and what does not, then trying again. Teams need room to make mistakes and grow. They need to feel comfortable and permitted to make mistakes then try again. Leaders and stakeholders who understand this concept support, and even request, that the teams take time to learn. Retrospectives also provide time for teams to inspect and reflect on things that go well and those that do not, and why. This can lead to greater learning, new approaches, and cohesion between members. This cycle of learning and experimenting will fuel the teams to higher performance.

The book, *"Managing for Happiness: Games, Tools, Practices to Motivate Any Team"* by Jurgen Appelo has an excellent visual tool called the Celebration Grid, shown in *Figure 3.04.* It facilitates a Retrospective by examining failures and celebrating the successes that resulted after understanding and learning from them. Everyone knows, but maybe not admits, that to err is human. Why not celebrate the errors that lead to progress and forward thinking! This often leads to rich ideas for more experiments and solidifies those experimental practices that should be incorporated into ongoing standards by the teams.

A very effective way for organizations to encourage learning is by organizing, what are often referred to as, Exploration Days, allowing teams to suggest

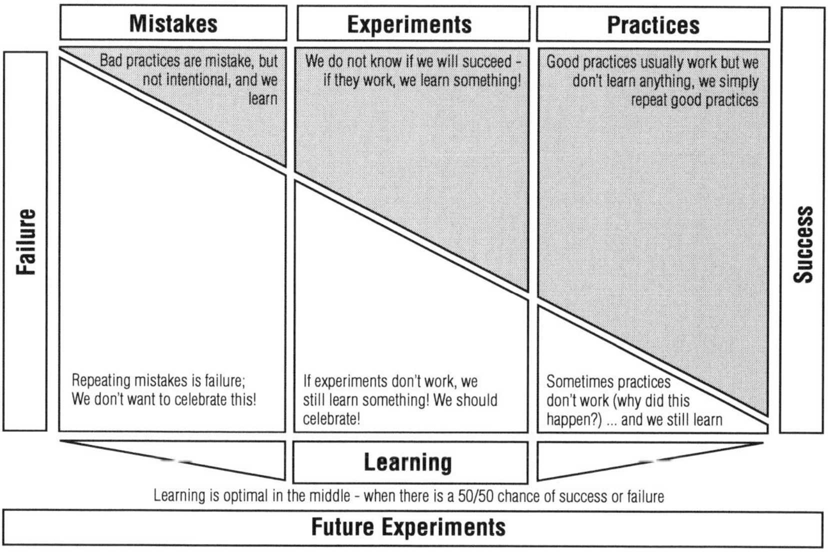

Figure 3.04 | Management 3.0 - Celebration Grid

ideas for experiments by setting aside time to develop new ones. Similarly, Atlassian conducts a ShipIt day every 3 months where a date is selected and product delivery must be within 24 hours. Not only is this fun for everyone involved, it promotes creativity, increases knowledge and often solves existing problems![4]

Organizational Culture Change for Agile Programs

When making changes to support the Agile transformation, many organizations fail in their scaled Agile approach because they do not consider the external support requirements. External, in this context, means outside of the teams. Several areas where executive support will be needed to nurture the culture shift that drives Agile success are:

- Support high performance and high trust within the organization.
- Break down organizational silos and impediments interfering with delivering fast.
- Support continuous improvement efforts, allowing experimentation and support for the right behaviors needed to deliver quality products and service that can be sustained and managed at reasonable cost to the organization.

Building a Culture that Supports High Performance and High Trust Organizations

Strong research into the factors impacting performance, specifically of IT departments, has recently been done looking at both high throughput and high stability as a valid way to measure IT performance. High throughput is measured in terms of lead time and deployment frequency. High stability is measured as the time needed to restore service after an outage or event that caused a degraded quality of service. The two other factors that correlate with, and strongly predict, high performance in IT are a high trust organizational culture and a lightweight, peer-reviewed change approval process.

The data shows that while external processes significantly decrease throughput, such as a separate approval team for changes going to production, they have a negligible positive impact on stability. Change approval mechanisms, such as pair programming or code review by other developers, are just as effective at creating stable systems as change advisory boards, but have a drastically better effect on throughout.

No matter how much process or control there is in an environment, it is impossible to compensate for teams who do not care about customer and organizational outcomes! Creating a culture in which people take responsibility for the consequences of their actions and customer outcomes is the solution.[5]

Although an in-depth discussion on building high trust is outside of the scope of this chapter, it is a key understanding for servant leadership. It stands to reason this extends to non-IT environments as well.

Breaking Down Organization Silos and Impediments Interfering with Delivering Fast

Over time, organizations accumulate "sludge" or waste as operational units, the PMO and business departments improve their efficiency and accumulate processes and routines once valuable, but have become less useful over time. It is often necessary to get executive support to incorporate continuous improvement techniques that will expose areas where change in systems and processes will improve overall delivery of product or services.

Analyses with Value Stream Mapping can provide vision and plans that connect all improvement activities. The process of mapping the complete Value Stream lifecycle from concept to delivery, provides a clear indicator of waste, in terms of wait time or inefficiency. The analysis allows waste to be seen across operational silos or Program organizational impediments, in what is referenced as, current state. From this, a future state can be determined and the plan to eliminate waste can begin by addressing the largest areas of waste first. Once the future state is reached, the next largest area of waste can be targeted for a new future state, allowing for incremental improvements. An overview of the Value Stream Mapping process can be found in the DevOps Chapter.

Support Continuous Improvement Efforts and the Right Behaviors Needed to Deliver Quality Products and Service

Everything is subordinate to good performance, to doing what is supposed to be done. The "True North" is a state of discipline (assuming software development) where developers building new Features, are able to push code changes themselves, after peer review. The exception is high-risk changes, which should be launched as a "dark launch". A "dark launch" can either be switched off in production or made part of an A/B test. Dark launch is a process where software is gradually released in order to get feedback and test performance. A/B testing, sometimes called split testing, is comparing two versions to see which one performs better. It is imperative that those involved in the code work be available for support when their changes go live.

In non-software Programs or Projects this would be different in terms of discipline, but the level of expertise and high-quality testing standards would be the same.

The goal of this cultural change of continuous improvement is to create an environment where learning new skills and progression are considered valuable in their own right and supported by management and leadership. People are able to make local decisions that are sound, which, in turn, rely critically on the flow of information, including feedback loops.

True agility means that teams are working to evolve processes to deal with their particular obstacles as they emerge. The Lean Improvement Kata, a very safe environment for teams to improve in an incremental manner and a natural practice technique for those using an Agile approach, is a good choice. The Improvement Kata is a management approach that entails repeating a routine of establishing challenging target conditions, working through obstacles, learning from what is encountered, adjusting, and meeting the targets, again and again. The Improvement Kata is a great companion to the Value Stream Mapping process.

When attempting to clone what has worked with individual projects in order to scale Agile, significant challenges will emerge. There are two main reasons for this. First, organizational impediments begin to surface with which the teams are ill equipped to deal. Second, adding just enough structure to maintain stability, without marring progress with excessive process or overhead, is very difficult to balance. Some examples would be:

- The facilities group will not allow furniture and space to be altered and it is against policy to hang posters on the wall or place whiteboards in the walkways.
- Human Resources wants detailed performance evaluations on all team members quarterly.
- Contract staff needs to be rotated every six months and developers cannot perform testing.
- The PMO wants detailed project status reports every week, all changes in scope to be reviewed and approved by the Change Board, and a detailed, integrated project plan updated every week, with timeline changed and percent complete for each detailed item.

These all become "sludge" in the product delivery pipes. Throughput goes down and overhead cost goes up! These are areas where executive support may be needed to resolve impediments.

Flexibility, Feedback Loops, and Adaption

One of the most difficult things when scaling Agile is the expectation setting around flexibility, feedback loops, and adaption. Stakeholders and executives, as well as Traditional Project Managers, who are not familiar with Agile, need to adopt a guiding or directing approach over a command-and-control approach. This will be covered more in the Planning section, but it is important to realize that setting expectations goes beyond the teams, and must also be communicated clearly at the Sponsor, stakeholder, and executive levels as well. Those external to the teams need to be prepared to be flexible. The additional time to go from fairly close in planning and estimating to precision is likely wasted time because change is liable to be around the corner in the next Iteration or Release. Get comfortable with ballpark numbers and prepare to adapt as information emerges.

The reason for the quick Agile feedback cycles is to allow for review and adaption as the teams learn. Risks will emerge; learning from experiments will uncover the best practices to follow and/or bad practices to avoid. There will be some failures, but the teams will learn quickly and adapt. Things will sometimes be messy. Step back and ask: is progress being made overall, is quality being built in, is the most important work being created first? If the answers are yes, don't sweat the small stuff, and continue to support the teams! Awesomeness is just around the corner!

This cultural change in thinking and behavior is difficult for many, including Project Managers. Utilizing a Coach can make a big difference!

Tools and Practices Recommendations

Encourage Communities of Practice

A Community of Practice (CoP) is an informal group of like-minded members that come together to share their experiences, learnings, and good practices around interdependent practices. These communities should emerge as needed and disband when not. They are typically enthusiastic, self-organizing volunteers requiring minimal structure. These communities come together to share Agile, engineering, or quality practices and should be encouraged as they help everyone develop their Agile skills and the right discipline.

Support Centers of Excellence

The Center of Excellence (CoE) structure tends to be more formal in nature and have a longer lifecycle than a CoP. These groups usually have management support and direction, with one or more members collecting data, evaluating results, and framing up good practices. Often this body of knowledge promotes continuous improvement efforts and can be responsible for evaluating and recommending tools as well as producing guidelines and minimum standards. Adequate leadership communication and support for this work will significantly improve this effort.

The Agile Program Charter

At the Program level a charter provides the Program Vision and boundaries. *(See Figures 3.05 and 3.06.)* It should be as short as possible so people will read it, but provide enough information that it will serve as a guide for trade-offs and decisions throughout the Program lifecycle. It should provide strategic guidance on:

1) How to coordinate across related projects (how will the synchronization on critical Program aspects happen?).

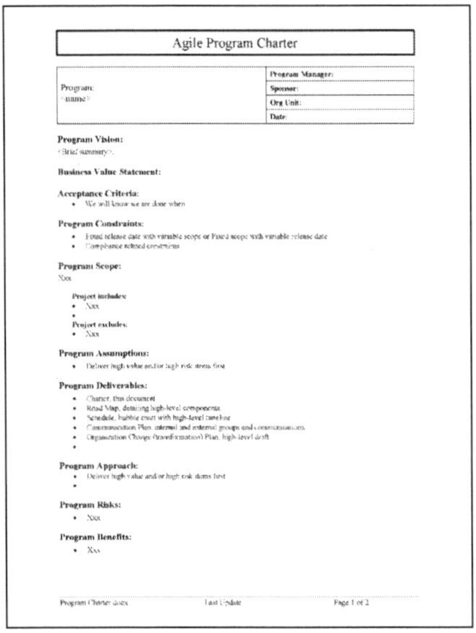

Agile Program Charter

Program: <name>	Program Manager:
	Sponsor:
	Org Unit:
	Date:

Program Vision:
<Brief summary>.

Business Value Statement:

Acceptance Criteria:
- We will know we are done when

Program Constraints:
- Fixed release date with variable scope or Fixed scope with variable release date
- Compliance related constraints

Program Scope:
Xxx

Project includes:
- Xxx
-

Project excludes:
- Xxx

Program Assumptions:
- Deliver high value and/or high risk items first

Program Deliverables:
- Charter, this document
- Road Map, detailing high-level components
- Schedule, bubble chart with high-level timeline
- Communication Plan, internal and external groups and communications
- Organization Change (transformation) Plan, high-level draft
-

Program Approach:
- Deliver high value and/or high risk items first
-

Program Risks:
- Xxx

Program Benefits:
- Xxx

Program Charter.docx Last Update Page 1 of 2

Figure 3.05 | Agile Program Charter

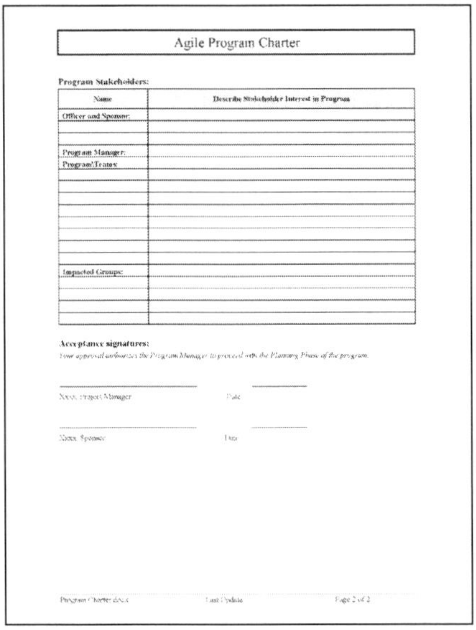

Agile Program Charter

Program Stakeholders:

Name	Describe Stakeholder Interest in Program
Officer and Sponsor:	
Program Manager:	
Program/Teams:	
Impacted Groups:	

Acceptance signatures:
Your approval authorizes the Program Manager to proceed with the Planning Phase of the program.

Xxxx, Project Manager Date

Xxxx, Sponsor Date

Program Charter.docx Last Update Page 2 of 2

Figure 3.06 | Agile Program Charter

2) How to collaborate across the various projects (e.g. geographic location, time zones, work hours, required tools).

3) How to know when the Program is Done (basic criteria for acceptance and closure).

In most Agile projects, scope is variable so the closure criteria have to be based around Releases, budget, or timeframe. In addition, since the customer/proxy can add or subtract scope at any time, process needs to be defined around acceptance and closure.

It is helpful to include a list of Features, but given that the Customer/Proxy can rearrange or change this at any time during the Program, a clear list of desired outcomes with a high-level potential Feature list, or links to separate live documents, provides better guidance. Establish guidelines, but leave room for flexibility.

Program Roadmap Radiator

This is a simple, at a glance, radiator of Program components. It should be prominently displayed and updated regularly. *(See Figure 3. 07.)*

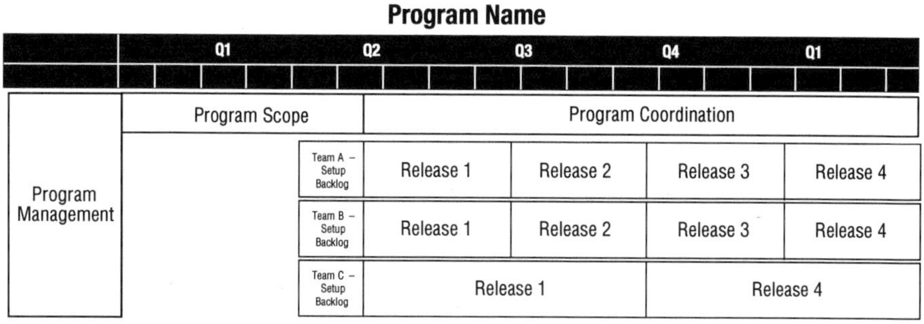

Figure 3.07 | Program Roadmap

Program Executive Status Report

See Figure 3.08 for an example of a Program Executive Status Report.

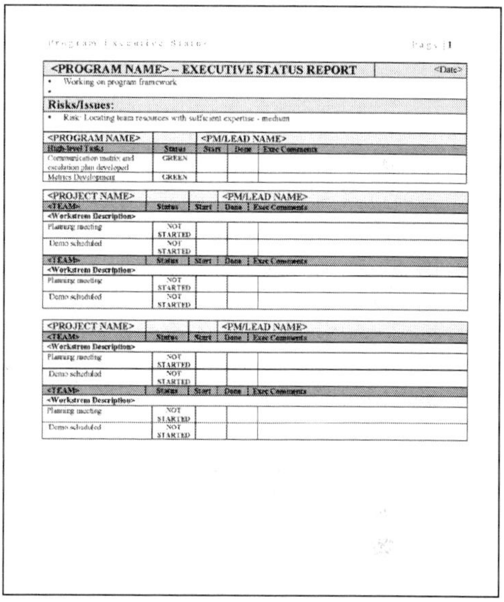

Page 1

<PROGRAM NAME> – EXECUTIVE STATUS REPORT	<Date>
• Working on program framework •	
Risks/Issues:	
• Risk: Locating team resources with sufficient expertise - medium	

<PROGRAM NAME>		<PM/LEAD NAME>		
High-level Tasks	Status	Start	Done	Exec Comments
Communication matrix and escalation plan developed	GREEN			
Metrics Development	GREEN			

<PROJECT NAME>			<PM/LEAD NAME>	
<TEAM>	Status	Start	Done	Exec Comments
<Workstrem Description>				
Planning meeting	NOT STARTED			
Demo scheduled	NOT STARTED			
<TEAM>	Status	Start	Done	Exec Comments
<Workstrem Description>				
Planning meeting	NOT STARTED			
Demo scheduled	NOT STARTED			

<PROJECT NAME>			<PM/LEAD NAME>	
<TEAM>	Status	Start	Done	Exec Comments
<Workstrem Description>				
Planning meeting	NOT STARTED			
Demo scheduled	NOT STARTED			
<TEAM>	Status	Start	Done	Exec Comments
<Workstrem Description>				
Planning meeting	NOT STARTED			
Demo scheduled	NOT STARTED			

Figure 3.08 | Program Executive Status Report

Program Backlog or Story Board

Inspired by Jeff Patton's Story Board Skelton and Backbone concept, this has been modified for Epics and Feature Decomposition and can be further modified into swim lanes for multiple teams or projects.[6] *(See Figure 3.09.)*

Program Schedule

The bubble chart is an easy way to show the overall timeline across multiple projects and teams. *(See Figure 3.10.)*

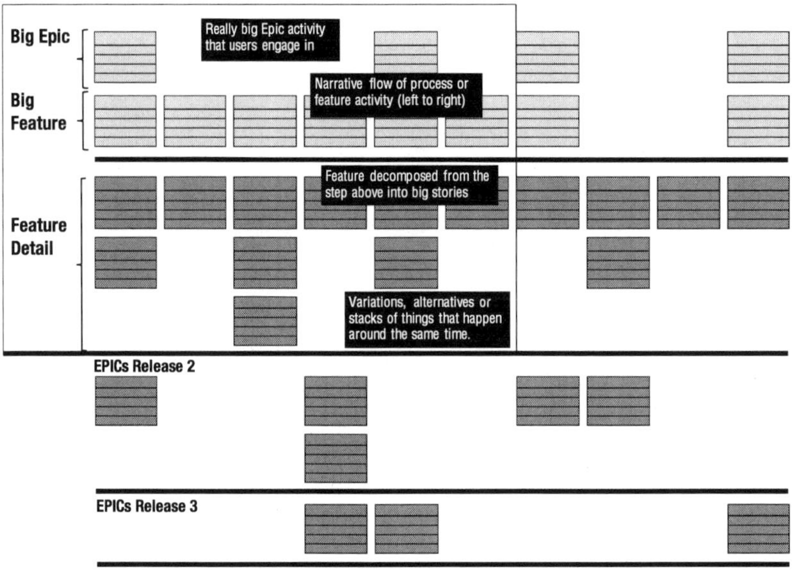

Figure 3.09 | User Story Roadmap

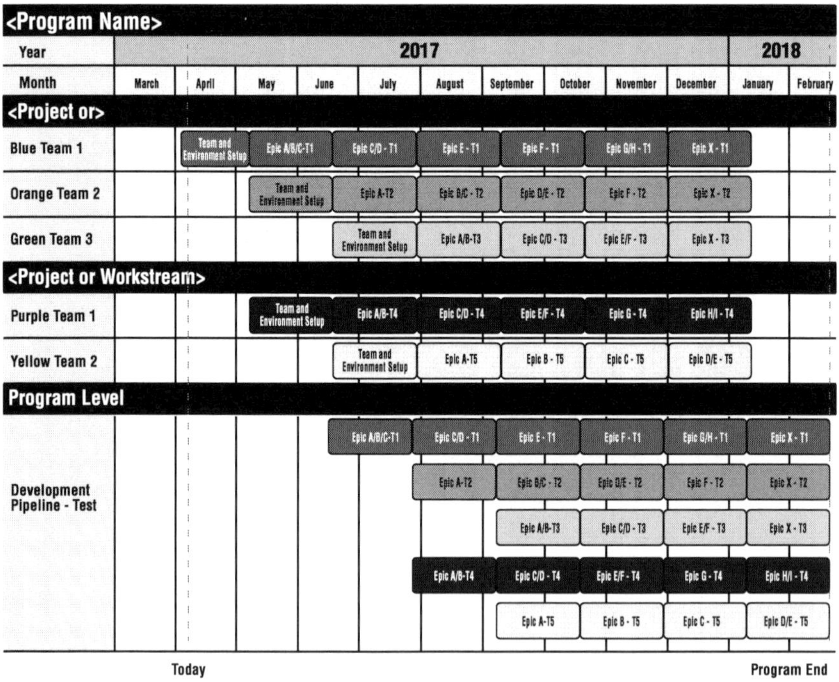

Figure 3.10 | Program Schedule

Escalation Plan Sample

A sample Escalation Plan is shown in *Figure 3.11*.

Escalation Plan

As issues or complications arise with regards to agile team deliveries and related work streams, both within our teams or external to them, it may become necessary to escalate issues if a resolution cannot be achieved within our teams. We will use the guiding principles below when it becomes necessary to do so. *Our guiding principles for escalation are:*

1) Resolve the issue at the lowest Team Level possible
2) Use the Priority Level below to determine the process steps
3) Always communicate to your direct resource and/or functional manager
4) Each team will define their own definition of critical as it deters from one application/system to the next

The table below defines the various **Escalation Levels**:

Escalation Level	Definition	Decision Authority
1	Team or individual	Team ScrumMaster and/or Team Product Owner
2	Agile Leadership Community (group or individual outside of your team)	Project Manager, ScrumMaster and/or Product Owner across affected teams
3	Manager – individual	Individual Manager or Business Relationship Manager
4	Manager – program	Program Manager of affected teams
5	Executive	Varies (necessary level of interaction determined by level 3 or 4 above)

The table below defines the ***Priority Level***, decision authorities, and timeframes for resolution.

Priority Level	Definition of Priority Level	Process Step
S1	Critical - work cannot move forward	If team levels 1 and 2 above have not worked, create a story with details to the criticality on the **Impediment board** and email Managers and include the link to the issue. If Team outside of Managers area are involved include them on the email. Also supply location of additional documents or business case that supports the current issue to needs to be addressed.
S2	Have a work-around but not sustainable (time limit should be	If team level 1 and 2 above, have not worked, create a story with details to the **time** urgency on the **Impediment board** and include the link to the issue. Alert your Manager and

Figure 3.11 | Escalation Plan

Impediment Board - Radiator

A sample Impediment Board is shown in *Figure 3.12.*

Cross Program Dependencies Radiator

A sample Cross Program Dependencies Radiator is shown in *Figure 3.13.*

Cross Program Risks Radiators

This risk radiator format was inspired by Mike Griffith's presentation at the 2006 Agile Conference. This standard graph has been modified to include multiple teams and works with a Story format similar to other Stories that make up an Agile risk game appropriate for team risk generation. *(See Figure 3.14.)*

Program Name										
Backlog Story	**Team A**	**Team B**	**Team C**	**Team D**	**Team E**	**Infrastructure**	**DBA**	**Leadership**	**Notes**	**Blocked**
Project or Workstream 1										
Infrastructure Setup Stalled		Resource Contraints - Need help resolving at a higher level	Resource Contraints - Need help resolving at a higher level		Resource Contraints - Need help resolving at a higher level			Joe has been sick- work delayed (any add'l resource?)		
Database Creation Dependency	Watch date for DB creation						Delayin DB Setup			
Project 2 Dependent Upon DB Schema	Watch date for DB/if it slips it is likely Schema will also be delayed						Delayin DB will affect Schema work- Project 2			
Project or Workstream 2										
Dependent upon project 1 for DB schema	Watch date for DBA on Project 1 Schema									
Project or Workstream 3										
Infrastructure Setup Stalled	Resource Contraints - Need help resolving at a higher level		Resource Contraints - Need help resolving at a higher level							

UPDATE THIS BOARD DAILY FOR THE PROGRAM STAND-UP BY 9:45 A.M.

Yellow - Potential Impediment

Green - Impediment or Dependency

Pink - Issue or Action Requested

Figure 3.12 | Program Impediment Board

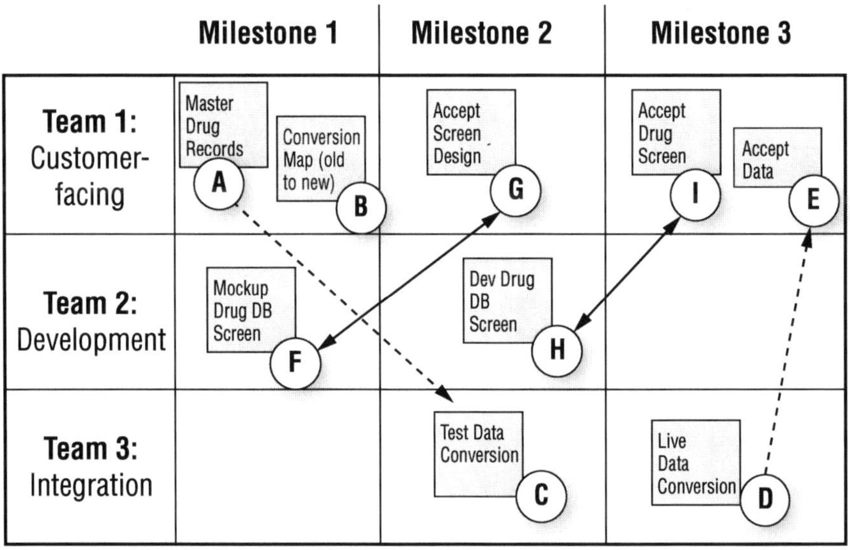

Figure 3.13 | Cross Program Dependencies Radiator

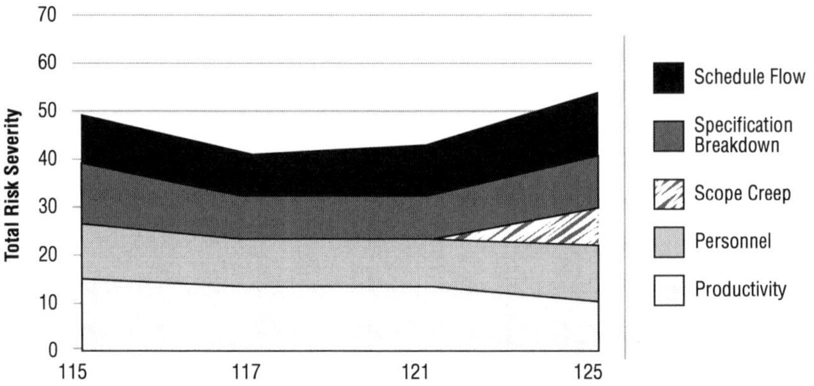

Figure 3.14 | Cross Program Risks Radiator

Conclusion

A lot of important information was displayed in this chapter, along with the tools and practices to help apply it. When deciding to make the transition to Agile, these will all be invaluable to making it smooth and successful!

Chapter End Notes

[1] Thompson, Loren. "HealthCare.gov Diagnosis: The Government Broke Every Rule of Project Management." Forbes. 3 Dec. 2013, *www.forbes.com/sites/lorenthompson/2013/12/03/healthcare-gov-diagnosis-the-government-broke-every-rule-of-project-management/#2fa8f3966b7f.*

[2] Denning, Steve. "The Boeing Debacle: Seven Lessons Every CEO Must Learn." Forbes, 17 Jan. 2013, *www.forbes.com/sites/stevedenning/2013/01/17/the-boeing-debacle-seven-lessons-every-ceo-must-learn/#6c45f89915c.*

[3] McIntosh, Susan. "What Exactly is the Agile Mindset?" InfoQ. 28 Aug. 2016, *www.infoq.com/articles/what-agile-mindset. Susan McIntosh is an author and Agile Coach.*

[4] For more information on the Celebration Grid or Exploration Days, visit Management30.com at *https://management30.com/practice/.*

[5] O'Reilly, Barry et al., *Lean Enterprise: How High Performance Organizations Innovate at Scale.* O'Reilly Media, 2015.

[6] Patton, Jeff. *User Story Mapping: Discover the Whole Story, Build the Right Product.* O'Reilly Media, 2014.

PART TWO

FRAMEWORKS

CHAPTER

4

Scrum of Scrums (SoS)

Overview

What is now known as Scrum was pioneered in the early 1990s. In 1995 Ken Schwaber and Jeff Sutherland collaborated in its first public presentation, where they suggested potential "good practices." The focus and success of early Scrum was single-team development and, as it succeeded in that arena, the next logical step was to scale Scrum to multiple teams. Scrum of Scrums emerged to meet that need.

The first use of Scrum of Scrums (SoS) was led by Dr. Jeff Sutherland at IDX Systems (now GE Healthcare) in 1996. In a 2001 paper, Jeff wrote that his intention was to "...turn the entire development organization into an interlocking set of Scrums." Jeff later commented that the original implementation even included "virtual teams for architecture, QA, to develop common strategies, tools, engineering standards, etc."[1]

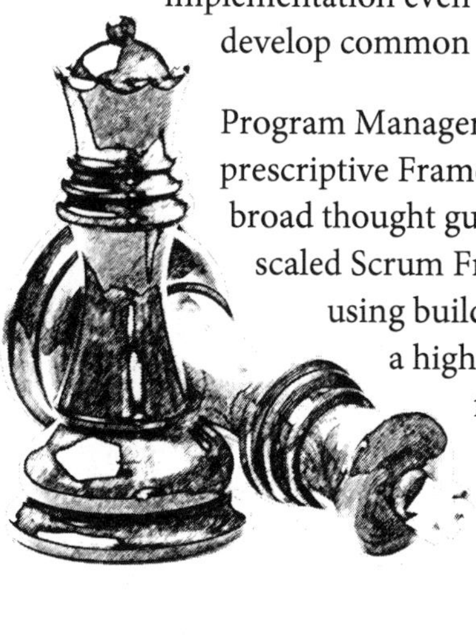

Program Managers should view Scrum of Scrums less as a prescriptive Framework and more as a set of general patterns and broad thought guidance to be used when constructing their own scaled Scrum Framework, customized for their organizations, using building blocks made from Scrum. Think of SoS as a highly customizable, lightweight proto-Framework for scaling Scrum.

This chapter will explore the commonly used techniques for scaling Scrum, generally referred to as Scrum of Scrums. It will explore both benefits and challenges to equip the reader for success using and customizing SoS where appropriate. It will also explore some recent updates to the thinking that spawned SoS and will touch on its new sibling, Scrum@Scale, which has been updated by Jeff Sutherland in order to provide clarity to some of the vague areas in SoS.

The Basics

Generally, SoS works with multiple Scrum teams, each pulling their own Sprint Backlogs from a single, central Product Backlog. Just like in single-team Scrum, each team holds a Daily Scrum meeting, but also sends representatives to the SoS Meeting where inter-team dependencies and obstacles, called blockers, are discussed. This meeting is usually held every day and provides the most granular and frequent opportunities for transparency, inspection, and adaptation, which are the three pillars of Scrum.[2] Remember, SoS is Scrum.

At the Program Level, one of the new ceremonies in SoS is a "Meta Scrum" or "Management Scrum" meeting for senior management and stakeholders, preferably held weekly, but no less than monthly, to resolve any escalated issues, review the Product Roadmap, make funding decisions, and set the direction for going forward. The meeting allows for frequent course corrections in response to learning from previous Sprints and spikes. Program Managers frequently customize this for their particular mix of product and organizational culture. For example, organizations with multiple, interrelated sub-products may have a larger Meta Scrum meeting, with more participants, in order to try to find the right combination of funding for all their initiatives. Other organizations may opt for smaller, or even less frequent, Meta Scrum meetings if that suits their needs better.

Although it was not a part of Jeff Sutherland's original SoS implementation at IDX Systems, many companies using SoS establish Communities of Practice to improve communications between members of different teams. This will be discussed at length later in this chapter.

In SoS, the work done at the team level remains the same as in single-team Scrum. Single-team Scrum was discussed in detail in Chapter 4 of the *Agile Almanac – Book 1*, but will be briefly reviewed here for clarity.

Scrum uses only three roles: Product Owner, Development Team, and Scrum Master. When combined, these people constitute the Scrum Team. Note that

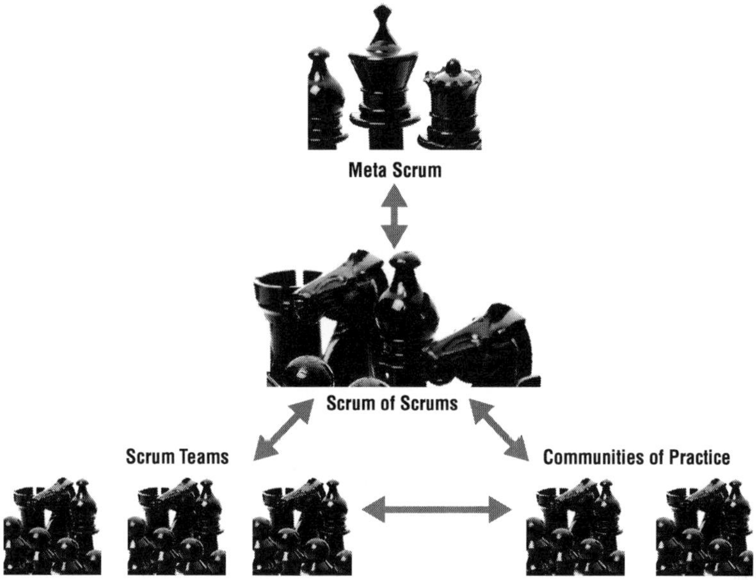

Figure 4.01 | SoS Lines of Communication

the Development Team is a subset of Scrum Team. The Scrum Team includes all the people and skills needed to complete a "Done" increment of product functionality. It is a cross-functional and self-directed team, usually consisting of five to nine people, following the "7 plus or minus 2" rule from leadership best practices. The Scrum Team uses an iterative, incremental process to deliver small units of value in short timeboxes called Sprints.

The Product Owner, as also described in Chapter 3 of this book, is primarily responsible for making decisions about product functionality, acceptance criteria, and assigning business value to Product Backlog items. They answer questions from the Development Team, solicit feedback from Users, and act as the voice of the Customer. They are responsible to the business for ensuring that the team is always working on the items with the highest value.

The Scrum Master is responsible for removing obstacles and ensuring that the Development Team follows the rules of Scrum. Similarly, to a Program Manager, a Scrum Master is a servant leader whose focus it is to help the team fulfill their goals without violating their autonomy as a self-managing group, by assigning tasks or making decisions about how the product will be developed.

In IT, for example, the Scrum Development Team includes all the coders, database administrators, business analysts, and testers without differentiating them. Everyone is simply a self-managing Development Team Member sharing collective ownership for producing the Product Increment.

In Scrum, the workflow starts with the Product Owner prioritizing the Product Backlog. Initially, this consists of the set of all the items the Product Owner identifies as being *potentially* needed for the Product. The initial creation of the Backlog is different from the ongoing Backlog decomposition and refinement that the team participates in during the Sprint. Experience has shown that teams starting with a deep Backlog of small Stories, ranked by value, have an easier time during Sprint Planning. According to Jeff Sutherland, teams who enforce a robust "ready checklist" and ensure that only fully decomposed, estimated Stories, with objective acceptance criteria, ever make it into Sprint Planning have *double the velocity* of teams who do not engage in this practice![3]

The Sprint begins with Sprint Planning where the Development Team selects the highest priority items from the Product Backlog that they think they can get "Done" within the Sprint timebox. Stories that are too large to complete in one Sprint are decomposed during Backlog Decomposition and Refinement until they are small enough to fit into one. The primary consideration for most Stories is business value, and the Product Owner will ensure that the Stories that provide the greatest value are pulled in first. Sometimes, however, for technical reasons, the team finds that they need to include a Story to create infrastructure or other architectural elements to support one. This would be discussed amongst the team during Sprint Planning and included in the Sprint Backlog only after total agreement. An example of this is a business that wants to upgrade their shopping cart functionality. Before they can do that, the Development Team needs to upgrade to a newer version of the database server.

Once the whole team has agreed on the Stories they will complete during this Sprint, the list becomes known as the Sprint, or Team, Backlog. During Sprint Planning, the team will also plan how they will get this work done, but does not necessarily assign Tasks since it is more typical for members to "pull" the highest value Tasks as they have availability to work on them. While all Agile methods, including Scrum, call for no Big Design Up Front (BDUF)," it is common for teams in single-team environments to plan their architectural and infrastructure components several Sprints in advance.

At the Program level it is common to have more rigorous architecture and infrastructure planning that extends even further into the future. This is covered in detail in Chapter 2 – Myths, Misconceptions, and Anti-Patterns.

Progress during the Sprint is guided by the Daily Scrum, otherwise known as the Daily Stand-up Meeting, which keeps the Development Team synchronized and where progress, risks, and impediments are made transparent. For example, if a software developer cannot make a required database change because the database server keeps crashing, that is something the Scrum Master would be interested in hearing about. The Scrum Master would, of course, first try to resolve this blocker himself, by working with the team responsible for that server. Failing that, the Scrum Master, along with any necessary team members, would take this to the SoS meeting for resolution with representatives of the other teams. The SoS meeting is covered in depth later in this chapter.

At the end of the Sprint, continuous improvement is enabled through two ceremonies – a Sprint Review and Sprint Retrospective. Continuous product improvement is driven by the Sprint Review Meeting where the work completed in the previous Sprint is demonstrated to any interested stakeholder for feedback. In the Sprint Retrospective Meeting, the team focuses on how to improve their process for the next Sprint.

Scrum ceremonies include Sprint Planning, Product Backlog Decomposition and Refinement, and the Daily Scrum, Sprint Demo, and Sprint Retrospective. The Daily Scrum facilitates team synchronization, provides visibility, and opportunities for inspection and adaption. These meetings are commonly followed by an "After Meeting" for problem-solving and working groups. The Sprint Demo and Sprint Retrospective are the final two ceremonies whereas Product Backlog Decomposition and Refinement occurs throughout the Sprint.

That wraps up the brief synopsis of single-team Scrum. If more information is desired, please consult the Agile Almanac – Book 1.

Benefits / Challenges

Benefits

Uses Best Known Framework and Existing Teams

One of the biggest strengths of using SoS is that it leverages the best known, perhaps most widely-accepted, Agile Framework. It gains added benefits from Scrum Teams who have previously used it for single-team projects. Therefore, the investment already made by the organization and practitioners in Scrum training is completely usable and provides a foundation for moving to the next level; SoS.

Fast Implementation
When teams are familiar with the Scrum Framework, SoS can be implemented relatively quickly, with minimal investment in additional training and minimal change resistance. SoS is also fast to implement because it is not very prescriptive. There is also little overhead of process and tools to start using SoS.

Easily Customized
Scrum of Scrums is easily customized to fit the organizational culture, product, team, and environment. Organizations can decide what additional support is required and add only what is needed, minimizing overhead and keeping the deployment as "lightweight" as possible.

For example, the budgeting and resource planning needs of a large organization will require more rigor than those of a smaller group or portfolio, and SoS can be adapted accordingly. The key idea is that managers closest to operational needs decide how to tailor SoS to fit the actual needs.

Note that just as in single-team environments, Scrum, itself, cannot be customized, only Program-level implementation details.

Challenges

Lines of Communication for the Product Owner and Scrum Master Roles
Scrum leverages the power of Osmotic Communication to reduce risk and speed development.

SoS becomes necessary because this inherent strength of Scrum Teams, unfortunately, reaches the point of diminishing returns far too quickly. The simple formula of n(n-1)/2 can be used to calculate the number of Lines of Communication for a team. That means, for example, that a team with 9 members has 36 lines of communication. While that is already a lot, simply increasing the team size to 15 creates 105 lines of communication. For a team of 25, the lines of communication balloons to 300! Clearly, size is a challenge to achieving cogent, adequate communication across the whole team as it scales up.

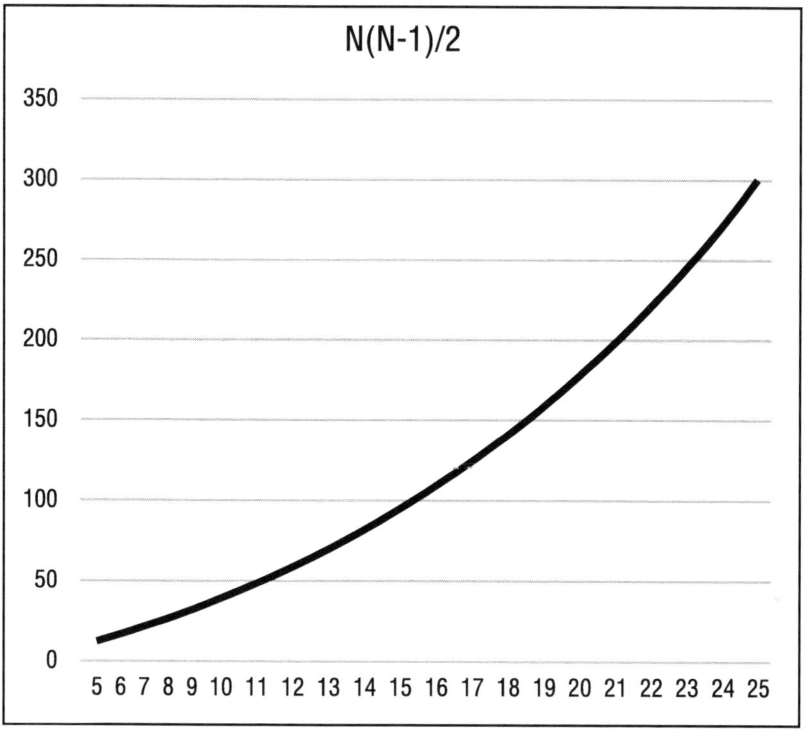

Figure 4.02 | Lines of Communication

Maximum Number of Development Teams per Product Owner and Scrum Master

As a rule of thumb, a fully allocated Product Owner can effectively manage no more than two Scrum Teams. There may be exceptions, but this should be treated more as a firm rule than a suggestion. Therefore, as Scrum scales, the Product Owner can easily be spread too thin and become the source of many dysfunctions. Methods for decomposing or nesting the job of the Product Owner are discussed later in this chapter.

Any guide for determining how many teams a Scrum Master can support is a little more nebulous. Many factors drive, and limit, the number of teams a Scrum Master can support including the Agile maturity of the team and organization, type of product being developed, experience level of the Product Owner, and number of issues and blockers that may arise. The more complexity and uncertainty the team faces, the more Scrum Master time and focus it will require.

No Built-in Budgeting Mechanism

Scrum of Scrums does not have a built-in mechanism for budgeting, unlike some other Frameworks for scaling Agile. This can be viewed as an opportunity to custom tailor an approach that fits the needs of the enterprise or portfolio, but since creating that approach consumes resources, it is listed here as a challenge.

No Built-in Resource Planning Mechanism

Scrum of Scrums also lacks a mechanism to do enterprise resource planning. The limitation is similar to the lack of a budgeting mechanism, except that at the enterprise and portfolio levels, this is a critical shortcoming. It must be addressed because it can be argued that enterprise and portfolio resource planning is trickier than budgeting. Planning complexity, because of the myriad of variables involved, can be non-linear or geometric while budgeting is more linear, allowing decisions to simply move more money from Project A to Project B. The elements for planning teams, skills, and non-compressible development logic, on the other hand, are not interchangeable dollars easily moved from Project A to Project B. That means that enterprises using SoS must also develop their own process for resource planning, being careful not to assume that an approach that works for another company will work for whatever unique blend of culture, product, and teams exists in theirs.

Culture Clash

One of the most common challenges faced when scaling Agile is a clash of cultures. Scaling Agile is commonly called an "Agile Transformation" for very good reason. Everything, or nearly everything, about the company culture will be changed or impacted. Obviously, change on such a broad scale is difficult to manage.

In the *11th Annual State of Agile Development Report* issued in 2017, the top challenge to any Agile transformation was an organizational culture that clashes with Agile values.[4] A whopping 63% of survey respondents listed this as a challenge. Successfully scaling Agile requires organizations to think long and hard about how they will manage the culture change that must occur for them to succeed with SoS. This cannot be overlooked.

Program-Level Attributes

What has been described up to this point in this chapter has largely been a recap of single-team Scrum. When things scale to the Program level, the need for new roles, not part of single-team Scrum, become important.

Roles

Chief Product Owner

Chief Product Owners incorporate guidance about vision and strategy from executives and other stakeholders and work with the Product Owners to maximize the value their teams are delivering toward that Roadmap.

It is important to note that for any given piece of functionality there can be only one Owner making the decisions if an optimal outcome is to be achieved. The Chief Product Owner is responsible for coordinating decisions and ensuring that communication happens, so appropriate visibility is created. They are not, however, an overlapping decision authority above the Product Owners. SoS does not dictate how to decompose the Product Owner role, but it is common to do so by functionality. *(See Figure 4.03)*

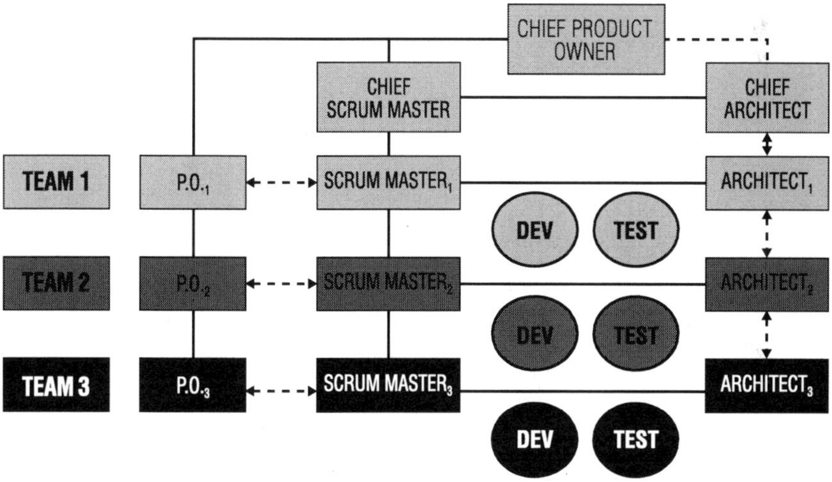

Figure 4.03 | Roles in Scrum of Scrums

Not only does the Chief Product Owner role help to scale Scrum by scaling the Product Owner role, it also helps reduce competition between Product Owners. Ideally, the Chief Product Owner will ensure that decisions to allocate resources or assign priority are made for the benefit of the product and not for the benefit of one particular Product Owner.

Chief Scrum Master

Once an organization has multiple teams working from a single Product Backlog, a need develops for someone to track and resolve issues transcending the individual team level. That person must coordinate planning, manage cross-team dependencies, manage and track risks, and resolve or escalate unresolved blockers at the team level. In IT projects, Chief Scrum Masters work closely with Chief Architects to ensure continuous integration. It is common for people in the role of Chief Scrum Master to also act as Agile Coaches when needed.

Chief Architect

Although it is not an official Scrum role, in single-team Scrum there is usually an Architect or Technical Lead on each team. However, at the Program level someone needs to coordinate all the Architects and unify technology decisions for the entire product. This person is the Chief Architect and they are responsible for making technical decisions that affect all teams. A working member of a Development Team can take on this extra responsibility. The Chief Architect works closely with each team's Architect or Tech Lead, and also with Product Owners and other stakeholders. For SoS, this role is critical for success with key technical competencies, such as Continuous Integration, Continuous Delivery, and DevOps.

Product Manager

As discussed earlier, a Product Owner can only contribute to two Agile teams at a time. While the Product Owner is in the team room working with the developers every day during development, some organizations find that they need someone to take on the product management tasks that are not development team related. Product Managers , when used, work closely with sales, marketing, finance, and executives to constantly ensure their Product Vision and Roadmap are in line with corporate strategy. They may also attend trade shows stay up-to-date with market trends and competition.

Although many organizations have success using this role, caution is warranted here. Remember that the rules of Scrum cannot be changed, and that everyone needed to deliver the value committed to must be on the Scrum team. When considering using this role, evaluate whether the value delivered by this person is needed for this product or not. If it is, they should be on a Scrum team. If it is not, reconsider their value altogether.

The beauty of SoS is that it can be custom fit to the organization's need rather easily. The two important things to remember about decomposing the Product Owner role is that there is never more than one person acting as the voice of the Customer on the team, and that the rules of Scrum cannot change.

Workflow

At the individual team level, SoS uses the existing Scrum Framework and should not represent a change to teams already using that. With multiple teams working from the same Backlog, additional work is needed to coordinate inter-team dependencies and blockers, communicate learning from Sprints and spikes to other teams, and possibly change funding priorities. The Scrum of Scrums and Meta Scrum ceremonies are added for these purposes.

Ceremonies

While the team-level work in Scrum stays the same in SoS, there are some new ceremonies and subtle changes to existing ceremonies necessary to succeed when using multiple teams. They include the Scrum of Scrums, Meta Scrum, Integrated Sprint Demo, Integrated Program Retrospective, and Backlog Refinement.

Scrum of Scrums

Purpose

The Scrum of Scrums meeting is the Daily Scrum for all the teams on the project. Think of the SoS meeting as a team responsible for delivering large Stories and Epics. While team progress is discussed, especially if a team is experiencing issues, the focus of the meeting is on identifying and removing cross-team blockers and managing dependencies. Like everything in Scrum, this meeting is timeboxed at 15-minutes regardless of the number of participants. Just like the Daily Scrum meeting, this is commonly followed by an "After Meeting" for affected members to discuss problems. Think of the Chief Product Owner as the Product Owner of the Scrum of Scrums. The leader, sometimes known as the Scrum of Scrums Master, is usually the Chief Scrum Master who is also empowered to bring blockers that cannot be resolved to the Meta Scrum team for resolution.

Membership

Although each team must send at least one representative to the SoS meeting, in practice there is some variation in the number of attendees for this meeting. . One representative, some members, or the entire team may attend, with a preference for the latter. If a subset of the team is selected to be representatives, the decision as to how many and which members to send is usually driven by current cross-team issues and blockers being faced and the results of the last SoS meeting. This meeting is held anywhere from daily to weekly, with a strong preference for the former.

An astute reader may now be thinking of the n(n-1)/2 formula for lines of communication and wondering how communication is maintained as the size of this meeting grows. Care must be taken that, as this meeting grows in size, the communication still happens. Like many things Agile, there is no firm rule about the size of this meeting. Some organizations have every Development Team, and member, attend this meeting and it is effective and limited to the 15-minute timebox while other organizations struggle with a meeting size of 20. This is an area where SoS can be tailored for an organization, but Program Managers are urged to do so with great caution and not violate the rules of Scrum.

Jeff Sutherland related an example of the best Scrum of Scrums meeting he has ever seen. The meeting was at Patient Keeper and every member of their 50-60 person development organization attended, what was described as, a "highly disciplined" SoS meeting that kept to its 15-minute timebox. He described this as "big room Scrum of Scrums" and noted that the organization was able to deploy at least four enterprise hospital systems per Sprint, and without fail, for years using this method![3]

Tools Used
Each Scrum of Scrums team should maintain an SoS Backlog of issues and blockers that team members are working towards resolving. If the SoS team chooses to do this, this information should be available on their information radiator, just like any other team. According to Scrum thought-leader Mike Cohn, during the SoS meeting, team members should answer the following four questions for their team:[5]

1. What has your team done since we last met?
2. What will your team do before we meet again?
3. Is anything slowing your team down or getting in their way?
4. Are you about to put something in another team's way?

Meta Scrum

Executives, Product Owners, and other stakeholders meet at least once per Sprint to make funding decisions, set direction, and discuss any issues that the Scrum of Scrums were not able to resolve. This meeting was originally called the "Management Scrum,"[6] but has come to be known as the "Meta-Scrum."

Purpose
The Meta Scrum is a product-centric meeting used to make strategy and funding decisions based on market feedback and new learning from the teams. A common trait of many organizations successfully using SoS is finding ways to incorporate the rapid learning occurring at the team level into Program-level decision-making. During this meeting, resources and budgets may be changed, or other projects funded based on prior learning.

Membership
Run by the Chief Product Owner, the Meta Scrum meeting is attended by senior management, typically those with budgetary or performance responsibility for the product and those who set product and corporate strategy and Product Owners. .

Tools Used
The Meta Scrum meetings usually incorporate information on work completed and remaining from the individual teams and track progress against a Backlog of products under consideration for prioritization and funding.

Integrated Sprint Demo

Like single-team Scrum there is a Sprint Demo in SoS, but it is scaled to include the integrated work of all teams. All teams must integrate their completed work into the overall solution for it to be shown in the Integrated Sprint Demo, which is held on the last day of the Sprint. These tend to be happy sessions filled with esprit dé corps and differ only slightly from single-team Demos. They are a primary mechanism for inspection and adaptation in Scrum. These meetings are owned by the Chief Product Owner who coordinates inviting outside teams, and external and offshore participants, as necessary.

For example, a road racing video game Program might have the following teams at its Integrated Sprint Demo:

- Key executives, Product Owners, and other necessary business stakeholders
- All the Development Teams that worked on the project, which might include:
    - Development Team A – Built the race track and the scenery
    - Development Team B – Built all the cars and their customizing options

    - Development Team C – Coded all the common graphics rendering modules
    - Development Team D – Recorded all the sounds
    - Offshore Development Team 1 – Coded the user interface
    - Offshore Development Team 2 – Wrote the online help
    - Onshore Vendor Team ABC – Conducted specialized testing
    - Onshore Vendor Team XYZ – Rendered graphic art components

- Stakeholders from other departments are also welcome, such as:
    - Sales
    - Marketing
    - Product Development
    - Accounting
    - Finance
    - Mailroom (OK, the mailroom isn't a key contributor and would not normally have a business need to be here, but Clyde, the mailroom manager, is a big road racing fan and was asked to attend this meeting to add an additional customer perspective. About nine months ago Clyde spoke up with an idea for a Feature that nobody had considered before. The idea was added to the Product Backlog, prioritized, built, and was released three months ago to critical acclaim. Not only was the publicity good, a whole new cohort of customers are signing up just for this new feature. Now Clyde is sort of a guest of honor at these meetings.)

Purpose

Integrated Sprint Demos are the primary method for the team to show its work to the business and user communities and for the Product Owner to solicit feedback. Many times, the priority of existing Product Backlog items changes or new ones are added based on feedback received at this meeting. The standard timebox for a single-team Sprint Demo is 4 hours for a four-week sprint and 2 hours for a two-week Sprint. Experience has shown that with more participants and potentially larger sets of functionality to demo, these meetings can easily go longer if not managed proactively.

Membership

Anyone who is interested in attending is welcome; this is an informal meeting. Sometimes external users, partners, customers, or even the mailroom manager are invited to attend.

Tools Used
Any tools needed for the entire room (or remote, virtual rooms) to see and participate in the demo. This may include screens, LCD projectors, desktop sharing software, and video conferencing.

Integrated Program Retrospective

One of the most powerful mechanisms in Scrum is the Sprint Retrospective. It is the ceremony that allows the team to apply continuous process improvement, reflect on how they produced the last increment, and how they can improve during the next Sprint.

As multiple teams are added, and are all executing against a single Product Backlog, the Integrated Program Retrospective provides continuous process improvement at the Program level. This way, individual teams improve as a result of their Sprint Retrospectives while the entire Program continuously improves by holding an Integrated Program Retrospective. During Sprint Retrospectives, any identified, Program-level areas for improvement are recorded and brought up at the Integrated Program Retrospective.

Purpose
Both individual team Sprint Retrospectives and Integrated Program Retrospectives are opportunities to identify and expose issues, impediments, and areas for improvement across the Program and are used by teams to inspect and adapt the Scrum and SoS processes, themselves. The team is challenged to find ways to make their next Sprint 1% more efficient. Mature teams will actually use this meeting to improve upon their Definition of Done.

Membership
At the Team level, Retrospectives are limited to members of the individual Scrum team. However, at the Integrated Program Retrospective, all team members in the entire Program are involved.

Tools Used
At both the Team and Program level, teams may employ whatever tools and methods they find useful. Commonly, Pareto Analysis is used to find the most impactful issues affecting the team. The team may create Fishbone Diagrams (also known as Ishikawa diagrams, after their inventor, Kaoru Ishikawa) to find the cause and effect relationships of the issues then use tools like "Five Whys" to get to the root causes. Finally, the teams may use

mechanisms like "Dot Voting" to decide on one or two issues to improve during the next Sprint. Sometimes these ideas for continuous improvement are memorialized in an Improvement Backlog.

At the Program level, teams are likely to be distributed geographically. Technology can be deployed to allow remote team members to participate if it is not feasible or cost effective for them to do so in person.

Backlog Decomposition and Refinement

The Scrum Guide does not list Backlog Decomposition and Refinement as a ceremony, but many individual Scrum teams treat it as a ceremony anyway, sometimes breaking it up over two days because the work can be demanding. Regardless of how it is accomplished, the teams should spend up to 10% of their time during the Sprint working with their Product Owners to refine and groom the Product Backlog. That means up to one day in a two-week Sprint, which may seem like a lot. Experience has shown, however, that this is time well invested.

With multiple teams, managing the Backlog becomes more demanding because of the number of people, parts, and issues involved. The Chief Product Owner and Product Owners need to be involved to rank Product Backlog Items (PBIs) by value. Products toward the bottom of the list are lower priority than those at the top of the list. They also usually have lower granularity than those toward the top of the list because the teams have not spent time analyzing and decomposing the lower priority items.

Initially, PBIs are given in T-shirt sizes because there is little detail, so any estimates would be a source of "false precision" and the time spent creating them would be a type of Lean waste. As the teams who will be building the PBIs analyze and decompose them, more becomes known to allow estimating with more granular units, usually Story Points. Only the team who will be working on the Story should estimate it.

Purpose

The Product Backlog must be constantly re-examined to ensure only the components that provide value and appropriate new entries are included. Teams work with their Product Owner to decompose large Epics into smaller Capabilities, Features, and Stories. Since Product Backlog Decomposition and Refinement happens during each Sprint, when the current Sprint ends, the Product Backlog will be up-to-date with small, high-value items at the top ready for the teams to pull into their Sprint Backlogs. This is critical.

Membership
While the whole Scrum Team participates in Backlog Refinement, only the Development Team doing the work actually estimates the Stories and only the Product Owner assigns it a priority.

Tools Used
The most common tool used here is Planning Poker, a modified Fibonacci series printed onto a deck of cards. Each team member flashes the card for the number of Story Points they think should be assigned. At the end, and as a group, they talk about their votes, starting with the high and low voters. The team re-votes until they reach consensus. This topic is covered in detail in Chapter 10 of *The Agile Almanac – Book 1.*

Artifacts

At the Program level, some important new artifacts are needed, in addition to those kept at the single-team level. A brief description of these artifacts is found here, with a detailed discussion of key artifacts in the Tools and Practices Recommendations section. You can also find templates and samples of key artifacts to download at GR8PM.com.

Working Solutions
The *Agile Manifesto* states that it values working software over comprehensive documentation. But because Agile has grown far beyond just software, and because scaling Agile often involves more than IT, it would be better to state and understand this principle as a preference for completed working solutions, or sub-components of the solution. Nowhere does it imply that no documentation is needed. The primary artifacts of SoS are completed work and necessary documentation!

Product Vision
In SoS, the Product Vision is a high level statement of what need the product will fill and who its consumers will be. This is typically no more than a couple of sentences long and the primary mechanism for aligning the team to a common Vision. This artifact takes on new importance at the Program Level since activities must be coordinated with more people.

Product Roadmap
The Product Roadmap is slightly more granular than the Product Vision and expresses a plan that includes the expected order of development for each Feature included in a Release. SoS does not consider it a commitment,

but rather a general idea of the order Features will be built in to inform stakeholders' expectations. As with the Product Vision, this artifact takes on new importance at the Program level because of the multitude of internal and external planning driven by the Roadmap.

Product Backlog
The Product Backlog is owned by the Product Owner and is a prioritized list of all the Features potentially included in the product.

Sprint Backlog
The Sprint Backlog is a subset of the Product Backlog that the team committed to delivering at the end of the current Sprint. As items are pulled from the Product Backlog into the Sprint Backlog they are decomposed from small Stories into Tasks by the team.

Program Improvement Backlog Items
It is common for teams to keep lists of items identified as targets for process improvement from their Sprint Retrospectives and manage them in an Improvement Backlog. This is also true at the Program level for the Program Retrospective.

Performance Measures
Scrum mandates that teams measure their progress toward meeting the Sprint Goal, however, the Scrum Guide leaves it up to individual teams to decide which performance measure(s) to use. At the Program level, the Chief Product Owner or the Chief Scrum Master usually decides which metrics to use.

Several common metrics are:

- Net Present Value (NPV) of Features delivered
- Internal Rate of Return and/or Return on Investment
- New customers obtained
- Retained customers
- Burn-down Chart
- Burn-up Chart
- Planned vs. Actual Story Points
- Escaped defects
- Business Value Delivered
- Risk Burn-down Chart
- Team Happiness or Engagement Index
- Team Burnout Indicator

How to Make it Work Effectively

Communities of Practice (CoP)

Although it was not part of Jeff Sutherland's original implementation, many companies using the Scrum of Scrums method have instituted Communities of Practice to foster cross team learning, increase the idea transfer rate across teams and, in some circumstances, coordinate cross-team dependencies and resolve cross-team blockers. This is especially useful with distributed teams, where the CoPs use conference or video calls, Wikis, and other technology to share data-rich communications. CoPs are usually role or interest based and provide a forum for team members from different teams to share ideas, insights, and shortcuts, review books, and learn new technologies. As CoPs mature new ones can be created based, not on role, but on a particular cross-team problem, a new technology being implemented, new regulations that need to be complied with, and so on.

Purpose

Speeding the "idea transfer rate" is the key idea behind Communities of Practice. Since teams will be working individually and experiencing rapid learning from Sprints and spikes, having a role-based CoP gives peers, who do not work together every day, a mechanism to share ideas, successes, and failures. Remember that in Agile the mindset is "fail fast to succeed sooner" so a "fast fail" is a good thing because learning and adjustments occur quickly, without wasting lots of time and resources.

Membership

Membership is usually role or position based. For example, on a software development project there could be Communities of Practice for C# developers, Java developers, database administrators, testers, Scrum Masters, and Product Owners. *(See Figure 4.04)*

Tools Used

Any collaboration tools that the Community feels are appropriate to share their ideas and documents can be used. Examples include SharePoint, Skype,

Video Conferencing, Voice Conferencing, and Desktop Shares. Experience has shown that having a small budget to provide food and refreshments at CoP meetings increases attendance and participation. Also, this should not be something employees are expected to engage in after-hours so plan time for CoP meetings during the work day.

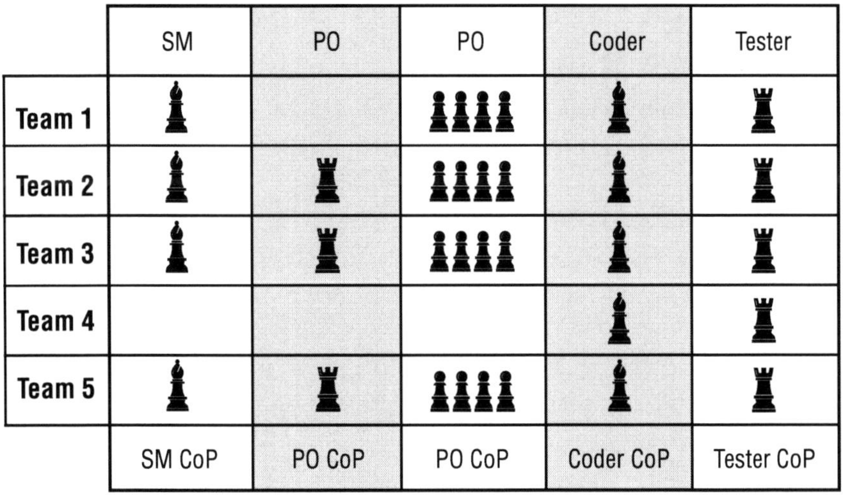

Figure 4.04 | Communities of Practice

Practical Application

Road-tested Advice courtesy of Jeff Sutherland - CEO, Principal Consultant, and Trainer | Scrum, Inc., One Broadway, Cambridge, MA 02142

During an email exchange with the co-authors of this book, world-renowned Scrum authority, Jeff Sutherland gave some advice that Program Managers, and all Agile leaders, would do well to note. He wrote:

"The first large scale Scrum at IDX in 1996 (now GE Healthcare) included virtual teams for architecture, QA, etc. to develop common strategies, tools, and engineering standards.

I don't use the word communities of practice as these are often information sharing only like the Guilds at Spotify. I am often at Spotify and they say the Guilds have little impact on development.

The Spotify Chapters, on the other hand, are led by people who would have [to] be traditional managers, who hire people and set engineering standards. Thus, they have a major impact on development. They train experts and deploy them to teams. They meet regularly to coordinate that which needs coordination across teams.

These Spotify Chapters are similar to the virtual team concept we used at IDX."

The point Jeff seemed to be making is to not get bogged down in the name or settle for meetings that boil down to information sharing and drinking coffee. Invest in having decision-makers in the meetings where standards are set and continuously improved!

And, by the way, spend time around smart guys like Jeff whenever you can. They 'accidentally' share great wisdom, often without even knowing it. Thanks, Jeff!

Scrum of Scrum of Scrums

By now, Program Managers understand that a key constraint in scaling Agile is the number of lines of communication between team members and that this is the reason why Agile teams become inefficient past a size of nine. But what do Program Managers do when the Scrum of Scrum meeting itself grows past a size of nine? To begin with, membership in the SoS meeting can be limited to one representative from each team, but that comes at the potentially high risk of not having key people in the room. Another approach is to have a Scrum of Scrum of Scrums (SoSoS) meeting in order to scale the SoS meeting.

In this case, each team has its Daily Scrum then sends a representative or two to the SoS meeting. The SoS meeting then sends key representatives to the SoSoS meeting. Note that membership and participation in the SoS and SoSoS meetings typically changes. Membership is flexible and can be decided on a day-by-day basis, depending on the agenda of the meeting. *(See Figure 4.05.)*

Scaling with Product Owner Meetings

Similar to the Scrum of Scrum of Scrums, Product Owners must also meet frequently to ensure they are aligned with the Chief Product Owner's Vision and resolve any dependencies or blockers within the jurisdiction of their role. These meetings are limited by the same lines of communication constraint limiting the size of individual Scrum teams, and like the Scrum of Scrums,

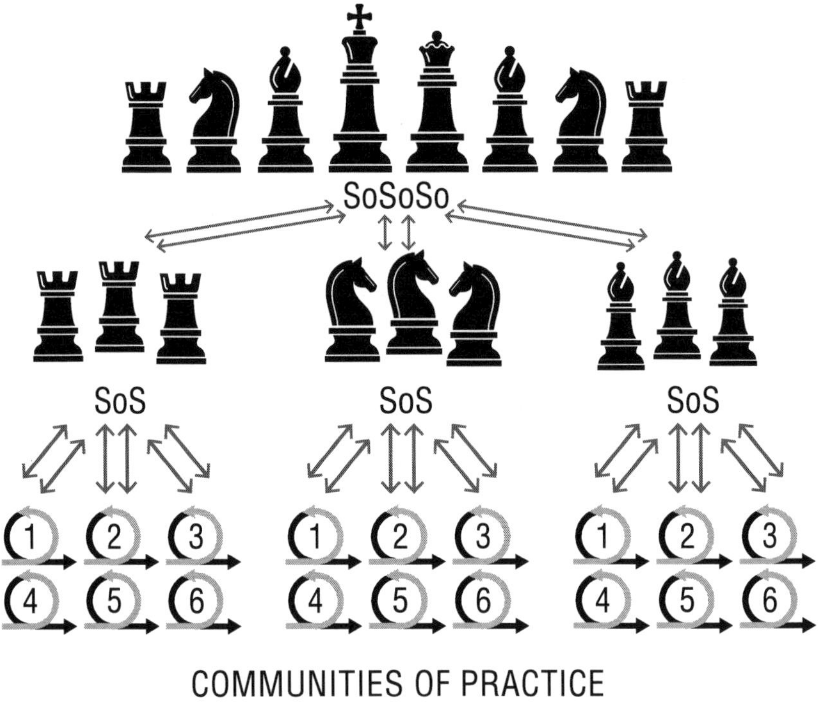

Figure 4.05 | Scrum of Scrums

this meeting must be carefully monitored to ensure that there is effective communication.

Product Owner meetings can be scaled any way that makes sense for the organization or the product. One typical method for scaling this meeting is presented in *Figure 4.06*.

Big Room Sprint Planning

For single-team projects, Sprint Planning is a fairly simple activity and consists of discussions between the Development Team members, the Product Owner, and the Scrum Master. In some circumstances, an Architect or other Shared Services SME may attend this meeting to provide context or perspective.

Once multiple teams begin to work from the same Product Backlog at the same time, complexity, dependencies, and contention for resources emerge quickly. What was a simple process for single-team environments becomes an incredibly complex activity where cross-team dependencies, blockers, and

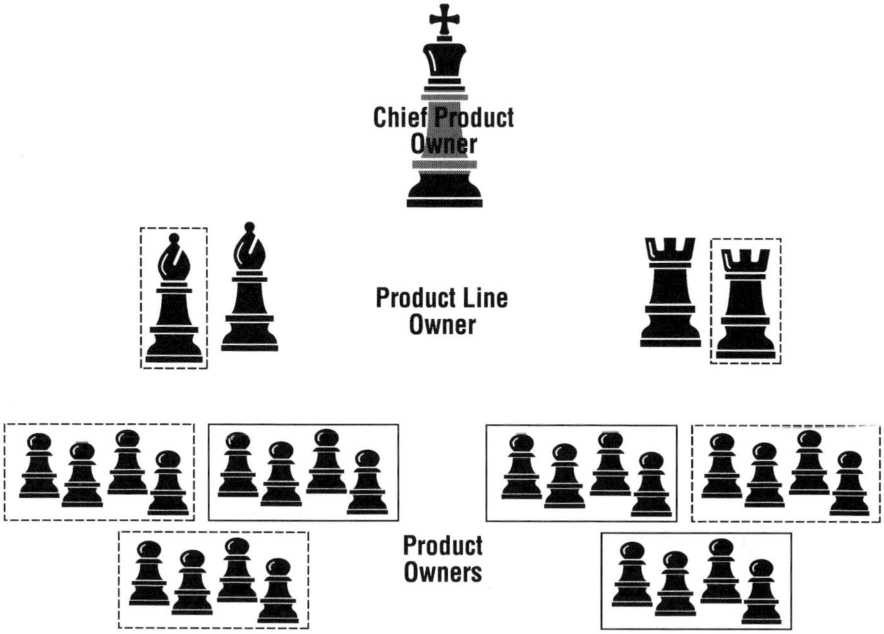

Figure 4.06 | Product Owner Scaling

risks must be made visible and managed. It is advisable to conduct Sprint Planning with as many of the teams physically in the same room as possible to foster osmotic communication. If some members must be in remote locations, technology should be deployed to allow them to hear and see their colleagues in the main room.

During this planning session, the teams will hear the Product Vision and Sprint Goal articulated by the Chief Product Owner. They will then pull their individual Team Backlogs from the unified Product Backlog. It is critical during this planning session to schedule multiple checkpoints so that as plans emerge, risks and issues can constantly be ferreted out, exposed, and managed.

At the end of Big Room Planning each team should have a Sprint Backlog they have committed to completing. The Chief Product Owner will review each Sprint Backlog to ensure that, when combined, they will make progress toward delivering the Sprint Goal. The Chief Scrum Master and Chief Architect will also analyze each Sprint Backlog for inter-team dependencies. Each team must agree and commit to this plan, and each risk must be recorded and assigned an owner. A plan for managing cross-team dependencies must be developed, which can be a nontrivial exercise in multiple team environments.

An alternate take on Sprint Planning with multiple teams was related by Jeff Sutherland during a conversation with the co-authors. He explained that at Spotify, the whole company prioritizes every initiative for the quarter at the Chief Product Owner level. Once these have been decomposed to the 50 – 100 point range they are small enough to be estimated by the individual teams who will be doing the work. Using this method does not require everyone to be in the same room or be involved in detail that is unrelated to their work.

Scrum@Scale

One of the reasons this chapter included so much input from Jeff Sutherland is because he has been doing exciting things with scaling Scrum since the mid-1990s. His most recent effort at scaling Scrum for the Enterprise is called Scrum@Scale, which is outside the scope of this chapter, but more information is available at www.scruminc.com.

Tools and Practice Recommendations

Big, Visible Information Radiators at Scale

A core concept of both Scrum and SoS is the idea of Information Radiators. Typically, these are walls where Task boards, Scrum boards, Kanban boards, Story cards, Burn-down charts, and any other information about what the team is working on, their progress, and any issues being encountered is displayed. In single-team environments, it is wise to place this material *outside* the team room so the information is available, without having to disturb the team, to any interested party who happens to be walking by. This works well in single-team environments, but when multiple teams or distributed resources are added to the equation, communication becomes exponentially more difficult.

The challenge with multiple or distributed teams is to provide this information in a "virtual" format so that any member of any team has complete visibility into any other team. Take an example of two teams who are coordinating dependencies on a Task affecting both. Both teams need to see the progress and blockers of the other team without having to disturb the other.

Regardless of the tools or the metrics used, practitioners must create a mechanism that allows any team member to have full visibility into all other teams instantly and without disruption.

There are a variety of strong tools for this task including CA Agile (formerly Rally), Atlassian, and Microsoft Team Foundation Server, to name a few. Tools will be discussed at length in Appendix B.

Synchronizing Multiple Teams

A challenge with SoS is coordinating the work, not only of Scrum teams, but of teams from other departments who may not use Scrum or SoS, outsourced and offshore team members, vendors, and such. Like most things with SoS, there is no prescribed answer, but rather general guidance. The key concept is that teams be as synchronized as possible. This means that each should have the same Sprint length and should all start and end at the same time. This greatly reduces risk and enables teams to manage dependencies more easily.

Program Level Artifacts

This section will expand on only the most important Program Level artifacts introduced earlier in this chapter. Remember that samples, examples, and more can be found at GR8PM.com.

Working Solutions

It's worth mentioning again that the whole point of Agile is to deliver value. The software, solution, or other product delivering that value is the primary deliverable and therefore the most important artifact.

Product Vision

Used in single-team Scrum as well as SoS, the Product Vision is even more important at the Program level because it is more difficult to align a large number of people to a common vision than a small number. At the Program level, potentially there are, not only multiple teams and internal departments, but also external vendors, offshore development teams, and many other resources. That highlights the need for an effective mechanism for focusing the extended team on a common vision. The Product Vision is the primary vehicle to align team members quickly. It is also important to note that the Program level is where learning from all the teams within the Program must be integrated as frequently as possible. The Product Vision is usually reviewed and revised, if necessary, after each Meta Scrum and Product Owner meeting.

Product Roadmap
Similar to the Product Vision, the Product Roadmap takes on new importance because of the number of people, both internal and external, who have to share a common vision of the Product Roadmap. Like the Product Vision, this is updated frequently.

Product Backlog
The Product Backlog at the Program Level serves the same function as the Product Backlog at the single-team level, but now has many more people to consult during refinement, looking to it for guidance, and contributing Features and defects.

Performance Measures
SoS allows Program Managers to choose the metrics that are important for their specific situation. Some of the most common performance metrics are:

- Net Present Value of Features delivered – This is a measure of the current value of the future cash streams expected to be realized by Features delivered.
- Internal Rate of Return and Return on Investment – These are measures of profitability of Features delivered that make it easy for executives and Program Managers to compare project performance and make funding decisions.
- New customers obtained – This is a measure of the number of new customers that have been, or are expected to be, secured by development of the completed Features.
- Retained customers – This simply measures the estimated number of customers who have not left because the completed Feature was developed.
- Burn-down Chart – This is the most common tool used by individual Scrum teams. It simply shows work remaining over time and is typically used at the team level. For a Program, it can be aggregated to show the progress of multiple teams.
- Burn-up Chart – This shows work completed and is more commonly used at the Scrum of Scrums level.
- Planned vs. Actual Story Points – This is a simple, easily-understood metric to track the accuracy of Sprint Planning and estimating.

- Escaped defects – This is a measure of the number of defects missed in testing. It can also include root cause analysis and cost impact analysis.
- Business Value Delivered – This measures the business value delivered with each Story at the end of each Sprint. It is a good idea to assign a business value along with a Story Point estimate to each Story.
- Risk Burn-down – This is similar to the Story Point Burn-down only it measures the mitigation of risk by showing risk remaining. It is easy to aggregate information from multiple teams into this chart.

Conclusion

Whether SoS is a destination for an organization or a waypoint on a journey to another Framework for scaling Agile, SoS offers Program Managers a quick and easy way to scale their existing Scrum teams to meet the needs of their programs. SoS is the most lightweight and flexible method for scaling Scrum and provides Program Managers with almost limitless options to configure their teams and ceremonies to meet their particular goals. This chapter and the tools at GR8PM.com should provide what is needed to get started scaling Scrum right away. Safe sailing and happy scaling!

END NOTES

[1] Sutherland, Jeff. "Agile Can Scale: Inventing and Reinventing Scrum in Five Companies." *Cutter IT Journal*, vol. 14, no. 12,2001. *www.researchgate.net/publication/290823579_Agile_Can_Scale_Inventing_and_Reinventing_SCRUM_in_Five_Companies]* Dr. Jeff Sutherland is one of the original signatories of the Agile Manifesto, a co-author of the *Scrum Guide*, and a globally recognized thought-leader in the Scrum domain. Through email correspondence with several of the Agile Almanac – Book 2 co-authors, he expanded his intent of SoS and shared experiences and advice. – 26 Aug. 2017.

[2] For more detail, download the Scrum Guide at: *https://www.scrum.org/resources/scrum-guide]*.

[3] Sutherland, Jeff. Telephone/Skype interview. 04 Aug. 2017. Several authors from this book held a video conference with Jeff where he elaborated on SoS, its successes, evolution, and best practices in great detail.

[4] Version One. "11th Annual State of Agile Survey." Apr. 2017, *www.explore.versionone.com/state-of-agile/versionone-11th-annual-state-of-agile-report-2.*

[5] Cohn, Mike. "Advice on Conducting the Scrum of Scrums Meeting, Scrum Alliance." 7 May 2007, *www.scrumalliance.org/community/articles/2007/may/advice-on-conducting-the-scrum-of-scrums-meeting.*

[6] Jeff Sutherland originally coined this phrase, but it is now commonly known as Meta Scrum.

CHAPTER

5

Kanban

Overview

Origins of Kanban

In the late 1940's Toyota began to develop what would become known as the Toyota Production System (TPS). This was the source of Lean principles and the manufacturing systems used to deliver products efficiently. TPS changed the auto industry and sparked a manufacturing revolution that has transformed more than just manufacturing worldwide.

Kanban is a key tool in the Lean process and can be likened to the central nervous system in the human body. Using visualization, environments with high complexity and uncertainty can more easily identify bottlenecks and when work is ready to progress. Kanban cards are the "nerve cells" that keep production instructions flowing through the manufacturing process.

The Kanban Framework used to scale Agile today has adapted from the concepts used in TPS to allow project deliverables to be produced more efficiently. Now, it is also being effectively used in operations for ongoing Program activities. To understand Kanban and how it can be applied to Programs, it is important to understand the key concepts that are the foundation of the Framework.

Workflow

Organizations have their own specific workflows, which define their business and drive competitive advantage by differentiating them from other companies. Their unique workflows directly impact the products and services they deliver while also exerting great influence on customer satisfaction and bottom line profitability. Workflows can be unique at the Program, Project, and Operational levels, often driven by the specific needs of the business unit served by the deliverable(s).

One of Kanban's strengths is its ability to improve any workflow. That strength, to be successfully leveraged, requires a comprehensive and critical understanding of the work activities and their interrelationships as they produce the desired deliverables.

The process can be broken down as simply as; "Work not started that needs to be accomplished", "Work-in-progress (WIP)", and "Work complete," as shown in *Figure 5.01.* It can also be as complicated as the process to build a car, develop a pharmaceutical, design document imaging software, or anything in between.

Figure 5.01 | Kanban Workflow

Pull vs Push

TPS was built on the core concept of pulling work through the manufacturing process instead of pushing it. This was a radical departure from the mass-production, based on the Ford Motors model that had ruled the world as the "American Manufacturing" approach prior to TPS.

TPS created important advantages because it reduced the cost of carrying inventory by eliminating bottlenecks in the workflow. The Kanban process means production never runs out of critical inputs to keep production throughput high, while also avoiding the cost of inventory and risk of it being damaged, lost, or becoming obsolete.

The Kanban Framework applies this core concept of pulling work to the discipline of project management. Work is pulled into the workflow as a result of a request from the Customer to provide a solution for a problem. Along each step of the process, a work item is pulled into a downstream step as a result of a team member requesting work from a preceding process step.

In this fashion, the work is pulled into the workflow and processed until the initial input becomes part of the final output.

Work in Progress (WIP)
Work in Progress is another core concept supporting Kanban. WIP helps manage and control the Kanban process so that optimal production efficiency occurs. The definition of WIP is work that is currently being processed.

Kanban manages WIP to achieve production control, which is completely differently than how Scrum achieves production control. Scrum arranges and manages the amount of work into timeboxes called Sprints. Kanban arranges and manages the amount of work into a single production step to optimize the team's ability to consistently deliver. As a result, Kanban does not use defined timeboxes and, instead, uses a continuous workflow approach with work being pulled through it. WIP limits can be placed on the workflow to ensure the correct amount is pulled and not too much, causing bottlenecks in production.

WIP limits can also be applied to an individual team member, the whole team, the project, or even the Program or Portfolio to help control the process or workflow with the goal to optimize production efficiency.

Focus
Focus is not a concept that Kanban prescribes, but is an important outcome. Some people take pride in being able to multi-task, but in reality, being able to focus on one task at a time improves productivity. To illustrate this, consider what occurs when several work items are in progress simultaneously.

In this simple example, the product consists of four Features each requiring four days to complete. If work is performed equally on each Feature during the first four days of the project, the product, and each Feature, ends up only 25% complete, as shown in *Figure 5.02.*

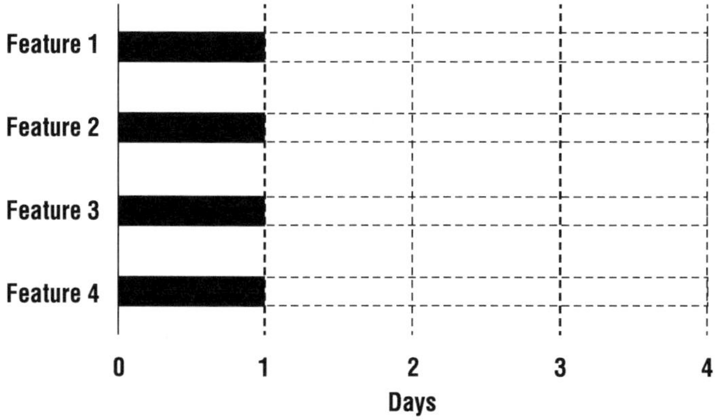

Figure 5.02 | Multiple Workflows Product Development

If instead, work is performed on just one of the Features, at the end of the fourth day, the product is still 25% complete; however, one Feature is 100% complete and could potentially be provided to the Customer. This is illustrated in *Figure 5.03*.

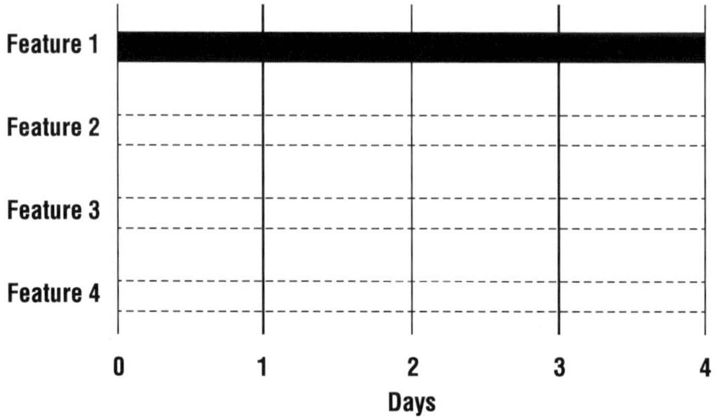

Figure 5.03 | Single Workflow Product Development

This allows for the Customer to receive a Minimal Marketable Feature (MMF) sooner. By way of contrast, it is likely to take longer to deliver the MMF to the Customer, due to the overhead of context switching, if the team works on all Features at the same time. This also enhances the opportunity to see any potential issues or risk within each Feature since focus is on one and not spread across many. By focusing on one Feature at a time, not only will the team complete an MMF sooner, but also learn from any mistakes or improve their technique as they progress onto the next one. This saves time, which leads to saving money; and that always results in Customer Delight!

Benefits / Challenges

Benefits

Easy to Implement

Kanban is easy to implement because the Framework advocates that you "start with what you do now". This basic principal of starting with what you do now, was identified by David J. Anderson of Leankanban.com as part of the Kanban Method, and encourages that existing processes and workflows be understood and kept in place while Kanban components are integrated into the process. Start by taking the time to visualize current workflows then add visual cues to begin managing them more efficiently.

Less Prescriptive
Frameworks do not get much lighter than Kanban. Unlike other Agile Frameworks that stipulate elements such as team roles, Feature size, Iteration length, and specific ceremonies, Kanban is light on ceremonies and other controls, facilitating quicker adoption within the organization.

Works with Existing Processes and Workflows
A key strength of Kanban is its minimal impact on existing processes and workflows. It is important to allow its practices to permeate existing activities. This means that processes and workflows do not have to change other than to include the visual cues and components aiding in the management and improvement of the workflow.

Continuous Improvement
David J. Anderson also advocates that there are six "general practices". They are:

1. Visualize
2. Limit Work in Progress
3. Manage Flow
4. Make Process Policies Explicit
5. Implement Feedback Loops
6. Improve Collaboratively, Evolve Experimentally

The final two, core practices go hand in hand with the key Lean principal of continuous improvement. Rather than attempting to correct problems in a workflow immediately, Kanban advocates the use of feedback loops, often in the form of visual cues. Team members are also encouraged to experiment and continually look for opportunities to improve workflow efficiency.

Effective for Programs
Program activities are often organized into projects and integrated with operations. Kanban is uniquely able to meet the needs of both projects and operational activities. Because Kanban's strength is managing and improving workflow, it does not matter whether it belongs to a project or to operations. In fact, due to the finite nature of a project, its workflow is often turned over to operations at the end of the project anyway. With Kanban cards or visual cues in place, operations can improve the workflow to make it more efficient

as they deliver the product or service to the customer. Additionally, limiting the WIP at the Project or Program level is a powerful lever to obtain better flow, focus, and quality.

Challenges

Mindset Change

To fully realize the benefits of Kanban, one must understand the Lean concepts that power the Framework. When applying Kanban and its principals, consider a familiar workflow and visualize how the process occurs. Look for places that have logjams, called bottlenecks, which slow down or hinder the flow. Visualizing the workflow is the key to leveraging Kanban.

Management Buy-in

Obtaining management buy-in to implement Kanban in the Program is likely to be a challenge. Like other Agile Frameworks, the methods and principals of managing projects is significantly different. Training at all levels is critical in the effort to fend off resistance, and through time the benefits will begin to overwhelm the challenges and result in management buy-in.

Understand Dependencies Between Tasks

In Traditional project management, a lot of effort goes into identifying Tasks and the relationships between them. Tasks can be described as having either a predecessor or successor relationship to other Tasks. With an Agile approach to projects, the emphasis is on understanding the Value Stream instead of the Task relationships. At times, this approach can cause confusion regarding dependencies between Tasks. If this occurs, it is possible for work to be pulled into the workflow prior to the completion of other needed inputs. The team should then work through the situation and take the appropriate actions to get the workflow moving again.

Program-level Attributes

Roles

As stated earlier, one of Kanban's foundational principles is to "Start with what you do now". It is important to get started now, so Kanban intentionally does not require changes to the organization, which would delay its implementation. As a result, the Framework does not prescribe roles, making it easy to apply to any Program. Current roles and responsibilities can be left in place and organizational changes are not necessary at the start.

Although Kanban-specific roles are not defined, these are a few things to consider when introducing Kanban into a Program because it might influence team responsibilities.

- Someone could be identified to educate the organization on Kanban principles and practices as well as the Lean concepts.
- Someone who is process-oriented must help identify and document the business workflows.
- The purpose of implementing Kanban is to apply continuous improvement to the workflow. Someone needs to encourage team members to look for opportunities to improve the workflow with things such as visual signals, buffers, queues, or even modifications to the workflow.
- Someone needs to lead regular reviews and analysis sessions using the artifacts discussed later to identify opportunities for continuous improvement.

Workflow

The key to successfully implementing Kanban in Programs and large projects is taking the time to understand and visualize business workflows. Visualizing workflow was discussed in detail in *The Agile Almanac – Book 1* along with a step-by-step approach to creating a Kanban Board. This chapter will build upon those concepts and scale them for Programs and large projects.

Visualize the Workflow

Each project within a Program could have a unique workflow. In addition, it is likely that operational activities being integrated with the Program will have one or more workflows. Those operational workflows could be specific to a workgroup or discipline, or even tailored to different delivery or support activities. As a result, Programs are likely to use multiple workflows to deliver the product or service to the Customer.

When multiple workflows are within the Program, it is not recommended to create one giant Kanban board to handle them all. Trying to do so would not only be an act of futility, but would also deter the natural outcome of Kanban – the continuous improvement of individual workflows. Each workflow could have its own Kanban board, which will evolve as it becomes more efficient.

Some organizations make it a policy to document their workflows and have processes in place to update that documentation as workflows change. More often, however, organizations do not take the time to document their processes and workflows, let alone maintain that documentation.

A Team Visualization Exercise is a straight forward technique that can be used to document a workflow and also provide a basis to convert it into a Kanban Board.

Team Visualization Exercise

Step 1: Assemble the team SMEs

Identify the key members of the team who understand the workflow, often referred to as Subject Matter Experts (SME). The individuals do not need to understand the whole workflow, but should have an intimate understanding of their portion and the team should represent all portions. Assemble the team in a room that has an open wall or large whiteboard.

Step 2: Identify Workflow Scope

Identify the boundaries of the workflow and the type of work items flowing through it then pinpoint the starting and ending points - what starts it and what designates its completion. Once that is done, determine points in the workflow where work items will exit and go to another workflow or some external entity.

Next, using different colored sticky notes, characterize the type of work items in the workflow. Examples could be enhancements, functions, defects, or documentation, in the case of a software development workflow. In the case of a physical product, those work items might include engineering, marketing, production, support, and management tasks.

Step 3: Identify Flows

Once the scope of the workflow is understood, the steps are identified. Working together, the team identifies each step of the workflow and writes the name of the step on a sticky note (using the same color for each step). Next, the sticky notes are placed on the whiteboard, in the order they occur in the workflow with an arrow drawn between each step to represent the flow the work items follow.

Step 4 – Test the Workflow

Test the flow of the work items, one at a time, by "walking" each of the work items identified in Step 2 through it. As that is done, consider the different conditions that might affect each work item to validate that the defined workflow captures each potential. For example, if the work item is a defect, does the defined workflow consider the potential for a defect that is critical and must be expedited?

Step 5 – Modify the Workflow

Finally, make the necessary modifications to the workflow based on deficiencies identified in Step 4. If, for example, it does not address expediting a defect, add the appropriate steps required to address that condition.

At the completion of the Team Visualization Exercise, you will end up with a documented workflow process similar to the example below in *Figure 5.04.*

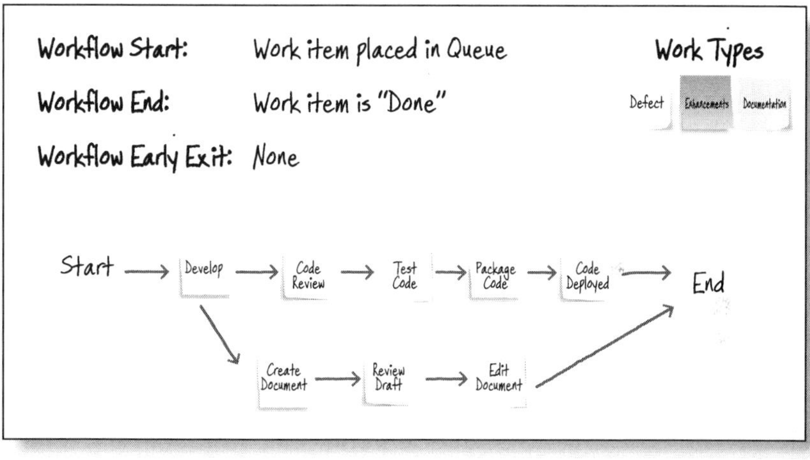

Figure 5.04 | Kanban Board

Creating the Kanban Board

Along with the documented workflow, there are a couple other components of Kanban to identify in order to build the Kanban board. They include buffers, queues, and WIP limits.

As described in Book One of *The Agile Almanac,* "Buffers and Queues are holding places for small inventories of work items used to insure instant availability of input when a downstream process pulls it." To build the

Kanban Board, review the workflow and identify where buffers or queues should be inserted to meet the goal of providing instant availability of a work item.

Each step in the workflow could have a WIP limit identified. A detailed discussion of WIP Limit is also included in Book One of *The Agile Almanac* where it says WIP Limits are "a tool for managing development bottlenecks by aligning the amount of WIP to the system's capacity, thereby creating planning options, accelerating throughput, and clarifying focus with transparency throughout the production cycle." To indicate the WIP limit for each step of the workflow documented during the Team Visualization Exercise that requires a limit, write a number in one of the corners of the sticky notes representing the workflow steps as well as each buffer and queue.

With that done, create the Kanban board showing each step of the workflow as a column on the board. In addition, add two columns, one to start the workflow (i.e., "Work Not Started") and one to identify completed work (i.e., "Work Complete"). *(See Figure 5.05.)*

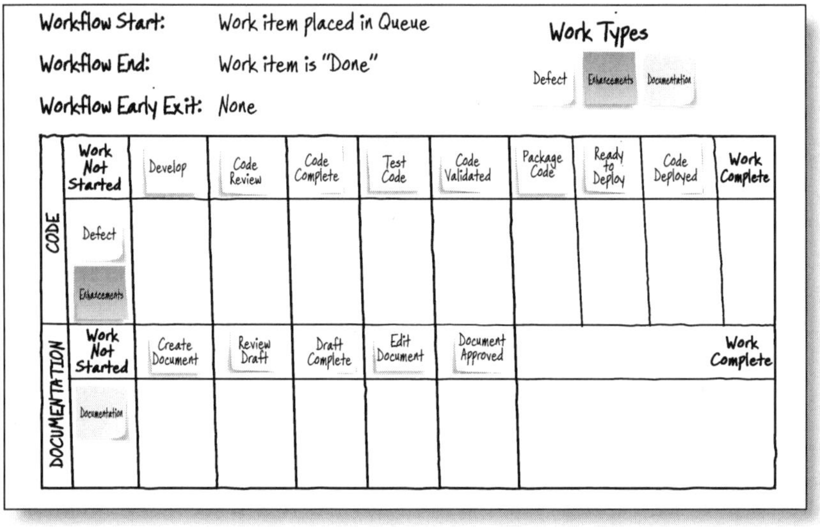

Figure 5.05 | Kanban Board

Many teams and organizations prefer physical Kanban boards, often using a whiteboard or wall. The columns can be made using vinyl tape for the lines or simply drawn on the board to allow for quick modifications as the workflow continues to evolve. Then Tasks or User Stories can be written on sticky notes allowing for the movement of the Tasks as they progress through the workflow. It is recommended to use different colored sticky notes to represent the different work types.

To provide increased visibility for Programs, electronic Kanban boards are recommended, with several software solutions available on the market. Most of them are web based, provide for customization of workflows and usually include the charts discussed later in the artifacts section.

Kanban Swimlanes

Notice that in *Figure 5.05* there are two different rows on the Kanban board. In this example, while both workflows run in parallel, documentation work items have a different workflow than the defect and enhancement work items. When this occurs, it is easy to represent the unique paths by creating swimlanes on the board.

On a Kanban board, different swimlanes can also represent each workgroup participating in the project. This becomes particularly powerful in Programs because it provides visual separation for the different resource types within. Additionally, each workgroup could have a separate workflow on the same Kanban board. *(See Figure 5. 06.)*

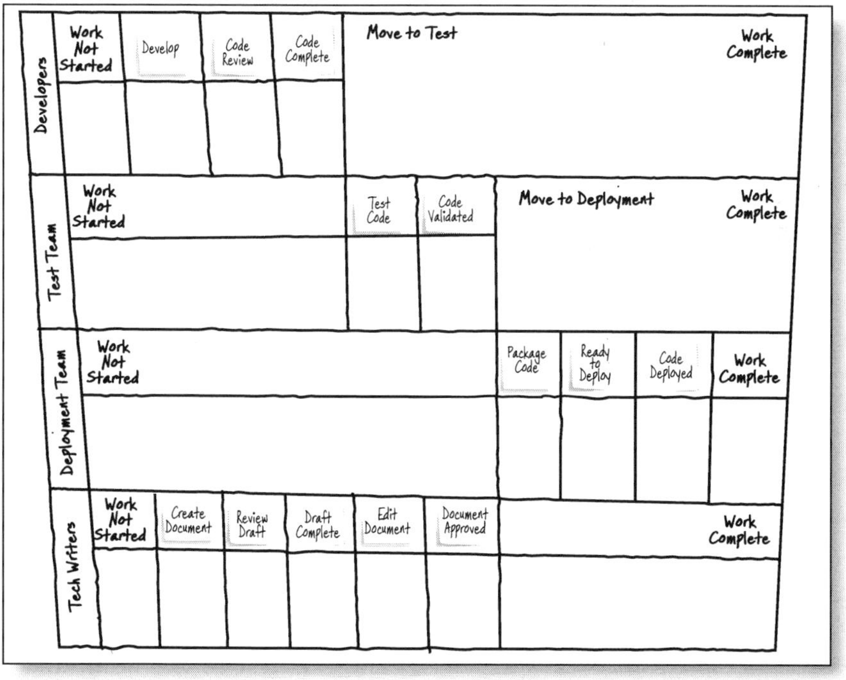

Figure 5.06 | Kanban Board with Swimlanes

Repeatable Program Workflows

The previous recommendation was to create separate Kanban boards for each project and operational workflow. Whereas this is still the recommendation, a lot of productivity gains can be realized by identifying and defining repeatable Program workflows. Using this method will aid in the scaling of Kanban for Programs.

Often, projects within a Program are similar in the sense that they follow the same workflow, and even have mostly the same Tasks, just delivering a different result. For instance, if the Program's objective is to produce new products within a certain category, it is likely that the workflow and its Tasks from product to product are nearly the same. When this is the case, a clear definition of the repeatable workflow, along with its Tasks, can be documented, making the successful repetition of each project perfect for Kanban.

Documenting the repeatable workflow is achievable using a Product Development Lifecycle (PDLC). A Product Development Life Cycle can focus on a tangible product, software product or solution, or even a service. Some industries might have a different name for the PDLC, such as System Development Life Cycle (SDLC), but the technique discussed below is the same.

The first step to documenting the Product Development Live Cycle is to identify the phases a product goes through from Ideation to Delivery, including post-delivery. In the example PDLC in *Figure 5.07*, there are four phases the Program follows to create a tangible product.

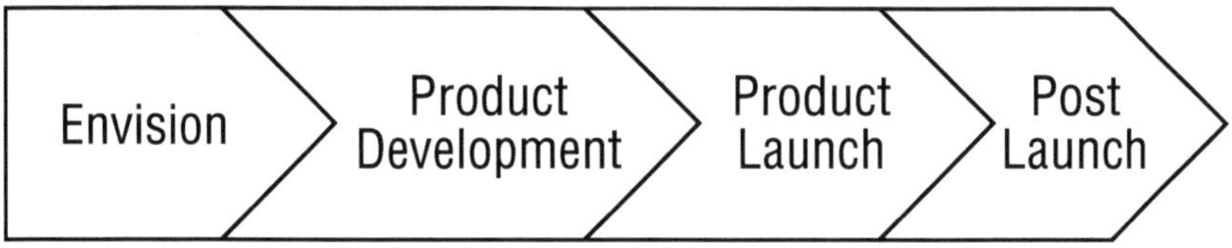

Figure 5.07 | Product Development Lifecycle (PDLC)

Once the phases are identified, document the PDLC workflow using the Team Visualization Exercise described earlier.

Upon completion of the high-level PDLC workflow, the development of the PDLC Phase Chart (PC) is the next step. The Phase Chart should include:

- A description of each of the phases in the workflow.
- Which group or role has activities in each phase.
- The desired outcome of the phase.
- The deliverables expected out of the phase.
- Typical time frame for each phase.

Note that the deliverables included in the Phase Chart are not Features of the product or service. They are the high-level components that are either expected to be delivered to the Customer or represent key milestones to stakeholders when coming out of the workflow. *(See Figure 5.08.)*

Phases	Envision	Product Development	Product Launch	Post Launch
Purpose	Identify Potential Products	Develop the Product	Launch Product to Customer	Deliver Product to Customer & Closeout
People/Groups	- Management - Marketing	- Management - Marketing - Project Management - Purchasing - Research & Development	- Management - Customer Support - Manufacturing - Marketing - Project Management - Purchasing - Research & Development	- Management - Customer Support - Manufacturing - Marketing - Project Management - Purchasing - Research & Development
Desired Outcomes	- Market Need Identified - Potential Solution Identified - Solution identified to meet market needs	- Market will support profitability - Final design is approved	- Product can be produced - Product is available for purchase - New product can be supported	- Project is closed out - Project Retrospective - Sustaining product plan in place
Deliverables	- Business Case - Project Charter - Approved Project - Assigned Team	- Prototype Products Finalized - Long lead time materials ordered - Tooling & Equipment Ordered - Approval to Proceed to Launch	- Website Built & Tested - Marketing Materials complete - Customer Service Processes in Place - Product Ready to Ship - Approval to Launch	- Product Shipped - Retrospective Actions Implemented - Product handoff to operations - Project Closed
Time	Ongoing	1 - 6 Months	2 - 4 Months	2 - 4 Weeks

Figure 5.08 | Phase Chart

Once the Phase Chart is complete, the Phase Task Chart (PTC) can be created. The PTC consists of the repeatable Tasks (or Stories) that should be included in each phase of the PDLC, as shown in *Figure 5.09*. It is helpful to group the Tasks by resource type to better visualize the work.

Unique Project or Program Tasks

Since each project has unique qualities and activities, they each have their own unique Tasks. At the commencement of a project the team should be assembled to identify its unique Tasks. They should also review the Tasks defined in the PDLC Phase Task Chart to validate the Tasks are appropriate for the project, removing any that do not pertain. This occurs in the Project Planning Meeting described in greater detail in the ceremonies section below.

Phases	Envision	Product Development	Product Launch	Post Launch
Tasks	**Management** - Develop Business Case - Assign Engineer **Project Management** - Develop Project Charter **Marketing** - Survey customer for needs - Identify potential products	**Management** - Approve Product Design - Approve purchases - Assign Production Launch Team **Project Management** - Create project plan **Research & Development** - Develop detailed design - Create prototypes - Test & evaluate prototypes - Create Bill of Materials (BOM) - Create Production Drawings - Design Tooling & Jigs - Identify Parts Pack - File Patent Papers - Create Plan for every part - Create Production Process **Marketing** - Conduct User Tests (external) - Create Branding Plan - Create Branding Materials **Purchasing** - Order long lead materials - Order long lead tooling - Order long lead equipment	**Management** - Approve Marketing Plan - Approve Customer Service Plan - Approve Launch **Project Management** - Facilitate Production Launch **Marketing** - Create Marketing Plan - Create Marketing Graphics - Create Marketing Video/Photo - Create & Test Website **Customer Support** - Create Customer Service Plan - Train Customer Service **Manufacturing** - Create Tooling - Create Jigs - Create Training & SOP - Modify Invoices - Create Kanban for Parts - Train Manufacturing - Build Launch Production Inventory **Purchasing** - Purchase Materials **Research & Development** - Support Production	**Management** - Review Financials vs. Business Case **Customer Support** - Receive feedback from users issues - Feedback to Envisioning for future products **Manufacturing** - Ship Product - Implement Product Sustainability Plan **Marketing** - Survey Customers **Project Management** - Conduct Retrospective - Implement Lessons Learned - Close Project **Purchasing** - Adjust Material Orders **Research & Development** - Evaluate Product Changes

Figure 5.09 | PDLC Phase Task Chart

The output of the Project Planning Meeting is the identification of the unique, known Tasks necessary for the project. Once they are identified for the project, the Kanban board should be created and the project Tasks placed in the Backlog or work-not-started column.

A similar activity should occur for each of the non-project workflows within the Program, with Kanban boards created for each operational workflow.

Ceremonies

Key ceremonies in the Kanban Framework were discussed in The Agile Almanac – Book 1. This section will expand on the important, and practical, ceremonies for a Program, including:

- Creating and Managing the Kanban Board
- Delivery Planning Meetings
- Project Planning Meeting
- The Kanban Meeting
- Retrospective Meetings

Creating and Managing the Kanban Board

In the workflow section, a lot of attention was placed on the creation of the Kanban Board because Programs require additional effort to manage it. Often, Program resources have competing responsibilities, distracting them from Tasks on a project within the Program. In fact, any one resource might have Tasks on several Kanban boards simultaneously! Defining and enforcing a Program-wide WIP Limit for each individual allows team members to focus and complete Tasks, thereby maintaining the workflow.

Delivery Planning Meetings

Delivery Planning Meetings are critical to managing the Program. Often, at any one time, multiple projects are in motion in conjunction with operational activities. The coordination of the release of Features across the Program occurs in Delivery Planning meetings. The purpose of the Release Plan is to deliver the Minimal Marketable Features (MMFs) that fulfill the Program Vision.

Project Planning Meeting

In Traditional project management, planning is a significant portion of a Project Manager's activity, which elongates the project schedule. In contrast, Lean thinking is focused on delivering MMFs to the customer, which provides value more quickly. In Kanban, this does not mean planning is ignored, rather, the emphasis is applied to defining the workflow and its continuous improvement to produce value more quickly.

The Project Planning Meeting is not typically promoted by the Kanban community, however, it is recommended to aid in scaling Kanban at the Program level. At the initiation of a project, a Project Planning Meeting could be held to kick it off. This has four main purposes:

1. Communicate the scope of the project to the project team.
2. Clarify the scope by identifying all the known Stories required to deliver the project.
3. Illuminate how the project aligns with the Program Vision.
4. Facilitate integration with other projects in the Program.

It is important to note that not all Stories will be known at the beginning of the project. However, using the techniques described in the workflow section, many predefined work items can simply be validated during the meeting, which eliminates waste and improves efficiency in line with core Lean principles.

"Sticky note planning" is a technique commonly used during the Project Planning Meeting to identify unique Stories. Once the scope has been communicated and the team has a clear understanding of the goals and deliverables of the project, they can step right into a "sticky note planning" exercise. This involves simply handing a stack of sticky notes to each member of the project planning team so they can create Kanban cards to document known Stories for the project. This typically occurs during a predefined timebox of 25-30 minutes. At the end of the timebox, the Kanban cards are placed in the Backlog of the Kanban board and the team collaborates to organize them, grouping the activities and removing duplicate Stories.

Using this technique the team will have populated the Kanban board by the end of the Project Planning Meeting and can begin work immediately. You don't get much Leaner than that!

The Kanban Meeting

The Kanban Meeting is held on a regular basis (often daily) to promote collaboration between team members. This is a self-organized team meeting and is typically held with everyone standing up, so as to promote quick accountability with a focus on what work has been completed and identifying any roadblocks in the workflow.

Retrospectives

In the spirit of Kaizen (continuous improvement), it is important to hold regular Retrospective Meetings, preferably once a month, at a minimum, for Programs, and at least bi-weekly for projects. Retrospectives provide teams in the Program the ability to continuously improve the process. That is why regularly gathering the team to identify ways to improve the workflow and processes is recommended.

Retrospectives are typically held both at the project and Program levels. At the project level, the team studies the process to find bottlenecks or impractical WIP limits that will reduce flow. At the Program level, the team analyzes the process to uncover issues, risks, and inefficiencies negatively impacting integration points across the Program.

Artifacts

There are several key artifacts needed to manage a Program using Kanban. These are listed in this section. Templates and samples with further discussion can be found in the Tools and Practices section and at GR8PM.com. Additional artifacts may be needed and this list should prompt thinking about others to add.

1. Kanban Cards
2. Kanban Board
3. Cumulative Flow Diagrams (CFD)
4. Flow Efficiency
5. Throughput
6. Cycle Time
7. Card Status

How to Make it Work Effectively

Kanban will only work effectively if the Kanban boards represent the actual workflow of the project or organization. It is important to take the time to identify and document the current workflow activity prior to creating the Kanban board. If the boards do not align with the workflow, work will stall and delivery dates will be missed. Additionally, it is likely defects will be introduced due to important steps missed in the process.

Therefore, the first steps to success when implanting Kanban in a Program, are identifying the workflow, documenting it on the Kanban board, and clarifying the Program integration points. These are only the first steps, as the true power of Kanban is centered on the concept of "continuous improvement". With Kanban, you are never "Done" because the process continues to improve the workflow, driving improved process efficiencies.

WIP Limits

Managing the Work in Progress is one of the keys to successfully managing work using Kanban in a Program. WIP should be controlled both at the project and operations level using the Kanban board so it can be managed across the Program. Establishing and enforcing WIP limits provides important controls and helps manage the flow of work through the process.

Establishing and adhering to WIP Limits is critical to successfully driving improvements and efficiencies in the workflows. Marcus Hammarberg, an Agile Coach and advanced reviewer of this chapter, recommends the following rules of thumb when it comes to WIP Limits:

- The lower the WIP limit the better.
- Stop starting – Start Finishing, i.e. it is preferable to finish work items rather than start more.
- If work gets idle ("I didn't have time to work with this yesterday"), then WIP is too high.
- If people get idle ("I have nothing to do without breaking the WIP limit"), then the WIP is too low, or start helping others to ensure a smooth flow.

Each phase or column on every Kanban board should be evaluated to validate the need for a WIP limit. To establish this, the team should agree on how many work items can reasonably reside in that column at any one time. Furthermore, this should be continually evaluated and modified against the rules of thumb to drive efficiencies in the workflow.

At the Program level, a WIP limit could be established to protect and support team members. The increased focus will improve work efficiency by limiting the number of work items one person can perform at any one time, thus minimizing the drain caused by context switching. A typical and reasonable individual WIP limit is two to three. In other words, no one individual will be working on more than two to three work items at any one time across the Program, even if they are a shared resource on multiple projects.

Continuous Improvement (Kaizen)
Kanban is simple to implement due to the "start with what you do now" mindset. The power of Kanban is unlocked when the Plan-Do-Check-Act cycle is followed. Remember to implement feedback loops in the workflow, which help identify bottlenecks and other gaps and process inefficiencies. These feedback loops can be measurements or metrics and may differ for each workflow. As issues are discovered, the team should be empowered to collaborate and identify improvements. Encourage the team to evolve the workflow through experimentation and Lean thinking!

Tools and Practices Recommendations

Kaizen Events

Eliminating waste and inefficiencies was one of the goals that drove Toyota to create TPS. Although the Kanban Framework is designed to continuously improve and eliminate waste in the workflow, at times, a concentrated focus on a troubled portion of the workflow is necessary to gain efficiencies. Holding a Kaizen event is an excellent way to provide that focus.

A Kaizen event is not a Retrospective, rather, it is a timeboxed event where key stakeholders, who understand the troubled workflow, gather together to identify the process inefficiencies. During the event, the Kaizen team is sequestered to either a dedicated room or at the location of the actual workflow, if appropriate, as in the case of physical products. A specific goal is provided by the workflow Owner and the team works through the issues to define an improved process or workflow.

The steps to holding a successful Kaizen event are as follows:

1. Identify the Kaizen team members who have a solid understanding of the workflow.
2. Remove any conflicting activities for the Kaizen team and assemble them in an environment, allowing them to focus on the event.
3. Identify the troubled workflow and decide on the processes to address it.
4. Review the existing workflow and associated processes to ensure all team members agree on the current state.
5. Measure the current workflow and associated processes. If measurements of the workflows are already available, the team should review them.
6. Evaluate the measurements and identify areas where improvements can be made.
7. Implement the recommended improvements.
8. Measure the impact of the changes to validate the success of the improved workflow and processes.

Kanban Board

The Kanban board is the central radiator of the Kanban Framework and periodic snapshots of it can be used as artifacts for the Program. As discussed previously, it is important that the Kanban board accurately represents the workflow. Due to the unique nature of each workflow, Program Managers must remember that creating and actively managing the Kanban board is critical for Program success. Important things to ask when doing so are:

- Is the workflow being followed?
- Are the WIP limits being adhered to?
- Are Bottlenecks being identified and removed?
- Are changes to the workflow reflected on the Kanban board?

Kanban Cards
Kanban cards represent the work items moving through the workflow. If the Kanban board is a physical board, the cards can be as simple as the sticky notes with a description of the work item, as discussed earlier in the chapter. Additional information, such as visual cues, can also be added to aid in the flow on the Kanban board.

The following are some of the fields to consider adding to the card:

- Title
- Description
- Card number
- Sub tasks
- Priority
- Due date
- Owner

Additionally, a method is needed to flag an impeded or blocked card from continuing through the workflow. Simply placing a uniquely colored sticky note or dot (preferably red) on any card that is impeded is one that works well. The impeded sticky note should also include a description of what is causing the roadblock and be recorded on the Impediment Board.

When using an electronic Kanban board, a method is usually provided to include all the concepts discussed above. To formalize a physical Kanban card, an organization could preprint customized sticky notes, such as seen in the sample card in *Figure 5.10.*

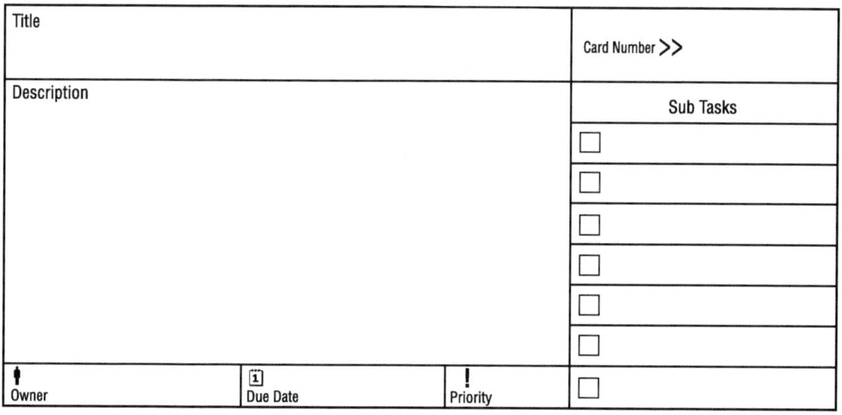

Figure 5.10 | Kanban Card

Cumulative Flow Diagrams (CFD) - Radiator

The Cumulative Flow Diagram (CFD) is the key radiator of Kanban and a great indicator of the health of the workflow. It provides the ability to identify issues as well as predict future progress. The CFD was discussed, in detail, in *The Agile Almanac – Book 1.*

The CFD provides the following information:

- History and quantity of the work in the Backlog
- History and quantity of the Work In Progress
- History and quantity of work that is Done
- Elapsed time between Ideation and Customer Receipt, also known as Lead Time
- Process throughput, also known as Cycle Time.

An example of a CFD using Card Count as the unit of measure is provided in *Figure 5.11.*

Flow Efficiency Radiator
Flow Efficiency is the measurement of how well work flows across the Kanban board. It measures the actual work time spent against total elapse time from start to finish. The higher the percentage of Flow Efficiency, the smoother the process is to deliver value to the Customer.

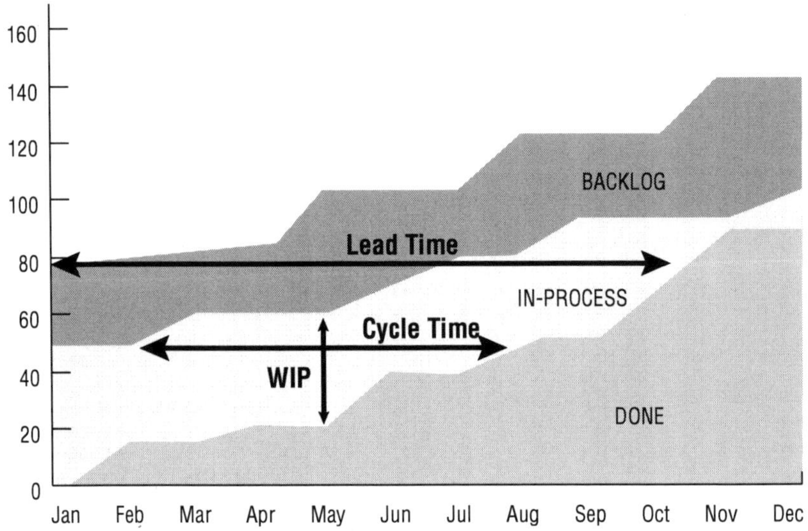

Figure 5.11 | CFD of Card Count

To calculate the Flow Efficiency, actual work time spent is divided by the actual work time plus any wait time during the workflow. This can be represented with the following equation:

Flow Efficiency = (Actual Work Time / Lead Time) x 100%

or

FE = (AWT / LT) x 100%

Where:

- FE (Flow Efficiency) = how efficiently work flows across the Kanban board, measured in percentage
- AWT (Actual Work Time) = the actual amount of time spent performing work, excluding time spent waiting
- LT (Lead Time) = the time it takes to get through the workflow from the time the work is requested to the time it is completed. The formula for this is described as: AWT + WT.
- WT (Wait Time) = the time a card is blocked by an impediment plus any time spent in buffers and queues.

The Flow Efficiency radiator is a measurement of the Flow Efficiency over time and shown in *Figure 5.12.*

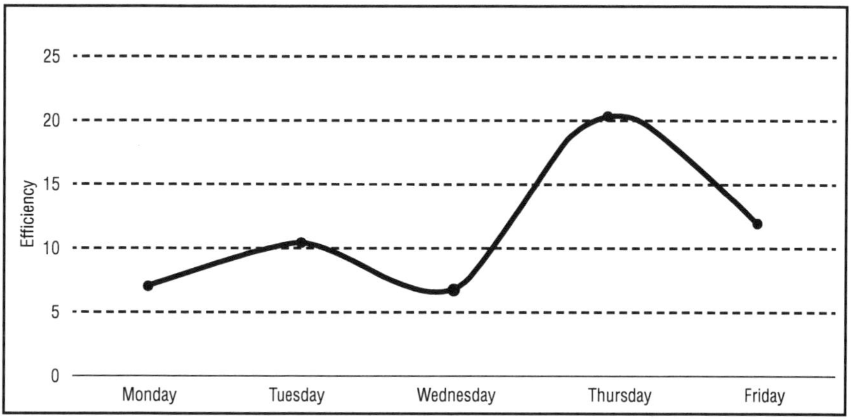

Figure 5.12 | Flow Efficiency

Throughput Radiator

Measuring the numbers of Kanban cards passing from the beginning to the end of the workflow, or a specific portion of it, can be presented in a Throughput chart. This displays the measurement over time and radiates improvement or deterioration stakeholders can use in decision-making. *(See Figure 5.13.)*

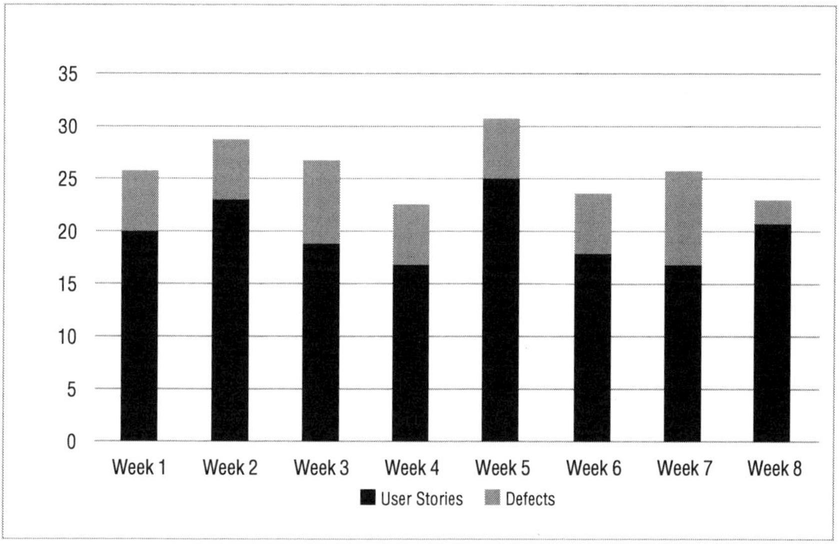

Figure 5.13 | Throughput Chart

Throughput is defined as the number of cards completed during a specific timeframe. For instance, it could represent the number of cards completed per day, week, or month. This could be measured by card count or averaged during a time window. Using a Throughput chart, one could predict the team's capability to complete work items.

Cycle Time Radiator
Cycle Time is a measure of process throughput, which is the time it takes work items to flow through the process. It begins when "work is in progress" and ends when the work is "Done". The Cycle Time radiator shows the average Cycle Time over a specified duration, illustrated in *Figure 5.14.* Low Cycle Time is targeted because that indicates work flowing efficiently through the process.

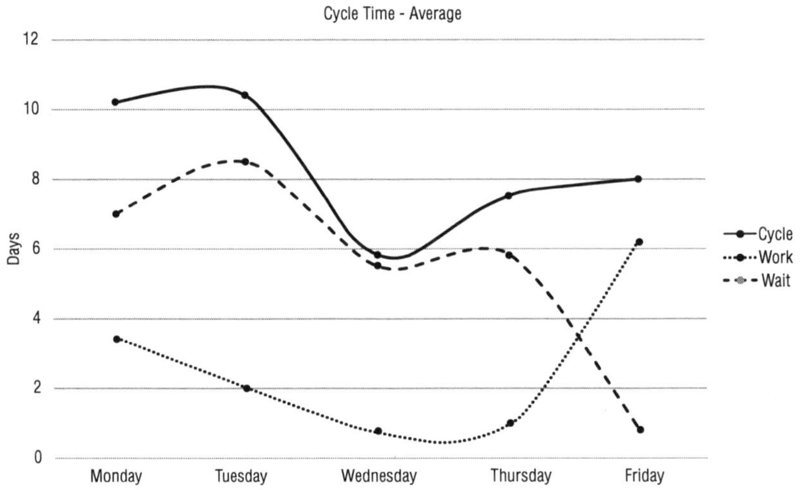

Figure 5.14 | Cycle Time Chart

Card Status Radiator
Program Managers report a project's or Program's status to the executive team. One of the difficulties they face is doing so without losing executive team interest or confidence. Failing to provide a percentage complete often causes management angst because they are accustomed to Traditional project management measurements. Agile uses the Card Status Chart as a tool to bridge this gap. *(See Figure 5.15.)*

A Card Status Chart simply records and reports total card counts and percentages for the following:

- Total Kanban Cards on the Kanban Board
- Total / Percentage of cards in the Backlog
- Total / Percentage of In-Progress cards
- Total / Percentage of Blocked cards
- Total / Percent of Done cards

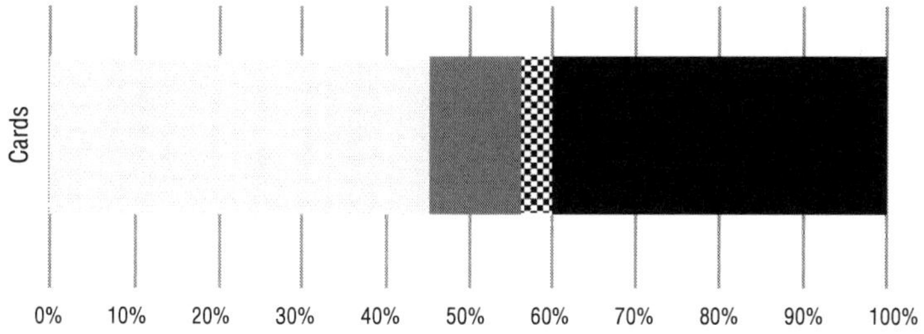

	Cards
Backlog	84
In-Progress	20
Blocked	7
Done	74

Figure 5.15 | Card Status Chart

Conclusion

Kanban is an Agile Framework with the lowest overhead of any Framework, making it easily implemented. It is a great Framework for Programs producing tangible or intangible products or services, and is especially adept for operational activities. In recent years, many software organizations have been adopting Kanban due to the fact that it is less prescriptive than other Frameworks. As more Program Managers and organizations adopt Agile, the benefits of Kanban to other industries become clear.

CHAPTER

6

DevOps

Overview

The word "DevOps" was coined in 2009 to describe Development and Operations teams working together to provide Continuous Delivery (CD). The DevOps approach started gaining popularity after Jez Humble and David Farley wrote *Continuous Delivery* where they described it as teams not only producing software (or other deliverables) in short cycles, but also ensuring it can reliably be released into production.

This chapter will delve into what DevOps is and is not; exploring the benefits and challenges and helping Program Managers develop a realistic plan for a DevOps adoption. DevOps is a unique set of practices. They can stand alone as a group of good practices, be incorporated into another Framework, as they are in SAFe and DAD, or be used independently of each other to suit the development environment. DevOps can be considered an emerging Framework due to being a combination of a mindset and core concepts supporting better systems execution. However, despite its mature practices, it is still emerging, which is part of why the formal Framework is not as mature as other Agile Frameworks. This does not make it less complex though. There are many critical success factors that must be considered when adopting any DevOps initiative. This chapter will provide guidance on those factors during, and after, the DevOps adoption process.

At this stage in the DevOps evolution, it is primarily focused on IT software development and operation support. However, others have begun using it outside of the software development field with powerful and exciting results. Some language used and processes described are directed towards software development, but the practices can translate to other endeavors.

DevOps is not for everyone. It requires a significant investment in training and support for most organizations. This includes learning the automation process, developing the disciplined approach, purchasing the necessary tools, and, of course, training in the use of these new tools and processes. For large organizations that must get to market quickly with their products, have issues with quality after product releases, or have a long, painful deployment process, DevOps may be a strong and workable solution. For other organizations, some of the principles and practices may have great value, but the full DevOps path may not be viable.

There will be vigorous debate about the fundamental features and future direction of DevOps. The latest edition of *The State of DevOps* report, released in late June of 2017, emphasizes the culture shift needed as well as the characteristics making organizations successful with DevOps. It should be noted that this report is supported by vendors in the DevOps space and DevOps thought leaders and is generally considered the authoritative record by most DevOps practitioners. It looks at statistical relationships between IT performance, organizational performance, technical practices, and cultural norms. This survey provides strong evidence that DevOps practices lead to higher IT performance, which, in turn, delivers improved business outcomes. These outcomes are measured by productivity, profitability, and market share.

The State of DevOps (2017) clearly outlined the characteristics of high performing organizations and the increasing number of them moving to the faster, stable DevOps model. Those characteristics are automation of configuration management, testing, deployments and streamlined team centric change approval processes, Lean product management practices, and loosely coupled architectures (services that can be developed and released independently of each other).

The word DevOps is a synthesis of "Development" and "Operations;" meant to convey a purposed interrelationship between the two, previously disparate, disciplines, leading to more efficient and effective delivery. Later, architecture was added. The key components of DevOps are collective ownership (breaking of silos), maximizing system flow, and developing solid technical practices. This means more than just automation tools, as some might think. It involves striving for the characteristics described in *The State of DevOps* (2017) report as well as technical practices including version control, continuous integration, trunk-based development, and automation.

Figure 6.01 represents all DevOps work-streams; effectively the whole delivery system.

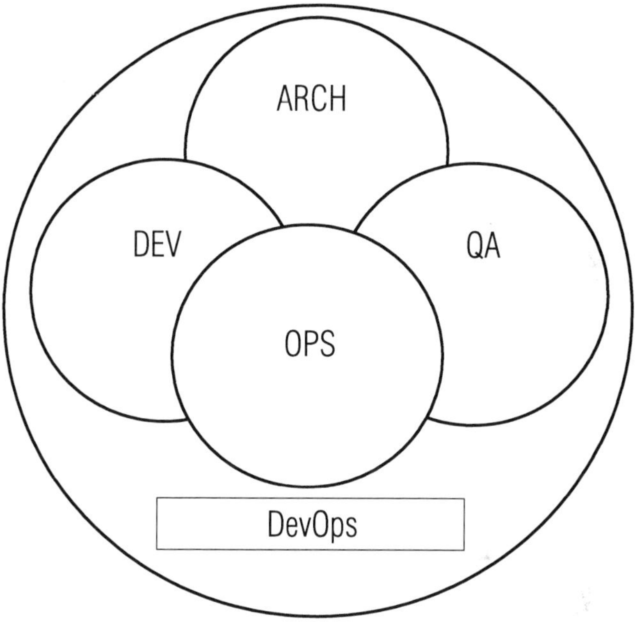

Figure 6.01 | The DevOps Team

Although there are many different ideas about what concepts and principles are considered part of DevOps, it generally encompasses the following components: whole system thinking, no silos, and full collaboration across business, infrastructure, development, and testing and support teams. DevOps promotes Lean Product Management, iterative delivery, rapid deployment, and useful feedback from customers. A key component is automation; everything that is repetitive in nature should be automated. Experiment, learn, and continuously improve. Measure in order to see trends and seek feedback on delivery. An important factor for executing quickly, the team must have the ability to try new ideas and update specifications without requiring outside approval.

For those just beginning their DevOps journey, this often requires an organizational culture shift. This includes greater collaboration, communication, integration, and automation across various groups in order to deliver reliable value, rapidly and continuously, as shown in *Figure 6.02.*

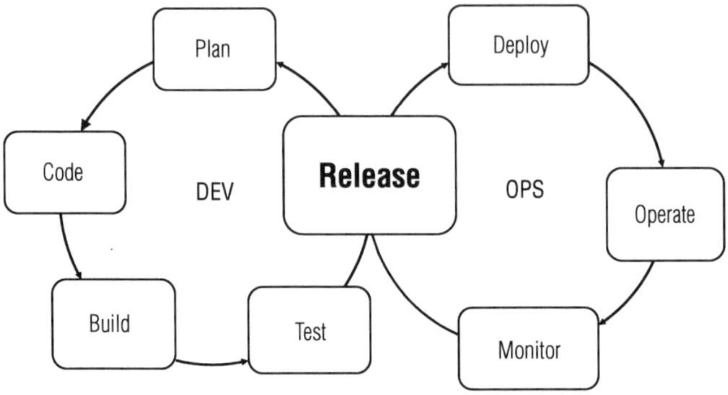

Figure 6.02 | DevOps Cycle

This presents some challenges as the operations team focuses on production stability, the development team on implementation of new functionality as quickly as possible, and the business team on usability. One of the major challenges in DevOps adoption is getting these groups to work cohesively as one unit.

Every organization depends on technology to provide value quickly, reliably, and securely to their stakeholders. How well organizations perform impacts their overall organization performance. According to the most recent *State of DevOps* report[1], high performing organizations were twice as likely to achieve key objectives including quantity of products and services produced, operating efficiency, customer satisfaction, quality of products or services provided, achievement of organizational and mission goals, and meeting external party measures.

Real World: Amazon Killing It With DevOps

Back when Amazon was still run on dedicated servers, it was a constant challenge to predict how much equipment to buy to meet traffic demands and pad estimates to accommodate for unforeseen traffic spikes. As a result, about 40 percent of Amazon's server capacity was wasted—and during the Christmas shopping season, when traffic could triple, more than three-quarters could be left unused—along with the money spent to purchase it.

Once the online retailer moved to the Amazon Web Services (AWS) cloud, it allowed engineers to scale capacity up or down incrementally. Not only did this reduce spending on server capacity, but it also spurred a transition to a continuous deployment process that allows any developer to deploy their own code to whichever servers they need, whenever they want.

Within a year of Amazon's move to AWS, engineers were deploying code every 11.7 seconds, on average. The Agile approach also reduced both the number and duration of outages, resulting in increased revenue.

"10 companies killing it at DevOps" by Christopher Null © TechBeacon, used with permission. *https://techbeacon.com/node/559*

Evolution of DevOps

Prior to the DevOps and Agile movements, release or integration of a software product was a big, painful event. *(See Figure 6.03.)*

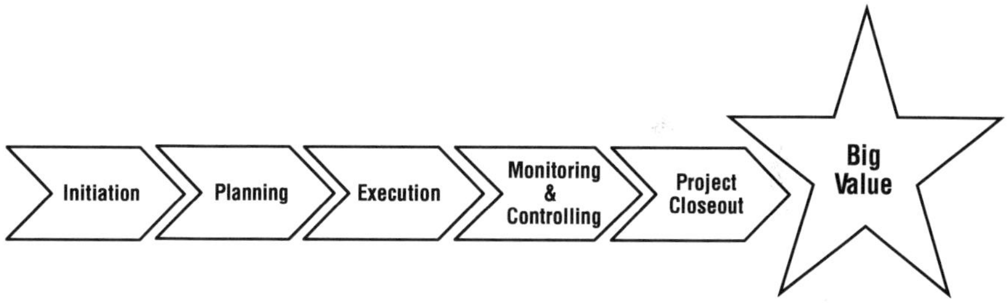

Figure 6.03 | Traditional PM Approach

Rational Unified Process (RUP) was an iterative development approach and early source of Agile principles, focusing on delivering business value and shortening the distance between business and development teams.

As part of the push for ongoing improvements, the focus turned to delivering reliable business value by adopting various engineering and quality practices such as Clean Code, Refactoring, Test Driven Development (TDD), Behavior Driven Development (BDD), Pair Programming, and Continuous

Integration. With this tighter discipline, developers and testers, along with rapid business team feedback, increased stability without sacrificing speed or quality.

DevOps began to emerge when Patric Debois and Andrew Shafer conducted a session on "Agile Infrastructure and Operations" at the Agile 2008 conference in Toronto, Canada. In 2009, Patric coined the term "DevOps" and started the DevOpsDays conference, which has become very popular globally. Finally, John Allspaw and Paul Hammond presented "10 deploys per day – Dev and Ops Co-operation at Flickr" at the O'Reilly conference in 2009. These three events gave rise to DevOps.

Once teams had predictably stable Iterations with consistent quality, efforts then turned towards delivering faster. Program Managers began to look at the painful hand-off between development and operations and how to better align these for faster delivery. Automation was the next target for improvement and, with development and operations teams collaborating closer than ever before, even greater innovations became possible! For many organizations, automation became a key differentiator, emerging as the backbone of a constellation of technologies and practices, which created a real competitive advantage.

Solid reference materials, based on lessons learned from countless teams who successfully implemented DevOps are now available and the practices first described have been adopted, further refined by practitioners, and are currently considered mainstream good practices. Thought leaders Jez Humble and David Farley paved the way with *Continuous Delivery* in 2010. Other seminal works in this area include Gene Kim and Jez Humble's *DevOps Handbook* and Gene Kim and Kevin Behr's *The Phoenix Project,* notable not only because of the groundbreaking ideas it contains, but also because it is written as a novel.

DevOps is the next step in disciplined practices using Agile values and principles as a foundation. It builds on solid practices and extends the cross-functional teams to include the support and operations teams. DevOps introduces new practices that build on those within XP, such as refactoring, coding standards, collective ownership, planning game, code peer review, and TDD, as well as continuous delivery, automation, and Lean Product Management.

Benefits / Challenges

Benefits

DevOps provides guidance on building the right culture among various required groups to yield fast, stable delivery of products. This is being referred to as "Shift Left" and at the core means building quality in, including security and performance, at every step in the process, not just at the end. This is achieved through disciplined practices and automation. Top benefits that can be achieved by DevOps adoption are listed in this section.

Time to Market – The "build quality in" culture, with a disciplined approach to delivery, ensures the DevOps adoption results in faster time-to-market and delivery times that eventually improve ROI. Organizations are able to deliver on new Features fast, resulting in sustained and increased market share. This is largely because they are spending less time doing unplanned and rework activities and devoting more time to generating business value.

Quality – Automation, at various stages, ensures consistent, high quality. Practices such as continuous testing, continuous release & deployment, and continuous monitoring not only reduce testing and deployment time, but also deliver a high quality product.

Continuous Delivery – The idea is to create a repeatable, reliable process for releasing products by keeping everything in version control, developing scripting for further automation, and implementing Release pipelines with continuous improvement feedback loops that lead to more predictable delivery and reduced cycle times.

Architecture – Shifting to loosely coupled services and components provides higher throughput and even higher quality and stability. In this context, loosely coupled means services can be developed and released independently of each other and teams are not dependent upon another team to complete their work. This leaves the infrastructure team with added time to invest towards more relevant activities.

Change and Release Management – Releasing 10 times a day requires change and Release management to step up in order to accept and absorb these frequent Releases. Weeks of communications and change management effort was previously required to bring a product to market. However, when processes are streamlined, the organization is far more efficient and effective. The result is vastly improved confidence in change and Release management processes.

Empowered Workforce – After a DevOps adoption, both the development and operations organizations will have greater responsibility throughout the lifecycle, leading to increased engagement and job satisfaction. Development teams will have better tools and procedures to reduce cycle times and improve quality. Operations teams will have enhanced opportunities to partner with the development teams rather than being the ones to 'catch' when a new system is 'thrown over the wall' for ongoing support.

Challenges

Steep Learning Curve

The learning curve is a challenge with DevOps adoption because the behavioral and development pattern changes required usually represent a sea-change in thinking from what an organization is currently doing. It requires all team members to increase their skills. Cross-functional teams must accept a new, much broader dimension of work. Thinking through all the possible downstream issues and potential support problems requires greater discipline and maturity. Collaboration with business stakeholders and quality assurance professionals is needed in order to have the adequate code coverage levels of automated unit and acceptance tests. Security and system performance concerns must be considered as part of the system build. While these validations and verifications can be automated, false positives will constantly appear and need to be addressed by professionals with a deeper understanding of information security and performance. Thought must be given to the effort to monitor and load balance systems. These are examples of items often addressed only after development and testing cycles are complete.

Embracing concepts like "building quality in" and "everyone is responsible for the delivery process" are major components of the "Shift Left" thinking – doing things earlier in the process. Everyone on the team should write some code using programming or scripting language in order to produce production code or automate repetitive tasks. But this goes beyond just code. The organization, as a whole, has to undergo some sort of transformation as well. The business needs to adapt to smaller and more frequent Releases, with "less complete" solutions and a broader interest towards experimentation. The operations and support teams must learn faster ways to troubleshoot the products and services through code or new artifacts. System resilience needs to be increased so infrastructure teams can decrease risk by changing the mindset from avoiding changes to doing them more frequently.

Organizational Culture Change

The organizational culture shift is significant as well. Asking release and operations managers to allow developers to release to production based on peer reviews and automated acceptance test passing is a big behavioral change. Leaders need to be urged to allow the DevOps experiments, remove some of the extra controls, and start releasing more frequently to production. To do so requires not only a better than average understanding of DevOps concepts and tools in order to present the compelling case, but also better than average influencing skills! Empowering the team must be combined with other capabilities like small batches, delivery process pipeline flow transparency, and customer feedback implementation.

Another element of the organizational culture change is centered on end-users and other stakeholders. They, too, must embrace the DevOps culture and be willing to accept more frequent, smaller Feature Releases. In some cases, end-users may be asked to perform more frequent usability testing in different environmental conditions.

Technology Fit

Research and analysis of tools takes a fair amount of time and resources. There are a number of possibilities to compare in order to choose the best fit for the organization. Using an outside vendor to help with the selection process is a prudent practice.

Once tools are selected, the implementation and use of tools, especially automated testing tools, can be a significant cost. Make sure to set expectations around securing outside assistance, training, and on-going support during ramp-up, adoption and beyond.

Program-level Attributes

A shift to DevOps will require significant investment for many organizations, both in tooling and in culture change, but this shift to Lean Product Management will drive higher organizational performance. This high performance, in terms of automation and configuration management, will fuel shorter recovery times when outages occur. In some cases the failures will be prevented due to the baseline monitoring of systems, configured to note changes. This will free the team to build new functions and Features.

A good practice is for teams to create Value Stream Maps of the current process as well as a future Value Stream Map with clear incremental plans to move toward this future state. This should include technical training, coaching, and change management components for cultural awareness. Present this to leadership as part of the initial steps of adopting DevOps. Also, be ready with a plan for tracking progress using appropriate metrics. See the Artifacts and Workflow later in this chapter.

Defining the right measurements and key performance indicators is essential. Displaying and clearly communicating progress will encourage the DevOps adoption process and provide motivation for everyone. More information on measurements is in the Artifacts section of this chapter.

This year, as part of *The State of DevOps* (2017) report, research was focused on leadership characteristics that help drive high performance. This is a great addition as leaders set the tone for the transformation, enforce the correct behaviors, and add their considerable authority and influence to obtain the budget for necessary added tools and training. In the research study used, the measure of transformational leadership included five dimensions taken from the Rafferty and Griffin 2004 model published in the Leadership Quarterly[2]. The characteristics of transformational leadership were found to be correlated with performance. High-performing teams reported having leaders with behaviors associated with these five dimensions as shown in *Figure 6.04.*

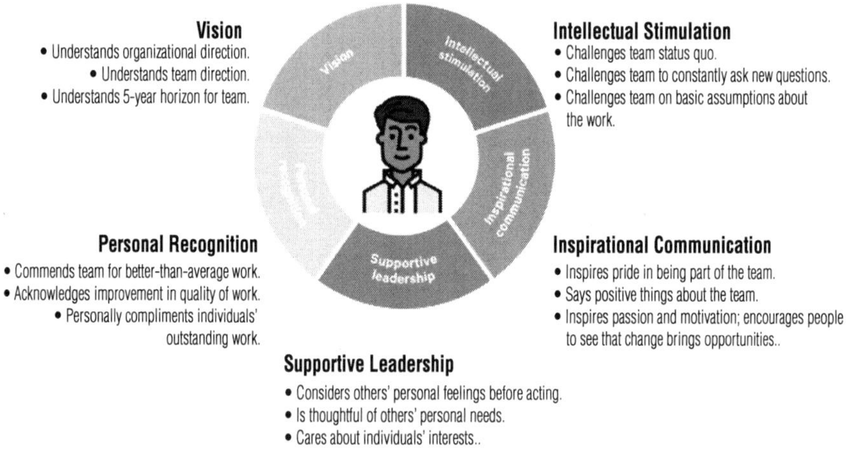

Figure 6.04 | Dimsnsions of Transformational Leadership

Vision –A clear concept of where the organization is going and where it should be in five years.

Inspirational communication – Communicates in a way that inspires and motivates, even in an uncertain or changing environment.

Intellectual stimulation –Followers are challenged to think about problems in new ways.

Supportive leadership – Demonstrates care and consideration of followers' personal needs and feelings.

Personal recognition – Praises and acknowledges achievement of goals and improvements in work quality; personally compliments others when they do outstanding work.

A transformational leader's influence also supports the teams' technical practices and product management capabilities. The data also indicated that the transformation leader's behavior, in itself, was not enough to be successful. Success depended upon the leader's behavior and many of the other key elements detailed in this chapter (i.e. the correct architecture, use of Lean principles, and solid technical practices). Transformational leaders that enable the values, processes, and practices embraced by the five dimensions, and support the set of practices outlined in this chapter, have a high probability of realizing the desired outcomes and benefits from a DevOps adoption.

There will come a time during adoption of DevOps when these leadership characteristics will be tested. People will resist change, challenge the direction, advocate abandoning efforts at the first sign of any hiccup or problem, or sabotage the process in some way. A large pitfall for Program Managers in this environment is reverting to command-and-control style behavior when things go wrong. People working in an Agile environment will see this change in behavior, and engagement and performance will reduce immediately. This can derail efforts and ongoing trust, and credibility will be difficult to win back.

Roles

There are no specific roles mentioned in DevOps. It is common to have great variation, from organization to organization, in staffing models and roles between DevOps implementations. There are new roles emerging, such as DevOps Engineer, Manager, Architect, Coach and so on. These roles are currently being defined by practitioners on the leading edge of implementing DevOps.

Workflow

The workflow for DevOps is dependent upon the organization's development process, compliance, and other regulatory requirements in the industry. When planning a strategy, the points in Chapter 3 for organizational culture change – removing silos and impediments, supporting high performance and high trust, and establishing True North – all apply to a DevOps transformation. Here are some considerations:

True North – Establishing the True North and purpose for the transformation to DevOps is critical. Everyone across all disciplines (infrastructure, quality assurance, support and maintenance, development, and their associated managers) will have strong feelings about the way they do their work, who approves and makes changes, and even, who belongs on the team. Program Managers must regularly remind everyone involved of the purpose so they stay focused and aligned.

Communications Plan – Prepare a high-level Roadshow to help people understand and communicate about what DevOps means for the organization and themselves. Typically, the Roadshow has three PowerPoint slides to prompt a dialogue with the attendees.

Figure 6.05 is an example of Slide 1, the True North Statement that is shared and explained.

> *Our system will produce and deliver:*
>
> - Produce defect-free responses that meet the customer's expectations,
> - Deliver responses, on-demand, only when requested by the customer,
> - Deliver responses with the least amount of waste possible, and
> - Produce them within the defined throughput parameters

Figure 6.05 | Roadshow - True North Statement

Figure 6.06 is an example of Slide 2, used to explain the communication resources and plan.

Communication:

- Where to find information on the DevOps transformation?
- Who will answer questions?
- What is the planned cadence and format for reporting on progress?

Figure 6.06 | Roadshow - Communication

Figure 6.07 is an example of Slide 3, where expected questions are displayed and answered in order to create an environment where attendees feel encouraged to ask questions.

Next Steps:

- What are the strategic steps in the overall transformation process?
- How will the first high-level Epics/Themes be implemented?
- How should we prepare to participate?

Figure 6.07 | Roadshow - Next Steps

Ground Rules – Establish some ground rules about team collaboration and behavior. Conflict will emerge. A strong dose of respect and trust, as well as reminders about good intentions, will be needed again and again.

Get a Coach – A coach with strong soft skills, a Lean background, and DevOps expertise is strongly recommended.

Plan the Transformation – Developing a high-level Roadmap for the DevOps transformation is key. It should be incremental and focus on the highest value areas first. Be prepared to communicate the high-level areas and benefits to executives, leaders, and teams and also the need for flexibility and adaption as new details emerge (and they will!).

Value Stream Map (VSM)

The Value Stream Map is an excellent aide in creating the DevOps delivery pipeline needed for the repeatable, reliable process of releasing products into production. This is recommended primarily because the VSM process helps to visualize and align different work-streams. Although a deep drive of VSM is beyond this chapter, a quick walk-through is included.

Value Stream Mapping Process

A Value Stream is the sequence of activities an organization undertakes to deliver on a customer request. The VSM purpose is to provide optimum value, as defined by the customer, to the customer, through the complete value creation process with minimal waste in design, build, and sustainability over time. Specifically, it is the activities required to design, produce, and deliver goods or services to a customer. VSM usually includes cross-functional departments and work-streams, and comes in many different forms. Often, the starting point is a high-level diagram that presents a major process, service or large function, referred to as a Product Family.

This Product Family is then decomposed into small work-stream segments with greater detail. The VSM process is an effective tool for establishing a strategic direction for making improvements. It requires participants to

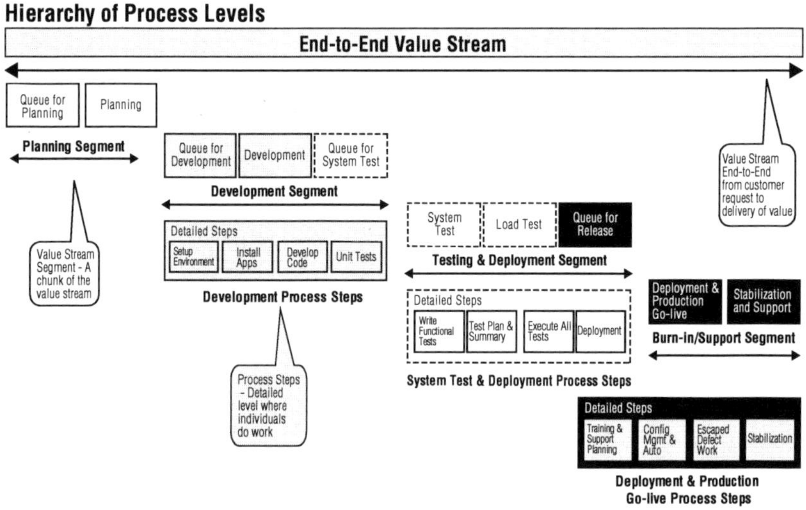

Figure 6.08 | Value Stream Map Segments

focus on who the customer is and depicts the components of the cycle of work: Information flow, Work flow, and Timeline.

Figure 6.08 - Example of the Value Stream Map Segments (work-stream)

The process of mapping out these components deepens everyone's understanding of the overall system, how everything relates to other components, and most importantly, the associated time to customer delivery, referred to as lead time or throughput.

Figure 6.09 - Example of VSM with Timeline section

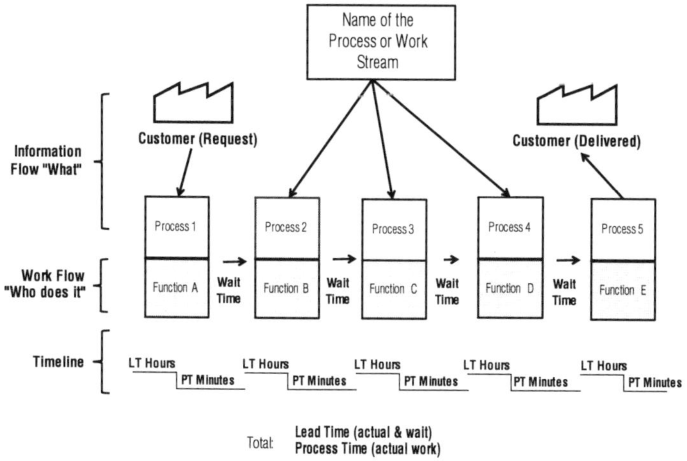

Figure 6.09 | Value Stream Map with TimeLine Section

VSM allows for the holistic system thinking necessary to systematically target areas needing improvement, develop a target state, track the throughput of changes, and get feedback; then iterate on the next best improvement.

Once VSMs are done across the different DevOps team work streams, the wait times and wasteful areas will begin to appear. Look for the best areas to improve and concentrate efforts there first. Double back to the leadership team with results and recommendations from the VSM process. These, coupled with evaluating tools and creating an implementation plan, are the prerequisite steps needed to launch the DevOps initiative. It is important to explain the process and set expectations appropriately. DevOps is a journey of continuous improvement, not a three to six month project. At each step data is collected and evaluated, and new ideas are targeted for improvement. This leads to the potential for continuous delivery and onto improvements to that process.

Continuous Delivery

As stated in the Benefits section, one benefit of DevOps practices is continuous delivery. This is the defined, repeatable, reliable process for releasing products. According to the 2017 *State of DevOps* report results, the biggest contributor to continuous delivery is teams that do all of the following:

- Make large-scale changes to the design of their system without outside permission.
- Make large-scale changes to the design of their system without depending on other teams to make changes in their own, or creating significant work for other teams.
- Complete work without needing fine-grained communication and coordination with people outside the team.
- Deploy and release their product or service on demand, independently of other services the product or service depends upon.
- Do most of their testing on demand, without requiring an integrated test environment.
- Perform deployments during normal business hours with negligible downtime.

This goes much farther than automation!

The following are the individual practices and techniques considered part of the DevOps continuous improvement journey.

Continuous Testing

Test Automation is not optional when it comes to DevOps practices. Testing is a critical part of the handoff between the development and operations group. Continuous Testing means executing the automated test cases, at various stages of the build pipeline, to get the feedback as early as possible. This requires a sound strategy and respect for the Test Automation Pyramid and application of the right combination of the Shift-Left testing approach.

Automate Build and Continuous Integration

In software development, build refers to a process in which source code files are converted into a final product that can run on a computer. This process commonly includes compiling source code files, packaging compiled files into compressed format, generating installers, and creating database schema along with master data from scratch. Other considerations are server configuration for web-based applications, application files, application configuration, and security.

These steps should be repeated each time a new change has been made to the code. In order to remove human effort and make these repetitive steps more reliable, they should be automated by creating an "Automated Build" for each product and service. Some of the most popular automated build tools are Maven, Make, MS Build, ANT, Gradle, etc.

Integration of multiple development work is a tedious, error prone, lengthy process. Until the early 90s, integration work was being done as a separate phase in software development. Later, with the evolution of eXtreme Programming (XP), many good practices came into existence, including Continuous Integration (CI). This practice emphasizes merging all developers' work to a shared repository several times a day. Build automation is a pre-requisite for Continuous Integration. This practice helps minimize the effort required in merging work at the end and enables stable working software to be delivered at any moment. Some of the most popular Continuous Integration tools are Jenkins, TeamCity, Cruise Control, etc.

Automate Provisioning

As demand for the product grows, the production system is scaled up by provisioning new servers and configuring infrastructure based on demand. This process should be flawless, seamless, and fast. That is the reason for automating this entire activity and why it is called "Automated Provisioning" or "Infrastructure as Code" (IaC). It is the process of scripting environments; installing operating systems, installing and configuring servers or VM instances, configuring how the instances and software communicate with one another, and much more. IaC is one of the key success factors in adopting DevOps. Developers help define configuration and operations teams get involved early in the development. Some of the most widely used tools are Puppet, Chef, Ansible, and Salt.

Automate Deployment

In the software industry, deployment is not easy. It is a complicated process requiring many steps related to package installation, configuring data sources, and even restarting servers. The purpose of deployment automation is to allow applications to be deployed across the various environments used in development processes and final production environments. It helps to achieve efficient, reliable, and predictable deployments, which eventually help both the development and operations team. It should also include an automated validation of the build, often referred to as "smoke testing". XL Deploy and UrbanCode Deploy are some popular tools for automated deployment.

Automate Monitoring and Feedback

Monitoring is a very important part of the maintenance phase. When the customer wants high availability and fault tolerance, any sort of downtime is unacceptable, so servers, networks, applications, databases, etc. are all continuously monitored. This also provides feedback from production used to further improve the overall system, giving DevOps teams the tools they need for continuous improvement.. This becomes more complicated as infrastructure scales. In order to manage this and quickly take corrective measures, automated monitoring is required. Some of the most popular tools currently being used in this area are Nagios, Zabbix, Sensu, ELK, SysDig, New Relic, AppDynamics, etc.

Ceremonies

There are no specific ceremonies suggested, or even required, for DevOps teams. Teams are left to decide for themselves what would be best for their particular organization and mix of product, technology, people, and culture. DevOps cannot be successful without strong collaboration between teams, no matter how much automation is achieved at various phases of development.

To promote the collaborative environment essential to DevOps success, there are a few recommendations.

- Specifically schedule meetings at regular intervals to keep different work streams aligned with work, both upstream and downstream (Value Stream segments).
- Make a point to invite other work streams' members to work sessions and establish agenda talking points so everyone can decide on the value of participation.
- Routinely conduct DevOps Retrospectives and solicit feedback on ways to improve.

Artifacts

There are no specific artifacts stipulated by DevOps, however, some key metrics should be captured to help monitor progress and determine the system health. Collecting data on the current state and progress toward targets should be discussed and decided upfront by the DevOps team so that once data collection has begun, everyone understands what is being measured and the reason for it. Sometimes DevOps metrics are nuanced and indicate nothing, or the wrong thing, until combined with other metrics. Determining the right mix of metrics is a challenging but necessary part of tailoring the DevOps implementation.

Metrics that are measured get everyone's attention. People will change behavior to align with measures that are tracked and rewarded, so carefully selected measurements are critical to achieving the results desired. Metrics that work for one organization will not necessarily work, or even be valid, for another organization. Mark Michaelis, Chief Technical Architect at IntelliTect, created an excellent mnemonic, TRACE,[3] for the Principles of Measurement referenced in *Figure 6.10.*

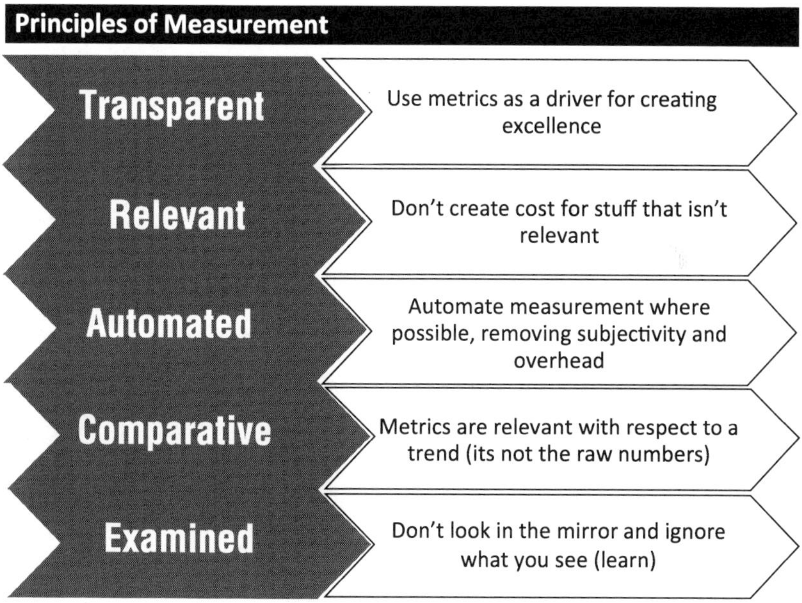

Figure 6.10 | Value Stream Map Segments

There are several metrics to consider that should be collected and radiated on a frequent basis so everyone can see progress. They are shown is *Figure 6.11.*

Metric	Description
Deployment Frequency	Throughput indicatorHow often is the team deploying new code?
Change Lead Time	Throughput indicatorThis is the cycle time required to deploy changes into production (code commit to code deployed and running successfully)
Change Failure Rate (% of failed deployments)	Stability indicatorWhat is the percentage of deployments which have caused an outage or negative user reaction?
Mean Time To Recovery (MTTR)	Stability indicatorWhen failure does occur, how long does it take the team to recover from the issue?
% Change in User Volume	Percent of change for number of new users
Availability	Is the Service Level Agreement (SLA) being met?
Performance (Response Time Indicator)	Is the product or service is operating within predetermined thresholds?
Cycle Time	Time to complete the task in a specific phase
Build Duration	Time to build the full stack

Figure 6.11 | DevOps Metrics

Warning signs, signaling risk or failure and their associated descriptions and/ or course of action, are described in F*igure 6.12.*

How to Make It Work Effectively

It is important to work as one team towards one goal. Many practices mentioned in the collaboration section can be used to enable DevOps culture. There are some technical practices that help smooth the DevOps adoption. These critical components are listed in this section.

Value Stream Map

The Value Stream Mapping exercise is useful in understanding how organizations deliver, breaking down elements of the delivery process and analyzing the work to determine ways to gain efficiency.

Build Quality In

The phrase "Build Quality In" refers to creating a testing strategy then executing that strategy by writing automated tests at multiple levels (unit tests, components tests, acceptance tests) and making them part of the Delivery Pipeline process. This means the tests will be triggered to run with every check in of code and will act as automated regression testing.

Event/Observation	Typical Means/Action
Down time is outside of SLA parameters	Determine what the process will be and routinely monitor/Investigate opportunities to improve
Customers express dissatisfaction with results	Determine what the process will be for gathering information, report results quarterly if possible/ Vigorously look for ways to improve satisfaction
Mean time to repair/recover (MTTR)	Ask the teams to determine what the process will be by individual area as appropriate and report results monthly/Ask the teams to recommend repetitive tasks best suited for automation
Cost of changes are unacceptable	Determine what the process will be by individual area as appropriate and report results monthly/Ask the teams to recommend high value improvements that will improve results
Releases lack expected functionality and quality	Determine what the process will be by individual area as appropriate and report out results monthly/Investigate opportunities to segment large releases into smaller, more frequent releases
Releases lack expected functionality and quality	Determine what the process will be by individual area as appropriate, report out results monthly/Engage customer more frequently; review backlog prioritization; drive shift-left behavior in the organization
Employee turnover is high	Determine what the process will be for gathering information, report quarterly/Conduct employee corrective actions based on feedback
Scheduled deadlines are missed	Determine what the process will be by individual area as appropriate, report results monthly/Do root cause analysis

Figure 6.12 | Warning Signs

Further, if this is part of the Build Delivery Pipeline, any other changes to configuration (infrastructure, architecture, or application) will also trigger the full range of testing automation. Build Quality In also means continually improving those automated tests and making sure they are valid. Some tests will need to remain manual, but automating as much of the repetitive test tasks as possible is the goal.

Build a Delivery Pipeline

The Delivery Pipeline consists of various stages of the delivery process. The Delivery Pipeline models the continuous integration and release management process necessary to build, test, and deploy. It is part of the entire process – from concept to cash – and can be modeled as a Value Stream Map for a Product, as illustrated in *Figure 6.13*, in a simple format. Process steps will vary depending on the organization's products and each stage is designed to verify the correctness of changes in the code from a different perspective. The goal of each stage is to validate new functionality or implentation and prevent errors from affecting end-users before reaching production. A failed test in the Delivery Pipeline is good, given it can potentially prevent this mistake from reaching users and customers. The pipeline's aim is to provide confidence, early feedback to the team, and visibility into the flow of changes to everyone involved in delivering new Features

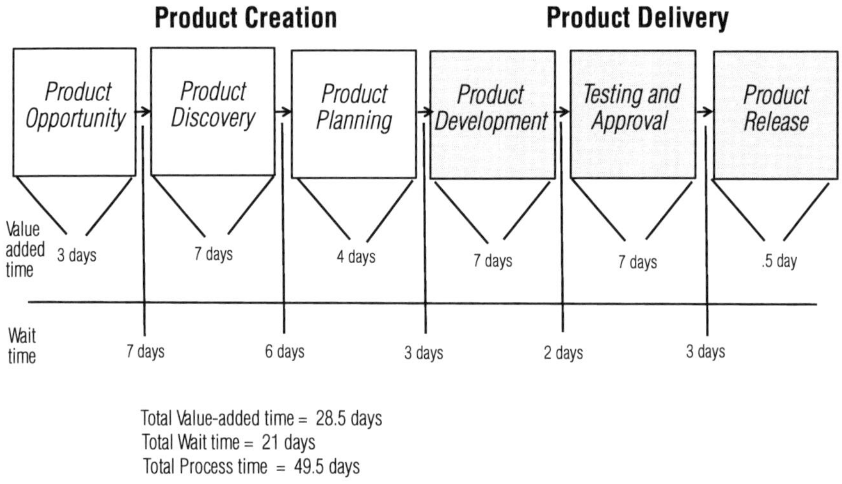

Figure 6.13 | Value Stream Map for a Product

Feature Toggle

This is a technique that allows for system behavior modification without changing code or rolling-back packaged code. It is also used as a safe technique to deploy or release un-finished Features into production along with finished Features by toggling off the unfinished Features. It is helpful to combine this with a soft release, sometimes referred to as a canary release, which is a technique used to reduce the risk of introducing code in production by slowly rolling out the change to a small subset of users before rolling it out to the entire infrastructure.

A/B testing, also known as split or bucket testing, is a method of comparing two versions of a webpage or app against one another to determine which performs better. This technique is used to get faster feedback, which is very important in case of Continuous Delivery or Continuous Deployment models, and can also apply a feature toggle.

These feature toggles need to be used carefully and it is recommended to remove them after the feature is completed or stable in order to keep the code and design clean.

Trunk Based Development (TBD)
Trunk based development is a branching strategy where all code is committed to a single branch, referred to as the trunk, with developers making frequent check-ins. Branches are created only for Release purposes. Bugs are also fixed to the main branch or trunk and, later, it is merged to the Release branch. In TBD, developers never commit changes to the Release branch. At the same time, Release branches are never merged back to trunk since they are short-lived and frequently replaced by other Release branches.

Clear strategies and processes should be in place so smooth code commits can happen frequently. Basic automation tests (unit and acceptance tests) should be in place so tests can be run to quickly confirm a good, or detect a bad, build. All broken code should be corrected immediately or the build is rolled back and completely reversed.

Myths and Anti-patterns

In Chapter 2, some general but key myths and misconceptions about Agile were covered. DevOps, however, is different than other Agile Frameworks in that it is very new, still emerging and changing rapidly, and there is not yet even a common understanding among practitioners about what is meant when an organization implements DevOps. Below are some common myths and misconceptions around DevOps.

DevOps is Only About Automation and Tools – DevOps is not about just adopting new tools and blindly automating processes. DevOps is, at its core, an Agile enhancement and uses the same good practices that other Frameworks, like Scrum, apply in areas, such as team size, collocation, and most importantly, communication. Program Managers must ensure that an environment of Personal Safety is cultivated and that unfettered intra- and inter-team communication takes place continuously. In fact, the key success factor in DevOps adoption is collaboration and communications among any area of the organization, not tool choice(s).

Developers Need to do Operations Jobs (NoOps) – Developers need to know and understand the processes and tools used by operations and vice-versa, however, that does not mean they will do, or even be capable of doing, the job of the operations team. This is part of the fallacy of "generalizing specialists" heard throughout Agile lore, but seldom seen in the real world. This was covered in more detail in Chapter 2.

Operations Teams Need to do Development – Similar to the above, the operations team members should also be familiar with processes and tools used by development team. In order to automate manual tasks in operation, they also need to write code and should know at least one scripting language. However, the operations team should refrain from writing (or rewriting) code that is already working and stable.

DevOps is Just Rebranding Your Ops Team as DevOps – Another common trend is organizations simply renaming their existing Ops team to DevOps. They continue working in silos and using the same processes as before, which is not, and cannot be, considered DevOps. Remember, DevOps is an Agile method centered on transparency, communication, collaboration, and collective ownership. All Agile transformations, or even limited Agile adoptions, can be difficult, even when led by experienced practitioners. The move to DevOps, however, is more difficult than most. Of all the Agile Frameworks and models, DevOps ranks toward the top of the list when it comes to requiring up-front investment and training, carrying the greatest risk, and generally being the most difficult to implement, particularly at scale. DevOps is definitely not a simple rebranding.

DevOps is All About New Skills – While it is true that both development and operations team members have to acquire some new technical skills relevant to DevOps related tools, this is not the major part of a DevOps adoption. The main parts are transparency, communication, collaboration, and collective ownership. It is all about the flow of delivery and continuous improvement of the flow.

DevOps Means Ten Deployments Daily – Much too frequently, Program Managers are overwhelmed by the fact that by DevOps adoption, companies could, if needed, make production deployments multiple times per day. Often times, executives will stop listening after they hear this, figuring DevOps could not possibly be for them because they never deploy that frequently, especially if they operate in a financial, insurance, healthcare, or other regulated environment. Just like Agile does not have one "right" length for an Iteration or Sprint, DevOps has no "right" frequency of deployment. Establishing the organizational ability to continuously integrate and deploy software is, in itself, an enabler of competitive advantage irrespective of deployment frequency. It is important to understand that if multiple deployments can be done in a day is the question, not if it is actually happening. If the answer is yes, then the processes and culture are well aligned in the DevOps mindset, which put another way, means if there is hesitation to release to production, the organization has not met the definition of DevOps.

DevOps is Only for Startups and Unicorns – Large organizations contain many reporting units, groups, and sub groups that mostly work in silos, as contrasted with unicorns and startups where workers are often in the same large room and anyone can talk to anyone at any time. In large organizations, the main barrier to DevOps adoption is not technical but cultural. Breaking silos between these departments and groups requires organizational level cultural change and executive support.

Tools and Practices Recommendations

DevOps Toolchain
Throughout this chapter many tools for multiple, specific applications have been discussed. The importance of automation and automated tools cannot be overstated for success at DevOps. Moreover, organizations with successful adoption of DevOps typically use multiple specialty tools for specific purposes, such as continuous build, test, release, deploy, monitor, etc. The constellation of tools deployed in a DevOps organization is typically referred to as the DevOps toolchain. Finding the right mix of tools can be difficult and often requires a fair deal of experimentation and continuous refinement to make sure that critical processes and hand-offs are effectively automated.

The choice of these tools and systems depends on the organization's unique needs and should be evaluated accordingly.

DevOps Progress Radiator
Figure 6.14 is a Change Lead Time graph that displays the number of minutes it takes to deploy code into production. The horizontal (diamond markers) line at 2400 minutes is the Target the team has set. The solid (star markers) line that starts at 3200 minutes and gradually slopes down toward the Target, but only reaches 2800 minutes, is the Planned Change forecast; showing how the team will get to the target. The line (square markers) that begins at 3400 minutes and slopes down until it plateaus at 2950 minutes is the Actual

Minutes performance through 4/1. The thick grey line (no markers) that begins at 3400 minutes and slopes down through 4/1 is the Trend Line. As the Delivery Pipeline process is executed and continuously improved, and automation is put in place, the Trend Line improves, even if the team gets stalled on a plateau trying to find the next breakthrough. The secret to reducing Change Lead Time is continuous improvement applied, again and again.

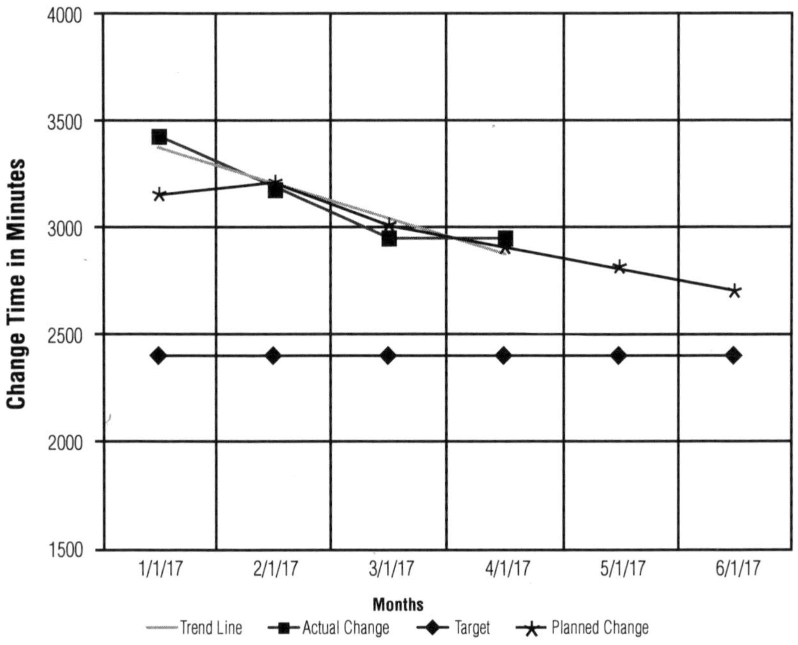

Figure 6.14 | Change Lead Time by Month (in minutes)

This chapter covered the most common metrics that will be of great value to many Program Managers. Many of these metrics can be communicated in ways similar to the *Figure 6.14.* For more information, tools, and tips on DevOps, please join the GR8PM tribe at GR8PM.com.

Recommended Practices for DevOps Teams

Configuration Management (CM)

Configuration Management is critical for any organization to be successful at delivering IT services, but in a DevOps environment, it becomes hyper-critical. CM activities include maintaining a robust version control system so that systems can be recovered quickly and reliably, and can just as quickly re-deploy code. The version control system also allows multiple developers to work on code simultaneously, while maintaining a "mainline" copy of everyone's integrated and tested changes. CM ensures that developers check their code into the version control system regularly (in many large organizations this is as often as every 6 minutes), keeping multiple versions of the code and allowing them to revert to previous versions if necessary. The CM team (usually other team members) can sometimes be the "code comment police," ensuring developers use the agreed on standard of documentation for their code.

Continuous Integration (CI)

Continuous Integration is another cornerstone capability essential for success with DevOps. Continuous Integration was first written about in Kent Beck's Extreme Programming Explained in 1999. The idea behind continuous integration, since quality is built in, is to commit new code to the existing codebase frequently to ensure everything is behaving as expected. This means every time a team member commits code, the software is proven to work with every change (this assumes there are comprehensive set of automated tests available to run). Bugs in the code are caught much earlier and cheaper to fix, providing significant cost and time savings. Examples of disciplined practices that CI focuses on are:

- Not checking in on a broken build
- Always running all tests locally (development workstation) before committing
- Waiting for commit test to pass before moving on
- Never going home on a broken build
- Always being prepared to revert to the previous revision
- Timebox fixing before reverting
- Not commenting out failing tests
- Taking responsibility for all breakages resulting from changes

The organization may need to consider investing additional resources to support DevOps in the area of Release Management and Test Automation. This will depend upon the current maturity of the practice(s) in the organization, number of professionals in these areas and their capabilities, the ability to shift staff laterally in the organization, and the desired maturity in the future state.

Conclusion

DevOps is a mature set of practices within Agile that are IT-centric, but not constrained to software. DevOps focuses on repeatability and reliability of processes, continuous integration, continuous delivery, cross-training, and like any Agile model, lots of high-quality collaboration.

Automation and tools are prerequisites for a significant gain with a DevOps implementation because only through them can testing scale to keep up with the massive productivity of Agile teams. A Deployment Pipeline is used because it guarantees that people will get repeatable processes at the push of a button. It is not necessary to automate everything at once; in fact this is not recommended. Start with the parts of the build, deploy, test and release process that are currently the bottleneck. Use the Value Stream Mapping process to pinpoint the best bottleneck candidate and continue over time to iterate improvements.

DevOps is focused on ensuring quality through automated testing early, and often, in the development cycle. Defects caught earlier in the lifecycle are less costly to fix than if they had been caught later or, even worse, if they had escaped to production! Continuous integration, automated testing, automated deployment, and monitoring provide the bedrock practices upon which stable production DevOps environments are built. Like all Agile teams, everyone on DevOps teams is responsible for quality and the delivery process.

DevOps is one of the more difficult Agile approaches to implement, but when the benefits are desired, it can really pay off and allow the organization to keep their competitive advantage!

END NOTES

[1] Forsgren, Nicole, et al. 2017 State of DevOps Report. Puppet. June 2017, *https://puppet.com/resources/whitepaper/state-of-devops-report.*

[2] Rafferty, Alannah E., and Griffin, Mark A. "Dimensions of transformation leadership: Conceptual and empirical extensions." Leadership Quarterly, no. 15, 2004, pp. 329-354, *www.researchgate.net/publication/222553147_Dimensions_of_transformational_leadership_Conceptual_and_empirical_extensions.*

[3] See Metrics that Matter for more on TRACE - www.slideshare.net/ITRevolution/does15-mark-michaelis-metrics-that-matter.

CHAPTER

7

Scaled Agile Framework (SAFe®)

Overview

Scaled Agile Framework® (SAFe®)[1] was created by Dean Leffingwell in 2011 and was the first method to dedicate itself entirely to scaling Agile. Since its launch, there have been many other scaling approaches brought to market, but SAFe has maintained its leadership and is still one of the most popular options.

SAFe is a freely revealed knowledge base of integrated, proven patterns for enterprise Lean-Agile development. It's a Lean-oriented approach for scaling Agile focused on aligning development with the enterprise's strategic focus. *(See Figure 7.01.)* It uses a unique blend of Agile principles along with some prescribed structure and workflows intended to improve throughput with the concept of an Agile Release Train (ART).

As the work is decomposed from Epics to Stories it allows the appropriate level of detail so delivery has a meaningful impact on a solution or system. SAFe creates a shared Vision of the work rooted in its Core Values and Principles, guided by a Lean-Agile mindset.

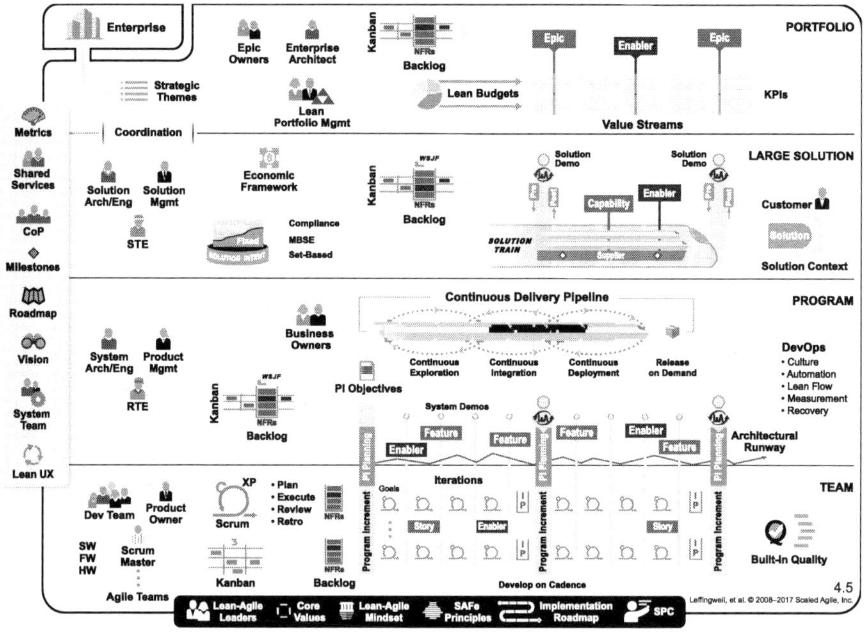

Figure 7.01 | Scaled Agile Framework

SAFe's Core Values are:

- Alignment
- Built-in Quality
- Transparency
- Program Execution

SAFe's Principles are:

- Take an economic view
- Apply systems thinking
- Assume variability; preserve options
- Build incrementally with fast, integrated learning cycles
- Base milestones on objective evaluation of working systems
- Visualize and limit WIP, reduce batch sizes, and manage queue lengths
- Apply cadence, synchronize with cross-domain planning
- Unlock intrinsic motivation of knowledge workers
- Decentralize decision-making

The SAFe House of Lean describes the Lean focus in the Lean-Agile mindset. It is a set of six constructs describing the frames, actions, and behaviors of SAFe teams. *(See Figure 7. 02.)*

Figure 7.02 | SAFe House of Lean

The roof displays the primary goal of having everything in the house support creation of maximum Value. Each pillar supports the roof (the goal) with a specific contribution or focus. The pillars included are Respect for People and Culture, Flow, Innovation, and Relentless Improvement. Each pillar will be explained in detail in the Workflow, Ceremonies and Artifacts sections. The entire house is made stable by resting on the foundation of Lean-Agile Leadership.

Benefits / Challenges

Benefits

Ease of Integration with Large PMO Organizations

One of the biggest strengths of SAFe is the ease of integration with large PMO organizations. The infrastructure and roles within the PMO are easily transferred into Agile roles within SAFe. Program Managers and Project Managers make excellent Release Train Engineers or Product Managers, as well as fulfill various other roles. At the Portfolio level, the PMO becomes an Agile PMO, changing its focus of working with Lean Portfolio Management to the Agile Program Guidance responsibilities, such as focusing on Essential SAFe, supporting communities of practice and sustaining and improving the Lean-Agile transformation.

Longer Time Box with Larger Committed Initiatives
SAFe's longer timebox is a great feature of the Framework. The Program Increment (PI) is a 10-week, 5 Iteration timebox that allows the team to take on and deliver larger Features and valuable Objectives. Shifting the focus from User Story delivery to Feature delivery empowers the team to breakdown objectives into meaningful Stories based on the acceptance criteria. User Stories are very specific and can be completed within a short Iteration. Planning at the Feature level reduces, what the team may consider, extraneous User Stories. User Stories are considered Tasks of the Features instead. This provides better visibility to the Agile Release Train's stakeholders.

Better Forecast Ability Leveraging Roadmaps
Another notable strength of SAFe is the focus on Roadmaps, which, in turn, enables the ability to forecast better. It is not that Roadmaps are a new concept SAFe brings into the picture, but that the Roadmap can be leveraged through a set of metrics and data to show roughly three PIs into the future with good accuracy. That means Agile management tools can create forecasts and future demand capacity models based on the Roadmaps being tracked in the tooling, while recognizing that plans will change.

Alignment of Multiple Teams Focused on Feature Delivery
SAFe does a very good job of aligning multiple teams and focusing their attention. The Agile Release Train (ART) is the cornerstone of the team alignment. ARTs bring cross-functional teams together to plan and deliver in the PI time box. The PI Planning event brings all SAFe teams and stakeholders into a two-day session to create an alignment of the business, solution, and architectural Vision. Agile teams then develop a best guess plan on what they can commit to deliver by the end of the PI. The PI Planning event is the crown jewel of team alignment, bringing many key bits of information presented into the ART. The business has the direct ability to guide their requests straight to the teams and ensure that the highest priority work receives the most focus.

Continuous Delivery
SAFe is a multiple Kanban Framework, which is continuously generating quality work on a regular cadence. With Kanban guiding flow throughout

the Program, there are no timeboxes to constrain delivering value to the customer. There is no need to wait until the end of the Program Increment to deliver completed work. Value is delivered when the Minimal Marketable Feature (MMF) is ready to release. DevOps practices and mindsets are represented by SAFe's CALMR approach (i.e., Culture, Automation, Lean flow, Measurements and Recovery) that enables continuous delivery.

Multiple Configurations of the Framework

The setup of SAFe is complicated due to the multiple layers of workflows and the introduction of the new roles, like Release Train Engineer (RTE) and System Teams. SAFe has 4 unique configurations of the Framework to provide direction on how to implement what fits right for the enterprise.

Essential SAFe is the most basic configuration, focusing only on the Program and team levels. *(See Figure 7.03.)* It works on the PI cadence for continuous delivery of value to the customer. With SAFe 4.0, an enterprise would implement either a 3- or 4-level Framework, depending on what best fits their delivery needs. With SAFe 4.5, there are four unique configurations of the Framework to provide guidance on how to implement what suits the Program. The roles and different levels of SAFe are discussed, in detail, later in the chapter.

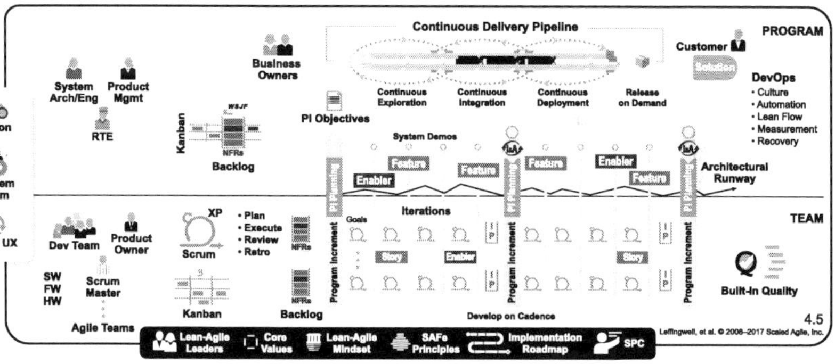

Figure 7.03 | Essential SAFe

Challenges

Keeps Traditional Delivery and Organization But Adds Overhead with New SAFe Roles

Since SAFe has multiple Kanban layers, naturally there are multiple roles that go along with those Kanban flows. As stated earlier, many of the PMO roles directly transfer into a comparable role within SAFe. But the new SAFe roles require training to ensure the person is capable and focused. Because SAFe decomposes Epics to User Stories, setting up a tree structure of work items that might look like a WBS or Task list, a risk is present when Traditional thinking mixes with the new Agile delivery model. Team members in the Program can revert to a Traditional mindset because it is what they know and have always used.

Allocation of Budgets to ARTs not Epics
SAFe leverages Lean Budgets for its accounting practices by focusing on funding Value Streams rather than projects. In contrast, Traditional accounting practices concentrate on funding projects. This can create a chasm to bridge in changing the accounting practices in some organizations and be a large point of contention during SAFe adoption.

Lack of Dedicated Scrum Master
Scrum dedicates a Scrum Master 100% to a team, but SAFe suggests that the Scrum Master is only needed part time. Many would argue that part time is too little time to properly focus on serving the team and actively participate in the Iterations. The Scrum Master leverages the power of osmotic communication to reduce risk and speed development. Their primary focus is on coaching the team, removing obstacles, and making sure the information radiators are projecting accurate information. That typically requires a more dedicated time commitment.

Need for Whole Organization to Embrace SAFe
In Essential SAFe it is not a requirement for the whole organization to commit to SAFe. But when the step into Full SAFe is made, there is a need to engage all aspects of the Value Stream from Accounting through DevOps. Since SAFe leverages Value Streams to deliver work, the transformation needs to include all aspects of the Value Stream, not just Development, QA, and Release.

Too Prescriptive
Many Agile purists will say SAFe is not truly Agile because it is too prescriptive. The assertion is that the Framework starts out with great observations across the ARTs, but as it becomes the company's standard way to do things, it takes away the ability for teams to self-direct – too much business focus, not enough team innovation. The prescriptive nature limits the way teams align and set their own practice of Scrum, Kanban or XP.

There is even an informal group who refers to itself as "UnSAFe". They believe that SAFe is RUP revisited and more of a Traditional delivery than Agile. As Ken Schwaber described in his post *unSAFe at any speed,* "Keep the values, keep the principles, think for yourself. A core premise of agile is that the people doing the work are the people who can best figure out how to do it. The job of management is to do anything to help them do so, not suffocate them with SAFe."[2]

Program-level Attributes

Roles

Business Owners

Business Owners are vital stakeholders who, while few in number, have the primary responsibility for business alignment, technical governance, regulatory compliance, and Return on Investment (ROI) of the solution developed by the ART. They evaluate critical variables like fitness for use and must actively participate in the ART events.

Business Owners focus on business outcomes in order to steer the ART appropriately. They must have reasonable technical competence in order to define a solution that works now, and in the near-term future. They eliminate impediments, in part, by speaking the language of development, business, and customer; fluently translating between the various stakeholder groups in order to create understanding and clarity. They defend PI plans while accepting that some stakeholder dissatisfaction is unavoidable. During PI Planning, they participate in mission setting, planning, various reviews, and problem-solving.

One of their most critical duties is to assign business value to Program PI objectives and approve the PI plan. Actively demonstrating an on-going commitment can be a determining factor in the success of the ART so they must stay involved. This is often a significant change in the common management mindset of "dash in, drop a load of manure, and disappear." Business Owners are fully committed Lean-Agile leaders who are accountable for understanding the Strategic themes that influence the ART and extending that knowledge into the enterprise and Value Stream context descriptions that drive the program Vision and Roadmap.

Product Manager

The Product Manager serves as the content authority for the ART, representing the business and communicating the business direction. They understand the customer needs and validate that the ART is delivering the desired solutions. They develop and communicate the Vision and Roadmap. The Product Manager owns the Program Backlog. The work is prioritized by leveraging Weighted Shortest Job First (WSJF) along with other factors like business value, alignment to near term Roadmap, architectural runway, or ROI. Well thought out and well written Features are an absolute must in order for the teams to succeed.

System Architect
The System Architect is a key member at the Program level. Their main responsibility is guiding the teams' development with high-level architecture of the System so that the team can have an accurate Vision during development. The System Architect also assists the Product Manager in defining and prioritizing Enablers to drive architecture and infrastructure, enabling the ART to run faster on a well-built architectural runway.

They also may assist in decomposing Epics into Features and give guidance to the prioritization of the work items. As the ART readies for the upcoming PI, the System Architect prepares architectural slides for the PI Planning Event to communicate the Architectural vision.

Release Train Engineer
The Release Train Engineer is a role unique to SAFe. The RTE facilitates Program events, including PI Planning, Scrum of Scrums, PO sync, system demos, and Inspect and Adapt. Coming out of the PI Planning session, the RTE tracks and escalates impediments affecting the ART delivery. They also coach Program leaders, Scrum Masters, Product Owners, and Agile teams on the Lean-Agile practices and mindset. For the business needs, the RTE monitors PI execution and reports against the metrics in the information radiators.

Agile Release Train
The Agile Release Train (ART) is a group of cross-functional Agile teams that focus on Feature and Capability completion. The ART aligns teams to a common business and technology mission. These teams plan together at the onset of the PI then deliver in a synchronized cadence. The ART brings its work together at the end of each Iteration for a System Demonstration, then present the completed Features at the conclusion of the PI.

System Team

The System Team is a special team in the ART dynamic. They work directly with the ART as a collaborator, bringing multiple teams' work together to form the system. This collaboration occurs during the Iterations, eliminating lag time for integration. They are the glue aggregating the teams' work into a larger working and tested System prepared for Release. They also assist in building an Agile development environment, as well as continuous integration and deployment tools.

DevOps

SAFe uses DevOps as an approach to development and automation for publishing to the production environment. This is a set of practices organizations use to plan, develop, test, and deploy working software or hardware into a production environment. SAFe has fully embraced the DevOps approach.

Workflow

SAFe has a series of Kanban flows that align the organization's strategy with the teams' execution. The Program is the sweet spot in the SAFe delivery model because of its focus on actual valuable work driving the completion of the Feature. The Program and teams are the core of every configuration of SAFe.

SAFe has 4 distinct configurations:

- Full SAFe
- Large Solution SAFe
- Portfolio SAFe
- Essential SAFe

Full SAFe supports a Portfolio implementation of SAFe with multiple Value Streams and one or more ARTs working on each. Organizational goals are defined in the Portfolio, via Strategic Themes, and communicate the organizational strategy to be reflected and executed throughout the Portfolio. This drives the bigger picture of how each team's work rolls up to the Features, Capabilities, and Epics. Epics represent centralized initiatives that cross Value Streams and are worked through the Portfolio Kanban then decomposed into Capabilities and Features for the ARTs to deliver. Lean Portfolio Management funds Value Streams through Lean budgets.

The next two configurations are less robust than Full SAFe. As described by Inbar Oren, SAFe® Fellow and Principal Consultant, Scaled Agile, Inc., "Large Solution SAFe is for enterprises who are building solutions that require multiple ARTs to develop, but do not need portfolio governance. The Large Solution level provides the roles, artifacts and events needed to coordinate the work of the ARTs within the value stream." Portfolio SAFe provides the roles, artifacts and events needed to coordinate the work of the ARTs for one value stream only. It includes portfolio governance and drives work from the strategic Portfolio level, similar to Full SAFe.

In all configurations, the Program and team levels are the same. The work that is in the Program Backlog has been refined through the Portfolio Kanban, the Solution Kanban, and is ready for the Program-level Kanban. The Features are managed by the Product Manager and prioritized using WSJF. The weekly PO Syncs are leveraged to refine the Features to ensure they include a well written description, hypothesis statement, and acceptance criteria so the teams are able to commit.

Once there are well written Features in a prioritized Backlog, the team is ready for a PI Planning event to kick off the PI. The RTE facilitates the PI Planning event and leverages the Readiness Workbook that SAFe provides to ensure the ART is ready and the event is organized. At the PI Planning event, multiple things occur.

The event begins with some basic introductions then jumps right into Business Owners providing insight to the business context of the solution under development. The Product Manager explains the Vision and Features in the Program Backlog, followed by the System Architect providing guidance on architecture. These three bits of information provide the team with a well-rounded context to answer questions as they work through the Features, shaping the team members' perspective as they prepare to fill out User Stories to deliver the Features in the PI.

The majority of the PI Planning event is iterating through the User Stories and Enablers needed to complete the Features. Enablers are Stories that set up the architectural runway for the teams. This could include infrastructure builds or spike Stories needed to "enable" the team to continue moving forward.

The teams break down the Features and begin to put User Story sticky notes on the PI Program Board, as shown in *Figure 7.04.* Once the teams define the User Stories needed to complete the Features, they write PI Objectives to

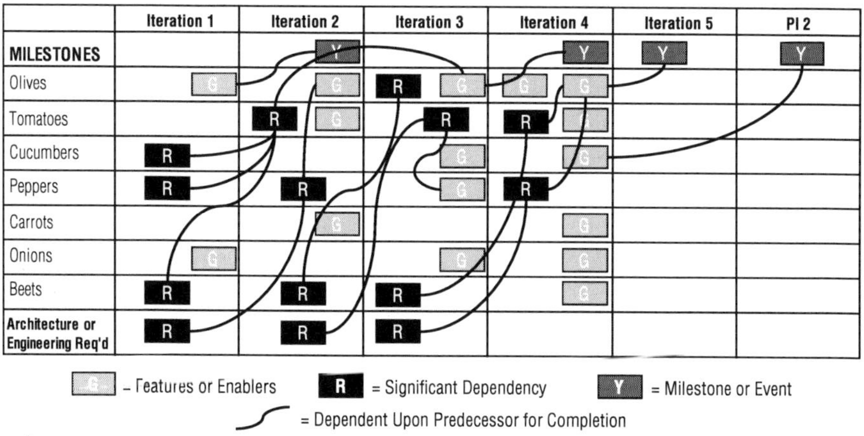

Figure 7.04 | PI Program Board

summarize the decomposed User Stories and articulate the expected business outcomes achieved for the PI. The Business Owners then go through and assign a business value to each objective, so that the business value delivered at the end of the PI can be measured. *(See Figure 7.05.)*

OBJECTIVE - DIGITAL WATER METER (DWM) SYSTEM	BUSINESS VALUE	
	Plan	Actual
Public Utilities Rate Adjustment Filing for DMW System	10	7
DWM Plan & Schedule for Partners	5	3
DWM WiFi Data-Collection Unit	4	4
DWM WiFi Data-Transponder Unit	4	4
DWM Mobile Data-Reader	6	6
DWM Public Hearings Road Show	10	7
DMW Phase 1 Roll-out	15	10
DMW Phase 2 Roll-out	20	20
DMW Phase 3 Roll-out	25	20
	99	81

Figure 7.05 | PI Objectives

Magic happens at the PI Planning Event. *(See Figur.06.)* The teams receive a jumpstart of contextual information to help frame the planning, and then work with each other to develop a plan to deliver committed objectives and solutions. Once the PI Planning event is concluded, the Product Owner

Figure 7.06 | PI Planning Event

transfers the User Stories into the Agile Program Management tool being used by the company and the teams begin working toward their Iteration commitment.

There is a Post-PI Planning meeting held with the RTE, Product Managers, and System Architects to recap the PI Planning event, review the PI Objectives and their business value, look at the Agile tool dashboards and information radiators, and confirm that ART Sync meetings are set up.

The Agile teams work in synchronized two-week Iterations using their own Agile method, such as Scrum, Kanban, or XP, with a System Demo at the end of each Iteration. During the System Demo teams show their work and demonstrate fully integrated system progress.

After four Iterations, the team goes through an Iteration called the Innovation and Planning Iteration (IP). In this, teams use the first week of the two-week Iteration to bring together the final Solution in preparation for the PI System Demo. The second week of the IP Iteration is used by the ART to hold its Retrospective, called an Inspect and Adapt event, as well as to prepare for the next PI Planning event. *(See Figure 7.07.)*

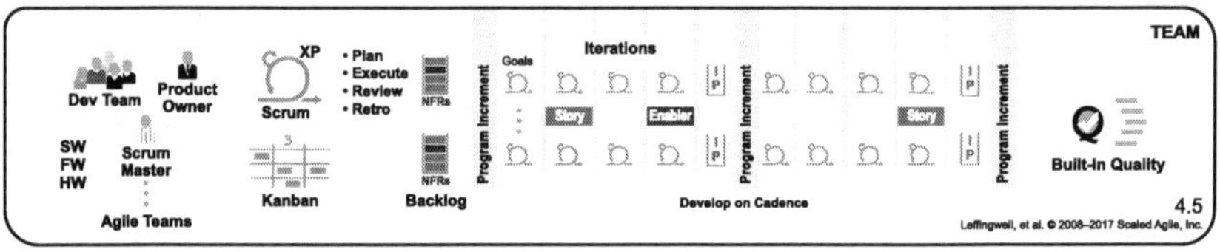

Figure 7.07 | SAFe's Team-Level

Solutions can be released at any time. It is common to have Releases occur on PI boundaries, but it is not required. Releases are not tied to Program Increments and can occur anytime if the Release Management requirements have been met.

This is a rinse and repeat cadence for Program Increments occurring in the Program.

Ceremonies

PI Planning event

This is a two-day planning meeting where the Business Owner expresses the Business Context, Solution Intent, and Architectural Vision for the proposed Features. Then, the teams plan what they can deliver by filling out the User Stories needed to complete the Features and committing to a set of objectives. The PI Planning event occurs every Program Increment and ART Teams, Product Owners, Scrum Masters, System Architects, Product Managers, Business Owners, and the RTE attend.

ART Syncs

These are Stand-up style meetings where the Scrum Masters and Product Owners walk through the Program Kanban board to review the current WIP, groom future Features and Capabilities, and discuss any dependencies and impediments that may stop the ART from meeting its committed objectives. Scrum Masters, Product Owners, Product Managers, and the RTE do this frequently within a PI.

System Demo

At the conclusion of each Iteration, as well as at the end of the PI, there is a system demo to show the progress of the integrated team work. This typically occurs every two weeks and involves ART Teams, Product Owners, Scrum Masters, Business Owners, and the Domain Architect (DA), Product Manager, and RTE.

Inspect and Adapt

During the IP Iteration, the ART comes together to assess its accomplishment and conduct a structured root cause analysis workshop of the problems it had encountered. Agile teams, Product Owners, Scrum Masters, Product Managers, Business Owners, and the DA and RTE attend the Inspect and Adapt event.

Artifacts

Roadmap

The Roadmap is a forecast for upcoming objectives for up to 4 Program Increments. A Roadmap is not a contract stating work will get done in the allocated PI, but more of a visual of where the work may get done based on current information. It is owned by the Product Manager.

Program Backlog

The Program Backlog is a part of the Program Kanban board where work is prioritized and groomed in preparation for the team's commitment at the PI Planning event. It includes the list of Features from which the team selects their work. It is owned by the Product Manager.

Readiness Workbook

The Readiness Workbook is a preparation artifact that aggregates all the pertinent information needed to run a successful PI Planning Event. This artifact contains information on everything from the team rosters to room logistics. In order to ensure that all the appropriate information has been accounted for and included, it is very comprehensive and owned by the RTE.

Weighted Shortest Job First (WSJF) Score[3]

WSJF is a process to prioritize the Program work items using a calculation to identify the highest priority work. It can be done with a tool like excel, or be internal to the management tool or system that captures the calculation results, referred to as the WSJF Score or value. It is owned by the Product Manager. WSJF is calculated as:

(User-Business Value + Time Criticality +
(Risk Reduction and/or Opportunity Enablement Value)) ÷ Job Size.

Where:

User-Business Value = Do our users prefer this over that? What is the revenue impact on our business? Is there a potential penalty or other negative impact if we delay?

Time Criticality = How does the user/business value decay over time? Is there a fixed deadline? Will they wait for us or move on to another solution? Are there milestones in the critical path impacted by this?

Risk Reduction and/or Opportunity Enablement Value = What else does this do for our business? Does it reduce the risk of this or a future delivery? Is there value in the information we will receive? Will this Feature open up new business opportunities?

Job Size = A proxy to give a rough estimate to work. A good example is, "If I'm the only one mowing my lawn, and the front yard is three times bigger than the back yard, the front lawn is going to take three times longer to mow."

PI Objectives
The PI Objectives are the culmination of the PI Planning Event. The RTE gathers up each team's PI Objectives and creates a master PI Objective list that is published for full visibility to all teams and stakeholders. It is owned by the RTE.

How to Make it Work Effectively

Leadership Commitment
It may sound cliché, but there is no substitute for commitment from Leadership. It is an unfortunate reality that workers do what their bosses say, so Leaders need to commit to and lead Agile delivery by example. There are many organizational shifts in the approach to complete the transformation into SAFe that will directly change how most of the people in the organization do their day to day jobs. Leadership needs to set the precedent for this change and evangelize the new Lean-Agile approach to delivering solutions. If they do not, everyone under them will follow suit and not accept the new mindset or commit to their maximum effort.

Commit to Self-Organizing Teams and ARTs
Companies walk a fine line in prescribing to the teams what they expect to be delivered versus how to deliver the expected solutions. *The Agile Manifesto* sets a clear standard to communicate the desired solution to the teams and empower the cross-functional knowledge workers to decide how to deliver on the Vision. This commitment changes the team dynamic and fosters the team's productivity so it is vital that their autonomy not be violated.

Full Value Stream Participation
Value Streams are the full end-to-end delivery of a solution, from initiation through Release to the customer. Most companies only focus on the actual development and deployment aspects of SAFe and forget to incorporate the beginning steps of the Value Stream. This myopic focus on Agile delivery

prevents the company culture from moving beyond its legacy mindset to adopt the new Agile way of delivering. By changing the entire Value Stream's interaction, the company shifts the focus away from a legacy mindset and begins reducing resistance to improving the overall delivery time to their customer. Improving the Value Stream improves total throughput and drives both top- and bottom-line organizational results.

Prepare for PI Planning Sessions

Prepare well for PI Planning sessions. These events are the cornerstone of the PI where teams plan and align around what and how to deliver together over the next PI. The PI Planning event contains a lot of information requiring effective communication to the teams. Without pre-planning, the event will be unsuccessful and, at a minimum, require more time to complete, driving up the cost.

Get Good at System Demos

Get good at System Demos. This is where the stakeholders get to actually see Value being realized. Too many teams get wrapped up in delivering User Stories, but Stories are just Tasks of the Feature and do not add Value on their own. The integration of the User Stories into a working system is where the power to change stakeholder perceptions really happens. It is vital to focus the team on the System Demos and stay vigilant about delivering Value, not just User Stories.

Get Great at DevOps

DevOps is an approach that improves integration into production. This practice requires technical expertise, but leads to massive increases in quality, thereby reducing the time of delivery to the customer. Take the time to set up solid DevOps culture and practices early in the adoption of SAFe.

Have Superb Retrospectives

As in all Agile Frameworks, teams continually look back and retrospect on their performance to identify what went well and what could be improved upon. Lessons learned are the output of the Retrospective. SAFe is no different. Leverage the IP Iteration and encourage the ART to come together to do an Inspect and Adapt event to identify areas of growth at the individual team and Program levels. Embrace the innovation that comes from within the ART.

Consistently Review Metrics and Dashboards

To borrow from Kanban, metrics and dashboards are visual cues of team's delivery. These information radiators are both valuable to the teams and Program to see progress towards the commitment made at the PI Planning event. Here are a few information radiators that are valuable and should be looked at often.

Program Kanban Board – The Program Kanban board is the essential visualization for the Program level. (See Figure 7 – 08.) This visualization shows the full span of work in the pipeline including the upcoming, current, and completed, deployable work. Program Backlog grooming should be done on the Kanban board to prepare work items for the team. Prioritization is also defined by using the Kanban board since work flows from the top of the Backlog.

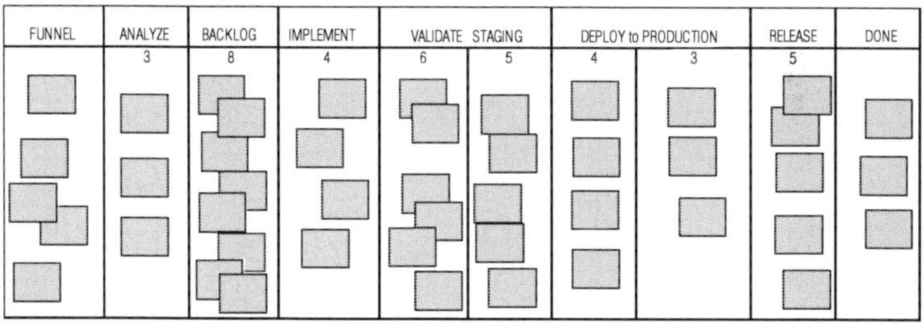

Figure 7.08 | Program Kanban Board

PI Burn-down – Similar to an Iteration Burn-down, the PI Burn-down shows the team's pace of completing the committed Users Stories against the ideal trend of Story completion for the PI. The chart shows the trend of the team's work completion rate and gives a quick forecast to see if the ART will meet their committed work goal.

Cumulative Flow Diagram (CFD) – The CFD is an excellent report that shows the trend of work in the different states of the Kanban flow. The area most focused on is Implementing and Validating. Cumulative Flow also shows the WIP over time, which can be used during Retrospectives to identify opportunities to improve efficiency. They can be quite simple or very complex. *(See Figures 7.09 and 7.10.)*

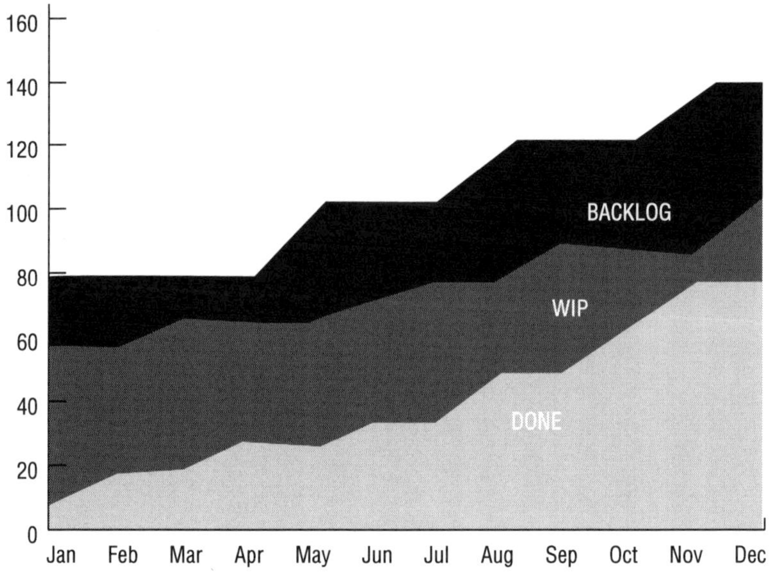

Figure 7.09 | Cumulative Flow Diagram (Simple)

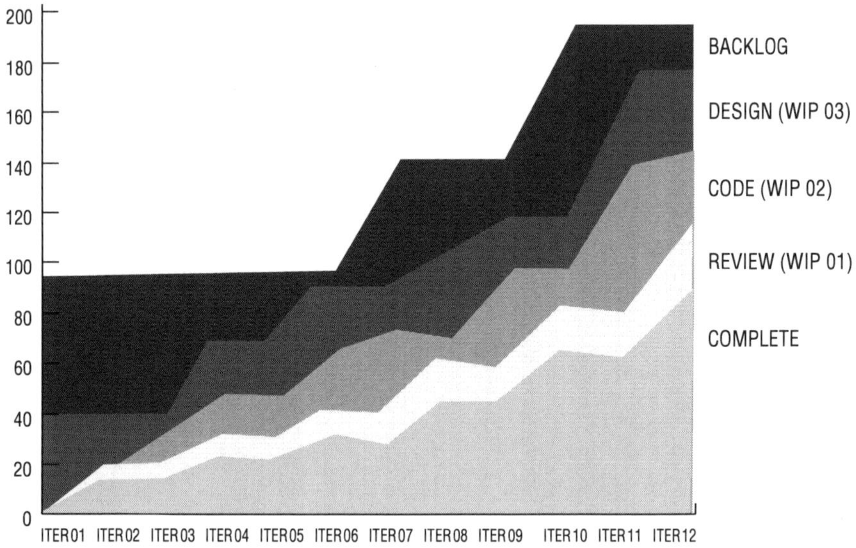

Figure 7.10 | Cumulative Flow Diagram (Complex)

Tools and Practices Recommendations

Tools

There are many different Agile management and reporting tools in the market, such as TFS, Atlassian, AgileCraft, VersionOne, and CA Agile Central. They all tout that they can scale effectively and are the best in the market. The reality is that it is not the tool; it is how an ART works together. Build the tool around the ART. Architecting the tool is important because of future reporting needs and visualizations. Forecasting and future demand capacity models can be created from the Roadmaps and the current work easily displayed through different dashboards and information radiators. The tools create a lot of transparency in a digital medium.

Despite the power of electronic tools, PI Planning events should leverage the proven power of "Low-tech, High-touch" in-person meetings using sticky notes and white boards. That way information can be taken and integrated into the electronic tooling to manage Program execution.

Practices

Embrace Kanban

Kanban brings a simple looking yet highly sophisticated method to delivering valuable solutions. The Kanban board is an easy thing to see and understand because it creates transparency to show the flow of work. The pull style of work assignment gives teams ownership of the work in progress, and allows them the ability to focus on finishing, rather than multitasking and delaying completion. To further your understanding of Kanban, refer to Chapter 5 in this book and also Chapter 7 in *The Agile Almanac – Book 1.* GR8PM.com has great references also.

Align Teams to Change the Delivery Model

Identifying and aligning the organization around Value Streams may require the reassignment of team members. This can be a shake-up at a company, but it is the right decision to make. Having the right teams together is the foundation for high performance and efficiency.

Manage Queues

Nothing breaks down a Lean delivery approach more than unnecessary waiting time. These are stopping points identified during the Value Stream Mapping that need to be addressed to improve efficiency. Be wary about areas ripe for miscommunication and potential defects. To mitigate that risk, eliminate as many queues as possible. Remember, always be as Lean as possible!

Do the ART Sync Meetings
ART Syncs are excellent ceremonies to keep ARTs focused on delivering the PI Objectives. This is when Scrum Masters and Product Owners identify and manage dependencies between teams and call out PI Impediments. There is no better to way to keep everyone's eye on the ball than to talk about it consistently.

Continuously Deliver Value
Build hypotheses; turn them into Minimal Viable Products and Minimal Marketable Features. Test them quickly and embrace the feedback, pivoting if needed without guilt or mercy.

Relentlessly Improve Processes
Focus on delivering value and keep measuring business results to learn which processes need work. This is true at all levels of SAFe.

Conclusion

This chapter has provided an appropriate exploration of SAFe to help assess whether a deeper dive is the next step in the Agile journey. Remember, SAFe uses a complex Kanban flow that integrates multiple layers together with lots of moving parts, so implementing it successfully requires an appropriate investment in training and study. Luckily, its structure provides enough flexibility to make it adaptable to any environment. Adapt the multiple configurations provided and the Framework will become unique to any organization as it implements SAFe.

END NOTES

[1] SAFe and Scaled Agile Framework are registered trademarks of Scaled Agile Inc.

[2] Schwaber, Ken. "unSAFe at any speed." Blog post, 2013, *https://kenschwaber.wordpress.com/2013/08/06/unsafe-at-any-speed/*.

[3] "Reproduced with permission from © 2011-2017 Scaled Agile, Inc. All rights reserved." *http://www.scaledagileframework.com/wsjf/*.

CHAPTER 8

Disciplined Agile

Overview

This chapter describes Disciplined Agile (DA), which provides process tailoring guidance on the integration of development, operations, and other support to deliver effective IT and coexist with SAFe, LeSS, and CMMI. Learning the DA process can be helpful to Agile leaders making the decision to employ Agile beyond an initial team level and evaluating the usefulness of various scaling methodologies. This chapter provides distilled information from a practitioner's perspective and references for a deeper dive, intended to support understanding this transformative Framework.

The goal of this chapter is to provide enough background to understand DA, appreciate its strengths, clarify tradeoffs, and determine when it can be used.

Scott Ambler and Mark Lines, co-founders of DA and thought leaders, provide several reasons why you should choose Disciplined Agile. Disciplined Agile:

- Picks up where Scrum leaves off, dealing with architecture, design, testing, Programming, documentation, and more.
- Is pragmatic, allowing a choice in how to apply it in response to each situation.

- Supports both Lean and Agile lifecycles.
- Is based on proven strategies used across multiple industries.
- Provides a foundation for scalability.
- Enables, and goes beyond, SAFe.
- Is constantly evolving as new Agile and Lean strategies emerge.

The DA process-decision approach provides light-weight guidance to help organizations streamline their processes in a context-sensitive manner, providing a solid foundation for business agility. The DA Framework calls out four process levels – Disciplined Agile Delivery (DAD), Disciplined DevOps, Disciplined Agile IT (DAIT), and Disciplined Agile Enterprise (DAE). The focus in this chapter is on the DAD portion of the Framework.

The strength of Disciplined Agile is in its governance and context-sensitive process goals. It prescribes phases with lightweight milestones, which is something every Project, Program or Portfolio Manager understands as a governance technique for simplifying execution oversight. Process goals are arranged by phase and offer optional best practice suggestions on how to accomplish that goal. Furthermore, its hybrid approach can blend with Traditional methods, making it an easy transition to Agile for an organization.

Background

Scrum remains the most used Agile methodology and is very effective at the team level. When Agile is scaled to the multi-team enterprise environment, additional dynamics take place requiring different roles, artifacts, ceremonies, and a new look at governance. Moreover, the integration of supporting teams becomes a driver for IT effectiveness. Therefore, being effective at IT is different from just delivering IT solutions.

The Disciplined Agile Consortium states, "The Disciplined Agile process decision Framework provides light-weight guidance to help organizations streamline their information technology (IT) processes in a context-sensitive manner. It does this by showing how the various activities such as solution delivery, operations, enterprise architecture, portfolio management, and many others work together. The Framework also describes what these activities should address, provides a range of options for doing so, and describes the tradeoffs associated with each option."

DAD, a hybrid Framework, adopts practices from existing methods and makes recommendations for when and how to use them together. DAD believes itself to be the mortar that fits and holds the Agile process bricks together *(Figure 8.01)*. In general, the DA Framework shows how various Agile, Lean, and other techniques fit together; and suggests when, and when not, to apply each one, and to what extent. DA provides choices and indicates the tradeoffs associated with each one.

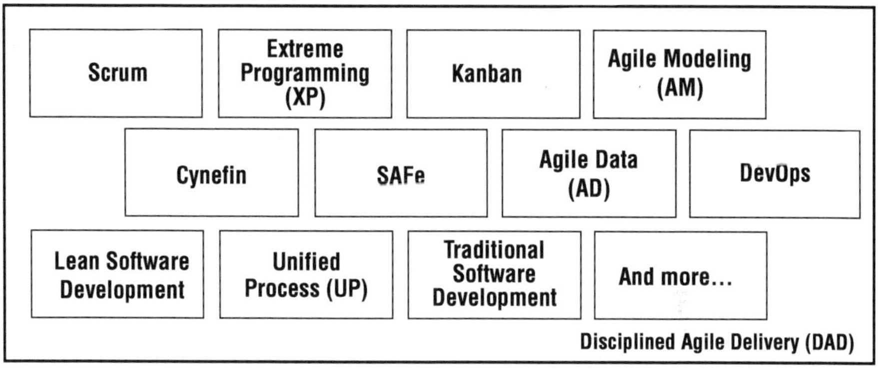

Figure 8.01 | Disciplined Agile Delivery

Lifecycle

The Disciplined Agile Delivery high level lifecycle view from concept through production and support is another strength distinguishing DA from other methods *(Figure 08.02)*. The explicit depiction of pre- and post-delivery

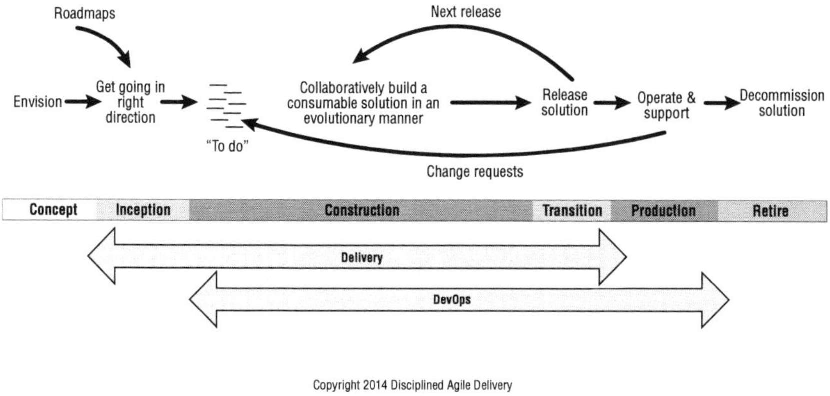

Figure 8.02 | Disciplined Agile full Lifecycle

activities, in addition to a three-phase delivery lifecycle, recognizes the need for preparation before building a solution, and operation and support in production. DAD provides five detailed lifecycles to choose from. They start with Agile/Basic, an extension of Scrum with elements of the Rational Unified Process. DAD then considers Continuous Delivery: Agile, a Scrum-based strategy where the team releases into production every Sprint, and Continuous Delivery: Lean, frequent continuous deliveries supported by DevOps practices. The fourth is Exploratory, using rapid build, deploy, and feedback cycles tested in the market based on Lean Startup. Last is Lean with continuous workflow as opposed to the iterative cadences and ceremonies of Scrum.

Phases and Milestones

DAD also indicates a full delivery lifecycle as opposed to just software development.

The high-level lifecycle consists of Inception, Construction, and Transition phases *(Figure 08.03).*

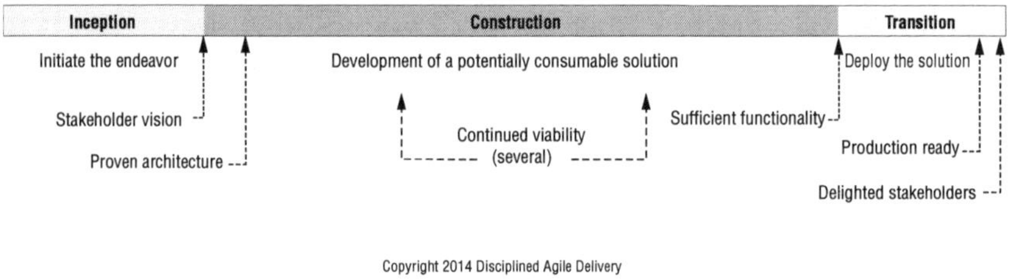

Figure 8.03 | DAD Lifecycle Milestones

These phases allow practitioners to corral concerns, risks, and actions into definable and manageable groupings as well as light-weight milestones to gauge progress.

The milestones allow process checks for inception and transition. The continued viability checks paired with sufficient functionality checks are key to governing the Agile project. Many Agile projects run past the point of delivering optimum value into diminishing returns because no one knows when and how to stop them. The constant review for viability reduces the risk of the interminable Agile project.

Scope of DA Process Framework

Disciplined Agile Delivery (DAD)
DAD is the foundation and addresses IT solution delivery as a whole to include an Agile lifecycle based on Scrum, a Lean lifecycle based on Kanban, and a lifecycle for continuous delivery.

Disciplined DevOps
DevOps is the streamlining of IT solution development and IT operations activities, and supporting enterprise-IT activities, to provide more effective outcomes to an organization. It combines and streamlines elements of security, data management, development, release management, IT operations, and business operations into a fluid cohesive whole.

Disciplined Agile IT (DAIT)
DAIT takes Agile and Lean strategies beyond development and balances enterprise architecture, data management, and portfolio management as well as IT governance.

Disciplined Agile Enterprise
A Disciplined Agile Enterprise is able to anticipate and respond swiftly to changes in the marketplace. It does this through an organizational culture and structure that facilitates change within the context of the situation it faces. Such organizations require a learning mindset in the mainstream business and underlying Lean and Agile processes to drive innovation.

Process Goals

To support complete IT solution delivery, practitioners need to think of more than design, build, test, and deploy. The DA Framework includes DAD, Disciplined DevOps, Disciplined Agile IT, and Disciplined Agile Enterprise. Each of these categories contains process blades, or collections of process options, practices and strategies, chosen based on the context of the enterprise. They can be tailored in consideration of process goals, decision points, and recommended options.

Combining the notation in *Figure 8.04* and the strong DA governance approach, the diagram in *Figure 08.05* can be used in tailoring a process to assure effective and efficient use of IT in enabling organization goals. Again, the first option is the most important and the bolded options indicate a good starting point for the average team in a situation with medium complexity.

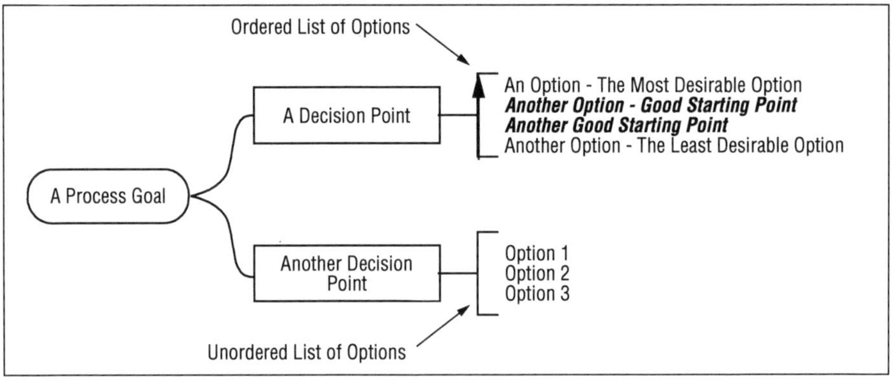

Figure 8.04 | Notation Standard for Graphing

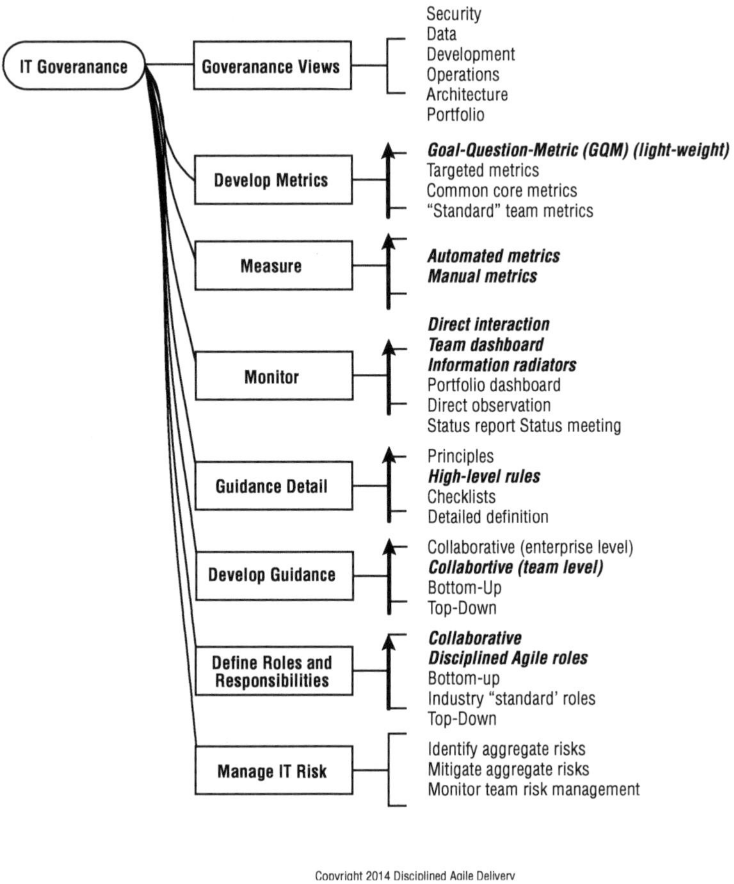

Figure 8.05 | DA Governance Mapping

There are twenty-three goals in total, each of which is described by a Process Goal Diagram. A disciplined Agile team will consider how to address each goal in a manner reflecting the situation they face. Most of the strategies and practices referenced in the goal diagram are described, including the trade-offs involved and considerations for when, and when not, to apply them, in the book *Disciplined Agile Delivery (DAD): A Practitioners Guide to Agile Software Delivery in the Enterprise.*[1]

The result is complete enterprise-ready guidance for Agile implementation across IT *(Figure 8.06).*

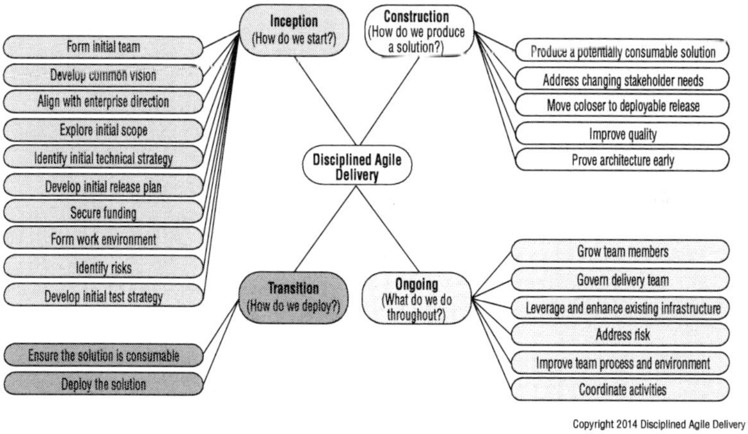

Figure 8.06 | Enterprise-Ready Guidance to Implement Agile

Principles

Mark Lines and Scott Ambler outline seven fundamental principles as the foundation for the DA Framework. They are:

- Delight 1low
- Enterprise Awareness

Delight Customers

Build with the customer in mind, work closely with them, build in small increments, and then seek feedback. Welcome change with the reality that the customer has a right to, and will, change their mind about Features and Capabilities to be delivered.

Be Awesome
Build the team around motivated individuals with the environment, support, authority, and cross-functional skills required to deliver quality products. People are motivated by the level of autonomy provided, the opportunity to master their craft, and a sense of purpose.

Pragmatism
Pure, prescriptive Agile does not work in all enterprise environments. DA realizes this and provides options for process choices when compromises must be made.

Context Counts
Individuals, teams, and organizations are unique in terms of processes and structure within the context of the problem they are solving. DA presents a comprehensive Framework for adopting an Agile approach that fits any context, with a variety of choices.

Choice is Good
DA provides process goal diagrams offering choices based on the intended goal. This provides both structure at the organization level, via process goals, and flexibility at team level by allowing choice of known strategies and likely options.

Optimize Flow
DA supports Lean and Agile strategies for workflow optimization with concepts such as sustainable pace, optimizing the whole, visualizing work, eliminating waste, learning experiments, measuring, and stabilizing teams *(see Figure 08.06)*.

Enterprise Awareness
The overall goals of the organization are considered in addition to the goals of the team. DA promotes seeking guidance from enterprise professionals, leveraging existing assets, following common guidance for consistency and quality, sharing team learning, and working in a transparent manner.

Scaling Factors

As an outgrowth of the Agile Scaling Method that Scott Ambler developed while at IBM, the Software Development Context Framework (SDCF) provides a situation dependent strategy for organizing people, processes, and tools for a software-based solution delivery team. The SDCF is generally applied at the Program or portfolio level. It calls for a selection strategy for people, processes, and tools then tactically scales that strategy based on six scaling factors.

The "radar" chart in *Figure 8.07* shows the scaling factors, with distance from the center representing increased risk.

Figure 8.07 | SDCF Scaling Factors

Figure 8.08 depicts how several selection factors drive the choice and tailoring of team members, delivery process, and tooling configuration.

Figure 8.08 | Selection Factors

Factors for Selecting a Base Strategy for People, Process, and Tools

DA leads practitioners through options and considerations for selecting their base strategy. They must consider whether the team members have the required skills for their roles or if they can acquire the role-based skills appropriately. Team members who are collaborative are also a better choice than those who prefer to work alone. This branches out into the organization, so it will be more difficult, but not impossible, for a more rigid, command-and-control style culture to adopt an Agile or Lean approach.

Problems can be solved in either a Traditional or Agile manner. It is DA's considered opinion that any problem with a decomposable solution can experience improved delivery via Agile. Whether the practitioner can decompose a series of deliverable solutions is the key. They must also factor in business constraints. The beauty of an Agile approach is the way cost and schedule can be fixed while allowing requirements variability. Often, stakeholders will want a fixed delivery date with a specified capability done within an assured budget. Decades of data prove that it is unrealistic to think all three can be "fixed" in situations with complexity and uncertainty. The three constraints, along with the dedicated availability of business product management and owners, influence how processes are tailored and the team is structured.

Factors for Scaling the Selected Strategy

DA guidance helps scaling by highlighting issues and considering several key factors. Geographical distribution has a large impact to success. It is important to develop a clear process for distributed teams, whether within a building or across continents. The same is true for the size of the team, especially as it increases to members in the hundreds. The correct processes and tools need to be in place to manage large or distributed teams, including those with members from different divisions or other companies.

Programs contain high complexity environments. A Program Manager must establish whether the domain is complex enough to require prototyping, modeling, or simulation and how to manage this along with the differing systems, platforms, and technologies that add more layers of complexity. Compliance requirements are another factor that can constrain teams so the Product Owner must consider their effect on architecture.

Benefits and Challenges

Benefits

Goal-Driven Approach

Experience and research indicate several fundamental advantages to taking a goal-driven approach like Agile solution delivery. A goal-driven approach, using the goal diagrams, provides straightforward process tailoring guidance. It does this by indicating the process factors that need to be considered explicit and potential strategies and practices to consider while addressing each factor. The goal diagrams can provide quick references to help teams identify potential improvements they otherwise might not have been aware of, improving the efficiency of Retrospectives. They also make process options very clear, articulating what issues need to be considered when tailoring an Agile solution delivery process to meet the unique needs of the situation faced by the team. In doing so, the guesswork is removed from extending Agile methods since a range of available options with detailed, context-sensitive advice is provided. Another benefit to the goal diagrams is their use as an easy and comprehensive "look-up chart" against which a team may be assessed, enabling process improvement.

DA provides a foundation from which to scale Agile approaches. An important part of scaling Agile is tailoring the strategy to reflect the realities of the scaling factors in the situation. By making process decision options clear, and by describing the trade-offs associated with those options, DA makes it very apparent what risks are being taken.

Hybrid Framework

DA builds upon other proven processes and Frameworks, allowing an organization to adopt the practices and strategies that fit, and provides guidance on how to tie them together. Scrum works very well within a team, but when it begins to scale the characteristics of projects, requirements and solution delivery require some flexibility to reduce risk. DA provides the process and decision guidance to tailor a single process from multiple approaches and practices.

DevOps Focus

DA supports streamlining development and operations activities along with enterprise practices, such as release, security, and data management. It includes explicit advice on a disciplined approach to DevOps. DevOps was discussed in detail in Chapter 6.

Strong Program and Product Governance

The enterprise's goals and strategy are enacted through chains of responsibility, authority, policy, standards, measurement, communication, and funding, which are the elements of DA governance. DAD uses phases and milestones to help guide teams and lower risk. At the enterprise level, the DA Framework includes an explicit IT Governance process blade and a Control process blade.

Benefits of Agile Transformation at Barclays

Barclays is a large financial institution with over 130,000 employees that has been in operation for over 325 years. Barclays has taken a holistic approach to their Agile transformation. It is not just a technology thing, linking up their various "islands of agility" to reduce the impedance mismatch between them.

- Barclays has the equivalent of over 1,200 Agile teams that have adopted DA approaches in progress.
- They needed to change both their funding and measurement strategies.
- They considered SAFe, LeSS and DA and settled on DA as it is not a "one-size fits all" approach.
- Results include a 300% increase in throughput (note: measured in terms of Story delivery), a 50% reduction in code complexity, and a 50% increase in test code coverage.
- More than half of teams are deploying into production at least monthly.
- Improved team happiness and morale.
- Improved business outcomes, such as quicker time to market.[2]

by Ben Linders on Sep 08, 2016

Challenges

User Group

According to Version One's *11th Annual State of Agile Report*[3] only a small percentage of the respondents indicated they were in some stage of adoption of DA. While this survey may be biased by the limited customer base surveyed, other surveys show different results. The fact remains that the DA market share is small, but climbing. This means the size of the User Group, and the resources accessed through one, is somewhat limited but improving.

Training and Knowledge Base
Training availability is not as pervasive as other options, but is increasing. Several books have been released and classes are becoming more common.

May Require Agile Consultants
The large number of DA options, while giving flexibility, may also be confusing to new adopters, and require some coaching. However, the goal diagrams do provide highlighted choices as likely starting points for small, near-located teams taking on a medium complexity problem, reducing initial tailoring risk.

Program Level Attributes

Roles

DA's full lifecycle approach prescribes more than the three roles in Scrum. It calls for fives roles on the team and an additional five, fractionally allocated to support scaling. Scrum focuses more on the construction phase where DA is much broader in scope. It is important to note that these are roles and not positions.

Roles are split into primary and secondary categories. Primary roles exist regardless of the scale of the team. They are:

- ***Stakeholder*** - A stakeholder is someone who is clearly impacted by the project. They may be an end-user or sponsor.
- ***Product Owner*** - The PO is responsible for the requirements and speaks for the customer. They are at the Program and enterprise level and part of a Product Owner Team.
- ***Architecture Owner*** - The architecture owner is the one who owns architecture decisions and is responsible for solution design. They are also at the Program and enterprise level, but part of an Architecture Owner Team.
- ***Team Lead*** - The team lead is a combination of a Scrum Master and Agile Coach. They act as the team facilitator and Coach and ensure process flow issues are resolved. Like the Architecture and Product

Owners, they are at the Program and enterprise level, but part of a Project Management Team.

- *Team Member* - A team member comprises any one producing the solution and taking care of design, build, and test tasks.

As a project grows in scale to enterprise, the following secondary roles may be added:

- *Specialist* - A specialist, such as business analyst or Program Manager, may be required.
- *Independent Tester* - This independent test team, operating in parallel, is typically needed for agility at scale situations within complex domains, using complex technology or addressing regulatory compliance issues.
- *Domain Expert* - In complicated domains, the Product Owner may not be the total expert, such as in Claims processing. An expert would be brought in to address a particular subject matter.
- *Technical Expert* - Technical experts are brought in on an as-needed, temporary basis to help the team overcome a difficult problem and transfer skills to one or more developers on the team.
- *Integrator* - An integrator is responsible for building the entire system from its various subsystems. In situations where there are sub-teams building subsystems and Features, the overall team may require one or more people in the role of integrator.

Workflow

The Agile/Basic DAD lifecycle is the most common, extending the Scrum model with ideas from XP and Rational Unified Process. The construction phase of this lifecycle is made up of timeboxed Scrum Sprints and will be familiar to those who have Scrum experience *(see Figure 08.09).*

The Lean/Advanced DAD lifecycle encourages use of Lean principles, such as minimizing work in progress, maximizing flow, reducing bottlenecks, and supporting a continuous work stream (instead of the fixed, timeboxed Iterations used in Scrum). Rather than a prescribed set of ceremonies (Daily Scrum, Sprint Planning, Retrospectives) held at certain cadences used in Scrum, Lean suggests that these events be done as needed. Lean/Advanced DAD suggests that, while the concepts behind Lean and the Kanban system

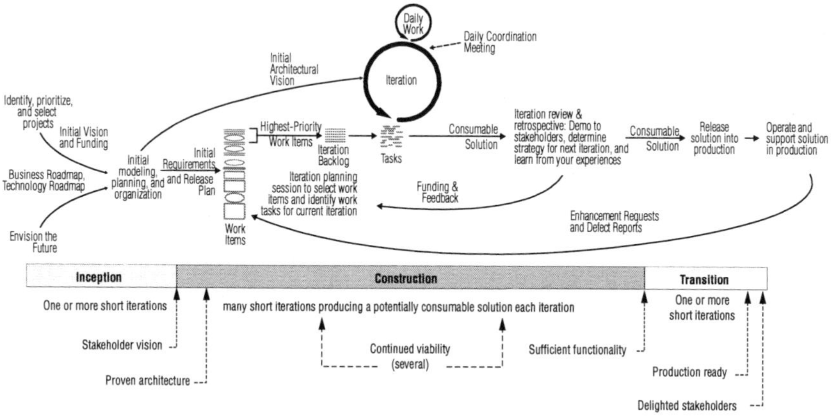

Figure 8.09 | Agile/Basic DAD

it uses are simple to learn, applying them properly to maximize throughput may be difficult to master. For this reason, Lean/Advanced DAD labels this lifecycle as advanced, hence its name *(see Figure 08.10).*

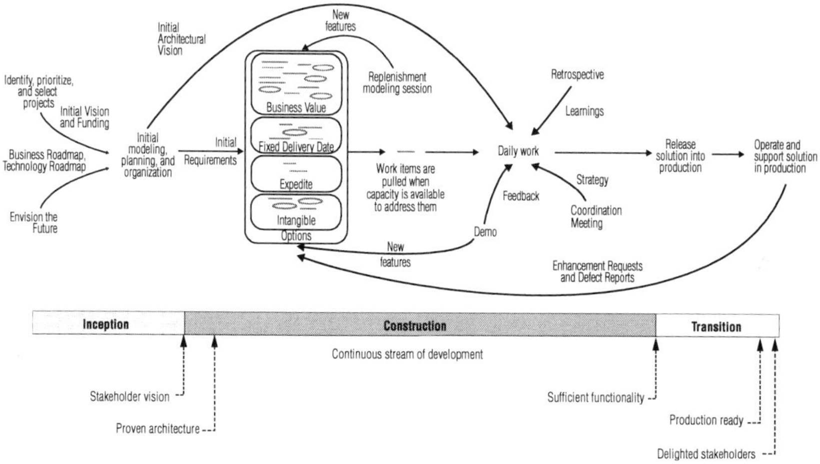

Figure 8.10 | Lean/Advanced DAD

The Continuous Delivery: Lean lifecycle supports more frequent delivery than other lifecycles. For this type of lifecycle to be effective, there needs to be mature processes around continuous integration and deployment and an infrastructure supported by advanced DevOps practices ***(see Figure 08.11).***

The Continuous Delivery: Agile lifecycle also supports more frequent delivery than other lifecycles, but unlike Continuous Delivery: Lean it adopts short

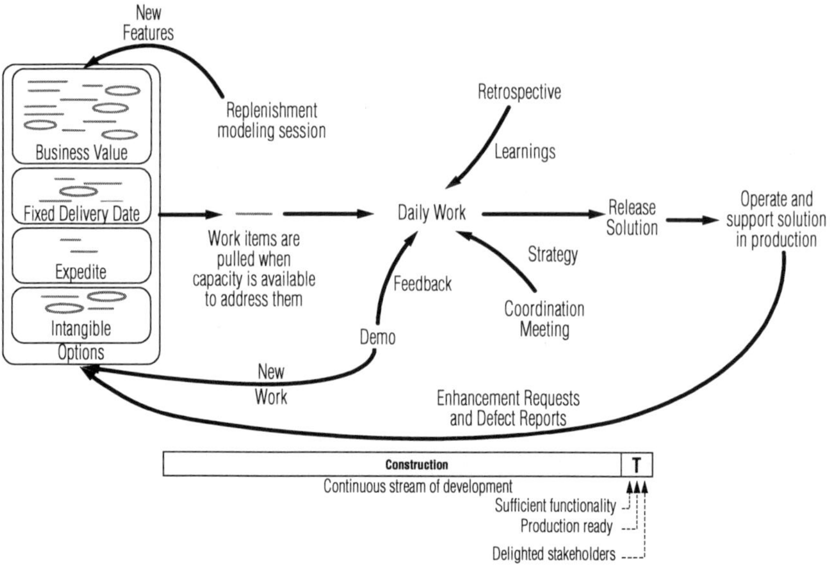

Figure 8.11 | Continuous Delivery: Lean Lifecycle

Iterations with delivery at the end of each. It is a natural progression from the Agile/Basic lifecycle *(see Figure 08.12).*

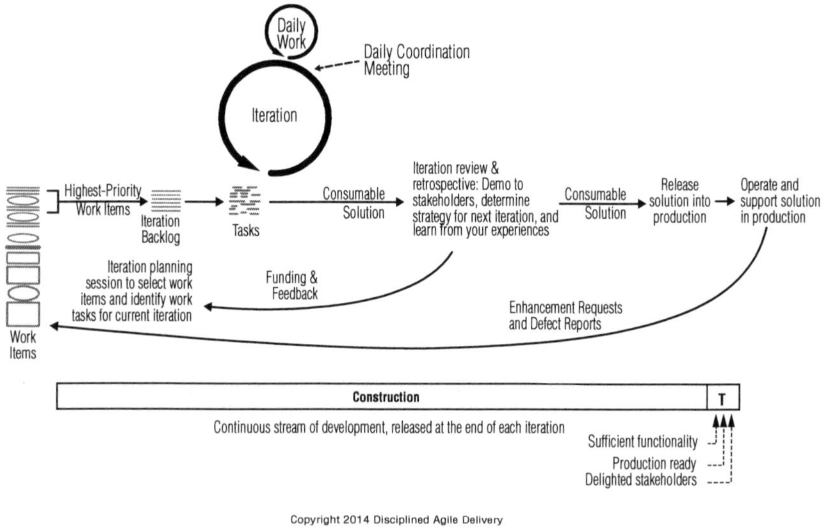

Figure 8.12 | Continuous Delivery: Agile Lifecycle

The Exploratory (Lean Startup) lifecycle minimizes upfront investments in favor of experimental applications that can be tested in the market and measured early and often during the project. Feedback from actual usage is used as the application is developed.

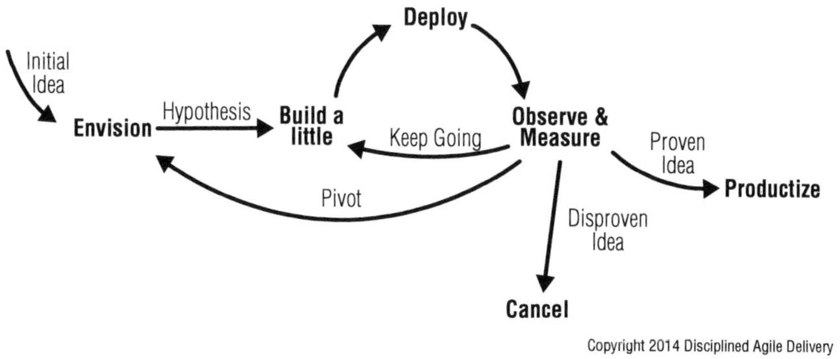

Figure 8.13 | Exploratory (Lean Startup) Lifecycle

Ceremonies

DA is infinitely tailorable with both Agile and Lean lifecycles each having their own "ceremonies". Scrum prescribes a very narrow set of options for doing things – one technique for a handful of process decision points – whereas DAD calls out a much larger range of decision points then provides several options and trade-offs for each. The following are some common ceremonies:

- ***Release Planning*** – Develop then maintain a high level project plan.
- ***Iteration Planning*** – At the beginning of an Iteration, plan what will be delivered and how the work will be done.
- ***Daily Coordination Meeting*** – Each day, hold a 15-minute coordination meeting.
- ***Iteration Demo*** – At the end of the Iteration show what was built to key stakeholders.
- ***Retrospectives*** – Take the opportunity to identify opportunities for process improvements based on information gathered throughout the project.

These ceremonies are rolled up to the leadership team level at the same cadence of the teams to provide Program level coordination. DA then provides a *"coordinate activities"* process goal to help the leadership address questions such as:

- If we're part of a larger team, how will we coordinate within it?
- How will we work with enterprise/IT teams such as enterprise architects and data managers?
- How will we coordinate our release/deployment with the rest of the organization?
- If we have geographically distributed team members, how will we collaborate with them?

Artifacts

Artifacts are a great example of why it is difficult to compare DAD with Scrum. Scrum prescribes a very narrow set of options for doing things - one technique for a handful of process decision points. In contrast, DAD calls out a much larger range of decision points then provides options and trade-offs for each, leading to a huge array of potential artifacts tailored to any given situation. The Product and Iteration Backlogs remain crucial to success.

How to Make it Work Effectively

As previously stated, Disciplined Agile is meant to be tailored to meet the needs of your organization, whatever its maturity. In addition to tailoring the process goals with decisions on the options recommended, an organization can make DA effective by selecting an appropriate lifecycle. An Executive Guide to Disciplined Agile provides the following advice for that selection.

Agile/Basic Lifecycle is the most common lifecycle and is recommended for the following situations:

- The work is primarily enhancements or new features
- The work can be identified, prioritized, and estimated early in the project
- Teams are familiar with Scrum and XP, or new to Agile

DAD Lean/Advanced Lifecycle is best in these situations:

- Work can be broken down into small work units of approximately the same size
- Work is difficult to predict in advance, such as maintenance work
- The team favors minimizing batch size and advanced planning

The Continuous Delivery: Agile Lifecycle is suitable when:

- Solutions can be delivered to stakeholders in a frequent and incremental basis
- Work remains relatively stable within an Iteration
- Organizations have streamlined deployment practices and procedures
- Projects require getting value into the hands of stakeholders rapidly, before the entire solution is complete
- Teams have mature DevOps practices in place including continuous integration, continuous deployment, and automated regression testing
- The team is long-lived (stable), working on a series of Releases over time

Continuous Delivery: Lean Lifecycle is best suited for:

- Projects or applications that can be delivered to stakeholders frequently
- Organizations that have streamlined deployment practices and procedures
- Teams that have mature DevOps practices in place, including continuous integration, continuous deployment, and automated regression testing

DAD Exploratory Lifecycle is useful:

- When the application addresses a new unexplored market
- When the stakeholders and delivery team can be flexible in adapting the application as it is being developed
- When you have a valid hypothesis/strategy to test with clear go/no-go criteria at test completion

Tools and Practices Recommendations

Process Tailoring Workshop

The Process Tailoring Workshop is where the team reviews the process goals and decides how they intend to work. It is held early in the Inception phase (what Scrum calls Sprint 0) and again at the beginning of Construction and Transition. DAD offers five lifecycles, 23 goals, and hundreds of options. In these workshops issues such as roles, lifecycle selection, practices and strategies, definition of done, and agreement on tools are agreed upon.

This workshop is key to the effective execution of DAD because it establishes the common vision of how the team will work with each other and within the Program. It is also a chance for the team to record how they will achieve repeatable results through lightweight, yet sufficient, Agile documentation.

Summary

The destination, as outlined in An Executive Guide to Disciplined Agile, is business agility. Wikipedia says that business agility is the ability of an organization to rapidly adapt to market and environmental changes in productive and cost-effective ways. Scott Ambler and Mark Lines offer Disciplined Agile as a map to that adaptive, Lean, responsive, and learning organization.

Agility of the enterprise requires agility of IT. All of IT. Disciplined Agile is the only Agile approach that addresses the full IT spectrum of solution delivery and its supporting practices.

"Diagrams used with permission of Disciplined Agile Consortium"

END NOTES

[1] Ambler, Scott W., and Lines, Mark. *Disciplined Agile Delivery: A Practitioner's Guide to Agile Software Delivery in the Enterprise. IBM Press. 2012*

[2] For more from Ben Linders, visit www.benlinders.com.

[3] Version One. *"The 11th Annual State of Agile Survey." 2017 www.stateofagile.versionone.com.*

CHAPTER

9

Large Scale Scrum (LeSS)

Overview

LeSS (Large-Scale Scrum) is the revolutionary view of Scrum translated into use for large corporations not only as a way to produce effective products, but to also help transform the organization into practitioners of Agile.

Consider what typically happens when more than 30 or 40 people start to work for an organization. There are organization charts, specializations, and managers to keep the organizational culture alive. The Scrum teams, in these organizations, trend towards component based work, with multiple handoffs to other coding, quality control, and testing teams. Now imagine 300 or 400 coders, each working on updating their individual pieces or components of a large web site. With only a component in mind, how does the team take ownership or efficiency into consideration? How do they keep to the overall Agile principles of keeping the Customer in mind first and releasing useful software updates as often as possible?

LeSS purposefully descales organizational roles and complexity, and flattens software development into Features, which each team codes, tests, and checks for quality as they prepare for Release at the end of each Sprint. Utilizing only minor modifications to single-team Scrum, LeSS suggests changes to the organizational model of the company, as well as changes to how the work is managed in the development team. Here is how LeSS came about.

Craig Larman is the author of *Agile & Iterative Development*[1]. Craig's book came out, not even one year, after the *Agile Manifesto* was published, and companies were eager to implement Agile practices. They contacted him and continued to push back on the general notion that Agile was designed only for small teams.

In 2005, Craig Larman teamed up with Bas Vodde and they worked with several large groups of developers in large corporations, running hundreds of experiments on how to do Large-Scale Scrum, which is where the acronym LeSS comes from. By 2010 they had published two books on the experiments, thought processes, organization, and communication work that goes into implementing LeSS. They also concluded that there needed to be two sizes of implementations to ensure success with the model. For companies running between 2 and 8 teams, LeSS works very well. LeSS Huge is suggested once the organization has 9 or more concurrent development teams. Larman and Vodde suggest a small addition to the oversight of the development effort by adding a new role called an Area Product Owner. This role is only to facilitate management of Features or items to the overall Product Owner, who still retains all responsibilities for the scope and flow of Product work.

The current state of LeSS has a core set of principles, learned and reinforced during the years of testing. These principles are governed by a minimal Framework of rules or, as Larman and Vodde like to say, "barely enough Framework to achieve empirical data to drive improvement." This Framework has a set of Guides to help implement the aforementioned minimal Framework needed in a particular environment or situation. The Guides were also created after the experiments, so future LeSS practitioners might not have to go through the same learning processes as Larman and Vodde. *(See Figure 9.01.)*[2]

Here is a brief overview and description of the 10 principles of LeSS, shown in *Figure 9.02.* Many of the concepts in this list drive both a benefit and a challenge in the next section of this chapter.

More with LeSS - The essential heart of LeSS, is simple to learn, but infuriatingly hard to implement. LeSS in not just Scrum for the development teams, it is Scrum / Agile / Lean for the entire organization.

Figure 9.01 | LeSS Complete Picture[2]

Imagine 20, 40, or 400 people essentially unhinged from the management Framework of most organizations with minimal roles, processes, and artifacts to keep the team efficiently focused on the Product the Customer wants. The team is more responsible without roles, more focused without process, and more successful without artifacts. More with LeSS!

Large-Scale Scrum is Scrum - Keep it simple! LeSS is the distilled implementation of the principles, rules, elements, and purpose of Scrum into multiple team environments.

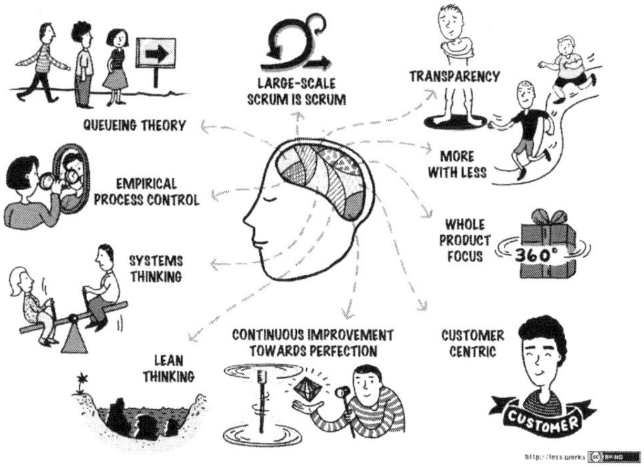

Figure 9.02 | Principles of LeSS

Transparency - By using short feedback loops, collaboration, and a solid Definition of Done, the teams will increase transparency and reduce workplace fear.

Whole-product focus - Regardless of team size or number of teams, everyone is focused on the Product the Customer wants. Each Sprint delivers a potentially shippable item to one Product Backlog, managed by one Product Owner.

Customer-centric - Always deliver value to the Customer and try to identify waste. Attempt to solve a Customer problem a new way. Each Sprint is delivering a shippable item and will be reviewed by the Customer. Everyone gets to work on Features the Customer will use.

Continuous improvement towards perfection - Are there any other Frameworks in this book that use the word perfection and mean it? LeSS envisions continual creation and delivery of low cost, minimal defect products to delight the Customer, improve the environment, and make everyone's life better. Everyone is expected to experiment towards radical improvement, with perfection as the goal.

Lean thinking - Lean thinking in the manufacturing space can be seen as a parent to Agile and Scrum to fill out the family of production facilities, including cars to the software that will drive them in the future. Keeping in mind the pillars, Respect for people and Challenge the status quo, a majority of Lean tools also appear as tools to make LeSS successful – Managers-as-teachers to teach development, manage to improve, promote stop-and-fix, and practice, "Go See," aiming towards the goal of perfection.

Systems thinking - The Customer sees nothing but the whole that the teams are delivering. It is a dynamic and complex system that works as a whole and needs to be worked on as a whole. Use modeling and team collaborations to avoid focusing on efficiencies or optimizations in parts of the Product. All parts of the system work together, and all teams should be coached to think in terms of an integrated system.

Empirical process control - Scrum introduced empirical process control to Agile, and LeSS amplifies it. The emphasis here is that 'best practices' do not exist for the solutions the team is creating, so every Sprint can be a learning and revising exercise as well as producing a shippable item. Engage with, learn, and own the process and its results.

Queuing theory - In an effort to reduce complexity, LeSS suggests removing queues from the development cycle. Hopefully, as the teams become cross-functional and the organization reduces excess policies, the queues will disappear as the Backlog Items become Features rather than components. During the transition, keep in mind that Queueing theory has little to do with the capacity of the teams and more to do with how distracting the work in the queue is.

Benefits / Challenges

The Agile movement, and Scrum in particular, have brought benefits in the efficiencies of producing software products. As software teams grow, specialize, optimize, and get organized into corporate management structures, they tend to be less Agile. When the organization grows into multiple teams, reporting to different managers, the problems of agility get even worse.

Because LeSS is built on a small set of rules, the typical corporate desire is to try and implement without changing the rest of the company. However, the power of LeSS comes not in how the teams are organized, but in how the rest of the company is so this Lean, Agile based methodology can succeed.

Benefits

The main principles of LeSS described earlier are also some of the primary benefits gained by implementing LeSS.

Easy to Understand

Large-Scale Scrum is Scrum! The retention of only essential layers of Scrum into LeSS make the Framework easy to comprehend. There is only one Product Owner, Backlog, team (set of teams), Sprint, Definition of Done, and Shippable Product Increment, no matter the number of people. Only when the number of teams approaches 9 is there the likelihood of adding one or more Area Product Owners to assist with Backlog management, so the single Product Owner can retain an overview of the product development.

Lightweight Framework

The real benefit here is that the full power of Scrum and Agile come into play on the whole organizational and management structure of the company, not just the development teams. The descaling of roles and organizational complexity allows the teams to take over their own management and responsibilities. This, in turn, drives changes back into the company on a cycle of continual improvement.

Scalable to Any Organizational Size

The LeSS Framework provides the ability to scale Scrum to any size organization with at least two development teams. By actually de-scaling organizational and management overhead, removing certain types of roles, and globally defining attributes, an effective workflow is achieved. The minimal rule structure allows the scaling to multiple teams while removing hindrances, re-work, or blockages in development work. LeSS has not just been theorized for large groups, it has been empirically proven to work with development groups numbering over 1,000 people.

Scrum Roles Familiar

An additional benefit of keeping things simple is the basic Scrum roles and functions, which people and organizations already know still exist in the new Framework. As suggested before, some traditional roles that exist on a

Scrum team, such as the Architect or Tester, will be rolled into team Member to achieve the functional end goal. Organizations adopting LeSS need to be prepared to simplify their list of positions to move from Scrum to LeSS. The only role that does not exist in traditional Scrum is the Area Product Owner, used in LeSS Huge for 9 or more teams in support of the Product Owner.

Focus on Product As a Whole

This benefit is listed in the Principles, along with the closely related Systems Thinking. Product focus gets everyone, in every team, aligned to Customer Value on every Sprint. As an organization builds teams using LeSS, there is an emphasis on the ability of each team to create whole features, which are integrated, shippable, valuable, and desired by the Customer. All the teams together, focused on the Product (and by corollary the Customer), start to value only those items that enhance the Product, and the process continues to improve to drive those enhancements.

Customer Centric

The Customer in LeSS is involved in every Sprint, and the Product Backlog contains items clarified and prioritized by the Customer. Not only that, but teams are encouraged to have direct communications with the Customer during the Sprint for their education or Feature clarification. Just as in the Product focus benefit, once all of the people, regardless of team affiliation, start working towards the same goals, efficiency starts to creep in.

Challenges

Change is the biggest challenge people ever face; especially in an organization where a level of authority and responsibility do not let them change things directly. Patience is required to play the long game of shifting the underlying system slowly while management starts to understand the benefits.

LeSS introduces some rules around teams and essentially asks that they be removed from the traditional corporate management structure. It also asks the corporation to take a look at these management structures and change them in the spirit of Agile. If the teams are already using Scrum, their transition is easier, although they will still have a new type of team to work with, most likely. It is the managers of the team members that are in the most conflict here, since LeSS proscribes allowing work into the queue only from the Product Owner.

In essence, LeSS allows an organization to implement with the development teams fairly easily, but the rest of the divisions have to change their view of the software development department.

Education

A fallacy about LeSS is that it is just Scrum, so there is no need to learn anything before implementing it. While the sentiment that LeSS is 'just' Scrum is true, there is plenty to learn before having a successful implementation . Mostly, the education is around the removal of process and rote, building an environment of experimentation and improvement, and explaining why this Framework is being put into place.

Cultural Change

Culture grows up around systems. In order to change culture, the underlying system has to change, and nobody likes change. LeSS is a systems change in terms of moving component teams to cross-functional teams, removing superfluous roles by integrating them directly into the teams, and managing the work into the teams directly. These system changes have implications for management not as easily defined. Just because LeSS is simple and light, does not mean it is going to be easy.

Implementing Without a LeSS Coach

For a smooth transition to LeSS, it is of paramount importance to have an experienced LeSS Coach available for the teams and the organization as a whole. For the organization, the Coach will help prepare and guide the changes needed to support the LeSS implementation. For the teams, they will work both on technical issues in coding or sharing, and operational integrations of automated testing or continual improvement techniques.

Lightweight Framework

The same simple Framework that allows us to understand LeSS easily and start working on implementation quickly has ramifications outside of the IT department. Getting managers to move from command-and-control to teacher and teams to focus on cross-functional learning rather than specialization, while allowing the teams to manage how they do their own work are hurdles this lightweight Framework creates for the organization.

Flow of Communication

Component Scrum teams are not used to working with other Scrum teams except to hand off pieces of code for testing or further development along the

Sprint. When the change to cross-functional teams happens, there is much more opportunity and requirement for communications across teams. These new opportunities need to be practiced and enforced to help align the single Product and Customer focus.

Program-level Attributes

Even though it is continually emphasized that LeSS is scaled Scrum, there are a few enhancements to the traditional processes and some extra meetings to coordinate. This is to be expected, once the number of people working in development climbs towards 100 or more. They certainly cannot all attend every meeting effectively!

Here are nine areas that may have slightly different definitions or requirements in the LeSS Framework than in traditional or single-team Scrum.

Sprint Planning Part 1 –
Sprint Planning is split into two parts to coordinate the division of Product Backlog Items (PBI) into the teams. The one Product Owner and people from all teams attend this meeting. The team members will self-manage, discuss shared work opportunities, and divide up the Product Backlog Items.

Sprint Planning Part 2 –
The second Sprint Planning is held at the team level. This may be a single-team meeting, but in most cases for coordination or learning opportunities, two or more teams will combine their meetings into one.

Daily Scrum –
This is also an independent team level gathering. To increase information sharing, a member of another team may observe, but the Scrums are not typically shared. This is primarily to keep the Scrum at its theoretical 15-minute limit, since two teams' worth of people could not likely finish in that time meaningfully.

Coordination –
This is where the need for extra and frequent communication shows up. While the teams are working on their Product Backlog Items, they need to coordinate with other teams. The main tools suggested for this purpose are familiar ones, such as Just Talk, Communicate in Code, Travelers, Open Space, and Communities.

Overall PBR -

Just as the Sprint Planning section is split into two parts, there may be an occasion to hold an Overall Product Backlog Refinement (PBR). This is a short, optional meeting designed to increase alignment between the Product Owner and all teams. It is attended by the Product Owner and members of all teams (not full teams) to decide which are likely to implement which items. Those items are then taken to the teams for their own individual PBR meeting.

Product Backlog Refinement –

Just as in single-team Scrum, the PBR is a required component of LeSS. This is emphasized as a single-team activity, but just as in other components of LeSS, there is the encouraged option for two or more teams to share this activity for learning and coordination.

Sprint Review –

This is another big meeting, attended by stakeholders, customers, the Product Owner, and members from all teams. During the inspection phase (or phases), where Product increments and new items are discussed, the recommendation is to have a 'science fair' or 'convention' style room(s) set up. Representatives from the team in each area, room, or 'booth' can show and discuss items developed by the team.

Overall Retrospective –

This is a new meeting not found in single-team Scrum and its purpose is to explore improving the overall system, rather than focusing on one team. The maximum duration is 45 minutes per week of Sprint. It includes the Product Owner, Scrum Masters, and representatives from each team.

Roles

One Product Owner

The ability of the LeSS Framework to enable one Product Owner comes from the reduction in roles and positions in other areas. A scaled Product Owner is conceptually equivalent to a single-team Scrum Product Owner, however, in LeSS their focus is on keeping the overview and delivering maximum ROI in the Product. They accomplish this focus by spending much of their time on prioritization and clarification of Product Backlog Items.

To facilitate this focus, the Product Owner becomes a connector in the business, rather than an intermediary through which information flows. There are five communication paths that the Product Owner needs to be cognizant of, understand, and nurture, shown in *Figure 9.03* graphically.

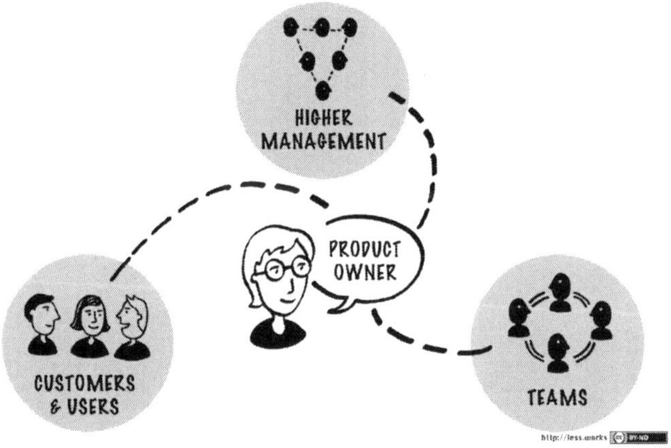

Figure 9.03 | Product Owner Relationships

- Product Owner ⟷ Teams
- Product Owner ⟷ Customers
- Teams ⟷ Customers
- Product Owner ⟷ Higher Management
- Product Owner ⟷ Scrum Masters

Because the adoption of LeSS creates the need for better communications, these areas are termed Relationships. Since the Product Owner is no longer just a conduit for information, they must have a better understanding of the entire work path, and these relationships are key.

The Product Owner / Team \ Customer communication triangle is the important piece of the relationship puzzle. Of course, the Product Owner has the Customer in mind and is trying to help the teams create the best possible Product, but in LeSS, it is also a requirement to have the teams talk directly with the Customer. This provides a secondary and validating link, as well as possible insights to customer needs rather than just getting information from the Product Owner.

The Product Owner / Higher Management relationship is geared towards the Product Owner taking complete accountability and responsibility for Product success on one side, and helping Higher Management create or implement organizational designs to improve adoption of LeSS on the other.

The Scrum Master helps as much as possible with the concerns, questions, and obstacles of the Product Owner. The SM gives feedback and educates the PO to enable them to adapt to personnel, organizational, or technical changes effectively.

Team Members

The term team does not normally define a role. When we look at what LeSS does with teams, however, we see that all the members of the team have the same responsibilities, therefore we can DEFINE this as a role. LeSS requires some definition and structure in a team that is not usually enforced in other Frameworks. Single-team Scrum could also organize this way, but it is not common to find. These well-structured teams have the following characteristics:

- **Self-Managing:** All members of the team have the same role, team member. This allows the team to have responsibility for their work (because they have to finish the entire Feature themselves), make decisions regarding their work (since they have communicated with the Customer directly for clarification), and manage their work within the team.
- **Cross-Functional:** This concept is a tricky one to manage, even with experienced Scrum practitioners. In the simplest terms, it means breaking apart the existing teams that work on components of a Feature and creating new teams, with people from each of those component teams able to create the entire Feature without handing work to another team. These new teams have all the skills required to complete a Shippable Product each Sprint or can learn them from other teams or team members in the time frame required. *Figure 9.04* shows how a component team may have to hand off work to other teams multiple times to complete an item, whereas the Feature, or cross-functional teams, develop complete items for delivery.
- **Relationship Management:** One of the responsibilities of the team is to communicate directly with customers or users to clarify the definition of work items. Once again, LeSS removes a common Scrum layer by allowing as needed communications with the Customer rather than through the proxy of the Product Owner. For the priority of work items, the team will still keep in touch with the Product Owner.

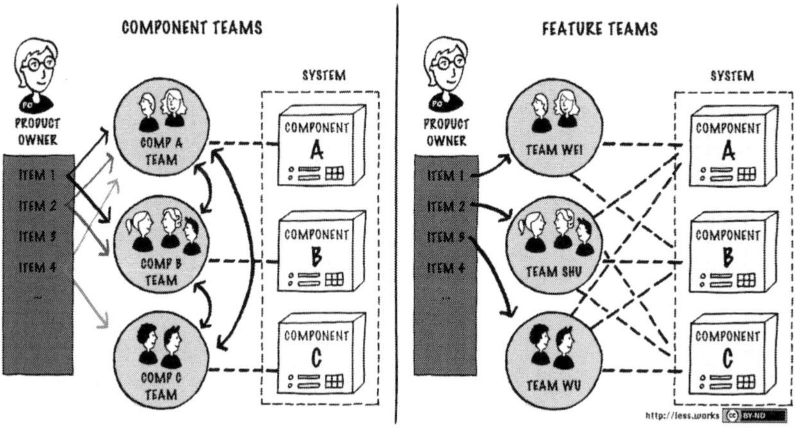

Figure 9.04 | Component Teams and Feature Teams

- **Long Lived:** A vast majority of studies on the dynamics of groups suggest that trust and efficiency increase the longer the group stays together. As part of the empirical process that brought LeSS into being, these results were proven yet again in the context of software delivery. Therefore, as part of the Framework, the team stays together forever, continuing to improve relationships, trust, efficiency, and knowledge – not just for one Sprint, Feature, or Product, but truly forever.
- **Collocated and Responsible:** Not all teams in LeSS have to be together, but within each, all members need to be in the same room. This drives knowledge sharing and trust, which increases responsible behaviors and efficiency.
- **Shared Team Goals:** This is more of an outcome than a requirement, something that happens when LeSS is implemented and starts to work. The long-lived, collocated, cross-functional team is tasked with some work items. Because they know each other, organize themselves, and know who to go talk to for clarification and prioritization questions, they all start sharing the same Goals to provide a quality shippable increment at the end of the Sprint.

Scrum Master

The Scrum Master in LeSS is a full time, expert level position. Let that sit for a minute and think about who the Scrum Master typically is in single-team Scrum. They are not expert developers, they are expert Scrum practitioners. Often in smaller organizations, the SM is named once the teams are formed or chosen as the lead developer on the team as well as the SM. In LeSS, the SM must be a full-time role, and certainly not part of the team (from a development point of view). Once the organization starts to think about implementing LeSS, they also need to think about who the SM is going to be, or potentially having to hire one. It is important not to get caught in the halo effect, which says, "You're our best programmer, we are promoting you to SM because you'll be great at it!" Go and find an Agile and/or Scrum certified SM. The two primary responsibilities of the Scrum Master are to the business and the teams. First, as a Scrum expert, they are expected to coach and teach the organization in Scrum principles, guiding them towards continual improvement. Second, as a facilitator, they lead the teams to their self-managing best, keeping everyone Product focused and creating an environment for continual learning and success.

Depending on the maturity of Scrum implementation and team self-management, a Scrum Master can be assigned to as many as 3 teams.

Area Product Owner (LeSS Huge)

As the number of teams in the organization grows beyond 8, it is recommended that the organizational principles of LeSS Huge be applied. From a Roles perspective, this means adding an Area Product Owner into the workflow. The overall Product is divided into areas, and the Area Product Owners prioritize and clarify work for the teams in their area. The single Product Owner still maintains scope and schedule decisions on the overall Product.

When LeSS Huge is adopted, this group of the single PO and multiple APO forms the Product Owner Team.

Workflow

An overview of the entire LeSS workflow is shown in *Figure 9.05.*

Again, the traditional Scrum architecture is present with just enough expansion to get items from One Product Backlog split down into small batches the teams can work on.

Throughout this chapter there are many references about 8 teams for LeSS, and 9 or more teams for LeSS Huge. This is not an exact number in all cases, but an empirically observed limit during the many years of experimentation

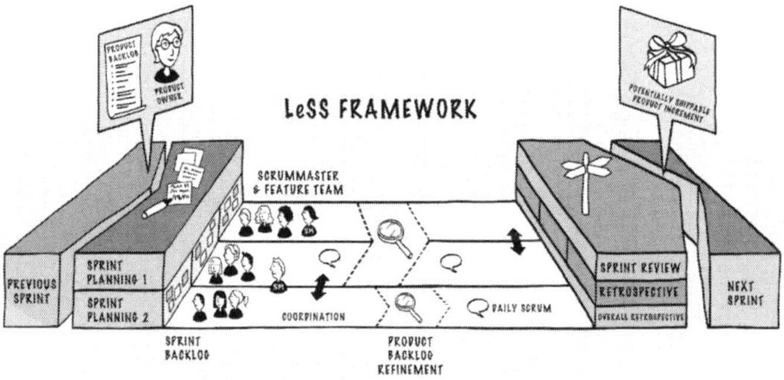

Figure 9.05 | LeSS Framework

and development of the Framework. It really has to do with the capacity of the Product Owner to maintain Product focus and the Backlog work, once the number of teams reaches 8. The guidance is flexible, like most things Agile. If LeSS works with 10 teams, by all means, keep it up. On the other hand, if an organization needs to implement LeSS Huge at 6 or 7 teams, certainly take the steps necessary to do so. As a note, remember the suggested minimum number of teams in a Product Area is 4, which makes it difficult to implement Less Huge 'by the rules' if you have less than 8 to start with.

Initial Product Backlog Refinement

Single-team Scrum does not describe a specific process for starting up development for a new Product. LeSS handles creating the Backlog for a new Product with an Initial Product Backlog Refinement. This is used singly at either the beginning of a new Product's development or when transitioning from another development model to LeSS.

In the case where LeSS is first being implemented, there are other important activities that also take place. The normal process would include gathering the Product Backlog items then splitting and refining them, identifying risks, and estimating. There are two other things that need special attention at this critical moment to help drive the success of the ongoing LeSS implementation. The Definition of Done is best defined before any work starts. Since this is how the teams will also define how their individual items are Done during Sprints, it is important to take the time and effort needed to start with a strong Definition of Done. Defining a vision is a second crucial step to take at the beginning of the development effort; giving the teams the platform they need to start work and improving how they work. A unified vision of the end Product will allow the teams to start working toward perfection immediately.

Sprint Planning

LeSS combines all teams and work into one Sprint. In single-team Scrum all personnel are involved in the Sprint Planning. Considering the number of participants in LeSS, and particularly LeSS Huge, this could run into multiple hundreds of people and coordination nightmares. To make sure the Product Owner sleeps more easily, the LeSS Framework has two planning meetings. *(See Figure 9.06.)*

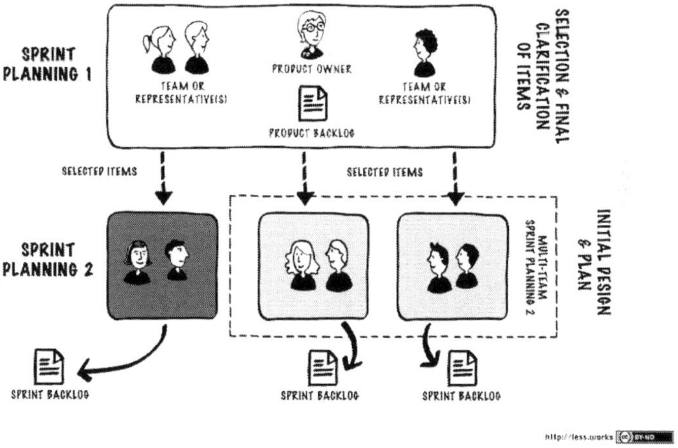

Figure 9.06 | LeSS Spint Planning

Sprint Planning One is attended by the Product Owner and representatives from all teams. In cases where LeSS is being implemented with 2 or 3 teams, it may be possible for all personnel to attend Sprint Planning One and would be the preferred mode in order to eliminate a communications handoff. The Product Owner discusses the Product Backlog Items, and the teams (or their representatives) decide which items they will take for completion.

Sprint Planning Two is a team level meeting attended by just team personnel. It is suggested and encouraged in the Sprint Planning Two meeting that multiple teams align their meetings and have them concurrently. This collaboration is used in the case where work the teams are doing is closely related, or even in some, cases shared. It is in Sprint Planning Two that the team decides how and when during the Sprint to work on each of the items.

The Sprint planning meetings generate the Sprint Backlog, which is a per team item, no different than single-team Scrum.

Daily Scrum

As described earlier, each team has a Daily Scrum. There may be a scout from another team present for information sharing purposes, but the Daily Scrum is a single-team meeting.

Coordination and Integration

One of the goals of LeSS is to get teams to Integrate their work often; not just often during a Sprint, but often during each day. This integration is also not into a test environment or branch, but directly to the mainline. These are not common practices and require a level of work coordination between the teams that is also not common practice. There are many common Scrum tools, and some described in the LeSS Framework, which can be implemented to help the teams achieve this goal.

Just Talk - Talking is encouraged. The best was to communicate with others is face to face, even about code, bugs, and test results. All team members, at any time, are free to go and discuss items or issues with members of any other team. Particularly if there is shared or common work, this is an important tool. In cases of distance, a video call would be a good substitute, or the phone works too. E-mail is discouraged as a Just Talk tool.

Communicate in Code - It is conceivable that between any two times code is checked in, many others have also had a chance to Integrate. This is when to notice if there are members or teams working on related items and a good time to Just Talk to someone about sharing work, creating efficiency, or checking Backlogs.

Multi-Team meetings - As described in the Sprint Planning section and also in other places in this chapter, the facility to allow multi-team meetings is crucial to keeping Backlog items on track. Just as in single-team, trust is growing amongst the members, which can be increased with communication and learning between two or more teams. Any excuse to get multiple teams involved in improving work should be encouraged.

Send Observers to the Daily Scrum - The Daily Scrum is the only meeting that has a limitation to one team. However, an Observer or Scout can attend another team's Scrum if there is shared or related work. Again, this is encouraged, but the Observer is there only to listen, since the Daily Scrum does not usually allow information other than team updates.

Travelers - In cases where there are limited numbers of experts in a technical area to assign to teams, there is a mechanism to supplement the long-lived team requirement. These experts become Travelers and share their technical expertise with a different team every Sprint. This sharing of knowledge then allows teams to collaborate about the technical area if the Traveler is assigned to another team in a remote area. Collaboration strengthens the network and increases coordination between teams.

Component Communities and Mentors - Just like the case of the Traveler, there may be a technical area or component being worked on by multiple teams. A Mentor for the component volunteers for any specialized coordination needed for successful development. The Mentor does not travel to different teams, but helps the coordination of work around the component. In cases where multiple people in multiple teams desire to volunteer to learn or help coordinate the work, a Component Community is formed. These are extra responsibilities taken on voluntarily due to a desire to learn, and, in the long run, help the overall improvement of development related to the component.

Leading Team - In some cases, a Feature is so large that there will be multiple teams working on it for multiple Sprints. Just as in the case of the Traveler and the Component Community, a Leading Team takes the lead on the work and development of the giant Feature then guides the education and coordination of other teams as they join in the work. This is how LeSS scales up coordination of experts – from a single Traveler, to a few in a Community, to an entire team as a Leading Team. In none of these cases are extra reviews of code or gates created. These are just the mechanisms used to keep everyone talking to everyone else about everything going on.

Product Backlog Refinement

This is a key activity to refine items to be ready for future Sprints. LeSS, again, creates a two-stage activity where single-team Scrum describes only one.

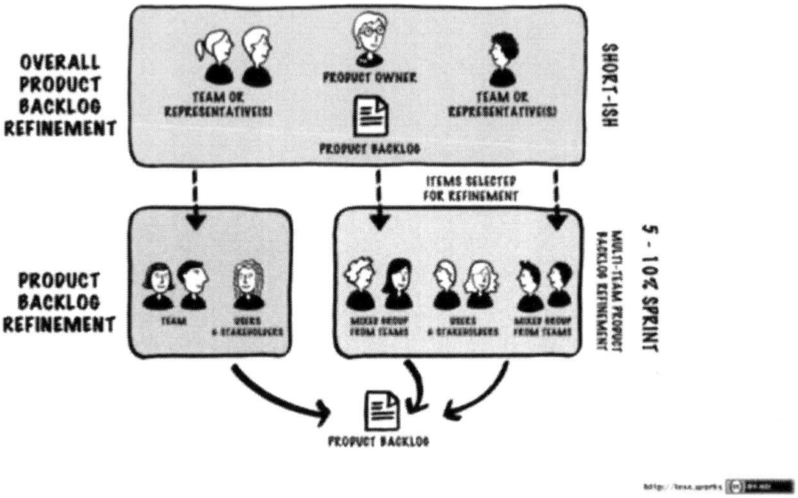

Figure 9.07 | LeSS Framework

The Overall PBR session includes the Product Owner, SME, and either all members of all teams or representatives of each. During the session the following are to be accomplished:

- Split big items
- Light-weight item analysis for basic understanding
- Estimate items
- Identify strongly-related items that suggest shared or common work, or coordination

The teams then each have their own PBR, or multi-team PBR, depending on the level of common work and coordination decided in the Overall PBR. The team-level PBR includes the team, users, customers, and stakeholders that work together on refinement.

Sprint Review & Retrospective

Just as Sprint Planning in LeSS is split into two parts, the Retrospective is done first at the team level and then on an organizational level, in reverse order of the Sprint Planning.

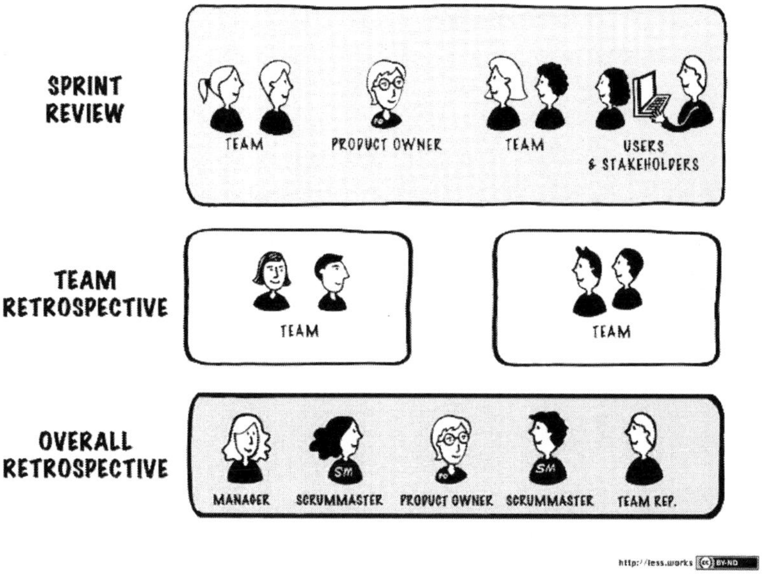

Figure 9.08 | LeSS Sprint Review and Retrospective

As described earlier, the Sprint Review is a large event, designed as an opportunity for everyone to discuss and collaborate about the Product.

The team Retrospective is the same in LeSS as in single-team Scrum. A practice encouraged in LeSS that adds value for all Agile practitioners is creating and maintaining an organizational improvement Backlog. This is described a bit more in the Artifacts section, as a way for the teams to communicate with the organization, as a whole.

The Overall Retrospective is an additional meeting in LeSS. Where the team Retrospective deals with the team's own assessment of their work and how to improve it, the Overall Retrospective addresses all the work done in the Sprint and how the organization is either helping or hindering it. Any manner of organizational problem, management process, or even cross-team collaboration issues are handled in the Overall Retrospective.

Focusing on teams, the discussion could range around cooperation and collaboration, how the Traveler / Component Community / Leader Team are handling their responsibilities, and any successes or learning opportunities to be shared across the teams.

Thinking about the Product Owner and Scrum Master, the discussion revolves around the strength and effectiveness of the five relationships, rapport and trust with the Customer, and ability to continue improving the management oversight of the developers to reduce problems.

This is also another time where the Organizational Improvement Backlog might be brought out and discussed to see how the perceptions of the team items line up with perceptions of others in the organization.

LeSS Huge

Once the number of teams get to 8, adoption of LeSS Huge becomes suitable and necessary for Product Owner sanity.

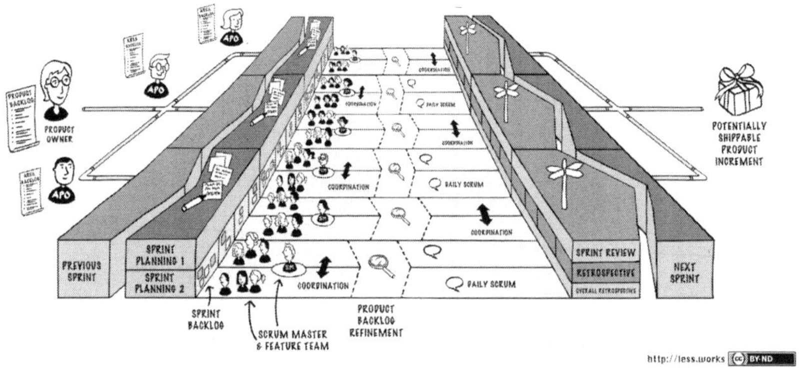

Figure 9.09 | LeSS Huge Framework

In terms of workflow and operation, LeSS Huge retains One Product Backlog, one Definition of Done, one Potentially Shippable Product Increment, one (overall) Product Owner, one Sprint, and all teams in one Sprint, with one delivery.

LeSS Huge creates 'Areas' in the Product, and assigns Area Product Owners to each. Essentially, LeSS Huge is equivalent to multiple LeSS implementations in parallel.

Ceremonies

There are organizational changes made to operations in order to keep LeSS working. Mainly, these aim at keeping all teams focused on the same goals, but still allowing each team to self-organize and do their work. Doing that, as explained previously, involves the use of the following ceremonies:

- Sprint Planning 1
- Sprint Planning 2
- Daily Scrum
- Overall PBR
- Team PBR
- Sprint Review
- Team Retrospective
- Overall Retrospective

All of the ceremonies align so that one common Sprint for all teams, working on the whole Product, ends in one Potentially Shippable Product Increment.

Artifacts

The Artifacts of LeSS are the same as single-team Scrum. (Of course they are, haven't we learned anything by now?)

Once the threshold for LeSS Huge is reached, Product Areas are added to the organization, and an Area Product Backlog is added to the end of the Sprint.

There is one item not related directly to the Product, not specifically an Artifact, but is maintained during the Sprint so it is included here – the Organizational Improvement Backlog.

Product Backlog - A date-stamped version-controlled record of the compilation of all the work that teams need to do on a single Product.

Sprint Backlog (Team level) - A record of all the work an individual team has done to complete the Product Backlog Items they selected during Sprint Planning

Potential Shippable Product Increment - A record of the integrated end result of all team work during a Sprint and delivered as the Potentially Shippable Product Increment.

Area Product Backlog (LeSS Huge) - Remember that LeSS Huge can be considered to be multiple LeSS implementations running in parallel on the same Product. Thus, a record from each Area of the Area Product Backlog needs to be communicated to the single Product Owner to support the understanding of all work being done.

Organizational Improvement Backlog - A record of the Organizational Improvement Backlog used by the teams to communicate directly with management, in support of or in parallel with the Scrum Master. The teams (and teams only) record impediments, improvements, and experiments in the Backlog, and managers report on appropriate actions done to implement the improvement items.

How to Make It Work Effectively

This chapter has discussed organizational and management changes, reduction in the number and types of roles, and simplification of rules. None of these are easy, even for small companies. By the time the organization grows to the point where LeSS can be adopted, there are likely to be strong beliefs about how the organization works and development happens. Successful adoption requires breaking assumptions, changing structures, and getting everyone on board with improving towards a shared goal.

LeSS is not just something an organization picks up and starts with next Tuesday. Even though the rules are simple and the Framework small, there is momentum in management and safety in the culture that all have to be overcome. Once the whole organization is convinced that LeSS should be implemented, the first decisions made are around the Three Principles:

- Deep and Narrow over Broad and Shallow
- Top-Down and Bottom-Up
- Use Volunteering

To start out, it is better to empower one set of teams, to really focus on one Product with organizational support, than to command all the teams to start and 'see how they like it'. LeSS is something that requires discipline from the organization as a whole, not just the developers.

The second Principle is Top-Down and Bottom-Up. Notice it is <u>and</u>, not or. Too much top control is a contradiction to Agile, which emphasizes the teams' needs to do its own organization and management. Too much bottom, or grass roots style, change might get moving in the right direction, but usually management tends to block processes not on the proscribed list. Both management and development (and everyone in between) need to be ready to test the changes being made to perform successfully. This brings up the third Principle, around how to staff the initial LeSS teams.

Volunteering shows that management has agreed to loosen some controls and allows for an initial feeling of trust in the team. The ability to make the decisions even before the work starts is empowering and will bring momentum to the change.

Following the Three Principles reduces the risk of the initial LeSS implementation failing and sets up the environment to continue forward. If the first attempt fails, there is learning and improvement. If the first attempt succeeds, the momentum will continue to grow as more teams join LeSS.

The organization will see what has to be changed, but blind adoption of a new process usually kills the creativity, innovation, and continual improvement desired in the first place. The next big steps in creating a winning LeSS implementation are Education and Definitions. This covers the entire organization and lets everyone know why LeSS is being instigated. Often, the help of a Coach is obtained to keep the initiative on track.

A broad Product definition and a strong Definition of Done are the balancing factors that guide work. A Product definition should be broad, to allow for a better overview of the whole Product. With that better view comes an understanding of how to deal with dependencies and solve problems rather than trying to continually provide solutions. It must be coupled with a strong Definition of Done to drive the critically important organizational changes LeSS requires.

Since the teams produce items of work during Sprints that are supposed to be Done, creating the Definition of Done that includes all work – including testing, for example – by necessity, drives the testing knowledge and capability into the team rather than having it be a separate artifact or handoff. The Definition of Done should continually be adjusted until it is perfect. This definition would include everything the organization, not just team, has to do to deliver the Product to customers. This also creates the focus of every Sprint creating potentially shippable items.

Once the key elements to a successful LeSS implementation have been achieved, getting the new teams Appropriately Structured in the new organizational scheme is the next hurdle.

Teams have been discussed previously as a 'combined role' in the Framework. Here, as the decision to implement is being made while wanting the best possible results, recall what Larman and Vodde say about the transformational possibilities of the team in an organization:

"These different—but proven—team concepts cause major change in organizations.

- Self-managing teams require a change from command-and-control management to manager-teacher. Instead of focusing on what people do, management should focus on how to create the environment for the teams to succeed.
- Cross-functional teams require breaking functional boundaries and working together across the whole organization to optimize delivering Customer Value. Instead of boxing people in functional groups, management should focus on cross-functional learning.
- Long-lived dedicated teams require giving work to existing teams and letting them decide how to do it. Instead of considering individuals to be the unit of performance, the focus needs to be on complete teams."[3]

Project Managers are probably thinking, "Hey! You haven't mentioned me yet!" Correct! Since the managers (in general) are going to stop directing the work of the team members, who are only going to work on items provided by the Product Owner, project management does not have a place in the LeSS Framework, as it tends to get in the way of self-organizing teams.

This is not to say that project management is not valid for other parts of the business, just not for the work on the Product handled by the LeSS implementation. Once the Product Owner and the teams start maturing, all the typical project management responsibilities are handled in the Sprints delivering completed work.

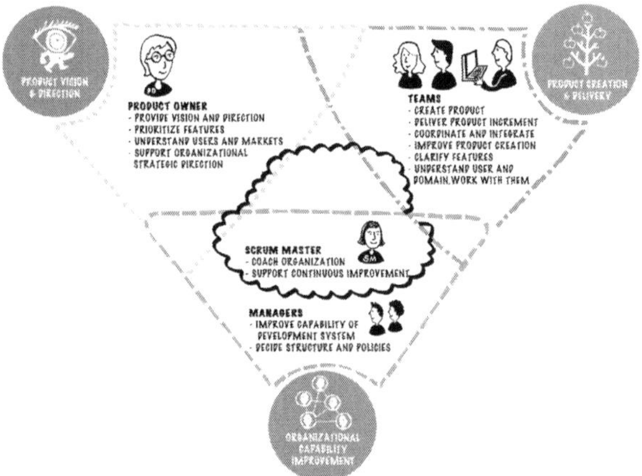

Figure 9.10 | Manager's Role

There is a continuum of definitions, even within the same company, of component, Feature, or specialization. The following graph is provided to guide an understanding of how those terms have been used in this chapter and how they relate to each other and a LeSS implementation.

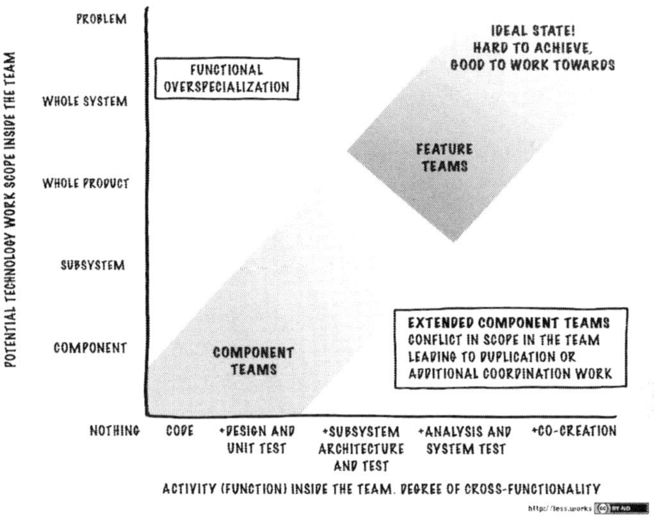

Fig 9.11 | Scope and Specialization

The last words in successful LeSS implementations are Continuous Improvement. What this really means is that it is never permissible to say, "We have finished our LeSS implementation." The continual drive towards Product development perfection will continue to uncover problems and demand ways to solve them be figured out. This is Lean. This is LeSS, where change becomes the new status quo.

In many ways, the organization will not realize what is possible until some results start showing up. Quicker Features to market, major revision times reduced by significant percentages, and successes of that nature start to get the attention of the business as a whole. It is with these successes that the Product Owners and Scrum Masters need to push the organization even further into the changes that will allow the teams to succeed even further. This vision of how far product development can go, fast it can happen, and successful it can be are what LeSS can help create.

Craig Larman and Bas Vodde have a 'perfection vision' they sometimes use for organizations striving to clarify and unify their own:

"Create the organizational ability to respond to changes by being able to deliver or change direction at any time without additional cost."

Do experiments, learn from failures, and focus on problems, not on tools. All of these things together will make the LeSS organization more successful.

Tools and Practices Recommendations

There are no such things as best practices in product development. There are only practices that are adequate within a certain context.

- Larman and Vodde

Many modern management teams have become so focused on performance and process that a quote like this can strike fear into a Product Owner's heart. How can a Framework, declaring from the outset that there are no best practices, be adopted by anyone? Never fear, there are many books of information to help, and even some good advice in this chapter. Adequate within a certain context means that Agile has to be adopted fully and tested constantly by all involved to get good results. The important thing to remember about practices is to avoid making them a process to follow – no matter what. Calling it a best practice would be to consider it already perfect (not likely). The entire point of Lean and LeSS is to continually improve and strive toward perfection. If a practice works for your team or organization, start using it while always looking to make it better.

In their books and other writings, Larman and Vodde discuss the adoption of LeSS and what that means for an organization. Some organizations need more help than others, so the LeSS Rules were formalized and published as a starting point for organizations. With this as the understanding, each will have to conduct their own experiments in continual improvement to make LeSS perfect for them. This follows the Shuhari learning model, which started

Fig 9.12 | Shu Ha Ri

out as a martial arts concept, but is now used to help describe the path from learning to mastery in other areas.

- Shu – Practice; Follow the rules and learn basics
- Ha – Bend; Test the rules to discover context
- Ri – Create; Adapt the rules to master the environment

Finally, when you have an occasion to celebrate and head to the Pub, remember the two unpublished rules. Larman's Rule: Beer is Belgian Tripel Karmeliet. Vodde's Rule: Cocktail is a Dirty Martini.

Enjoy yourself!

END NOTES

[1] Larman, Craig. *Agile and Iterative Development: A Manger's Guide.* Addison-Wesley Professional, 2003.

[2] All images used by permission of Bas Vodde and Craig Larman, source *http://less.works*

[3] LeSS website - *http://less.works*

CHAPTER

10

PMBOK® Guide Sixth Edition

Overview

It sounds strange to call the *PMBOK® Guide Sixth Edition* an "emerging Framework" since the *PMBOK® Guide* has existed for more than 30 years, starting long before the *Agile Manifesto* was written and the current season of Agile began. But the emerging Framework classification is appropriate when we consider what the Sixth Edition release embodies. A bit of historical perspective will help create clarity.

In 1996, the *Project Management Body of Knowledge* underwent a radical revision similar to the revision occurring in the *PMBOK® Guide Sixth Edition.* The two revisions are comparable because both included a combination of significant mindset change and an overhaul of the published standard supporting the project management profession.

In 1996, the standard now known as *A Guide to the Project Management Body of Knowledge* was known as the *Project Management Body of Knowledge.* The new title added the words, "A Guide to the," which demonstrated a significant mindset change. It changed from the *Project Management Body of Knowledge (PMBOK®)* – a static, circumscribable foundation – to A Guide to the *Project Management Body of Knowledge (PMBOK® Guide)* – a growing, adapting, improving set of practices and principles curated and managed by a central body, PMI, for the benefit of all stakeholders, not just project management practitioners[1]

The revisions advance the Stakeholder Management processes added in the Fifth Edition, which are renamed and expanded in the Sixth. Also accompanying the additions to the *PMBOK® Guide Sixth Edition* is a set of proven, real-world tested practices and principles with Agile being added to every Knowledge Area! The impact on project management can only be described as unprecedented, making the *PMBOK® Guide Sixth Edition* an emerging Framework, or perhaps even more accurate, a *re*-emerging Framework as it sets the groundwork for scaling Agile in truly powerful ways also unprecedented.

It is also worth noting that PMI invested in a comprehensive survey of academic research[2] as well as serious market research into how Project Managers perform their jobs – in the real world – prior to the Sixth Edition update. Based on that investment, the structure of the processes, inputs, tools, techniques, and outputs were reviewed to assess how well the Fifth Edition reflected the growth and evolution of the profession. They also used the understanding of real-world practitioners to quantify the reasoning behind the changes that had occurred, then architect those changes into the *PMBOK® Guide Sixth Edition.*

The new *PMBOK® Guide Sixth Edition* has been revised, retaining relevant information from previous editions while integrating the new practices and principles that reflect the evolution of the project management profession as a core competency to support organizational change and drive increased customer value and enterprise growth. It integrates terminology and practices from a wide spectrum of newer project management practices, particularly in Agile.

In the next chapter of this book, the *Agile Integration Framework (AIF)* will be explained in detail. The AIF is a powerful, practical interdisciplinary model for fully engaging critical business stakeholders and vital customer interests using a common lexicon, proven principles, and autonomous, self-directed teams.

Scope of the Revisions
In Project and Development Life Cycles, Section 1.2.4.1, the addition and discussion of adaptive lifecycles, including Agile, iterative, and incremental approaches, begins. The various approaches are categorized as "Agile or change-driven life cycles" and an Appendix covering them is included.

Section 2 focuses on "The Environment in which Projects Operate."

It includes information on Enterprise Environmental Factors (EEFs), Organizational Process Assets (OPAs), processes, policies, and procedures (Section 2.3.1). The Process Groups are the same, but three new processes have been added. First, Manage Project Knowledge was added to the Executing Process Group where it intersects the Project Integration Management Knowledge Area. Second, Implement Risk Responses was also added to the Executing Process Group where it intersects the Project Risk Management Knowledge Area. Third, Control Resources was added to the Monitoring and Controlling Process Group where it intersects the Project Resource Management Knowledge Area. Estimate Activity Resources remains in the Planning Process Group, but now intersects the Project Resource Management Knowledge Area. Also, some processes have been renamed to align with the process intent and clarify understanding.

The processes have been categorized into three groups – processes that occur once or at predefined points, periodic processes done as needed, and repeated or continuous processes. There is detailed coverage of this topic in Section 1.2.4.4 of the Sixth Edition.

Two Knowledge Areas have been renamed. Project Time Management is now called Project Schedule Management and emphasizes the critical nature of scheduling. Project Human Resource Management is now called Project Resource Management and covers both team and physical resources.

Section 3 explores the role of the Project Manager, covering their organizational responsibilities and the skills and competencies required to be effective.

Sections 4 through 13 of the Sixth Edition contain the Knowledge Area discussions and are laden with the new Agile content. Knowledge Areas in previous editions of the *PMBOK® Guide* started with an introduction, outline, and overview illustration. In the Sixth Edition, each Knowledge Area begins with four elements, *Key Concepts, Trends and Emerging Practices, Tailoring Considerations, and Approaches in Agile, Iterative, and Adaptive Environments.*

Key Concepts covers the information in previous editions. *Trends and Emerging Practices* expresses what is considered a good practice for a majority of projects, most of the time, and also includes a limited discussion of industry trends not practiced on most projects and explains why they are part of the process inputs, tools, techniques, and outputs (ITTOs). *Tailoring Considerations* highlights options for tailoring the processes, ITTOs, and lifecycles, and includes a list of questions useful to practitioners as they customize their project management approach. *Approaches in Agile, Iterative, and Adaptive Environments* covers development methods, techniques, artifacts, and practices specific to the use of Agile, iterative, and adaptive approaches. Because Agile techniques have been integrated throughout the Sixth Edition, specific ideas to help practitioners identify and integrate them into their projects is also provided.

One interesting area, likely to be actively debated and refined over time in the near future, is coverage given to differentiating between Project and Product Scope. This idea has interesting ties to the principles in Lean and Agile that focus on continuous process and product improvement. The discussion will significantly enhance the awareness that program management and scaled Agile are more *process* oriented, while project management and Agile are more *product* oriented.

The release of the *PMBOK® Guide Sixth Edition* and the discussion contrasting process versus product orientation will have significant implications for *The Standard for Project Management®* as well as *The Standard for Program Management®* and scaling Agile.

In a certain sense, the release of the *PMBOK® Guide Sixth Edition* is strangely Agile for the typically bureaucratic PMI organization because it is being released before reaching a more robust level of maturity. One of the important facets of the value of this book is its ability to fill the 'maturity gap' and set the stage for useful, powerful discussions among professional practitioners. This book helps clarify the parts of the Agile content that are not only immature, but factually wrong, thereby helping the reader protect themselves. But the critical point is that any shortcomings are far less important than the value of releasing a standard that can be debated, refined, and improved by the whole community of practitioners before the *PMBOK® Guide Seventh Edition* is released, four years from now.

Spirited debate is expected over the coming years. The *Agile Practice Guide,* currently being developed jointly by PMI and the Agile Alliance, is an encouraging sign of healthy future dialogue and engagement. The *Agile Practice Guide* is planned for publication in September 2017, concurrent with the *PMBOK® Guide – Sixth Edition.* The coverage in this chapter will provide insights to help foster significant dialogue as the community focuses on integrating customer value and enterprise growth.

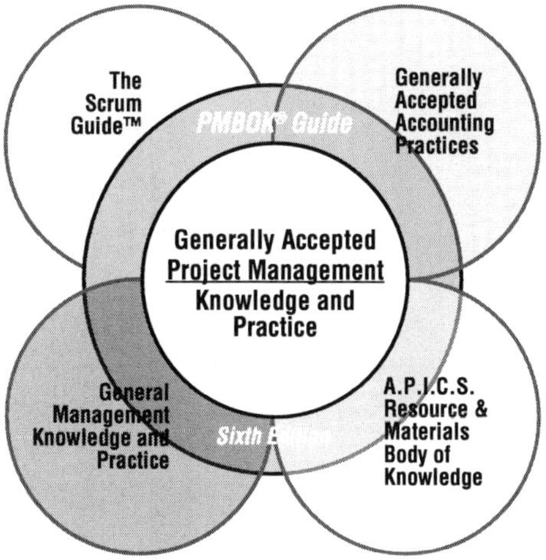

Figure 10.1 | *PMBOK® Guide Sixth Edition*

Benefits / Challenges

Benefits

Leverages the Best-Known Framework Adding Significant Credibility
One of the biggest contributions the PMBOK® Guide Sixth Edition makes to Agile practitioners is credibility! As described in Chapter 1, the vision of this book is to be a Rosetta stone to help Program Managers speak in understandable terms with customers, management, and all the various technical professionals involved in the Program. With over 770,000 certified PMP®s globally, and over 3 million copies of the *PMBOK® Guide* in print, it is arguably the most broadly known and accepted lexicon available. Integrating Agile into the lexicon gives Program Managers a common vocabulary that is credible with significant numbers of customer and management stakeholders. It is also a foundation that technical professionals are familiar with, even those who disagree with portions of the *PMBOK® Guide.*

Leverages Decades of Process Development and Refinement
It is a core Lean principle that continuous improvement is the path to perfection. And even though no one suggests the *PMBOK® Guide* is in a state of perfection, it is in a process of continuous improvement and the integration of Agile principles is a logical step in the progression

towards better project and program outcomes. By leveraging the decades of development reflected in the *PMBOK® Guide*, a Program Manager can sidestep many mistakes that are a source of avoidable waste.

Integrates With "The Standard for Program Management®" published by PMI
In addition to the *PMBOK® Guide* there is a second resource, The Standard for Program Management® published by PMI, shown in *Figure 10.02*, that holds an immense amount of practical insight specifically for Program Managers. By extending and focusing the principles and practices in the *PMBOK® Guide* specifically for managing the additional challenges present in Programs, *The Standard for Program Management®* sheds light on very specific opportunities and risks, commonly present in the large-scale environments considered in this book.

Figure 10.02 | The Standard for Program Management

As previously noted, the release of the *PMBOK® Guide Sixth Edition* will have significant implications for *The Standard for Program Management®* and scaling Agile, as the best ways to align the varying process- and product-oriented perspectives are worked through.

Includes Proven Options for Budgeting and Advanced Scheduling
As mentioned throughout this book, one of the major strategic weaknesses of the current Frameworks for scaling Agile is the lack of serious, in-depth guidance on managing budgets and complex, large-scale schedules. By comparison, the *PMBOK® Guide and The Standard for Program Management®* contain sophisticated, proven, detailed insight into how these significant requirements can be properly managed in Traditional environments. This book extends those insights into the scaled Agile arena.

It is an odd paradox, and one that validates Henry Ford's observance about thinking being hard work, that a vast number of PMP®s, who lay claim to being professionals, actively seek to avoid using Earned Value Management (EVM) and, instead, pursue a shortcut around it. It is not that there isn't a tool for sophisticated budget and schedule management; just that they do not like it because it is not point-and-shoot easy. EVM can be mastered with comparatively little effort when taught correctly, but too few teachers or students are engaged in the diligent effort needed to master it. It almost seems they expect stakeholders to rely on their judgment as professionals when they say, "Trust me. A miracle will happen." *(See Figure 10 .03.)*

Figure 10.03 | Odd Paradox

In spite of any silly paradoxes, the impact of the *PMBOK® Guide Sixth Edition* on Agile credibility for Program Managers, who invest in understanding and mastering the required skills, practices, and principles, will be truly remarkable.

Challenges

Misunderstanding the Paradox of Knowledge Workers
In 1999, Peter Drucker emphasized the need for organizations to empower the knowledge worker to make decisions that they – more so than management – are in the best position to make; and also to avoid having the knowledge workers leave, damaging the organization.[3]

Knowledge workers are persons who combine various forms of structured and unstructured data and use creative thinking to solve mostly non-routine problems. They are commonly described as thinking for a living and examples include engineers, architects, scientists, and lawyers.

In, *Drive: The Surprising Truth About What Motivates Us*[4], Daniel Pink describes three factors that motivate knowledge workers, who, by the way, happen to be the largest portion of the technical professionals working in Agile programs. Those three factors are Autonomy, Mastery, and Purpose.

Together Drucker and Pink circumscribe the paradox of Knowledge Workers where senior or Program Managers, misunderstanding Agile, wrongly believe that Agile in the *PMBOK® Guide* means teams will run marathons at the pace of a 40-yard dash. They do not understand that Agile is not fast; it creates speed by leveraging innovation in the face of complexity.

The challenge is to empower teams to learn as much and as quickly as possible, and use that capacity to respond swiftly to the future as it unfolds, so it creates an unassailable competitive advantage for the enterprise. Dan Pink's formula – Autonomy, Mastery and Purpose (AMP) – is the key to unlocking learning that, "AMPs up your team's voltage!"

Figure 10.04 | Agile Creates Speed Through Innovation

The challenge is to create a light-weight structure based on *PMBOK® Guide* principles that optimizes the whole of organizational throughput, while simultaneously protecting the creative, non-linear, and imaginative insights that only come from fully engaged knowledge workers.

Flexibility is an absolute requirement for knowledge workers to successfully deal with the challenges of developing goal-centric, integrated, high-functioning solutions in the dynamic, program environment as it moves through the Cone of Uncertainty.

Instead of expecting more documentation or additional planning to find the answer, teams must be given the autonomy to prototype different ideas, and refine, test, and repeatedly improve them. They must be given security to exercise their autonomy in a process where they fail faster to succeed sooner.

Program Managers and enterprise leaders must work to understand and embrace participatory decision-making and develop the difficult, sophisticated leadership skills needed to set clear, long-range objectives, facilitating a thorough interrogation of the requirements so that realistic expectations are defined and influence the development of healthy, durable, mutually-respectful relationships. Otherwise, high attrition rates and the immense cost of knowledge workers leaving the Program for a better opportunity elsewhere will ultimately damages the enterprise.

Overcoming this challenge requires leaders to take seriously the advice of William McKnight, the fabled Founder and leader of 3M Corp., who was fond of saying, "Hire good people, and leave them alone."

PMBOK® Guide Framework Requires Dedicated Effort to Master
Developing gravitas by exhibiting serious, logical, cogent arguments for the new Agile program management processes requires dedicated effort to learning and mastering Agile skills, practices, and principles. That is an unfortunate, somewhat intimidating, and unavoidable challenge.

> ***"Clear thinking requires courage rather than intelligence"***
> – Thomas Szasz[5]

Program Managers must choose to invest the time and energy required to think seriously, analyze, test, and master the Agile Frameworks and tools they intend to use. Opting in must be a conscious choice and accompanied by a commensurate commitment of time and energy.

Risk of Installing Heavy-Weight Processes that Disable Agile Advantages
One sadly humorous aspect of the current state of scaled Agile Frameworks is the pushback exhibited by groups, like UnSAFe[6] for example, who appear to oppose any kind of structure or guidelines being prescribed for scaled Agile development. They seem to think that Agile is divinely revealed dogma that magically makes unfettered, freewheeling development successful on a large scale. They also seem to believe they can be persuasive, telling bosses they will have to wait and see what will be delivered, how long it will take, and how much it will cost *(Figure 10.05)*.

Figure 10.05 | Just Wait and See

Perhaps they completely missed, or denied, the fact that Agile has a pedigree underpinning whichever Framework they adhere to as their preferred method. The primary source for much of the Agile principles is Lean, and there is nothing in Lean that rejects the need for structure and guidelines in order to scale a process or product. A visit to any manufacturing facility using the Toyota Production System[7] and Lean principles will provide ample evidence for the critical role that structure and guidelines play in scaling an Agile environment.

In fact, no Agile team has ever rejected the corporate burden of accurately completing timesheets as imposing too much structure, preferring, instead, to not get paid. Yet those same teams will struggle mightily in a battle to reject a common standard or template for a Burn-up chart. It is a case of selective blindness or being completely tone deaf to the reality of an enterprise.

However, accepting the reality that some, or all, teams must embrace practices that sub-optimize their micro-dynamic in order to optimize the whole of the Program or enterprise must be balanced against the risk of requiring heavy-weight processes that disable the advantages of using an Agile Framework.

Risk of Budgeting and Scheduling Misalignment

Chapter 1 introduced the concept of Defined Granularity. This was expanded on in several subsequent chapters and will receive deep-dive treatment in Chapter 11. Here, it is simply worthwhile to note that a misalignment in the level of granularity being applied to planning versus the level being applied to budgeting or scheduling can create an immense amount of confusion and waste.

To illustrate, the *PMBOK® Guide* provides guidance on levels of estimating described as Rough Order of Magnitude (ROM), Budgetary, and Definitive. The levels acknowledge that various degrees of mathematical granularity exist and therefore should be taken into account. Yet it is not uncommon for Programs to spend an inappropriate amount of resources – time and money – creating Definitive estimates for budgets and schedules when ROM is the only mathematically reasonable option. The result is irrational stakeholder behavior due to false confidence based on illogical estimates feeding into plans, schedules, and budgets.

Program Managers, who allow a misalignment between the granularity being expressed in planning presentations and the mathematical, statistically reliable granularity possible in large and long-range estimates, induce irrational stakeholder behavior and suffer a loss of respect from them since they expect the Program Manager to operate more professionally.

Program-level Attributes

For this section and purpose, the *PMBOK® Guide* will be emphasized to guide a broader range of professionals and industries, with the understanding that *The Standard for Program Management® (The Standard)* supplements or expands upon these attributes.

Both The Standard and the PMBOK® Guide have refined a development approach referred to formally as Traditional, or casually as Waterfall. That approach has now been redefined to include Waterfall, Iterative, Adaptive, Agile, and Hybrid development approaches. See, for example, Section 5.1.1.2 Project Management Plan in the *PMBOK® Guide.*

That means Program-level attributes now require professional Program Managers to speak effectively using analogies that stakeholders understand. One example they can use is Storyboarding. Storyboarding is a prototyping technique used to help sequence development (process orientation) or define navigation using illustrations (product orientation). For an example, see Section 5.2.2.8 Prototypes in the *PMBOK® Guide.*

Story boards are actively used in Agile, both as a process management tool and product development tool. By acknowledging that they are also proven in industries like advertising, film production, and instructional design, Program Managers, using a Traditional approach, can coherently embrace Agile and explain it to stakeholders.

Roles

Research consistently demonstrates that the top Program Managers exhibit skill in tailoring or customizing their approach to benefit their teams and the enterprise. They are now expected to be skillful at blending both Traditional and Agile methods to maximize the probability of Program success. They must embrace emerging trends like using fusions or hybrids of Traditional, Agile, and other iterative practices promoting team engagement and customer involvement. This is discussed in detail in Section 3.4.2 Technical Project Management Skills in the *PMBOK® Guide.*

The *PMBOK® Guide* recognizes that success means shifting away from a command-and-control structure toward a more collaborative and supportive management approach, empowering teams by delegating decision-making to the team members. This new approach seeks to optimize resource utilization through self-organizing teams with a minimum of centralized control.

The *PMBOK® Guide* incorrectly states that self-organizing teams are used mainly for the execution of IT projects and that they usually consist of generalized specialists, instead of subject matter experts, operating in the absence of a Project Manager while continuously adapting to the changing environment and embracing constructive feedback. In Chapter 2 of this book, the myth that "Agile is Only for Software" was shown to be false, and two significant examples were provided. The canard of "generalized specialists" was also exposed for the inadequate and unhelpful myth that it is. Real world experience irrefutably debunks the idea of teams working in the absence of a PM except in the tiniest of companies, operating in the smallest of niches.

Collaborative teams are often critical to the success of Programs and projects with high degrees of complexity and uncertainty. They provide innovative responses to those challenges by utilizing improved communication, increased knowledge sharing, and fail-fast flexibility to overcome barriers and impediments. Unfortunately, the *PMBOK® Guide* inaccurately ascribes this to collaborative teams' variability and rapid changes, suggesting less time for centralized testing and decision-making.

Nonetheless, as noted earlier, these inaccuracies are far less important than the value of releasing a standard that can be refined and improved by the whole community of practitioners before the *PMBOK® Guide Seventh Edition* is released.

Workflow

Since the *PMBOK® Guide Fifth Edition,* adoption of Agile and Adaptive methodologies has exploded into the project management domain. The Sixth Edition includes an important subsection called *Considerations for Adaptive Environments* at the beginning of Sections 4 through 13. It also includes an Appendix describing the use of Agile, Adaptive, Iterative, and hybrid approaches from the perspective of Project Management Process Groups.

The *PMBOK® Guide* Appendix explores the nuances of the Project Management Process Groups and *The Standard for Project Management®* with respect to how they are performed within the project environment and lifecycle. For example, Section 1.4.2.1 of the *PMBOK® Guide* states that the "project life cycle needs to be flexible enough to deal with the variety of factors included in the project." That implies that projects must evolve and adapt as detailed information becomes known. The ability to evolve and adapt is crucial to success when a Program or project faces high degrees of complexity and uncertainty, not the least of which is the wide variations that occur in stakeholder expectations.

The *PMBOK® Guide* Glossary describes the project lifecycle as "the series of phases that a project passes through from its start to its completion." A project lifecycle is understood to include one or more phases of development, sometimes called the Development Lifecycle, of a product, service, or derivative of the two. Development lifecycles can be Traditional, which typically means they are predictive and can be subjected to plan-driven management. They may also be Adaptive and therefore require an Agile or Iterative management approach. Lastly, development cycles can also be hybrid, which appears to be the fastest growing approach.

The Appendix includes an interesting figure that aims to show a continuum of project lifecycles using a table listing how requirements are processed, plans handled, involvement of key stakeholders guided, and risks and costs managed. The point it seems to make is that workflows for plan-driven project lifecycles emphasize specifications and detailed planning combined with milestones for key stakeholder involvement. It contrasts that view with the perspective that workflows for Adaptive or Agile lifecycles emphasize progressive elaboration of requirements and short, iterative cycles of planning and execution that keep key stakeholders continuously involved to provide frequent feedback. It then suggests that workflows in the middle of the continuum emphasize optimizing development outcomes by utilizing hybrid methods. The most useful conclusion is that projects within a Program may benefit from being executed differently.

The project lifecycles, or workflows, in the *PMBOK® Guide* are defined as phases where "a collection of logically related project activities culminates in the completion of one or more deliverables." See, for example, Section 1.2.4.2 in the *PMBOK® Guide*. This concept has an almost identical parallel in Agile where Iterations produce increments that are integrated to fulfill the acceptance criteria for the Release.

The *PMBOK® Guide* Appendix explores the two Adaptive patterns referred to as Sequential Iteration-Based Phases and Continuous Overlapping Phases. Sequential Iteration-Based Phases says Adaptive projects are delivered with a sequence of Iterations utilizing a cadence of predictable timeboxes to aid scheduling and the application of relevant project management processes. From a Lean perspective, these Iterations incur overhead considered necessary, unavoidable waste for effectively managing projects with high degrees of complexity and uncertainty. Continuous Overlapping Phases apply the process groups continuously throughout the lifecycle to aggressively refine and improve both development and planning. The workflow continuously pulls work items from a prioritized Backlog.

The *PMBOK® Guide* inaccurately describes the aim of Continuous Overlapping Phases as minimizing the overhead of managing Process Groups by removing the start and end of the Iteration activities. It compounds the distortion by saying that continuous pull systems can be viewed as micro-Iterations, with an emphasis on maximizing the time spent on execution rather than management. Since a workflow continuously pulling work items from a prioritized Backlog is a Kanban system, it is much more accurate to say it minimizes overhead by focusing on optimizing throughput and minimizing the cost of Work In Progress (WIP). Increasing throughput by optimizing the efficiency of the workflow has nothing to do with Iterations – micro or otherwise.

Traditional and Agile workflow practices share an arbitrary logical device for bucketing and managing information at various levels of granularity. The PMBOK® Guide refers to this device in Traditional terms as a Work Breakdown Structure (WBS) whereas Agile calls it a Feature Breakdown Structure (FBS). In both cases, the decomposition of the higher-level Features, Functions, or Capabilities, collectively referred to as components, are subdivided into the work items for each of the deliverables or subcomponents that can be reintegrated as tangible or intangible products, services, or a derivative of the two. It is common in Agile to describe the process as taking Epics and decomposing them into User Stories. Reference Sections 5.4.2. Create WBS: Tools and Techniques and 5.4.2.2 Decomposition of the *PMBOK® Guide* for more specifics.

Workflows have an obvious correlation to schedules because both express work across time. Traditional approaches to creating schedules commonly involve creating logic networks and analyzing them with tools, such as the Critical Path Method. The Agile approach is less detailed, and perhaps less sophisticated, by design. Schedules in Agile are expressed in three levels of detail or granularity. The highest, and least, granular level is the Roadmap, where details are comparable to the idea of Rough Order of Magnitude (ROM), as described in the *PMBOK® Guide*. The middle level is the Release Plan with details either at the ROM level or the Budgetary level, as described in the *PMBOK® Guide*. The third level, with the highest granularity, is the Iteration Plan, where, depending on organizational standards, the details are at the Budgetary or Definitive levels, as described in the *PMBOK® Guide*. The logic behind the more limited granularity of Agile schedules is three-fold. First, since long term estimates simply cannot resolve details at a higher level of granularity, attempting to do so creates, what Lean would categorize as, expensive, avoidable waste. Second, presenting such inherently flawed information to stakeholders creates unrealistic expectations based on the false precision of the evidence, which subsequently destroys stakeholder confidence in the process and the Program Manager when the truth becomes evident. Third, trying to estimate and schedule at such a detailed level disempowers the team, making them feel micro-managed or untrusted, and removes the energy, creativity, and disciplined focus needed to solve the problems and challenges the project and Program face.

The iterative scheduling of work items from a Backlog, as practiced by Agile, is a form of Rolling Wave planning where the work to be accomplished in the near term is planned in detail, while work further in the future is planned at a higher or less granular level. Rolling Wave planning is a form of progressive elaboration that has been part of the *PMBOK® Guide* for many years. It means work items can be defined with various levels of detail, depending on where they are in the project lifecycle. In Traditional planning, Work Packages are decomposed into Activities, whereas in Agile planning, Epics are decomposed into User Stories. See, for example, Section 6.2.2.3 Rolling Wave Planning in the *PMBOK® Guide*.

Agile improves the long-time Traditional approach by using it to deliver incremental Value to the customer or concurrently develop large quantities of Features using multiple teams. Agile relies on decoupling as many interconnected dependencies as possible to accomplish this result. Doing so allows Adaptive lifecycles to drive product development that welcomes change, which maximizes customer and marketplace value.

Kanban, advocated as an Agile approach, extends this practice centered on the pull-based scheduling concepts pioneered by W. Edwards Deming[8] in the Toyota Production System that defined the Lean manufacturing principles, and expanded by Eliyahu Goldratt in his seminal work on the *Theory of Constraints*[9] and the *Critical Chain*[10].

Adaptive approaches are generally characterized as using shorter development cycles so work can be reviewed and adapted more frequently. These shorter cycles provide more rapid feedback, which creates insight into the alignment of deliverables with suitability or fitness for a specific purpose.

Programs scaling Agile often manage workflows across projects and initiatives using a hybrid approach, such as defining workflows starting with long-term Roadmaps, then decomposing them into Releases and Iteration plans that optimize factors like regulatory compliance, organizational governance, and geographic dispersion. It requires successfully adapting workflows to manage technical complexity spanning the full delivery lifecycle by utilizing plan-driven, adaptive, and hybrid approaches simultaneously.

Ceremonies

Managing the workflows requires ceremonies to create activity lists as part of the project schedule then update the activity lists periodically, using Rolling Wave planning or Agile techniques, to report progress. The purpose of the ceremonies is to facilitate decision-making using techniques like the "Fist of Five," popular in Agile settings. For examples and elaboration on this, see Sections 6.2.3.1 Activity List and 6.4.2.7 Decision Making in the *PMBOK® Guide.*

Ceremonies include meetings to estimate activity durations and User Stories, plan Iterations, prioritize the Product Backlog, and have the team commit to specific work items for the next Iteration.

The *PMBOK® Guide* correctly identifies the important practice of including stakeholders in ceremonies, even those from outside the project or organization, where appropriate, as an emerging trend. It advocates that this common Agile practice can be applied to all types of projects. Unfortunately, it <u>incorrectly</u> states that the practice of including stakeholders only extends to "short, Daily Stand-up meetings."

The *PMBOK® Guide* continues by <u>mistakenly</u> suggesting that the team breaks down User Stories to low-level Tasks, with estimates in hours, at a meeting attended by the Product Owner, Scrum Team, and Project Manager where the outcome includes information on assumptions, concerns, risks, dependencies, decisions, and actions. The *PMBOK® Guide* inaccurately describes Release planning as allowing the Product Owner and team to decide how much needs to be developed and how long it will take to have a releasable product based on business goals, dependencies, and impediments. For more details see Sections 6.4.2.8 Meetings and 6.5.2.8 Agile Release Planning in the *PMBOK® Guide.*

Ceremonies play a vital role in Program-wide communication, as well as internally to each project. In addition, posting artifacts from the ceremonies delivers transparent communication that improves management and stakeholder satisfaction. Despite the inaccuracies in the *PMBOK® Guide,* the discussions they will generate become great educational launch pads, bringing the opportunity to either teach other colleagues or learn from them!

Artifacts

The *PMBOK® Guide* does not prescribe any Agile specific artifacts, assuming that the artifacts common to whichever Agile method being used will become part of the archives of the project and Program.

How to Make It Work Effectively

As mentioned before, differentiating between Project and Product Scope, in order to align with the Lean principles of continuous process and product improvement, has important ramifications for Program management and scaled Agile. The environment will have to be more process oriented while supporting the team's need to be more product oriented.

The *PMBOK® Guide* Appendix acknowledges that the Project Management Group of processes occurs across the project lifecycle continuum and interacts differently in adaptive life cycles. Specifically, it states that the Initiating Process Group will revisit and revalidate the Project Charter as the project progresses, and competing priorities and changing dynamics cause project success criteria to evolve. This is so because adaptive projects rely on the voice-of-the-customer to provide feedback on the emerging deliverable on a continuous basis. That feedback ensures a correct project result.

It also states that the Planning Process Group of processes in adaptive lifecycles will develop high-level plans and progressively elaborate them to an appropriate level of detail. It suggests that practice should involve as many team members and stakeholders as possible, incorporating a wide base of input to overcome uncertainty.

The *PMBOK® Guide* Appendix goes on to describe the Executing Process Group processes in Agile, iterative, and adaptive project lifecycles as operating within Iterations that conclude with a demonstration of completed functionality. The processes manage stakeholder engagement by showing increments of work done and soliciting discussion of future work.

The Monitoring and Controlling Process Group includes processes that track, review, and regulate progress and performance by maintaining a Backlog. As work is completed, various trends and metrics are calculated so changes to future Iterations can be made, grounded in real progress rates. Using that information, work is scheduled in the next Iteration based on business priorities and team capacity. The metrics, performance status, and projections are shared with project stakeholders via trend graphs called information radiators.

Lastly, the *PMBOK® Guide* Appendix describes the Closing Process Group processes used in iterative, adaptive, and Agile projects as focused on undertaking the highest business value items first. The benefit is that when a project or phase closes prematurely, perhaps because of budget or schedule restrictions, some useful business value still gets delivered, creating early benefits realization instead of a loss of sunk costs.

Organizational Standards of Practice

Given the perspective of the Process Groups just described, enterprise standards of practice, commonly called governance, need to be suitably tailored for Agile programs.

A primary concern requiring appropriate governance is ensuring that the sponsor and customer representative stay consistently engaged with the project and Program. Their feedback must occur as deliverables are created because it drives the Product Backlog grooming process, ensuring it stays aligned to their current needs. That means projects in Agile Programs will repeat the Validate Scope and Control Scope processes during each Iteration.

Tailoring governance for projects with evolving requirements, often due to high-risk, high-complexity or substantial uncertainty, means accepting the deliberate choice of Agile methods to conserve resources by spending less time defining scope that cannot be known in detail early in the project, and embracing a process that commits to ongoing discovery and refinement.

A common aspect of this process is building and reviewing mock-ups and prototypes in order to refine the requirements before releasing later versions.

When organizations are new to Agile approaches it is vital to see that Traditional processes used in Control Schedule are adapted to focus on the current status of the project schedule for continuous product improvement and Retrospective meetings for continuous process improvement. Continuous product improvement results in reprioritizing the remaining work (i.e., Backlog) whereas continuous process improvement results in evaluating the rate at which deliverables can be produced (i.e., team velocity) per Iteration. The combined insights of the two determine how the project schedule has changed and the best options for responding to the actual changes occurring.

The Agile approach also creates unique governance needs for tailoring the way project cost is managed and reported. Trying to produce highly-detailed cost estimates for projects with high uncertainty will probably lead to waste due to frequent changes. Instead, focus on light-weight estimation methods that generate fast, low-cost forecasts aligned with the level of granularity being used for planning and decision-making. The level of cost granularity can then be adjusted as progress is made, changes become known and understood, and detailed decision-making must occur. Detailed estimates should be reserved for the short-term planning horizon defined in the governance choices. Governance should also include recognition that projects dealing with high-variability must include scope and schedule flexibility in order to meet strict budgets or tight cost constraints. See, for example, Section 7 Project Cost Management in the *PMBOK® Guide.*

Agile Programs include high-uncertainty projects which, by definition, incur more risk. Therefore, they must use frequent reviews of incremental work products and cross-functional teams to accelerate discovery and learning that ensure risk is understood and can be managed. Governance needs to ensure that risk is considered during the selection of the Iteration Backlog, even if an informal process is used to identify, analyze, and manage it. It should also adapt planning based on a continuously updated assessment of the risk exposure. See, for example, Sections 11 Risk Management and 11.3 Performed Qualitative Risk Analysis in the *PMBOK® Guide.*

For enterprise standards of practice and governance to be suitably tailored for Agile programs, they must achieve significant levels of stakeholder engagement and participation. Agile methods accelerate information sharing that creates optimal transparency so stakeholders can identify any misalignment, dependency, or other issue as early as possible. Otherwise, the critical, timely, productive discussions and decision-making that enable a dynamic co-creative process will not happen. Governance must cultivate an open, engaged environment or the result will be a failure to mitigate risk, build trust, and support early adaptations that reduce costs and improve the probability of project success. See, for example, Section 13 Project Stakeholder Management in the *PMBOK® Guide.*

Tools and Practices Recommendations

To properly select the right tools and practices it is critically important that the Program Manager select between Agile and Traditional methods correctly, and that the use of hybrid approaches not be shunned. The distinguishing characteristics of projects that benefit from Agile are prominent levels of complexity and uncertainty, or a combination of the two. Extensive experience suggests that, perhaps, only one-third of the projects for enterprises, in the size range of the Fortune 2000, benefit from the added overhead of Agile approaches. Luckily, that one-third are the source of innovative-advantage the organization needs to succeed in the battle for constituent tax dollars or consumer spending. Interestingly, it also seems that about one-third of the people in those same organizations are well suited for, and desire to be part of, Agile projects.

For projects using Agile methods there are some very valuable tools and practices to use.

Osmotic Communication
Agile methods require a huge amount of communication "bandwidth" to creatively solve problems and produce robust, reliable planning. Requiring collocation of resources at critical times is the "insurance premium" for mitigating risk and optimizing throughput. Granted, full-time collocation, as advocated by single-team Agile Frameworks, is an unrealistic and unattainable standard for large Programs. However, temporary collocation at the beginning of a Program and project, as well as for planning Releases or responding to significant breakthroughs or setbacks is mandatory.

Low Tech, High Touch
Collocating the right resources for planning Releases or responding to

significant breakthroughs or setbacks must be coupled with planning done the right way. The right way means that low-tech, high-touch methods must be used at these strategically and tactically significant meetings. Two examples that prove the value of such an approach are Intel Corp. and Siemens who are both successful powerhouses. Intel has MAPP (Make a Project/Program Plan) Day and Siemens has PACT (Project Acceleration Control Technique) Day and both are low-tech, high-touch rituals that fuel their continuing success in highly competitive, extremely complex and uncertain environments.

Low-tech, high-touch methods are epitomized in any "sticky notes on a whiteboard" process that every stakeholder has experienced. While the method and goal of the sticky note meeting may vary, they all leverage the human-engagement that they create. Leveraging that wisdom is highly recommended. The cost of gathering key stakeholders for planning at significant points is vastly exceeded by the value of opportunities captured and the costs of risks eliminated.

Unrelenting Focus on Customer Satisfaction

There is no substitute for an unrelenting drive to understand, assess, validate, and refine the clarity of customer requirements so that expectations are met and exceeded. The elusive target lies at the intersection of conformance to requirements and fitness for use. Every process must contribute to ensuring the project produces the intended result and that the result satisfies a real need. Therefore, test-driven development and frequent quality reviews must be built into the core project process and not be added to the end of the project.

Lean principles have proven that managing quality is everybody's responsibility, even though different roles have a different emphasis. For Agile Programs, and the projects they contain, every team member owns an aspect of quality management throughout development. See, for example, Sections 8.2 Manage Quality and 8.3 Control Quality in the *PMBOK® Guide.*

Conclusion

As time marches forward, and the vigorous functional discussions that will unavoidably happen as the *PMBOK® Guide Sixth Edition* is debated, refined, and improved by the whole community of practitioners before the *PMBOK® Guide Seventh Edition* is released, remember that PMI's uncharacteristically Agile decision to release a less robust version with the Agile content still immature was bold and of far greater importance than any value added maturity might have created by delaying the release of the standard.

Kudos to PMI! Now it is time for the PMP®s of the world to make it great.

END NOTES

[1] The PMBOK® was originally published in 1987 as a stand-alone document to guide project management information and practices. In 1996, revisions were made to create an official guide to advance the development of project management by documenting and standardizing accepted project management information and practices. These changes superseded the previous document and became the PMBOK® Guide – 1st Edition. The 2nd edition was published in 2000 and contained new materials reflecting the growth of the project management profession and corrected any errors in the 1st edition. The 3rd edition, published in 2004, included similar revisions made in the 2nd edition as well as incorporating "good practices" applicable to most projects. In 2009, the 4th edition was published with the aim of making the contents more accessible, developing the widely recognized "triple constraints" by expanding them to six, and modifying existing, adding new, and removing obsolete practices. The 5th edition was released in 2013, incorporating updates, further standardizing terms, processes, inputs and outputs, and including advancements, such as rolling wave and adaptive lifecyle. The PMBOK® Guide – 6th Edition, published in September 2017, completely restructured its format and focus. It is now structured by process group, not knowledge area and focuses largely on project plan components and project document examples and updates. A huge addition to the 6th edition is the expansion on and amount of Agile project management coverage, in response to Agile becoming one of the fastest growing methodologies in recent years. The PMI Talent Triangle was also added, amongst other things. Because the PMBOK® Guide is recognized as an American National Standard by the American National Standards Institute (ANSI), it must be updated approximately every four years to reflect the latest industry practices.

[2] For more information on how PMI develops their standards and gathers the information to do so, please visit PMI.org or, specifically, *https://www.pmi.org/pmbok-guide-standards/about/development* to learn more about the standards development process; *https://www.pmi.org/learning/publications/project-management-journal* to learn more about research published and used in the development process; and *https://www.pmi.org/pmbok-guide-standards/about/get-involved* to learn more about the activities used in the development process.

[3] Drucker, *P. F. Management Challenges for the 21st Century.* HarperCollins, 1999.

[4] Pink, Daniel H. Drive: *The Surprising Truth About What Motivates Us.* Riverhead Books, 2011.

[5] Thomas Szasz (April 15, 1920 – September 8, 2012) was a Professor Emeritus in Psychiatry at the State University of New York Health Science Center in Syracuse, New York, and a noted critic of the moral and scientific foundations of psychiatry.

[6] UnSAFe is an informal group of people who believe that SAFe is RUP revisited and more of a Traditional delivery than Agile. This is discussed in Chapter 7 of this book.

[7] For more information on the Toyota Production System (TPS), revisit Chapter 5 of this book or Book 1 of the Agile Almanac.

[8] William Edwards Deming (October 14, 1900 – December 20, 1993) is perhaps best known for his work in Japan. He taught how to improve product quality through the application of statistical methods. Deming made a significant contribution to Japan's later reputation for innovative high-quality products. Despite being a hero there, he was only beginning to be recognized in the U.S. at the time of his death.

[9] Goldratt, E. M., *Theory of Constraints.* The North River Press, 1999.

[10] Goldratt, E. M., *Critical Chain.* The North River Press, 1997.

CHAPTER

11

Agile Integration Framework (AIF)

Overview

Agile has fostered undeniable successes interfacing technology and the real world, which has led to its broad adoption and acceptance. At the same time, the world – or more accurately, the expectations of customers and key stakeholders – has moved beyond the current body of knowledge shared and published in Agile circles. In response, various Frameworks have been developed and deployed to scale Agile in the marketplace with some degree of success, but also with undeniable limits. Those Frameworks appear to share a common paradigm because they all started with the perspective that to scale Agile, a Framework must start from Agile, stay within Agile, and extend its processes and practices from that Agile foundation.

The problem with selecting that paradigm as the baseline model can be seen in Einstein's remark, "We cannot solve our problems with the same level of thinking that created them!"

Applying Einstein's insight also suggests that the best path to creating value with scaled Agile may require practitioners from both Traditional and Agile backgrounds to surrender their allegiance to old models and choose carefully-crafted, Lean-centric Frameworks, methods, and systems. Readers are urged to view scaled agility as choices on a continuum and remain open to innovative ideas.

As Mike Cohn shares so clearly and eloquently in,

"Let Go of Knowing: How Holding Onto Views May Be Holding You Back[1]", even convictions that have served well in the past could hinder processes in new situations. There are brilliant thought leaders in both Traditional and Agile domains – and even some professional peers – whose opinions are the exact opposite of each other's. Biases often prevent even very smart people from questioning assumptions because embracing new information is hard but vital, nonetheless.

The Agile Integration Framework (AIF) explained, explored, and proven in this chapter starts with an entirely different paradigm because scaling Agile often requires major organizational change to be successful. Further, getting all the key stakeholders to explore, accept, implement, and embrace the changes required by scaled Agile has a much higher probability of success if important principles, methods, processes, and practices can be shown as a mere evolution of beliefs they already hold as true.

The foundational approach of the AIF is that the many decades of developing advanced business school models and strategies, appropriately combined with five decades of developing the *PMBOK® Guide* and the Standards for Program and Portfolio Management, while leveraging the distinct improvements of Agile drawn from Lean principles provides the most robust, most reliable, and most flexible approach for scaling Agile. That is true, in large part, because the AIF reduces stakeholder resistance by making the perceived risk of change dramatically lower, as shown in *Figure 11.01*.

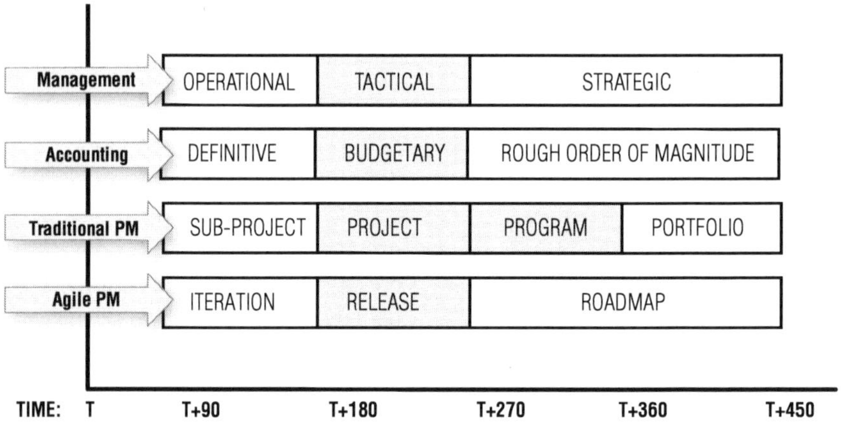

Figure 11.01 | AIF Foundational Paradigm

The vision of the Agile Integration Framework is founded on the acknowledgement that the management, accounting, and Traditional and

Agile project management domains share a great deal of common ground in their understanding of the environment in which products, both tangible and intangible, and services are delivered, regardless of whether the provider is a public agency or a private enterprise.

The AIF is a Rosetta stone for Program Managers, providing a cogent, flexible Framework that works in any setting and has a common lexicon to make it understandable for stakeholders, executives, and technical development professionals alike. The AIF is an organizational model that empowers and enables teams and individuals to be self-directed while optimizing the throughput of the whole enterprise.

Recall that the trajectory of increased transistor capacity on integrated circuits (IC) unlocked profound and nearly unimaginable improvements in the capabilities, miniaturization, and integration of devices of all kinds. *(Look back at Figure 1.01 for reference.)* Evidence of the change can be seen in the growth of the Internet, which is the most universal platform for communication in the history of humanity. It also induced a non-linear increase in communication complexity that has been amplified by the number of ways the Internet can be accessed and leveraged to create products, services, and derivatives of both based on the unbridled growth in sources of information, channels for accessing it, and tools for manipulating it. The result has been an exponential growth in the complexity of customer expectations. *(Look back at Figure 1.04 for reference.)* The result is a business environment of chaotic, unrealistic expectations enabled by seemingly unlimited technological advancements that every Program Manager must respond to in order to be successful.

Initially, project management was an antidote to the chaos, but the increase in complexity soon left it in need of better tools and thinking, as evidenced by the biennial *Chaos Report*[2]. Scrum, then, appeared as a more robust antidote with a focus on iterative development anchored by customer involvement. Scrum turned out to be 'synthesized genius' that provided a path forward to better results in a chaotic environment, but on a limited scale. It now shares the same challenges as Traditional project management because of the continued non-linear growth of complexity and uncertainty. *(Look back at Figure 1.08 for reference.)*

The very significant work of the thought leaders who developed the advanced business school models and strategies, the *PMBOK® Guide* and the Standards for Program and Portfolio Management, and the Frameworks of Agile drawn from Lean principles has enabled the AIF to be the next step in the evolution of how enterprises drive success by using Programs to deploy the products and services constituents and customers expect. The AIF builds on these foundations by integrating those sources of insight to produce a highly-intelligent way to scale Agile amid the unavoidable complexity, uncertainty, and chaos.

At the same time, it is important for every practitioner reading this to understand that the advanced business school models and strategies, the contributions from Project Management Institute (PMI®), and the various Agile Frameworks – while each being important – are not the sole source of the solution. The solution provided by the AIF is founded on integrative thinking – a "both and" model, not an "either or" model – where the unique integration of the parts is what unlocks success.

The solution employs principles proven to be effective across many industries, not limited to just one, such as software. It will exhibit a comprehensive understanding of the marketplace challenges caused by non-linear complexity and uncertainty. It will apply proven principles supported by a set of tools equipped to cope with the demands of iterative, interactive planning and development while also complying with rigorous Generally Accepted Accounting Principles (GAAP), the demands of PMOs and enterprise leadership, and other similar constraints. It will accomplish all of that by integrating prior insights and adding important new ones regarding the demands of planning for, and responding to, customer requests in an environment where the level of change is historically unprecedented. The AIF will apply proven principles and be a comprehensive model that supports robust, reliable decision-making amid the non-linear distortion caused by the extended time horizons and massive sizes of the desired Program-level results.

The AIF is an elegant solution found at the overlapping intersection of the Agile Frameworks, the *PMBOK® Guide* and its related standards, and strategic business models. *(See Figure 11.02.)*

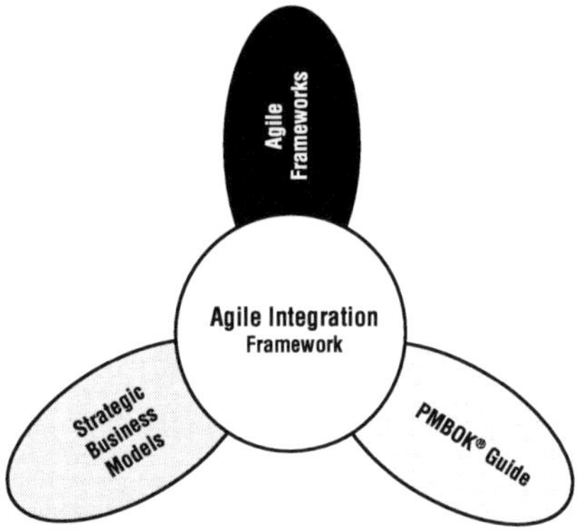

Figure 11.02 | Source of the AIF

The AIF optimizes the whole in a far broader and deeper way than other Frameworks by applying the concept of Defined Granularity to unify the key ideas in the business school models, the PMBOK® Guide, and various Agile approaches to effectively articulate the impact of non-linear distortion caused by time and size. It is a full response to the technical, communication, and customer expectation complexity and uncertainty facing Program Managers and organizations everywhere. *(See Figure 11.03.)*

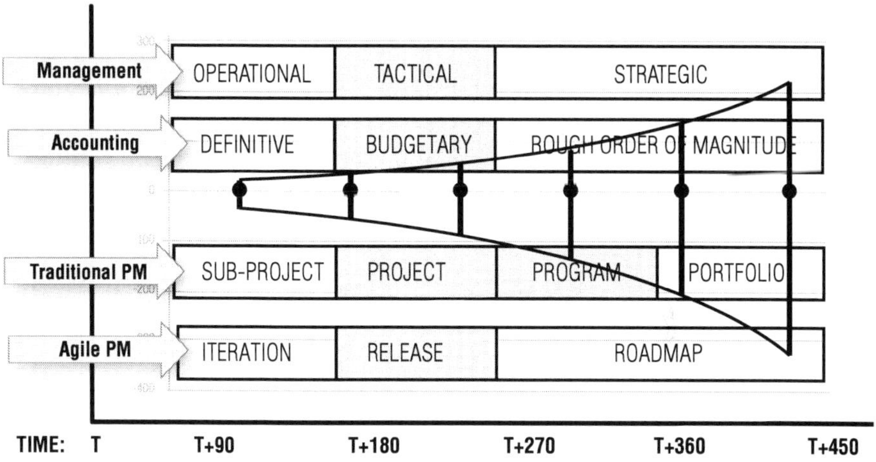

Figure 11.03 | AIF Foundation & Defined Granularity

Defined Granularity means the organization, or the Program Manager, has defined the appropriate time boundaries for applying Rolling Wave decomposition to the requirements whether they are Epics and User Stories or Work Packages and Activities. By effectively articulating the non-linear nature of the unavoidable time and size distortion, often referred to as the Cone of Uncertainty, seen in *Figure 11.03,* the AIF provides Program Managers with a powerful tool for sharing a perspective that can effectively influence and guide stakeholder expectations and help align them to the reality imposed on Program execution.

For example, the proper thresholds for increasing granularity in a ship building enterprise might be 6 months, 1 year and 3+ years, while in a website development business it might be 8 weeks, 16 weeks, and 9+ months (or 2 weeks, 4 weeks and 8 weeks, where granularity might go from medium to fine to super fine!). In most environments, the near-term granularity is definitive, the mid-term granularity is budgetary or Planning Poker, and the long-term granularity is rough-order-of-magnitude (ROM) or Affinity estimates.

Notice that the Cone of Uncertainty, which reflects the level of estimating accuracy possible, is not perfectly symmetrical around the center line. Instead, it shows that the tendency to underestimate is greater than the propensity to overestimate. But more importantly, notice that estimates about items farther in the future, or similarly, items that have a larger scope, are distorted in an unavoidable non-linear way. The distortion is not someone's fault – as if they are too lazy to provide proper scope definition or calculate the size of the sub-assemblies – it is an immutable reality, like the law of gravity.

Program Managers can use the influence gain by demonstrating an expert grasp of this reality to guide stakeholders through decision-making processes, leveraging Defined Granularity. For proper decision-making to occur, granularity must be properly scaled to the purpose of the Program, whether it is organization innovation, product differentiation, or technical stability. It must be properly scaled to the size of the initiative, whether it is project, Program, portfolio, or enterprise. And, granularity must be properly scaled to time horizons, including near-, mid- and long-term. Defined Granularity means setting parameters or standards for framing the Definition of Done to apply to the pertinent facets of granularity that guide Program execution to success. For example, the Definition of Done at the strategic level of granularity cannot be estimates that are accurate to within one day of total effort. Nor can definitive level of granularity estimates be accurate to within one month of total effort and be accepted.

Program Managers must understand that there is a direct correlation between the complexity in scaled Agile and chaos. Scaled Agile generates many powerful insights the Program Manager can leverage, but only when the linkage between ever increasing technological capabilities and the non-linear increase in communication demands is properly managed (i.e., recall the formula for communication paths in a group [n*(n-1)/2]). As the gatekeepers to success in complex chaotic environments where Programs can make, or miss, the best choices for developing systems that delight customers, Program Managers have a critical role to fulfill. The Agile Integrated Framework, covered in this chapter, will provide vital insight into the perception Program Managers must have to succeed.

Benefits / Challenges

Benefits

Integrates Well-Accepted Principles to Influence Stakeholders' Expectations
One of the most important contributions Agile has made to business execution is the rigorous application of a development cadence designed to systematically integrate customer feedback to validate and formalize incremental steps of progress as the truest measure of successfully delivering a final, desirable outcome. That contribution is based on the definitively proven Lean principle of continuous improvement.

Program Managers do well to articulate that the AIF foundation starts with Lean's insistence on continuous improvement to establish credibility with stakeholders. They can then use that influence to explain to stakeholders that Program-level execution requires extending that Lean baseline by adding DevOps' metrics and measurements that may be more technical or abstract, but are nonetheless as important as customer interactions. Having a more comprehensive view and understanding helps guide stakeholders through decision-making processes that leverage Defined Granularity to document the Program purpose, properly size the initiative, and define scaled time-horizons for planning, executing, and reporting.

Having a documented Program purpose properly articulating the size boundaries of the initiative and defining transition points of the scaled time-horizons for planning, executing, and reporting clearly benefits every stakeholder, and especially, the Program Manager.

Leverages the Best-Known Project Management Authority for Significant Credibility
It is an undeniable fact that PMI is the most widely recognized and respected source of project management expertise. Leveraging PMI standards and vocabulary, where appropriate, gives the AIF, and Program Managers and practitioners who use it, implied credibility! That credibility is vitally important because cultivating the stakeholders' perception that scaled Agile is an evolution – not a revolution threatening their existence or requiring them to learn a completely foreign language before they can understand and use it – opens their minds to embrace the inevitable changes it will demand.

The AIF uses and extends key principles, such as Rolling Wave Planning, Progressive Elaboration and Decomposition from the *PMBOK® Guide,*

The Standard for Program Management® and The Standard for Portfolio Management®, as well as the *Agile Practice Guide®*, to create sophisticated insight into planning, executing, and reporting on the Programs using scaled Agile. Doing so decreases stakeholder resistance by reducing the perceived risk.

Industry-Independent Rosetta Stone

The key principles of the AIF are broad and deep enough to provide robust support in environments delivering tangible and intangible products and services. The AIF serves as a Rosetta stone that makes vital communication across stakeholder groups not only possible, but coherent and insightful.

Every experienced Program Manager can testify to the fact that executive, operational, accounting, and technical development stakeholders may as well be speaking different languages, given the number of significant communication breakdowns that typically occur. It is no coincidence that these are the single biggest driver of risk and Program failures.

In 2014, the Gartner Group published research that established the hierarchy of success as People, Processes, Data, then Technology. People either communicate effectively, or they don't, and the probability of Program success hangs in the balance and is dependent upon processes using the correct data that is collected, curated, and delivered by technology in ways that enable decision-makers to act in timely, rational fashions.

The AIF helps the key stakeholders – the people – define a resilient, effective process that aids and supports making deferred commitments at the last responsible moment to optimize the total throughput of the Program.

Unified Model of DevOps and Critical Metrics

Agile's synthesized-genius was to insist on iterative development anchored by customer involvement to define business Value. Unfortunately, and typically, one of the key questions left unanswered by Agile Frameworks has been, "How does the business determine, then parse Value so that it can be delivered in small increments using short Iterations?"

Pursuit of an answer to that question has led to many responses, with DevOps, perhaps, being the most robust. DevOps required extending metrics and measurements beyond simply those from the customer and adding more technical or abstract ones that were equally important. The AIF embraces that more comprehensive understanding and extends it by combining it with insights from the *PMBOK® Guide* to greatly improve stakeholder understanding and acceptance.

When the *PMBOK® Guide Third Edition* was revised to the *PMBOK® Guide Fourth Edition*, one of the most talked about changes was the evolution of the Iron Triangle to the Helluva Hexagon *(Figure 11.04)*.

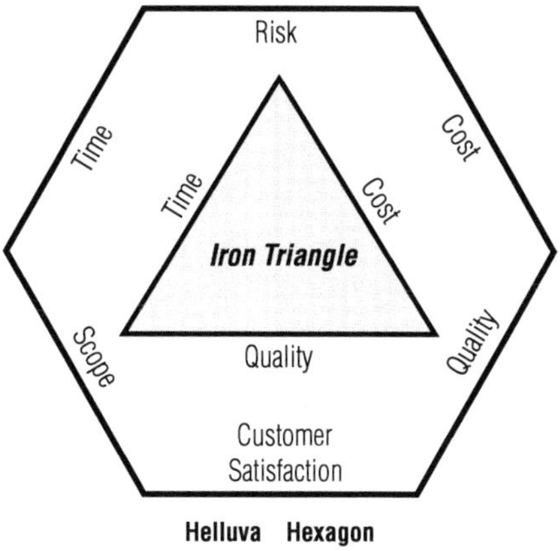

Figure 11.04 | Iron Triangle Evolution

That change implied the centrality of metrics to project and Program success, as illustrated in *Figure 11.05*. It also meant metrics would be compelled to become more sophisticated, but no specific guidance on how to accomplish that feat was provided.

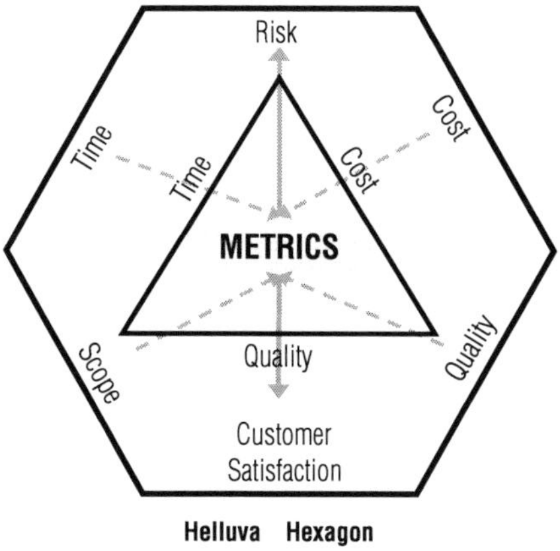

Figure 11.05 | Centrality of Metrics

Perhaps without even knowing it, DevOps wrestled with the same issue. It recognized the need to find a response to the challenge of how experts in the business domain could determine then deconstruct and articulate Value so it could be delivered in small increments using short Iterations. It became clear that the key was to apply quality assurance best practices to create more sophisticated techniques for defining metrics that support both technical practices and product outcomes *(Figure 11.06)*.

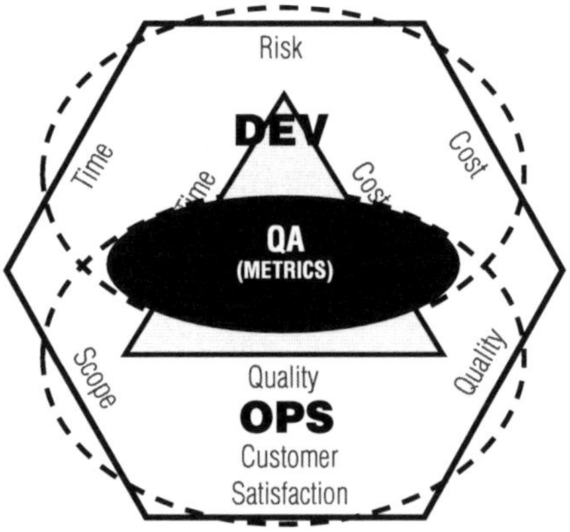

Figure 11.06 | DevOps & the Helluva Hexagon

The AIF empowers Program Managers and practitioners to use more advanced techniques to guide stakeholders to significantly better metrics, producing a profound increase in the probability of Program success by partnering domain experts from all three sources as equals *(Figure 11.07)*.

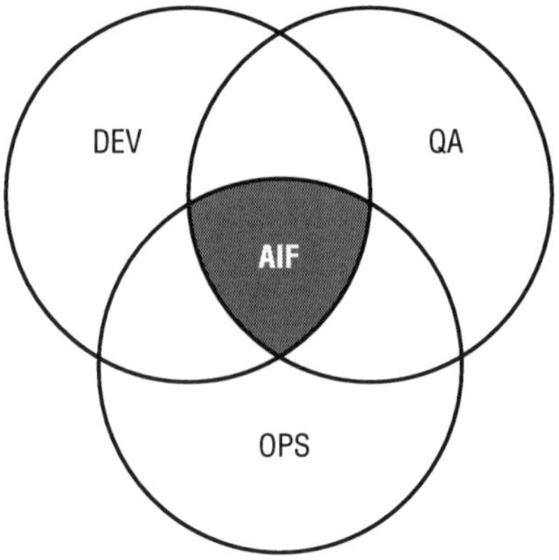

Figure 11.07 | DevOps & the Helluva Hexagon

Includes Proven Options for Budgeting and Advanced Scheduling
As previously mentioned in several other places in this book, one of the major strategic weaknesses of the current Frameworks for scaling Agile is the lack of serious, in-depth guidance on managing budgets and complex, large-scale schedules. By comparison, the *PMBOK® Guide and The Standard for Program Management®* contain sophisticated, proven, detailed insight into how these significant requirements can be properly managed Traditionally.

The AIF treats budgeting and scheduling according to the Lean concept of required, non-value-added activities that should be minimized in order to reduce waste. It applies a light-weight, "barely sufficient" philosophy to combine the guidance of the *PMBOK® Guide, The Standard for Program Management®* and Agile's iterative, incremental development process to define a credible option for Program Managers to use.

Supplies a Useful, Light-weight Context for Big Design Up Front (BDUF)
To succeed in scaling Agile, it is incumbent on Program Managers and other practitioners to recognize the "No BDUF" canard as a ridiculous over-simplification that will lead to Program failure! The AIF is a solution that cultivates an understanding of how to combine granularity for decision-making with support from appropriate technical architecture and engineering, robust planning and scheduling, and sound progress and financial reporting.

Delivers a Powerful Set of Metrics to Track and Improve Quality
The cornerstone of a functional quality management process for Programs and Program Managers is a reliable, light-weight approach that can be consistently applied across the spectrum of Traditional, Agile and hybrid projects. The AIF provides a structure that acknowledges and respects the different needs of the various projects and supports them to advance Program success. Responsible, engaged stakeholders demand a transparent approach that consistently and cogently applies a uniform understanding of how metrics are selected and defined. The metrics must show how they impact Program success and provide direct access for all stakeholders to monitor them. Such metrics are essential in energizing stakeholders' interest in Program progress because they embrace their personal accountability and rights.

Program Managers unleash the power of Lean and empower project teams to exercise continuous improvement, which directly increases the probability of Program success. The chapter on Quality Management details how the AIF simplifies creating and using the right Program metrics to become a minor task the Program Manager facilitates.

Challenges

Accepting the Limitation of Good Enough

Every Program Manager has heard the aphorism, "Perfect is the enemy of good," which is an English version of the saying, "Better is the enemy of good," coined by Voltaire. Agile's insistence on starting with a clear Definition of Done is a safeguard against this trap, yet many stakeholders fall victim to it because Program Managers lack the vigilance or commitment to guide them away from it.

The *PMBOK® Guide* clearly states that the deliverables should be everything, and only, what the stakeholders have 'contracted for', even if the contract is informal and internal. Anything more is commonly referred to as "gold plating" and anything less is a failure to deliver. Agile names the same concept "barely sufficient", suggesting that it is not insufficient nor is it overly sufficient. Lean principles align to this fundamental assumption by insisting on avoiding waste.

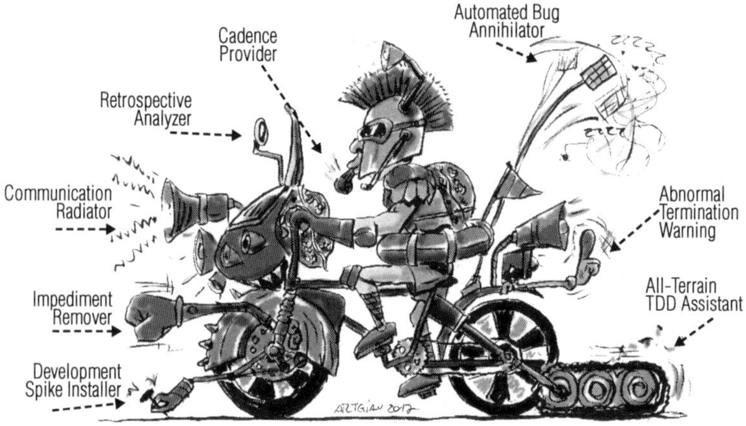

Figure 11.08 | Limitation of Good Enough

Despite the well-known, indisputable truth that "good enough" embodies, getting stakeholders to accept it as the correct standard is a persistent problem. This is a challenge for and duty of the Program Manager to effectively communicate to stakeholders so they accept reasonable and appropriate limits for the deliverables and avoid this pitfall. *Figure 11.08* illustrates the limitation of "good enough". The rider cannot possibly need both a suit of armor and a flotation device! Safety does not require a whistle, horn, three headlights, a fist in front or a disapproving finger (for tailgaters) in back.

Resistance to Proper Testing

Getting stakeholder expectations adjusted and aligned to the challenges of managing a Program, which by definition includes the AIF, requires effectively communicating the true impact of improper testing. As Fred Brooks explained in his classic work, *The Mythical Man-Month*, quality control and testing are non-compressible activities and because they occur at the end of development, the only decision is to do, or not do, proper testing. It is a matter of pure fact that testing cannot suddenly be resized or recalibrated to force-fit it into an arbitrary, unplanned time bucket remaining at the end of the schedule. Program managers must competently address the cost of not testing to overcome stakeholder resistance to appropriate scheduling practices that include proper testing. *Figure 11.09* illustrates the cost of not testing.

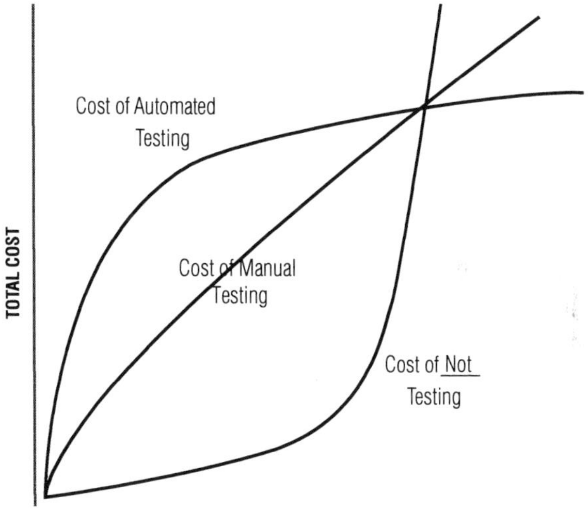

Figure 11.09 | Cost of Not Testing

The How to Make it Work Effectively section of this chapter will address how to manage testing to optimize benefits and minimize costs, but Program Managers must thoroughly understand and be committed to scheduling standards that do not avoid the challenges of maintaining proper testing.

Integrating Traditional and Agile Teams

Integrating Traditional and Agile teams in a Program is unavoidable and therefore Program Managers are required to be skilled at planning-by-design and avoiding planning-by-accident if they want to ensure success. The challenge is that the cadence for Traditional teams is totally different than that used by Agile teams. That doesn't mean it cannot be done! But, it does mean that it is a challenge not to be taken lightly.

In practice, the most important principle is to focus planning on being effective first and efficient second. Identifying the points where effectively delivering Customer Value is possible supplies the context for defining how to efficiently deliver it. Being effective must have priority over being efficient in the development approach.

The following sections will demonstrate how to integrate Traditional and Agile teams by combining the Traditional technique of building logic networks with enhanced Agile practices focused on delivering Customer Value efficiently.

Culture Clash

Just "going Agile" with a team or two invokes fear for many stakeholders. The perceived risk is amplified many times at the thought of scaling Agile. For stakeholders it sounds like Agile aficionados are saying, "Trust me! Just jump. Everything will be OK. Really!"

But, as the saying goes, "Perception is reality!" and perceptions are at the root of the all too common culture clashes that follow. It is of paramount importance for the Program Manager to take seriously the need to demonstrate to stakeholders that Agile is an evolutionary step forward that combines the strengths of Traditional and Agile approaches while integrating Lean principles. Program communication must exhibit serious, well-founded thinking before asking stakeholders to adopt them. It is not enough to imply "Everybody's doing it" or "Everybody says it's right." It is necessary to describe the logic behind each change in terms that validate, for example, the statistical science behind the use of Affinity Estimating and Planning Poker. By explaining the mathematical, logistical, or behavioral science behind the new practices, Program Managers cultivate stakeholders' confidence that careful, cogent thinking has occurred before they are being asked to take the leap.

Coincidentally, the Program Manager also gains a significant level of vitally important influence and gravitas when they exhibit serious, logical, cogent arguments that support the processes they have selected to use to maximize the probability of a successful outcome for the Program.

PMBOK® Guide Framework Requires Dedicated Effort to Master
The AIF makes careful use of key concepts from the *PMBOK® Guide*, which means Program Managers are required to dedicate the time needed to have a professional command of it. The benefit of that investment is the significance of the Program Manager and the ability to influence stakeholders that will follow.

"Continuous effort – not strength or intelligence – is the key to unlocking potential."

– Winston Churchill

Program Managers must invest the time and energy to succeed by committing to seriously analyze, test, and master the *PMBOK® Guide* and the Agile Frameworks and tools they intend to use. Opting in must be a conscious choice, accompanied by a commensurate dedication of time and energy.

Risk of Installing Heavy-Weight Processes that Disable Agile Advantages
Acceptance of the assumption that some or all teams must embrace practices that sub-optimize their micro-dynamic operating environment in order to optimize the whole of the Program or organization must be balanced against the risk of requiring heavy-weight processes that disable the advantages of using an Agile Framework.

Program Managers must maintain the balance between optimizing the whole and sub-optimizing the teams. They must take responsibility for controlling how much process standardization is required and communicate, perhaps even "sell", it to the various stakeholders. They have to push senior management into relenting when too much process standardization is required and pull the team into engaging when the standardization is important or unavoidable, as in regulatory requirements. Doing so will, once again, demand that the Program Manager develop logical, cogent arguments for the requirements and not simply adopt a "Do it because I said so!" attitude. The effort invested in communicating coherent reasoning works to mitigate the risk of malicious obedience occurring when teams become alienated. The return on that investment is very high indeed!

Risk of Budgeting and Scheduling Misalignment
Program Managers do well to realize that a misalignment in the level of granularity being applied to planning versus the level being applied to budgeting or scheduling can create an immense amount of confusion and waste. For example, if senior management makes planning decisions on

a quarterly basis with monthly updates yet requires daily collection and reporting of Program or project activities, the cost of daily reporting is an avoidable waste according to Lean principles.

Another aspect of this problem occurs when Program Managers allow the granularity of details being expressed in planning presentations to create stakeholder confidence based on false precision. For example, when the statistically reliable granularity possible for a large Feature with a long-term expectation for delivery is presented with a definitive-looking estimate during a presentation, it induces irrational stakeholder behavior because their expectation is distorted into thinking the estimate is exact. They then suffer a loss of respect for the Program Manager who was expected to operate more professionally.

Four-Dimensional Communication

As a brilliant associate, Ariane Schmidt, Regional Project Manager with Spokane County and the City of Spokane, observed, this age of technology allows for communication in up to 4 dimensions. One dimensional communication is written. Two-dimensional communication is experienced via YouTube and WebEx technologies. Three-dimensional communication takes place in face-to-face exchanges. Four-dimensional communication occurs asynchronously when technology intermediates conversations, making them independent of time. The use of email combined with mostly unlimited access to the Internet has made this common. Communicating virtually, as it is often called, is, in fact, a fourth dimension that produces by-products like attention fatigue, contextual alignment exhaustion, and, quite often, completely inaccurate and very unrealistic expectations.

Program Managers, and indeed every professional practitioner in the organization, have a duty to remember that electronic communication is a weak, and often fatally flawed, channel for the exchange of complex, technical information. It is a nearly guaranteed-to-fail channel for the nuanced, interdependent conversations required to keep stakeholder expectations aligned with the cycle of discovery and innovation occurring in scaled Agile Programs.

Program-level Attributes

This section aligns with Gartner's hierarchy of People, Processes, Data, and Technology by discussing Roles, Workflows, Ceremonies, and Artifacts.

Roles

The AIF is a scaled Agile Framework so the roles only exist in the environment of a Program, or perhaps an uber large project. The AIF has no application in small scale situations such as single-team projects. It embraces the need for appropriate structure and roles to guide execution in Program settings unlike some Agile Frameworks that appear unable or unwilling to acknowledge that basic truth.

As a Program management Framework, the AIF centers on the Program Manager role and has three roles external to the Program, one role external to the Delivery Team, but internal to the Program, and one role external to the Delivery Team that may be internal or external to the Program. Some roles have only one practitioner per Program, by design, while others have multiple people sharing the role. The roles are shown in *Figure 11.10.*

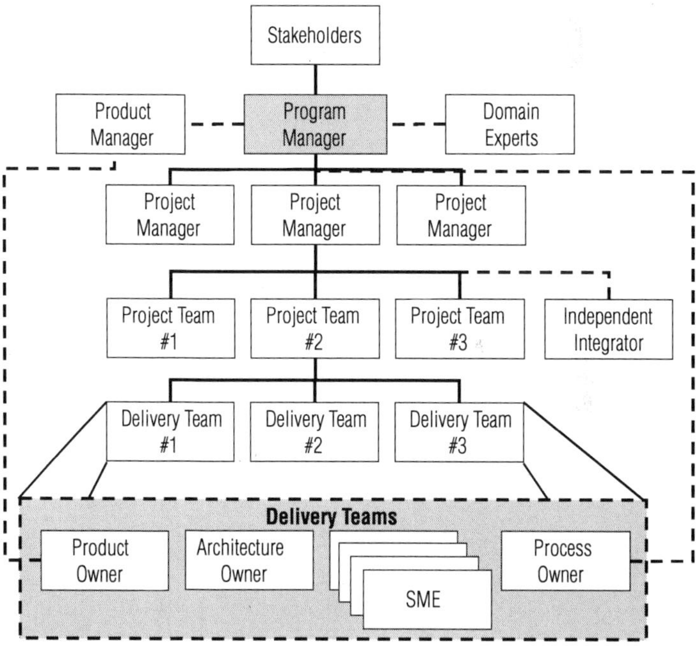

Figure 11.10 | Program Organization Chart

Pivotal Role

Program Manager

Program Manager is, by design, a role that is filled by a single person. Their highest responsibility and chief domain of concern is the people in the other roles. Both Gartner's hierarchy of success and the experience of any senior leader or seasoned Program Manager can confirm that people are the source of the greatest innovations and break-throughs as well as the deepest failures and challenges, making them the top priority.

Related to that, without the Program Manager acting as the champion of both the actual change and communication related to it, everyone – from the enterprise leadership team to the security guard watching the parking lot – will default to an expectation of failure.

Program Managers serve their people by facilitating planning events, synchronization and communication ceremonies, and responding in a timely way to issue escalations. They provide coaching, when appropriate, to continuously cultivate a deeper understand of Lean principles and application of Agile practices and mindset. Doing so improves the Program Manager's ability to successfully monitor and interpret progress reporting against the set metrics.

The Program Manager closely aligns with both the Product Manager for defining, refining, and communicating the Vision and goal of the Program and the Project Managers to optimize discovery, learning, and execution. Together, the Program and Product Managers maintain the Freeway Plan, Roadmap, and Program Backlog, which cover long-, mid-, and short-term needs with proper granularity.

Three External Roles

Stakeholders

Stakeholders include customers, end users, sponsors, organizational managers, and anyone else clearly impacted by the Program, or who perceives themselves to be impacted. They may be positive champions of the change, product or service or they may be negative resistors and detractors. Regardless of their persuasion, they all benefit from properly aligned communication and can contribute insights during various ceremonies and improve the probability of Program success. Therefore, they must be properly engaged.

Domain Experts

Domain experts are far more common in Programs than in smaller Agile situations because scaled Agile environments are complicated domains with frequent cases of non-linear uncertainty. Domain experts typically serve as outside counselors for the Program and Product Managers, supplying expertise and advice on matters atypical of "general" knowledge, such as medical billing, aerospace engineering, and atomic power generation. These experts are utilized, typically, on an as-needed basis although, for some Programs, having them on retainer is the preferred option.

Product Manager

The Product Manager speaks for the business and stakeholders, communicating decisions about the scope and direction directly to the Program and Project Managers, and indirectly to the Delivery Team. They communicate customer needs by outlining and refining the Vision of the portfolio in the Freeway Plan, which they control. They specify desired results by building the Roadmap and Program Backlog together with the Program Manager.

The Product Manager communicates customer needs with granularity appropriate to the planning time-horizon so the Features and capabilities that fulfill those needs can be developed. They participate in validating the results from the Delivery Team during Product Review Meetings so accurate assessments of the progress towards successful fulfillment can be made.

As the leader of the Product Owner Team they facilitate periodic Product Team Gatherings to integrate the assessments from the Product Review Meetings with the Roadmap, Program Backlog, Epic Work Packages (EWPs), and even significant User Stories from individual projects to create a "compiled" view of the Program as a unified body of work.

Together with the Program Manager, they prioritize the Program Backlog to align the work with factors like business Value, near term opportunities, and availability of architectural designs, engineering specifications, or required infrastructure. Doing so commands a solid understanding of a useful Definition of Done, therefore the Product Manager and Program Manager involve Domain Experts, as needed, to design the Freeway and Roadmap and write the descriptions of FFCs that must flow down successfully for the Delivery Team to succeed.

The Product Manager serves, with the Program Manager, as the guide keeping the Program tracking positively forward towards the goals of the customer and organization. They must maintain a cohesive, high-functioning relationship because they succeed, or fail, together.

One Internal Program Role, External to the Delivery Team

Project Manager

Project Managers are responsible, first, for the people within their domain, and second, for the processes used for execution, without losing sight of the Product deliverables. Processes serve the Delivery Team to enable the delivery of the agreed upon results, which is the primary responsibility of the Delivery Team. By focusing on the people and the process, in the priority prescribed by the Gartner Group research, Project Managers ensure success for the project and, ultimately, the Program.

Project Managers sometimes integrate specialists comparable to Domain Experts. The specialists may be business analysts clarifying requirements or facilitators to help with ceremonies. They can also be technical experts who help identify and assess designs, impediments, or risks. Sometimes they are experts in team dynamics and interpersonal communication, used to improve team functionality.

Project Managers plan and guide execution and report progress using information radiators populated with information from the Delivery Team. They manage escalations and remove impediments or blockers when needed.

Delivery Team Roles

The Delivery Team is a set of project-specific teams. The teams may be organized and executing based on Traditional practices or they may be organized and executing as cross-functional Agile teams. Regardless, their focus is wholly centered on delivering outcomes that can be integrated into Features, Functions, and Capabilities the customer Values, as defined by the Product Manager in the Freeway Plan and elaborated on in the Roadmap, Release Plan, and Program Backlog.

The project teams participate in defining proposed Milestones for Traditional project teams and Iteration Backlogs for Agile project teams, drawn from the Program Backlog and aligned to fulfill the Release Plan. Teams plan as a Delivery Team unit, regardless of the methodology they are using, during the Bi-Monthly Release Planning and Iteration WAG Planning ceremonies. They plan independently during the Iteration SWAG ceremony.

The planning ceremonies create a segmented but unified strategy for developing deliverables, following a synchronized cadence that leads to a solution demonstration at the pre-agreed time of the Integration Point

Review (IPR). The IPR interfaces the Traditional Milestones and the Agile Iterations together for stakeholders to see and respond to solution deliverables and provide actionable-insight on the outcome.

Product Owner
The Product Owner is an agent of the Product Manager and part of a team or teams. They usually come from a business or business-analyst background, but also have technical skills, often from the quality assurance and testing domain.

As the acting 'voice of the customer,' they are responsible for making decisions that clarify the detailed nature of each component of the Iteration or Milestone deliverable. They are the liaison between Product Owners on other teams, escalating and expediting issues with the Product Manager to keep them from becoming impediments or obstacles.

Typically, they meet regularly as part of the Product Owner Team, bringing back valuable information to their team and socializing it as appropriate.

Process Owner
The Process Owner is an agent of the Program Manager and part of a team or teams. They often come from a Lean, Agile, Traditional or CMMI technical background. Having solution integration experience is particularly valuable for them, but they must also have well-developed coaching and mentoring skills. They act on behalf of the Program Manager to ensure their "Processes serving People" goal is being met.

They are responsible for clarifying process requirements while supporting allowable, needed flexibility and communicating team needs to the Program Manager. They guide the team on creating and maintaining a culture of integrity and personal safety, vital to the core principle of incremental progress at an infinitely-sustainable pace. Without a sustainable pace, due to the long time-horizons and stressful complexity of Program deliverables, Programs fail from high attrition rates that deprive the Program of longevity of critical participants powering the development cycle.

The Process Owners liaise across the program with the Process Owners on other teams to manage cross-project issues, escalating and expediting issues with the Program Manager when needed to keep them from undermining the team. Typically, Process Owners meet regularly as part of the Program Manager Team, bringing back vital updates to their team and integrating it as needed.

Architecture Owner
Architecture Owners are responsible for the architecture and engineering decisions made by the team. Their decisions are guided by governance standards, typically established by a department of the organization outside the Program. They make decisions about, and are responsible for, the team deliverables being successfully integrated into the solution for IPR ceremonies and final Release or roll-out.

The Architecture Owner is critical to Program success because no matter how well the deliverable works in the micro-environment of a project, it will be judged by how well it integrates to the macro-environment of the Program. To fulfill their responsibility, they must guide development for their team and effectively communicate with other infrastructure owners on their behalf. They must have highly developed technical skills in the domain of the project and Program deliverables as well as the ability to accurately communicate the vision of their team's development approach to others.

Architecture Owners must also successfully assist the Product Manager and Program Manager in decomposing the Roadmap and Release Plan into Features, Functions, and Capabilities by giving guidance on the dependencies impacting the prioritization of work items. They act as the liaison with any external integrator or system provider.

Typically, Architecture Owners meet regularly as part of their department's Center of Excellence (CoE), and often voluntarily participate in Communities of Practice (CoP), both inside and outside the organization, to stay current on organizational governance and developing industry trends and tools. They bring back useful improvements to advance the maturity of their team's integration capabilities.

Subject Matter Experts (SME)
Team members are indisputably the most important part of the entire Program organization. Ultimately, every other role is designed to enable, protect, cultivate, and value the team members because that's where the magic happens! "The best laid plans of mice and men oft go awry[3]" if the team is not properly empowered and informed to harness their personal gifts to synthesize their genius for solving problems and producing desirable outcomes.

As part of the Delivery Team, SMEs are selected based on their specific skills for creating the solution the customer envisions and it is, therefore, impossible to specify the required technical skills in a book. It is possible, however, to say that their individual success, and that of their team, is far more dependent on their interpersonal awareness and skills – the subject of a myriad of books in another genre entirely.

Team members need to have the "right stuff" and be supported in using it!

One Internal or External Program Role, External to the Delivery Team

Independent Integrator

Depending on the size, maturity, and strategic business model of the organization, Independent Integrators can be internal or external. Many Fortune 500 companies and similar-size public agencies and military commands have internal Independent Integrators. Most smaller organizations use external professionals to supply those needs. In either case, it is usually one group or company that provides the expertise and services.

The Independent Integrator's System Team specializes in providing and configuring the platform, such as cloud-based servers, or designing and building the environment, such as manufacturing lines in a production facility. They work with the Project Team, under the watchful eye of the Program Manager and contracting authority, to ensure the system is ready and will not cause lag time for integration and Product release. Usually, the System Team also interfaces with governance or release managers to ensure compliance with regulatory or organizational requirements. The System Team supplies the setting the Integrator Team uses to aggregate the deliverables from the project teams into a working and tested solution that fulfills the Program goal and is prepared for release.

The Independent Integrator may be one or more people who assemble the subcomponents and subsystems into the overall solution and are responsible for constructing a cohesive solution that expresses an entire system, or a major portion of it, being released into production. To achieve agility at scale in such complex domains, sophisticated, independent testing must occur and usually it must operate in real time, parallel to the integration.

Workflow

Elegant sophistication often looks basic to the uninformed. For example, $E = MC^2$ looks unimportant to the uninitiated, but clearly its simplicity belies its sophistication. While no one is suggesting that the AIF has Einstein's level of gift embedded in it, do not be distracted by its deceptive simplicity. If Lean, Scrum, and the explosion of Agile Frameworks have proven anything, it is that in environments of high-complexity and high-uncertainty, the most reliable path to progress and systematic solution development is discovery and learning. At a high level, the picture of a successfully scaled Agile Framework looks like *Figure 11.11.*

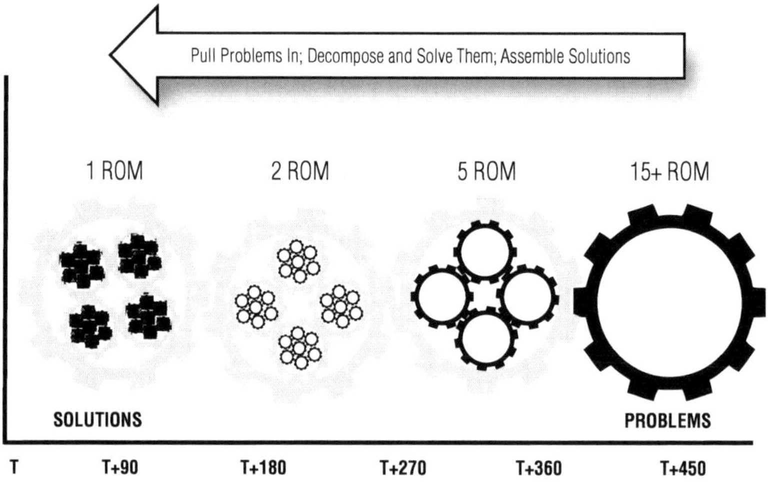

Figure 11.11 | Systematic Solution Development

The empirical approach of transparency, inspection, and adaptation is the principle underpinning the AIF. It is an approach where problems are made transparent by decomposing them into more and more granular components. In the *PMBOK® Guide,* those levels of granularity are defined as Objective, Phase, Work Package, Activity, and Task. The equivalent levels in Agile are most commonly described as Product, Theme, Epic, Story, and Task. What they share in common is the perspective that large things with low granularity, akin to boulders, are at the top level and very small things with high granularity, akin to gravel, are at the bottom level. In between are things in various stages of transformation, akin to stones that are large but not boulders, medium, and small but not gravel. *(See Figure 11.12.)*

The Work Decomposition Structure (WDS) in the AIF starts with information from senior leadership and organizational governance guidance, provided by a PMO or equivalent mechanism. The senior leaders define the composition and priorities of the Portfolio and organizational governance guides the process of defining product deliverables. In Book 3 of *The Agile Almanac,* practices for effectively doing that and enabling the

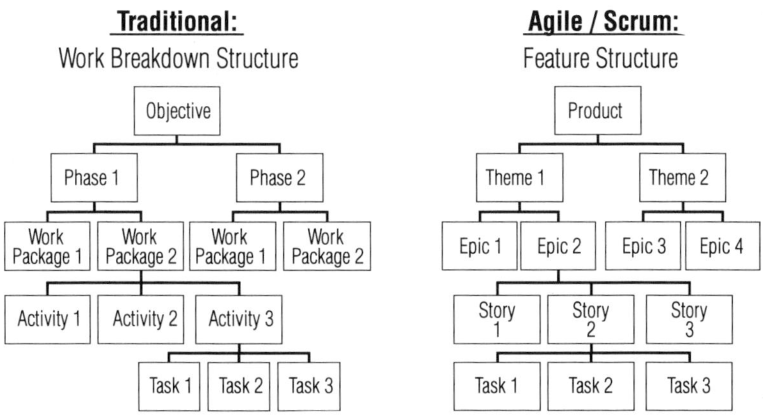

Figure 11.12 | Work Breakdown and Feature Structures

Agile Enterprise will be covered, but that is outside the scope of Book 2. The WDS in the AIF begins with a defined Program scope, one or more of which aggregate into the Product Deliverable. *(See Figure 11.13.)*

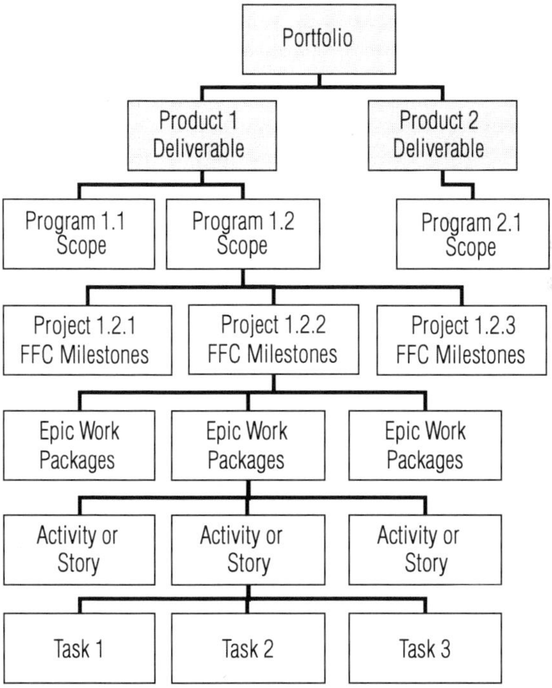

Figure 11.13 | Work Decomposition Structure

The AIF workflow begins with fracturing the Program scope into Feature, Function, and Capability (FFC) clusters that are natural classifications such as engine, transmission, and differential for automobiles, or propulsion, stabilization, and vector control for rockets. Think again, of boulders being split into large stones that will undergo additional fragmentation in order to refine the details about them. As the workflow progresses it creates more and more transparency, enabling inspection in the form of analysis and testing so that discovery leads to learning and innovative adaptation.

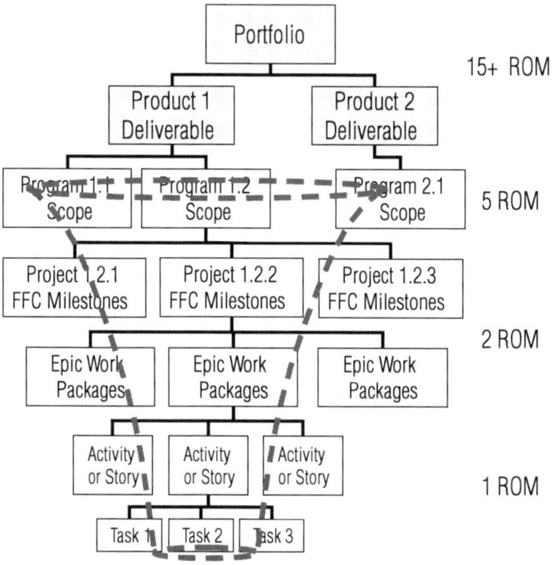

Figure 11.14 | WDS and AIF Workflow Results

Decomposition transforms Program-level information, with a range of potential variance in outcomes of perhaps 5 ROM, into details with perhaps a single ROM of potential variance. *(See Figure 11.14.)* The critical improvement is that Program-level problems that could not be developed become work items that can be iteratively constructed in such a way that discovery and learning leads to the creation of clusters of partial answers that can be assembled into a useful solution. *(See Figure 11.15.)* The process reduces the boulders into gravel that can then be mixed with water, sand, and cement and reformed to become the foundation of a large skyscraper.

The first round of decomposition results in defining the FFC Milestones. FFC Milestones can be used in Traditional project execution as schedule Milestones to measure progress or in Agile project execution as the elements of the Themes that lead to a successful Program outcome.

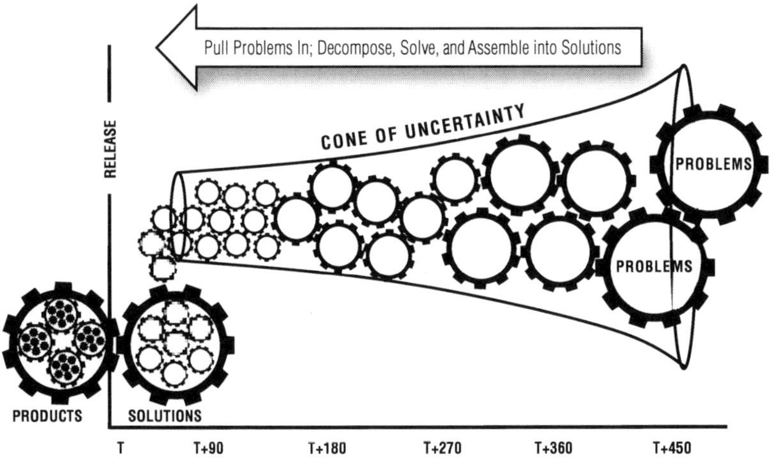

Figure 11.15 | Workflow Results Over Time

But decomposition does not operate in a vacuum. It serves the purpose of creating plans and schedules that will deliver the building blocks of customer Value. It is an essential step, but without care, the Program can fall victim to a common and insidious assumption that is always imprecise and often downright wrong, as explained in the CVLN section.

Customer-Value Logic Network (CVLN)

The first Iteration of planning uses the FFC Milestones to create a Customer-Value Logic Network (CVLN) that ensures effective choices regulate efficient ones. It is common wisdom that "Doing the right thing is more important than doing things right!" Yet, many Program Managers appear to do planning with the insidious assumption that everything stated in the Program scope will be completed. And if everything will be completed, the logical way to plan their Programs is to design it for the highest efficiency. However, when any group of Program Managers is polled about the percentage of Programs that end up cutting scope in order to achieve compliance with deadlines and budgets, the response is always greater than 85 percent. That means that Program Managers know that effectivity is paramount, but 85 percent of their plans are prepared as if it is not. This is a simple-sounding but extremely important step because it addresses one of the biggest problems in project management – being forced to make major, indiscriminate reductions in scope because of an impending budget or delivery date constraint. Since development team efficiency rarely aligns with the customer's value-hierarchy, when money or time is running out, the remaining scope invariably contains Features, Functions, and Capabilities of greater Value than some that have already been completed. Ultimately, to meet the deadline, the customer is forced to sacrifice items of greater Value than those previously delivered, leaving them very unhappy!

The CVLN is the governance tool that corrects that mistake. Creating the CVLN is a simple – but not easy – process of writing the name, and brief description if needed, of each FFC Milestone on a sticky note then arranging them as a flowchart from left to right, starting with the one having the highest customer Value and proceeding to the one having the lowest. The process identifies the logical order of development from a customer-Value perspective, knowing that the development work will be staged for efficiency later.

The process is simple, but the sophistication can be increased if the CVLN planning participants are willing to analyze the FFC Milestones to see if they can be split or combined to create a more useful view of how customer Value is created. At times, the added granularity renders amazing insight. In any case, the FFC Milestones should not number more than 30 and usually total around 25. Book 1 of *The Agile Almanac* also included a discussion on how to use FFC to do initial planning that may be useful to review.

The process is simple, but determining and agreeing upon the amount of customer Value in a specific FFC Milestone is not easy. There are numerous ways to assess the amount of customer Value and, regardless of which is used, the biggest risk is that senior stakeholders will subvert the process to prioritize their preferences regardless of the customer Value present. The second biggest risk is that they will not commit to being available to participate appropriately.

A variation of the CVLN creation process is to have the participants brainstorm a list before creating the sticky notes, as shown in *Figure 11.16*.

Only after the value drivers have been defined should considerations of efficiency enter the planning discussion. The need for this level of clarity can be seen in the historical evolution of Enterprise Resource Planning (ERP) systems and the best practice for their deployment.

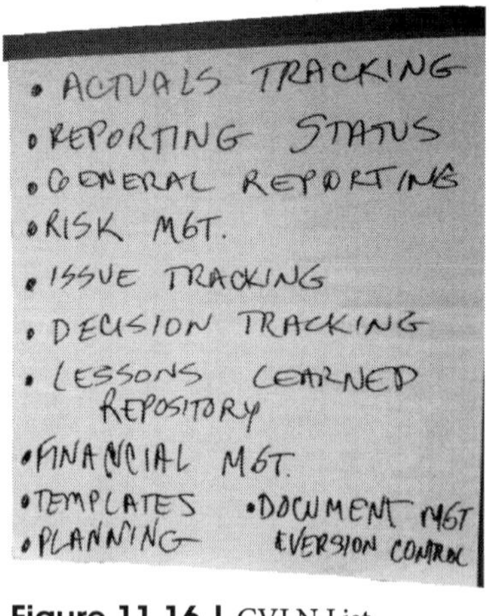

Figure 11.16 | CVLN List

Back in the mid-1990s when ERP systems were the magic panacea for company growth, the best practice was to implement as a "Big Bang!" It meant going live, for example, on January 1 and abandoning all legacy systems at the same time, on the assumption that the new system would work properly and do everything the old system did, but better. After catastrophic losses at Hershey Chocolate[4] and Whirlpool Appliances made the national news, the new best practice became Rolling Wave. Big Bang was highly efficient but potentially fatal. Rolling Wave was effective for avoiding lethal outcomes while also being efficient.

Changing "Big Bang" Best Practice to "Rolling Wave"
When a big ERP project involves the global reputations of the system creator, SAP, its flagship product, SAP R/3, a publicly traded company, Whirlpool, and its implementation partners, Deloitte Consulting in New York, a lot of finger-pointing can be expected when things go sour.

Whirlpool, Deloitte, and SAP made a risky implementation decision to go live with the SAP R/3 Enterprise Resource Planning (ERP) system using a "Big Bang" approach knowing red flags had been identified. The Big Bang choice was aligned to the "Go Live" event over the 3-day Labor Day holiday, and fixing the red flags would have caused the launch to miss the holiday weekend.

The outcome was a crippled shipping system that had been scheduled to go live on September 7th, but significant problems, reportedly, dogged the system until November 1st. The Big Bang best practice caused appliances to be stuck in warehouses, leaving stores with delays of up to eight-weeks for receiving new inventory. It caused major problems for many smaller stores who got a significant percentage of their income from selling Whirlpool appliances. As the stores started recommending competitors' products to their customers simply because that is what they had in stock, the loss of sales negatively impacted revenue for Whirlpool.

An SAP AG senior vice president reportedly blamed the client, Deloitte declined to comment, and Whirlpool refused to discuss the details of the catastrophe, saying only that the company would hit its fourth-quarter earnings targets.

Whirlpool, like Hershey before it, became the face of complicated ERP implementations failing. Soon after, Big Bang got replaced by Rolling

Wave as the industry best practice.

For more information, see *SAP: Whirlpool's rush led to shipping snafus*, by Stacy Collett, Computerworld, November 5, 1999

Program Managers must be as adamant as needed in getting the right stakeholders to put the proper effort into defining the CVLN because it governs Program planning and execution, for better or worse.

Execution Logic Network

Once the CVLN has established the effectiveness drivers, the second round of decomposition begins to define how to maximize efficiencies. The FFC Milestones are fractured into their constituent parts, the Epic Work Packages (EWP), and used to build the Execution Logic Network (ELN). The resulting EWPs should not exceed 125 or the ELN becomes unmanageable. It is usually better to limit the number to 100 or less. When the team of planners is new to the process, it is wise to use smaller batches so the process can be learned and mastered before the complexity driven by larger quantities is introduced.

Each EWP is written on a separate sticky note, using a well-recognized name, and placed on a whiteboard or wall. The sticky notes are arranged from left to right, indicating timing from start to finish, while showing the logical order of the development process. The predecessor and successor relationships between the Tasks are shown by drawing arrows between the activities.

The EWP stickies describe their attributes with granularity for planning that transforms the long-term time-horizon into the more detailed mid-term horizon. The information elements include name, brief description of desired outcome, known conditions of satisfaction, and any other critical content used when assessing where it fits in the development process. Because the granularity of the details increases as EWPs are decomposed into Activities or Stories, then ultimately into Tasks, summarized information at this level will still effectively focus the dialogue needed to identify the logical approach and align development work with the goal.

Each sticky contains one, and only one, EWP. *(See Figure 11.17.)*

It is important that the arrows be carefully and clearly indicated, and that the resulting network graph not look like the result of a failed game of Pictionary. There are two reasons for this. First, the ELN is an influential tool for

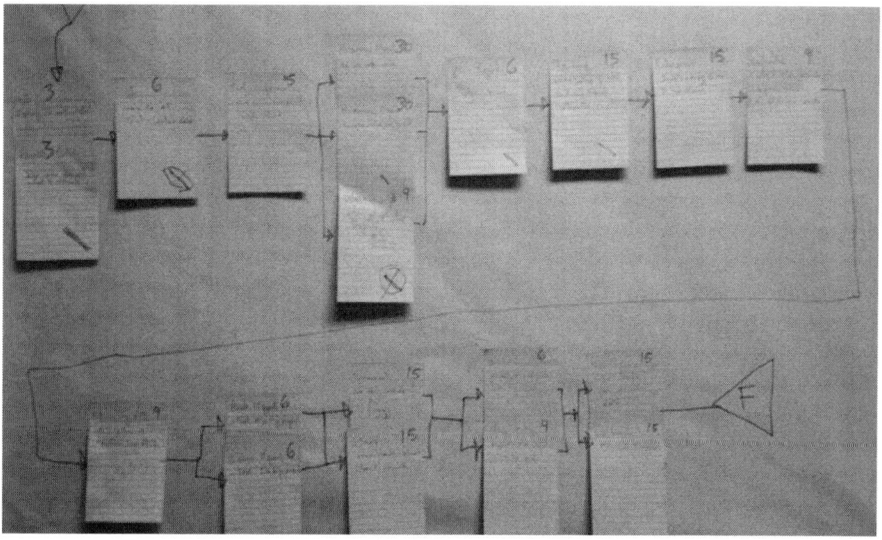

Figure 11.17 | Execution Logic Network (ELN)

stakeholder communication, but it is only credible if it looks well-conceived. Second, the EWP will be subjected to Affinity Estimating and the values assigned will be added to the sticky notes so that the ELN can be subjected to Critical Path analysis.

Affinity Estimating

The EWPs must include a size assigned to them. This is where explaining it in a book gets a bit tricky. Some teams prefer to size the EWPs then create the ELN, and some teams prefer the reverse. Usually the determining factor is whether the order of development impacts the assumed scope of the EWP. In *Figure 11.18*, the whiteboard, where the EWPs were sized before creating the ELN, can be seen.

Figure 11.18 | Affinity Sizing

Size is decided using the Affinity approach. Affinity Estimating is a technique used to quickly size EWPs, typically to plan a CVLN or ELN for a project, Program, portfolio, Roadmap, or Release, as shown in *Figure 11.19.* Later, those sizes are refined, using Planning Poker, to produce more granularity.

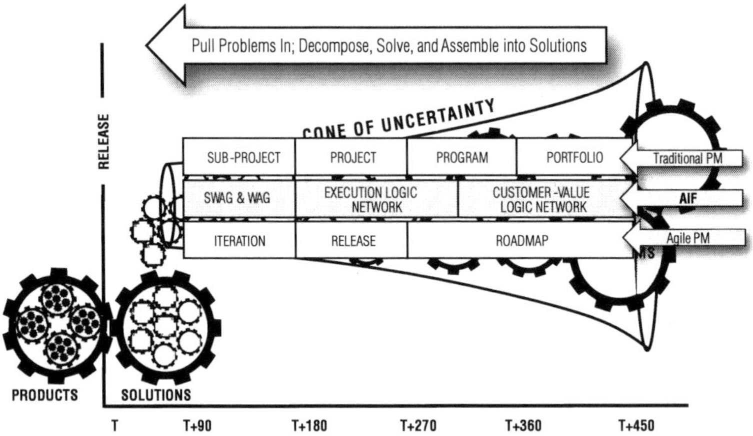

Figure 11.19 | Correlation of Estimating Time Horizons

Affinity Estimating, or Affinity Sizing, leverages the human ability for determining the relative size of things and avoids the human limitation for assessing the time required to complete something, especially in the abstract. It compares work items to each other to assess their relative size.

The Affinity Estimating process organizes the EWP stickies according to their relative size by sorting them into columns labeled with a scale – typically, the "T-Shirt" scale of extra-small (XS) to extra-large (XL), plus a Parking Lot column. The leader usually populates the columns with their first guess at the relative sizes and the team takes over and finalizes them.

The process follows these simple instructions given to the participants:

- All of the participants will approach the workspace together.
- They will work in complete silence and simultaneously assess the first draft currently posted with each participant evaluating the proposed size of each EWP sticky relative to the others, based on the complexity, effort, and uncertainty involved with delivering it.
- If the proposed size seems correct to the participant, they will leave it alone.

- If the proposed size seems incorrect to the participant, they will move it to the correct column, and place a small diagonal line in its bottom right corner. If a diagonal line already exists there, they will add a second line, perpendicular to the first, such that an "X" will be created. If an X already exists, the participant must leave it or move it in the Parking Lot column.
- When everyone is satisfied, as indicated by the cessation of cards being moved, the entire team will step back from the workspace.
- A team discussion will follow to size the stickies in the Parking Lot because when a sticky ends up there, it usually indicates a lack of clarity about the scope of work on it.
- The last step taken is to discuss each participant's thought process when they applied the sizes then convert that to its assigned numerical value by writing it on the sticky note.

The more shared time spent in the domain, the more likely it is that all participants thought Small was 2 days, Medium was 5 days, and so forth. The reason that the process uses t-shirt sizes is to minimize the waste that occurs in the form of arguing over whether a task is 2 or 3 days, or 2 or 3 weeks, or 2 or 3 months, etc. Arguments, at this point in the planning cycle, are a negative investment in false precision and should be avoided. There is less disagreement about whether something is small, medium, or large. The definition of each t-shirt size can be agreed upon much faster once all members agree on the size of each EWP. At this point, the goal is planning-level accuracy aligned to the Defined Granularity guidelines. The purpose is to get a basic plan in place so better planning can occur for the EWPs on the near-term time horizons.

Once the ELN contains EWP stickies with sizes assigned to them, the next step can occur.

Critical Path Analysis

Once the ELN has been created it can be analyzed using the Critical Path Method (CPM) to evaluate the network and turn information about EWP relationships into knowledge about time constraints. Understanding and managing the critical path allows a Program Manager to allocate resources so they can best help Delivery Teams stay on schedule while balancing the cost and value of those trade-offs. (Because CPM has been written about extensively elsewhere, its value will be highlighted here with only a summary of the technique. The summary is quite technical and dense but also important. If unfamiliar with CPM, investing time in expanding professional command of it is recommended.)

A typical ELN has activities happening simultaneously in several different facets of the Program. These different activities often occur on separate "logic paths" running both sequentially and in parallel. In addition, cross-project dependencies create a potentially intricate web of dependencies. CPM clarifies two vital pieces of information so they can be communicated to the Delivery Team and other stakeholders. First, which activities, if allowed to slip, will cause a directly related slip in the completion of the Program and, second, which activities can directly improve the total performance of the Program if different resources are applied to them, or if dependencies are changed by altering the development approach.

CPM uses the term Float to accomplish the job of identifying the critical path. Float is the time difference between when an activity, not on the critical path, is scheduled for completion and the latest allowable time it can be completed without negatively impacting the finish of the Program. When the scheduled time of completion equals the latest allowable time, Float equals zero. Therefore, any slip in completing the activity directly impacts the Program completion date.

Starting with the ELN, the process of applying CPM occurs in five steps. First, convert the ELN to a CPM flowchart. Second, conduct a 'Forward Pass' calculation. Third, conduct a 'Backward Pass' calculation. Fourth, calculate Float. And, fifth, evaluate the Critical Path.

To convert the logic network into a CPM flowchart, each sticky must have room for numbers to be added to the left, middle and right along the top and bottom of the sticky. *(See Figure 11.20.)*

EARLY START DATE	DURATION	EARLY FINISH DATE
NAME (and other info, as needed)		
LATE START	FLOAT	LATE FINISH

Figure 11.20 | CPM Sticky Note

The center section includes information such as Activity name and owner, and other brief information to make clear what it is. The number of the Affinity size is written in the top center cell, and typically called Duration. The remaining information – Early Start Date, Early Finish Date, Late Start Date, Late Finish Date, and Float – will be filled in as the calculations are completed.

Early Start and Early Finish dates are computed during the Forward Pass calculation that applies the equation Early Start plus Duration equals Early Finish (ES + D = EF) through the entire network from the start to the finish. The result of each calculation is recorded in the appropriate cell of each sticky.

The Late Start and Late Finish dates are computed next, as part of the Backward Pass calculation that occurs in a reverse-sequential order through the entire network. The Backward Pass calculation applies the equation Late Finish minus Duration equals Late Start (LF - D = LS) and the result of each calculation is recorded in the appropriate cell of each sticky.

Lastly, Float is computed using the equation Late Finish minus Early Finish equals Float (LF - EF = F). The calculation for each activity is independent of every other activity. Therefore, the Float computations may be done sequentially or in parallel. The result of each is recorded in the appropriate cell of each sticky.

With the three results recorded, the critical path can be identified, by tracing the path of activities with zero Float, and more importantly, evaluated by the Program Manager. The normal convention is to highlight the arrows connecting the zero Float activities with a red marker.

For most Program Managers, by the time the Program has been assigned to them, a delivery date has been established by the customer and marketing team or a senior stakeholder. That is why it is critically important to test the probable accuracy of the expressed and implied assumptions that went into choosing the delivery date. As is often the case, both the date and budget are unrealistic, making it vital for the Program Manager to present the results of a rational analysis in the hopes of influencing the expectations of those key stakeholders.

Common risk factors reviewed include whether the Program has multiple critical paths because when many EWPs are time critical, it automatically increases the inherent risk. A closely related risk is the number of activities with very low Float, referred to as "near critical" activities. Additionally, the number of integration points or Milestones on the critical path is evaluated. Each integration point carries an inherent risk that rises in direct proportion to the number of paths that merge. Another risk factor to assess is whether too many activities on the critical path are the responsibility of the Delivery Team on a particular project.

Three big advantages emerge from the work done to develop the ELN and run an initial set of critical path calculations. First, communicating with stakeholders shifts from a battle of differing opinions to a discussion of the implications of the mathematical analysis. That shift raises the influence of the Program Manager so the Program can be programmed for success (pardon the pun, it was hard to resist). Second, the manual flowchart can be used as a draft to error check the results produced by the software. This is important because a simple slip at the keyboard can produce data entry errors that incorrectly define the relationships between predecessors and successors, and remain undetected until they have induced grave problems in Program execution. Third, decisions made about software configuration drive the results delivered by the software, and ELN and CPM evaluation provide critical insight for the Program Manager to understand the impact of those configuration settings. By comparing the manual results with the computer-generated ones, the Program Manager can confirm that the software is processing the data in the way expected.

Defined-Granularity Scheduling

Defined-granularity schedules are created by applying a Rolling Wave of decomposition and the CPM analysis just described to the appropriate planning levels, at regularly scheduled time intervals. The process begins at the enterprise level with Annual or Semi-Annual Strategic or Freeway planning, flowing down to CVLN and ELN planning as part of quarterly Roadmap planning, and bi-monthly Release planning, then finally reaching Iteration and Milestone planning, at both the WAG (Wild Ass Guess) and SWAG (Scientific WAG) levels.

As part of building the various schedules, work items are sized using Affinity Estimating, then Planning Poker, and finally estimated in the Traditional sense of Definitive estimates, as defined by organizational governance and the PMO. The estimates start with five shades of granularity, progress to 50 and reach final, high-definition granularity with thousands of shades of grey. Each cycle adds more granularity, and comes at an increasing cost, so additional cycles should only be applied if the added cost is justified by the needs of decision makers and the decision-making process.

Progressively Elaborated Budgets
Budgets are progressively elaborated, using the defined-granularity schedules to increase the reliability of financial forecasts. They incur the same added cost for data collection as granularity increases. So, if senior management makes planning decisions on a quarterly basis with monthly updates, budgeting and reporting of Program or project activities should be calibrated at the same level to avoid waste, according to Lean principles.

Ceremonies

Agile ceremonies, or meetings as they are called in the Traditional world, are a double-edged sword – high-value when done right, resource drain when not. Ceremonies are in the category of things where less is more. Consider this when reading the explanation of each of the following ceremonies.

Annual Freeway Planning
As depicted in *Figure 11.19*, the CVLN is applied for Agile Roadmaps and Traditional Programs and portfolios to ensure effective choices govern efficient ones. The CVLN is a governance tool that solves a problem present in many of the other scaled Agile Frameworks –poorly defined long-range planning. It guards against being forced to make major, indiscriminate reductions in scope that violate the customer's value-hierarchy because of an impending budget or time constraint.

The Annual Freeway Planning ceremony is when stakeholders, with a vested interest in strategic success, formalize the budgetary and resource commitments creating the Freeways that connect and support the Roadmaps. As with the CVLN, it is a simple, but not easy, process because the outcome must be political transparency about priorities. Transparency is achieved by avoiding the "What's the priority?" game, where everything is a "Gold 'A' #1" priority, and getting to the brass tacks of *"Show me the money!"* discussions. When done correctly, it stops confusion from flowing down and impeding Programs or project teams.

Figure 11.21 shows the result for a client that went from 941 Programs in their portfolio to 37, and only 6 of the "Top 10" were funded. According to the CEO, "The organization went from marginal progress in a chaotic environment to extreme progress with laser-like focus in a disciplined environment full of excited teams."

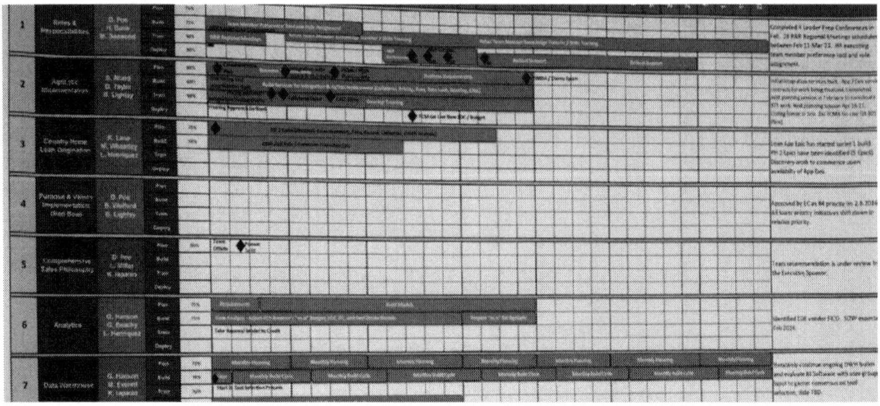

Figure 11.21 | Annual Freeway Planning *(based on funding choices)*

The process is tailored to the organizational environment and the marketplace in which it competes, including factors like whether the competition is for public or private dollars, runs on 3-year or 3-month development cycles, and produces premium or generic products. The granularity is at the Affinity Estimating level for Agile Programs and the ROM level for Traditional ones within the portfolio. Agreeing upon the amount of resources to commit and how adequate progress, in reasonable time, will be measured, gated, or approved is not easy but vital.

Semi-Annual Roadmap Planning

Semi-Annual Roadmap and Program-level planning sessions deliver results as either, or both, CVLNs and ELNs, depending on governance choices and regulatory requirements. It is where choices that drive effectiveness are integrated with those that maximize efficiencies. In both Agile and Traditional Programs, the granularity is refined to the FFC Milestones and sometimes the EWPs.

The outcome is a cogent network graph for each Program that can be directly correlated to the Freeway Plan. Governance choices, made to enhance stakeholder communication, will establish whether the Affinity and ROM estimates must be refined to 50 shades of granularity using Planning Poker, and also whether the network must be subjected to more detailed Critical Path analysis using the new values. *(See Figure 11.22.)*

Governance choices will also determine rules for synchronizing the inter-project cadence at this level or during the Quarterly Release Planning session.

Figure 11.22 | Semi-Annual Roadmap *(with Programs circled)*

Quarterly Release Planning

Quarterly Release planning sessions typically deliver results as ELNs focused on driving Program efficiencies. The granularity is refined to the EWPs, with Planning Poker or Definitive Estimate values assigned.

The outcome is a cogent network graph for each Release that can be directly correlated to the Roadmap or Program plan. Stakeholder communication commonly demands Planning Poker granularity and a detailed Critical Path analysis of the network. It is also typical that the Agile and Traditional projects' cadence gets synchronized so that Milestone reviews or phase gates are aligned with completing Iterations. This is crucial because successful integration of the final Program deliverables demands it and the Integration Point Review ceremony confirms it.

Iteration & Milestone WAG or SWAG

The more conservative or regulated the organization is, and the tighter the margins are between profit and loss, the more likely it is that Iteration- and Milestone-level estimates and plans will be required. Lean principles would suggest that, even though it is counter-intuitive, requiring WAG or SWAG estimates is a mistake with tighter-margin Programs and products because the additional estimates and plans increase overhead at precisely the time when external decisions cannot change the outcome.

Integration Point Review (IPR)
Following the Quarterly Release planning ceremony, the appropriate stakeholders discuss any issues that will impact the solution demonstration at the Integration Point Review (IPR) ceremony. The IPR brings stakeholders together to see and respond to solution deliverables that combine results from both Traditional Milestones and Agile Iterations.

The IPR keeps teams, using different development approaches, focused on the shared responsibility for successful integration, and gets them into the process of doing it before the final integration and "Go Live!" event occurs. It reduces many significant risks that materialize as problems during the actual "Go Live!" when this ceremony is not used.

Monthly Program Steering Meeting
While the name of this ceremony may carry a lot of negative baggage, Program Managers significantly increase their influence, as well as the efficiency of all projects within their Program, by having a regular, predictable meeting for all stakeholders to "see the whole story." When professionally presented, it is invariably well-received and eliminates having more meetings for the stakeholders of each project.

For the best outcome, it is presented jointly by the Program and Product Managers, reviews every in-flight project, and validates their alignment to the strategic goals of the Program. It begins by summarizing the status of each project as:

- ***Continue*** – The project is delivering the expected strategic value according to the defined metrics.
- ***Slowdown*** – Unexpected development success (positive) or resource over-consumption (negative) have caused the project to lose inter-project alignment, creating Program risk and calling for analysis and a realignment plan.
- ***Swarm*** – The project needs to get back on track so contingency funds or alternate resources have been allocated to accelerate it back into alignment.
- ***Pause*** – The project remains strategic, but a new initiative or Program Backlog reprioritization has claimed the resources allocated to the project so it is paused until resources become available again.
- ***Cancel*** – The project is no longer strategic so sunk costs are not a factor in the decision, although considering them is a common mistake. The project is terminated.

Ceremonies are a primary source of artifacts.

Artifacts

Artifacts shown already include the:

- Program Organization Chart *(Figure 11.10)*
- Work Decomposition Structure *(Figure 11.13)*
- CVLN List *(Figure 11.16)*
- ELN Diagram *(Figure 11.17)*
- Affinity Estimates *(Figure 11.18)*
- CPM Sticky Notes *(Figure 11.20)*
- Annual Freeway Plan *(Figure 11.21)*
- Semi-Annual Roadmap *(Figure 11.22)*

Additional artifacts include Planning Poker Estimates, Definitive Estimates, Budgets, and Schedules that should be archived and version controlled so that Retrospective ceremonies can use the data to identify and analyze opportunities for improvement.

How to Make It Work Effectively

"I would not give a fig for the simplicity this side of complexity, but I would give my life for the simplicity on the other side of complexity."[5]

– Oliver Wendell Holmes Jr.

In an earlier section, Ariane Schmidt's insight was noted about four-dimensional communication because making scaled Agile work effectively, including the AIF, requires Program Managers and enterprise leaders to remain conscious of the attention fatigue and contextual alignment exhaustion that can be induced if they set irrational, quite often inaccurate, and simply unrealistic expectations.

For leaders and Program Managers familiar with chaos theory, Ariane shares another piece of highly useful insight by comparing a Cartesian approach to analysis with using a Julia Set approach instead. Consider that the Cartesian approach, that is "normal geometry", shows every point as just an intersection of the x and y axes leading to really cool graphs, but the equations always produce the same output unless you change something. The approach is tidy and useful when the situation is not inherently dynamic. But, scaled Agile is only used in unavoidably (and some would say, frustratingly) dynamic situations.

In those situations, using the Julia Set approach that "adapts" depending on where the Program's viewing lens is located is much more useful. With a Julia Set approach, a complex, gnarly ball of proverbial string can look like a sphere, line or even a point, so mapping it in a system that supports different viewing lenses is very valuable. The underlying concept of Chaos Theory (or Fractals) is that dynamic systems have feedback loops of self-similarity. However, it is very important to note that feedback loops have boundaries, called "Attractors."

For example, a Program can have any combination of risks or problems, but all are bound by the scope of the Program, which is the boundary set. For any given Program, the risks, assumptions, and resources could all be the Attractor, the dynamic feedback loop that is the boundary set of the Program. The boundary set is the "line" between chaos and order that the Program Manager and executives are responsible for managing. When they don't manage that line, they induce chaos and irrational, undesirable outcomes.

To make AIF (or any of the scaled Agile Frameworks) work effectively, Program Managers must consider not only the Programmatic drivers of complexity and uncertainty, but also the "social" drivers because both factor into the boundary set. They must dedicate unflinching focus to questions such as, "What are the constraints, and symptoms of those constraints, that will cause non-linear uncertainty to appear or increase?" Knowing the constraint and defining the symptoms identifies the risk and the triggering events that underpin professional responsiveness. Because complexity and uncertainty have a compounding effect in Programs and uber-large projects, Program Managers must commit themselves to thinking.

> ***"No problem can withstand the assault of sustained thinking."***
> – Voltaire

An odd result of such clearly focused thinking is that it may lead to the most counter-intuitive step in "Making it Work Effectively."

Kill Bad Projects

Programs often provide a warm, damp environment for the 'bacteria' known as bad projects to multiply until they kill the host.

Michael O'Brochta, PMI-ACP®, PMP® once said, "Bad projects abound. They waste money and resources, divert attention from good projects, and undercut future projects by sowing seeds of doubt about organizational competence. In an ideal world, bad projects would not be allowed to continue; they would be killed. But, all too often, bad projects are not killed, they live on; they are often hard to kill."[6] Programs live in the real world, not in "an ideal world", but that does not excuse a Program Manager from exercising whatever tools are needed to kill a bad project hiding in their Program.

Michael then described the heart of the problem saying, "...clouded judgement can lead to cognitive dissonance. Throwing good money after bad leads to sunk cost, the desire for harmony and not making waves leads to groupthink, over investment in a previous decision or course of action leads to escalation of commitment, and trying to have it both ways leads to conflict of interest."[6] Program managers cannot afford cognitive dissonance because they must make bad projects easy to kill.

Optimize Testing Practices

In the Challenges section, *Resistance to Proper Testing* described how the Program Manager was required to effectively communicate the true impact of improper testing. Competently demonstrating the cost of <u>not</u> testing to overcome stakeholder resistance to proper scheduling practices that ensure adequate time for testing was shown to be vital. *(Shown in Figure 11.09.)* The prior discussion will be extended here to show one way a Program Manager could approach this critical topic with key stakeholders.

Setting a clear foundation about testing is the first step that must be taken. Depending on the sophistication of the stakeholders, it is possible to open the discussion with a little satirical humor. At the right time in another meeting, or at the start of a meeting specifically intended to discuss the governance standards for testing, the Program Manager could open by saying something like, "We decided that since testing could hurt the feelings of the developers who might interpret testing as a lack of faith in their amazing skills, we won't do any testing!" If the stakeholders are primarily from the business, another popular opener is, "We decided to use the Microsoft best practice and let our customers do the beta testing for us. We'll save a lot of time and productivity will soar!"

After the humorous opening, a serious discussion must start with an honest dialogue of the cost, both in terms of time and money, that is required to do testing that meets the standard of a recommended practice. Testing will vary between industries, tangible and intangible products, perhaps even

Figure 11.23 | Cost of Testing

the various uses of a specific product, such as hiking boots for occasional recreation versus serious mountain climbing. What remains the same in every environment is that the cost of testing varies according to the number of test being done over time, as shown in *Figure 11.24.*

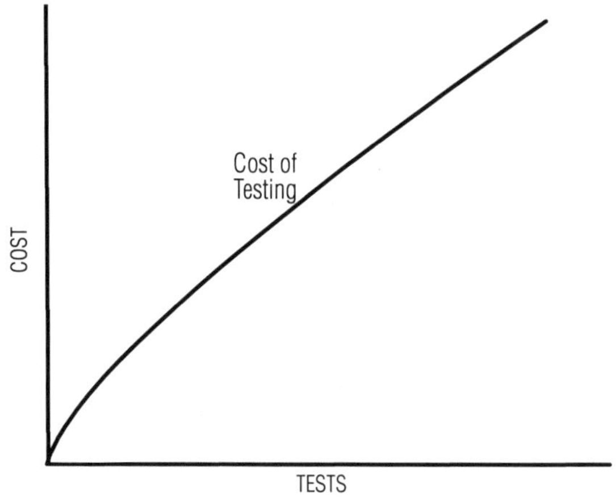

Figure 11.24 | Cost of Testing

The second point that must be credibly explained is that the cost of not testing, which starts out low in the beginning, rises in a non-linear fashion because issues, problems, and "bugs" tend to compound. Many Program Managers are PMP® certified, and every PMP® had to memorize the simple formula **n(n-1)/2,** explaining the non-linear growth of communication paths in a group, to pass their exam, so it is suggested that Program Managers use it to add some "scientific weight" to their presentation of this principle. *(See Figure 11.25.)*

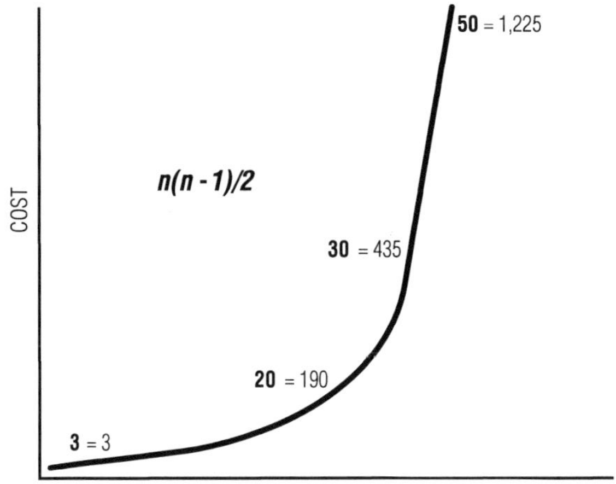

Figure 11.25 | Cost of Not Testing

With that groundwork in place, the next step is to explain that complexity and uncertainty need to be factored into the governance standard by "scoring" them, using *"figurative mathematics"* (i.e., insight not algebra) to calibrate the impact of testing requirements and balance the cost of testing and not testing against the impact on development productivity. *(See Figure 11.26.)*

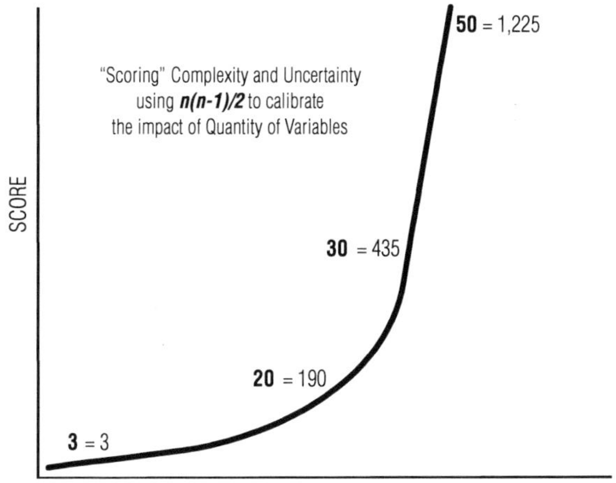

Figure 11.26 | Cost of Not Testing

Project A has 20 test variables with an impact score of 190, while Project B, with 30 test variables, scores 435, but Project C, with 50 test variables (the sum of variables for A and B), has a score of 1,225. Explaining that the score for C is almost double the combined score of A and B because of the non-linear interdependencies inherent in the environment of Project C generates stakeholder insight. *(See Figure 11.27.)*

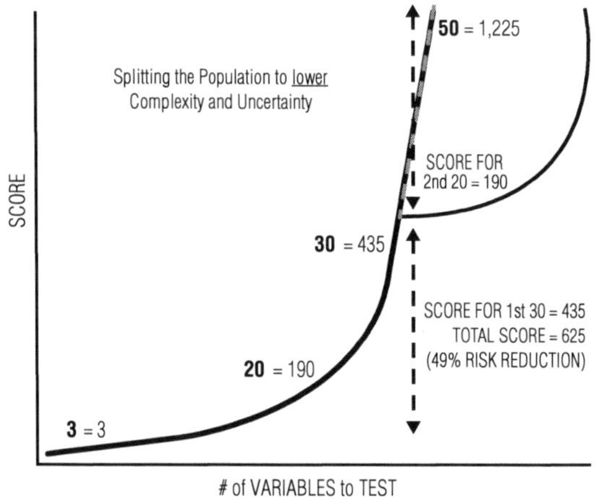

Figure 11.27 | Value of Population Splitting

Introducing senior stakeholders to the idea that splitting populations (i.e., 20 and 30 instead of 50) could have the potentially huge benefit of reducing risk often motivates those, who otherwise resist committing, to make themselves available for Freeway and Roadmap Planning sessions.

To further illustrate, consider the impact of an architectural design element used in multiple locations of a building. If the transformer that reduces 480v input to 240v output is connected to electrical junction boxes that get used 30 times on each floor (treating each floor as an Iteration), the score for testing each floor is 435. But, because an electrical failure can cause a potentially catastrophic fire, the safety system tests are integrated, so the score for testing two floors is 1770. Even worse, if testing is done after completion of all 10 floors, the score rises to 44,850 and the cost of fixing a problem to meet the grand opening deadline skyrockets!

The number of tests grows exponentially if the system gets more complex as development continues, so a Program with 50 variables has a much higher testing score than one with two projects containing 20 and 30 variables each.

Getting key stakeholders to see the value of using planning to split populations also opens the door to another highly valuable conversation. Automated testing has all the benefits of splitting populations and, in many cases, even more. As *Figure 11.28* shows, the cost curve of automated testing, which rises more quickly in the beginning, rapidly flattens out, and with each incremental variable added for automated testing, the average cost per variable tested goes down.

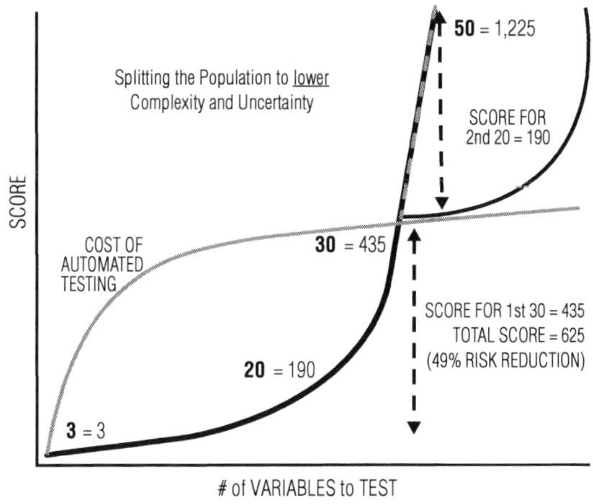

Figure 11.27 | Value of Automated Testing

The use of the formula, *n(n-1)/2*, produces a figurative calculation or score representative of the increased complexity when variables and test cases increase over time. If this test complexity score is applied to the number of defects that would be found, either in a test environment or production, it also gives an indication of the positive or negative opportunity of testing as well as the cost of each option. The following example uses a few key assumptions to provide a comparison that will aid stakeholders in vital decisions regarding the cost of not testing.

Figure 11.26 shows three projects with increasing quantities of test variables. Adding the following assumptions to illustrate an example shows how it gives a view into the cost of Automated versus Manual testing, and the cost of defect fixes in a test environment versus production.

Assumptions:

- Each Manual Test case costs $60 to execute.
- Each Automated Test case costs $30 to execute.

- The base cost of Manual and Automated Test cases are equal.
- For each variable tested the team will identify 0.5 defects.
- Each defect manually identified costs $120.00.
- Each defect identified using Automated testing costs $60.00.
- Automated testing is half the cost of Manual testing once it set up. One-time cost of Automated set up needed as well as cost of documenting all test cases.
- The cost of a defect fix and successful re-test is $270 (assumes 4-hrs Dev + 1-hr Test).
- The cost of a defect fix, re-test and release to production for an issue found in production is $540 (plus potential cost of lost reputation when customer-facing).

Project	#of Test Variable	n(n-1)/2	Test Complexity Score
Project A	20	20(20-1)/2	190
Project B	30	30(30-1)/2	435
Project C	50	50(50-1)/2	1,225

Project	# of Defects	Manual Testing Cost	Automated Testing Cost	Defect Fix	Production Issue Resolution Cost
Project A	10	$600	$300	$2,400	$5,400
Project B	15	$900	$450	$4,050	$8,100
Project C	25	$1,500	$750	$6,750	$13,500

This example is representative of the increased cost of not testing. The opportunity to identify and resolve defects with testing, especially using automated testing, protects the organization's reputation and brand value, and does so at a significantly reduced cost.

None of that suggests that using an indiscriminate testing strategy rises to the standard of a recommended practice. But requiring tests that will, or should be, run frequently and repetitively, and be automated, is a very good practice. Decades of experience conclusively demonstrate that human beings are far less likely to frequently perform an unpleasant or difficult task, compared to a pleasant or easy one. Automated tests are a pleasant, easy task that can be done while the person required to do them is having a coffee break. Therefore, testing gets done more often, which directly reduces the risk and cost of rework, resulting from them not being done.

A sophisticated testing strategy can also nuance governance so that it suggests avoiding the cost of automating non-repetitive tests, or ones occurring so late in development they will only be run a few times. The idea is to manage testing so it optimizes benefits and minimizes costs. Program Managers who do it effectively will also tie testing governance to a commitment to scheduling standards that support proper testing.

Carve Out Program Manager Time Blocks
Perhaps the most intuitive, yet least honored step in making planning work effectively is to carve out specific Program Manager time blocks to carefully create, analyze, and comprehend the budget and schedule so a realistic understanding can be continuously shared with every stakeholder.

Gartner Group made the hierarchy of success clear – People, Processes, Data, and Technology. None of them can be skipped, and all of them need to be properly integrated. That means the Program Manager must invest time and energy in a personal process of leadership and management because complexity and uncertainty will automatically compound otherwise.

People need communication by design, not by accident. Communication by design requires well thought-out content that requires time to create, then effectively manage, budgets and schedules. Those budgets and schedules must have reliable data, cost effectively gathered and processed, which means having the right tool correctly configured. (The Tools appendix is included at the end of this book to help with this.)

How to integrate Traditional and Agile teams by combining the Traditional approach of building logic networks with enhanced Agile techniques was demonstrated within this chapter. Preparing before, and analyzing after, are critical to effectively using those techniques to deliver Customer Value. None of that can, or will, get done unless the Program Manager exercises the discipline to use the concept of Block Time, as taught by Stephen Covey in books like *Seven Habits of Highly Effective People*[7].

Tools and Practices Recommendations

The foundation for making recommendations about tools and practices starts with acknowledging that, for Programs, there is never a "pretty outcome" in real-world situations like the ones often cited in the "demo" or "canned scenarios" proposed by some aficionados in their blogs and presentations. Life is messy and Program Managers must prepare for success with that as a very real understanding. "Life is messy!" never qualifies as a reason for being ill-prepared, no matter how much someone likes that excuse.

Osmotic Communication

Osmotic communication is the undisputed, best way to communicate because it maximizes communication bandwidth, but Programs seldom consist solely of collocated teams where this is possible. Therefore, every intelligent communication plan – designed to support the people, the stakeholders – must include strategies and tactics to overcome the loss of bandwidth with operational interventions. The options are limitless, but the Program Manager must choose to do something, and it must be something adequate!

Low-Tech, High-Touch

Every successful leader will confirm, "You can forget the plan but you better do the planning!" Properly understood, that means planning must be done the right way. The right way means that low-tech, high-touch must occur at strategically and tactically significant times. The cost of gathering key stakeholders for planning at significant points is vastly exceeded by the value of opportunities captured and the costs of risks eliminated. Intel Corp. and Siemens are successful powerhouses. Intel has MAPP (Make a Project/Program Plan) Day and Siemens has PACT (Project Acceleration Control Technique) Day and both are low-tech, high-touch rituals fueling their continuing success in highly competitive, extremely complex and uncertain environments. Leveraging that wisdom is highly recommended.

Process Governance Toolchain

Throughout this chapter, multiple tools have been shown with general and specific applications. Taking the time to develop an enterprise-specific Process Governance Toolchain has value that cannot be overstated. Having well-defined governance options saves valuable time, and a light-weight minimum standard gives Program Managers the freedom to exercise their unique insight to make the right choices. Defining the constellation of tools available to Program Managers, while leaving them free to choose the right mix, unlocks profound value.

Kanban and DevOps

Nearly every environment imaginable benefits from wise and effective usage of Kanban and DevOps. Take the time to understand how they can help every Program and enterprise reach their desired maturity and future state, better, faster, and cheaper!

Conclusion

The Agile Integration Framework (AIF) embraces the simple fact that the management, accounting, and Traditional and Agile project management domains share a great deal of common ground. It is a Rosetta stone for Program Managers that provides a cogent, flexible Framework and lexicon that stakeholders, executives, and technical development professionals understand. The AIF supports an organizational model that empowers teams and individuals while optimizing the throughput of the whole enterprise.

The AIF has been explained, explored, and proven so that Program Managers can leverage a paradigm that scales Agile by facilitating successful organizational change with important principles, methods, processes, and practices shown as non-threatening evolutionary extensions of existing beliefs. The foundational paradigm of the AIF embraces the value of advanced business school models and strategies, five decades of developing PMI® intellectual property, and the distinct actionable-insight of Agile and Lean principles to provide the most robust, reliable, and flexible approach for scaling Agile.

The AIF acknowledges the deep debt owed to the very significant work of the thought leaders from business schools, the PMI®, and Agile and Lean communities. The AIF hopes to help Program Managers be the next step in the evolution of how enterprises drive success by creating delight among constituents and customers. Program Managers must choose to integrate the AIF with their own insight to produce a highly-intelligent way to scale Agile amid the complexity, uncertainty, and chaos that is unavoidable.

May safe sailing and an exciting journey be yours!

END NOTES

[1] Cohn, Mike. "Let Go of Knowing: How Holding onto Views May Be Holding You Back." Mountain Goat Software. 3 Apr. 2015, *www.mountaingoatsoftware.com/presentations/let-go-of-knowing-how-holding-onto-views-may-be-holding-you-back.*

[2] "The CHAOS Report" *The Standish Group*, published annually. *https://www.standishgroup.com.*

[3] Burns, Robert. *To a Mouse, on Turning Her Up in Her Nest with the Plough.* November, 1785 (as paraphrased in English).

[4] "Hershey's Biggest Dud Is Its New Computer System," *The Wall Street Journal.* 29 Oct. 1999, *https://www.wsj.com/articles/SB941156105920533040.*

[5] Common adaptation of direct quote: Holmes, Oliver Wendell, Jr., *Holmes-Pollock Letters: The Correspondence of Mr. Justice Holmes and Sir Frederick Pollock,* 1874-1932, 2nd ed., 1961, p. 109.

[6] O'Brochta, Michael. "Why Bad Projects Are So Hard to Kill." Project Management, 21 Apr. 2017, *www.projectmanagement.com/articles/379634/Why-Bad-Projects-Are-So-Hard-to-Kill.* A brief biography of his work and credentials is also available through the link provided.

[7] Covey, Stephen R. *The 7 Habits of Highly Effective People. Free* Press, 1989. Covey (1932 –2012) was an American educator, author, businessman, and keynote speaker.

PART THREE

APPLIED SCALED AGILE

CHAPTER

12

Virtual, Distributed & Multi-Team Environments

Overview

Modern organizations have become virtual work systems composed of complex, highly distributed, collaborative teams, requiring greater connectivity and sharing among an increasing number of individuals and groups. Large scale Programs are often complex, especially when working with a mix of virtual and collocated teams. Knowledge sharing and decision making often end up distributed across many people throughout the organization. Agile brings practices that potentially increase the autonomy of these teams, but regardless, they must coordinate the integration of important information. Business domain knowledge is often held uniquely by one or more subject matter experts (SMEs), which are vital for teams to achieve Program and organizational goals. Virtual work increases the risk that decision-makers will not have the critical knowledge needed to support good choices.

Significant effort is required for the organization and teams to develop and maintain a shared perspective. It will not happen by accident!

Collocated and remote teams work on interdependent tasks to achieve a common goal. One main difference between the teams is that virtual team members may be working in different locations and, often, in different time zones. Today, most remote teams work on projects and their membership varies from relatively stable to constantly changing.

The nature of the project sometimes drives the need to work outside of a collocated team, using remote, distributed, or virtual members. Other times it is a strategic business choice, driven by expectations of competitive advantage. In either case, to work together effectively, Program teams must become more than a collection of individuals working to reach a business goal. They must connect at both the task and interpersonal level, getting together for task-related requirements such as planning, estimating, and scheduling. To be successful they must have a social connection that expresses trust or they will not maximize performance.

Recognize that having remote teams are an intentional organizational design choice expected to engage individuals with the best skills to develop a specific deliverable, provide around-the-clock support, or integrate resources while saving time and money. But those goals do not erase the challenges created by teams depending on technology to create the bandwidth needed to solve complex problems and collaborate when implementing solutions, both of which are difficult activities even when working face-to-face.

Before buying into the hype of virtual teams and collaboration technologies, it is crucial to understand the challenges of launching and sustaining effective virtual teams, especially for large Programs. While technology can do a lot to manage quantitative variables, like time and distance, the qualitative variables that haunt virtual teams, like language, trust, and behavioral norms, are amplified, not minimized. That means specific leadership expertise is required to avoid falling victim to the old adage, "Fools rush in where angels fear to tread!"

Having the latest technology is far less important than ensuring teams develop the ability to comfortably interact, communicate regularly, and successfully foster commitment. Trust, cultivated by effective communication, will propel the teams and the Program forward. In practice, this means having confidence that team members are doing their best, given what they know at the time, their skills and abilities, the resources available, and the situation at hand. Complexity in this realm occurs concurrently at many levels, magnifying the potentially negative, unintended consequences.

This simple fact makes training in problem solving and collaboration essential. To achieve real problem solving within the Program, the team's idea transfer rate must be comparable to the rates enjoyed by smaller, collocated teams. To collaborate effectively, decision making and communicating, with true cultural awareness, despite language barriers, is also imperative.

None of the above will happen by accident. It will only occur by design, which requires expert-level meeting facilitation, virtually and in person, when working with remote teams. It also requires that problems, like incompatible technology platforms and inadequate training, be addressed before they cripple trust and create insecurity and skepticism.

Time

For Programs with virtual teams, time differences create both advantages and disadvantages. For example, Programs that require a wide pool of talent and have a short delivery timeline can create a twenty-four-hour work cycle by moving work from the U.S. to Europe then on to Asia before returning it to the U.S. While it may be challenging to schedule meetings with a globally distributed team, it is a possible strategy. Of course, this can bring risks for communication when questions arise, requiring responses from a group in a different time zone. The wait time for an answer or decision can stretch to several hours, or more, and tension can rise as differing cultural attitudes surface about working outside normal office hours.

The point is that complexity rises and will not be managed correctly without purposely designed processes, procedures, and systems. This chapter aids the reader by providing specific guidance, instructions, and samples that can be used immediately.

Distance

Teams at least 100 feet apart are considered remote. Large Programs can, and often will, contain teams located on different floors or even in different buildings in the same campus. Basically, if teams send emails instead of getting out of their chairs to communicate with the other teams working on the same Program, it is an indication that some of the challenges of working with remote teams may apply.

For larger distances, teams will face some common and different advantages and disadvantages. Distance imposes barriers to the "natural" process of building trust and teamwork present with face-to-face interactions. Because virtual teams do not share a physical work environment the subtle, often highly nuanced, process of forming a team identity, where the commitment of each individual to the goal is made and reinforced by things like shared experiences, common jargon, office location, and even fashion norms, insignias or logos gets truncated.

Nevertheless, virtual teams can create elevated levels of interpersonal connection related to goals and commitments when a sense of appreciating and caring for one another is cultivated using periodic face-to-face meetings and professional "exercises" with the purpose of building and maintaining a team identity that supports a social network. In this chapter, a tool called, "Team Photos in the Workspace" fits this purpose.

Creating standards that build trust, support group norms, and reinforce work expectations is more of a challenge and requires diligent and disciplined effort. Check out "Meeting Norms" in the Artifacts section of this chapter to use as an inspiration for turning your implicit norms into explicit.

Unfortunately, not all organizations have the staffing capacity to commit one individual to each project role for every project or product endeavor underway. Fractionalized assignments of professionals are a common response to tackle the lack of a specialized workforce and the highly competitive markets in each industry.

This chapter provides Program Managers critical insight for working with Programs using Agile Frameworks and multiple teams in distributed and virtual environments. It will share experiences, challenges, benefits, and good practices to inspire a new cycle of experimentation so that Agile's power can be unlocked as teams apply an inspect-and-adapt approach to the Program's context.

Benefits / Challenges

Benefits

Staffing From a Larger Talent Pool
By having a mixed strategy for staffing with collocated and remote teams, Programs may leverage the benefits of having a much larger talent pool. Cost reduction is one, given salaries tend to be higher in first world countries and there are many, equally qualified professionals in other parts of the world that are less expensive. Also, a higher engagement level may be achieved

because being part of large Agile Programs can increase motivation for some professionals seeking that experience as a basis for future work assignments. It may also be a good way to recruit professionals from abroad.

More Work per Schedule-Day Consumed

Offshore and nearshore teams are widely used in Programs. Among the advantages of Agile Frameworks, improved delivery time, increased quality, and a much wider talent pool are three. For example, a development team working in Brazil and an integration testing team in China may not overlap in their local working hours, but may still work very effectively together, while speeding delivery by using a "follow the sun" tactic of passing work back and forth. As the integration testing team finds and reports defects, the development team fixes them then passes the work back to be tested again. The quality of the software being delivered increases because more testing can be done in the same number of days of schedule time because of the distributed teams in this strategy. Each team had a clear purpose and their acceptance of responsibility was the key to success.

Diversified Cultural Background

Culture is the collection of behaviors and beliefs impacting team members on a daily basis. Program Managers must remember that the organizational culture has a very strong influence on team formation, collaboration, and trust among team members. It has an even bigger impact on the inter-project bonds that will directly affect the probability of a Program being successful. It can, and must, be diligently managed to drive success.

The diversity brought in by different cultural backgrounds has an enormous value for the business and Program. It generates different perspectives and promotes healthy debates that can mitigate risks to a Program's scope, process, and tools. It may even redefine a business model! A well-communicated culture of unity will improve the quality and speed of the project results and Program deliverables.

Challenges

Cross Team Appraisals and Recognition

Even though each organization follows different strategies it is important to make sure that team members are not solely measured individually, but also as a team unit, in terms of performance appraisals. Otherwise, it is likely that individual best interest will come before helping another colleague to benefit the Program team. Teams must be aware of the overall Program and continuously focus on optimizing the whole, not just on their own team or personal interests. When individuals do not clearly understand what the Program and organizational culture are, and how it will impact their performance assessments, it can generate any number of counter-productive issues and challenges.

Program Team Size
Leadership principles clearly articulate that the ideal team size is between 5 and 9 members. Program Managers need to recognize the inherent challenge of working with offshore or nearshore teams, especially if their team size grows beyond 9, increasing the difficulty of self-organization, communication, and collaboration. Good practices suggest that properly sized, self-organized teams tend to communicate and collaborate better with other similar teams.

Language
Unless you are working on a Program where the entire staff has native proficiency in the same language, which is unlikely, expect that language will be a challenge to team communication. Distributed teams are often working from different parts of the world and most of the time their native idioms are not the same. Even differences, such as American and British English, or even regional differences in dialects, will generate the equivalent of signal noise or background static in electronic communications. Team members will find their ability to understand, contribute, and collaborate affected depending on their fluency or familiarity, and regardless, it will always be a negative factor if it is not dealt with by design.

Luckily, in the Tools and Practice Recommendations section there is a powerful practice called, “Eyes Train Ears” that solves this conundrum.

Program-level attributes

Offshore and Nearshore Staffing
Hiring offshore professionals to staff multiple teams is a practice that has been used by IT and IT dependent companies for a long time. One of the big selling points for offshore development is the lower price. However, it is myopic to think exclusively about cost per hour when measuring productivity remains a big challenge. In many industries, knowledge of the business domain and the quality of the deliverables makes a lot of difference and may have a big negative impact on the company’s overall operations. While Time

and Material (T&M) is the most common contract model, there may be benefits to using other alternatives, such as outcome-based compensation or Story Points correlated to business value added.

Hiring nearshore staffing is similar to offshore staffing. The main difference is that the provider usually works in a similar time zone, which enables more collaboration and better communication between staff and the provider.

One of the strategies for overcoming the risks of losing sight of the business knowledge on any team is to always have at least one representative of the company who is "hands on" as part of the team, even if they are not physically present. A potential challenge is making sure the teams see these representatives as a valuable team member. At the Program level, it may also be beneficial to create a network of these professionals to support a holistic view and promote the exchange of knowledge and experiences. The Center of Excellence (CoE) and Communities of Practice (CoP), mentioned in several other chapters of this book, are great ways to have oversight, receive solid guidance and advice, and create an inclusive, collaborative Program environment.

When it comes to quality assurance, think of it as test-driving a car before buying it. No one likes the process of buying a car – narrowing the selection down, choosing features, agreeing on the price, applying for financing, waiting for it to be detailed and gassed up – it can take hours! It is tempting to take any, and all, short cuts to decrease the amount of time spent sitting at the dealership. However, no one would advise purchasing a vehicle that has not been test driven. Without testing out the ride, comfortability, and features, there is no way to know if that vehicle will serve the value sought. The time it takes to do this is well worth the confidence in the product being purchased.

If a company invests in unit and automated functional tests, automates their infrastructure provisioning, and has an effectively automated pipeline, risks of having defects or failures on systems, products, and services are decreased by catching them early. This applies equally to building airplanes, pharmaceuticals, and software, despite the vocabulary just used being from software. If the teams are not already following the DevOps practices explained previously in this book, they should consider developing such competences. Teams should not focus just on improving quality, they should also understand that stakeholder confidence in the level of functionality in each deliverable of the Program is required, and strive to achieve and maintain both.

Some years ago, companies made staffing decisions that outsourced software development to big consulting firms. One of the reasons behind this was the ability to upscale and downscale their IT workforce as demand varied. Flawed logic made the process look viable, but did not make it possible. They discovered that throwing developers at an unrealistic expectation is not a solution. Two developers will not always solve a problem twice as fast. In fact, growing teams abruptly increases the risk for poor team performance. According to Bruce Wayne Tuckman[1], each time a team changes its core members or the scope of development, the curve of forming, storming, norming, performing, and adjourning restarts.

When working with multiple virtual teams, be conscious about the distribution and relationships of remote and in-house staffing. Make sure there is a knowledge sharing strategy so the information does not stay exclusively in one domain.

Continuously inspect and measure the cost and progress of each team against key Program metrics to be sure that the trade-offs are favorable. What can initially appear as a cheaper option, can become more expensive very quickly.

Lastly, keep an eye on attrition from both teams because higher than average attrition it is probably a symptom of other problems that can also rapidly become very costly.

Crowdsourcing

Crowdsourcing consists of opening real business challenges for any number of individuals, that can be pre-screened or completely random volunteers, to solve. Their background and expertise can vary and, depending on the project or initiative, the crowd could be a mix of amateurs and professionals, but the collective result will potentially still add more value to an organization than if it was executed by their own staff. Some individuals use such crowdsourcing opportunities to learn, explore new domains, or demonstrate skills in order to find a new full-time position. It is fairly common to have software projects and products tested using crowdsourcing.

Roles

"Coming together is a beginning; keeping together is progress; working together is success."

– Henry Ford

A collection of professionals working together becomes a team when there is trust between the members, well-defined roles and responsibilities, and a very clear purpose to be achieved or maintained that each member understands and commits to fulfilling. For Program Managers, one of the challenges is how to properly communicate and keep goals aligned while mitigating the risks of shared dependencies. With virtual teams, the risks are increased so integrating certain practices is needed to mitigate that risk.

The practice of having team members select a "Stick-Buddy" or "Remote Buddy" is very helpful because it accelerates the development of trust by ensuring communication through pairing teammates across teams working from different physical locations. The idea is that each person has someone else representing them at the other site. This can build stronger relationships between remote team members, enable better collaboration and communication, and create or generate different channels of communication. For example, two individuals might be more keen on using a specific instant messaging tool that the whole team isn't using.

It is common for Program Managers to work closely with multiple Project Managers or team leads and use them as points of contact during the development and delivery of each project. The Sticky Buddy role is an extension of this practice, enabling every team member to connect with other team members at different working sites. It provides the ability to interject and represent others that are willing to contribute, even if they are not physically present in the room at that specific moment.

Workflow

As just mentioned, Program Managers face challenges creating durable communication so goals stay aligned while mitigating the risks of shared dependencies inherent with virtual teams. That means they must integrate communication by design into all of the other workflows where the teams are involved.

Workflows do not change just because there are virtual, remote, or distributed elements in the team organization, but a crippling lack of communication is likely to occur if the workflow is not enhanced with ceremonies and practices that prevent it.

Ceremonies

Virtual Daily Meetings

Daily Stand-up Meetings promote faster decision making and create a 24-hour plan for the work to be tackled before the next Daily Stand-up.

Virtual Daily Meetings require a higher level of discipline. It is not uncommon that participants have issues with the technology, like the camera, microphone, or audio not working, that will disrupt and sabotage the meeting. Getting the technology right and tested before a daily meeting is critical. Being virtual increases the importance of preparation, because the team needs to not only summarize and structure their thoughts, but also communicate them efficiently, aiming to avoid miscommunication. A very high level of discipline is required in order to be effective with Agile Frameworks and communicating effectively during Daily Meetings is a core practice supporting that discipline. When the team is remote, being on time and following the team norms becomes even more important.

Program Managers must be careful to look forward and have the right tools that support the information transfer needed for the meetings to be opportunities to help the teams be more productive, map out risks, and suggest mitigation plans.

Cross-Team Daily Meetings

For large scale Agile transformation initiatives, where multiple teams are working on developing and delivering different products and services, the Cross-team daily meeting is a good practice. Points of integration, issues, and learning should be the main focus.

The Program Manager must ensure that there are facilities that support the opportunity for specific teams or individuals to gather in an alternate virtual space and continue the conversation right afterwards. Both collocated and virtual teams use "After Meetings" to solve problems and deliver the Program.

Virtual Planning

Programs have remote elements so it is necessary to have a tool to centralize, support, and manage requirements and Program Managers must own the process that supports changes to them. It is often a good practice to delegate its management to the Product Owner because they typically facilitate any remote planning sessions and also have the responsibility to keep the Backlog updated and prioritized. Earlier chapters in this book shared many ways to coordinate effectively across teams. What is vital and different for virtual teams is the added discipline to define and communicate the governance standards and follow through with the technical support that facilitates its fulfillment.

Big Demo or Big Showcase

A Big Demo, also called a Big Showcase, typically dedicates a full day each quarter to present what was delivered during that quarter. Every team presents what they have accomplished and members of other teams choose which presentations they want to attend. They use the opportunity to better understand aspects of solution deliverables such as architecture, tech stack and business impact.

The goals of each team were aligned from the beginning of the quarter until the end, and this big review serves as an opportunity for teams to present and share what was accomplished with other teams and all stakeholders. It also serves as a forum for sharing and learning about new technologies used and solutions adopted, thereby increasing "tribal knowledge." Often, teams and individuals learn about something that was created then reuse or expand on it during the next quarter.

For a Program, this is a great ceremony to get a holistic view of the deliverables across different environments. It is an opportunity to give and receive feedback from everyone engaged in the deliverables.

Virtual Retrospective

During Retrospectives, it is important to see and hear all participants. It is easy to use tools to collect data, generate insights, and create action items for improving. It is challenging to run a Retrospective while distributed because of the need for very high levels of communication bandwidth. Asking participants at each site to write on sticky notes and stick them on a wall often fails because webcams do not work quite well enough to share what is written on each sticky note.

Leveraging the Stick Buddy technique can come in handy when one team is off site. The pair can help each other contribute with their notes and thoughts.

While it might be financially impractical to bring the teams together for every Retrospective, Program Managers should be prepared to exert influence for gathering them following the delivery of a Release or completion of a Roadmap. The money saved on risks mitigated, and the money gained on opportunities realized, will more than offset the cost of the Retrospective at major Milestones. The logic behind this good practice was explained in detail in an earlier chapter.

Artifacts

Code as Living Documentation

In Agile Software development, having business rules documented through unit tests with Acceptance Tests Driven-Development (ATDD) or Behavior Driven-Development (BDD) ensures that it is a living document, always running on the team's and cross-team's integration pipelines and updated as part of the software development lifecycle.

Structuring documentation as code helps onboarding new team members, improves collaboration with business and stakeholders, and also supports knowledge sharing inside and across teams. The DevOps chapter in this book included several useful practices for documenting with code. But this concept should not be limited to just software development. In construction, the entire industry does something similar and refers to it by the name, "As Built Drawings." Creating "living documentation" can reduce future risks and increase tribal knowledge that protects and enhances the organization's future.

Meeting Norms

Meetings are a pain for many, but there are ways to reduce the hurt. Creating lists of collaborative norms for more effective meetings is one way. A few things to consider are:

- What is the tolerance for being late?
- Are attendees allowed to drink/eat?
- When there is a meeting invite, is the agenda and purpose of the meeting provided and adequate?
- How to proceed when the timebox is over for the meeting.
- Are attendees allowed to play on smartphones during the meetings?

Of course, not all of these questions will be applicable for each Program, but the idea here is to avoid "common sense" assumptions and give visibility to the team agreements. A good approach is to post agreed upon norms on the team's wikipage or website, and periodically review parts of them so everyone is reminded of their existence and each team member can help ensure they are either being followed or adapted.

How to Make It Work Effectively

There are many alternatives and models for multiple teams to align and collaborate effectively. The biggest challenge is often convincing the organization to commit to the necessary changes in order to work with Agile across multiple teams.

Fractional Workforce Considerations
Coordinating fractionalized professionals at the Program-level is vital to minimizing the challenges they can bring to the Agile process. Clarifying who has the responsibility to manage each team member's agenda and time, even if that member will have a high level of autonomy, is imperative. Multiple projects may need to negotiate with operational leaders and other Program Managers to properly prioritize and share the availability of fractionalized team members.

A fractionalized team member must commit to attending the ceremonies used by the team and delivering value. When members are working on multiple projects within a Program, the Program Manager must work with the Project Managers to make sure ceremonies are scheduled at times that avoid creating conflicts for the fractionalized team members. The next accommodation required is establishing fixed work windows within the Iteration so everyone can reliably participate, contribute, and be available for the team. This clarity, added to a consistent commitment, will enable the team to plan their work so that the fractionalized member is able to deliver and contribute effectively.

While not optimal, some teams will either be partially or completely composed of fractional members. When that is the case, a good practice is to synchronize their work windows so they can collaborate and work together despite being distributed. This will also require adjustments to team ceremonies, such as daily meetings, being held during the committed work window. The work and reality of the team's time commitment must guide decisions on where to make exceptions to the Agile Framework and process being adopted.

A good practice for an organization beginning the transition to Agile practices is to set up pioneer teams for success. The goal of these pioneer teams, even when they are not fully exploiting all of the benefits of Agile, is to show what is possible and continue to advocate the next step towards agility.

Golden Hours or Core Hours

Golden or Core Hours are an application of the concept of Block Time first defined in Steven Covey's seminal work, *The 7 Habits of Highly Effective People*[2]. They are protected time windows, agreed on by team members, so they can dedicate higher levels of focus to problem solving and thereby increase productivity. The PM needs to protect the teams from interruptions during these periodic 60- to 90-minute spans so they can solve development and production related issues. This will help Program Managers get a higher visibility of when the fractionalized members will be working with the rest of the team. Begin with assigning two or four Core Hours a day, regularly assessing the results during Retrospectives, and adjusting the hours accordingly.

Using Core Hours enables a higher level of autonomy for the team member and ensures dedicated focus for the whole team. If any member is not following the agreement, any other team member can call them out and help bring everyone back on track.

Tools and Practices Recommendations

"Eyes Train Ears"- A Technique to Improve Communication

The Eyes Train The Ears!

A Proven Cure for ESL in Virtual Teams
by John Stenbeck

core concept courtesy of

Karen Schneider, Public Sector Programs Manager, IBM
with contributions from

Megan Moore, Project Manager, R&D,
Schweitzer Engineering Laboratories

Introduction

Today, project management and business teams must respond ever more quickly to changing customer demands and market constraints. Information sharing and decision-making are pressed into tighter and tighter timeboxes. To make matters even more complex and uncertain, many of the people involved have different priorities and perspectives that must be worked out in a virtual environment that removes most non-verbal communication. And finally, many of them are communicating using English as a Second Language (ESL).

English shares a unique distinction in human history as the first language to be spoken by more non-native speakers than by native speakers. Native speakers will tell you that the various dialects spoken, whether from the "Deep South" in the USA or the "Queen's English" spoken in India and Australia, can make it hard to understand the words being spoken. But those difficulties pale in comparison to the challenge faced by non-native speakers trying to communicate with one another. Consider for a moment the trials awaiting a team where ESL members are from Brazil, Eastern Europe and the Far East.

Virtual teams are becoming more popular for many reasons. One of the big reasons is the unavoidable financial constraint encountered when using a globally distributed development model to find and produce viable and effective solutions.

Virtual teams can offer great advantages, but they also face difficulties inherent with online and technology-intermediated relationships. Without the benefit of body language traditional management styles, based on seeing teammates frequently and sharing the same workspace, do not translate successfully for virtual teams. While communicating in person seems easy enough, the frequency of miscues and misunderstandings is well known. Inserting technology as an

intermediary, such as email and conference calls, can create a battlefield as miscommunication takes hold.

To overcome the virtual team challenge it is necessary to have communication by design, not by accident, where structural support is provided and a shared team experience is created. The structural components guide the behavior of team members while the shared team experience influences the motivation of each member.

The approach described here has been described by many users as the most powerful tool they have ever discovered for helping Virtual Teams overcome the barrier of English as a Second Language (ESL)!

Understanding Context

Research has shown, and common experience has validated, that communication includes far more than just the explicit meaning of the words being used. The context of the conversation supplies important information about the message being conveyed and received. Non-verbal behavior implies a great deal about the message regardless of whether it is expressed intentionally or not.

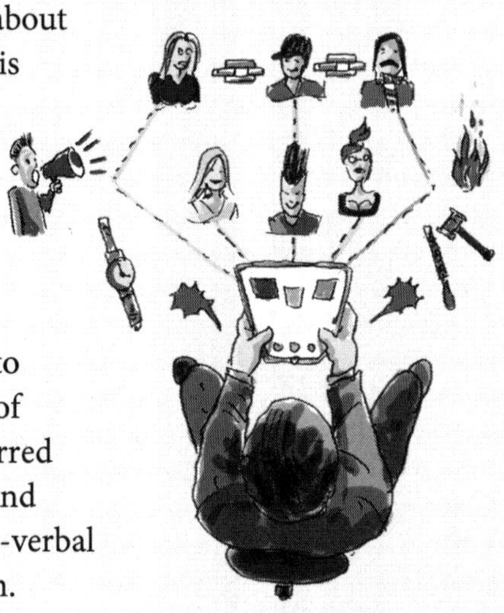

Non-verbal communication includes everything from facial expressions and visible reactions, to gestures and body language (technically referred to as kinesics), to the posture and physical separation of the communicators (technically referred to as proxemics) and even the tone and pitch of the voice, which are the non-verbal attributes of the spoken conversation.

Non-verbal signals provide vital clues that are used to reinforce or reinterpret what is being said, understand the political or emotional load of what is being said, and provide real time feedback or manage the pace of the interaction.

In addition to being vital, non-verbal communication is very culture-specific. Consider the common stereotype of Italians using big gestures and lots of hand motions or Americans being Cowboys and Lone Rangers who do not embrace consensus-based decision-making. Or consider the thumbs-up gesture commonly used to express approval in England but considered offensive in Greece.

Despite its complexity and uncertainty, non-verbal communication plays a major role in forming an accurate and reliable exchange of information. The kind of information that is vital for project team success, yet is severely limited for virtual teams due to the inescapable intermediation of technology.

Implementing a Solution - Using Eyes to Train Ears

Cultivating a team spirit enables exciting productivity. It does so, in part, because servant leadership becomes the operational norm so cross-functional teams become self-directed and fully accountable. Collocated teams enjoy a host of communication advantages in this regard whereas very real challenges arise for virtual teams.

In order for the team to stay engaged and synchronized they must have clear communication. The most common challenge for virtual teams is to understand the language being spoken with a non-native accent so they can decode the message with a minimal risk of misunderstanding.

The "secret" to overcoming this important conundrum became apparent to me during a conversation with Karen Schneider, Public Sector Programs Manager, IBM. During our conversation, Karen described a technique she used that I named, "The Eyes train the Ears" because, amazingly enough, that is exactly what occurs.

The technique creates communication by design by providing a structural support that greatly improves the shared team experience. The structural component guides the team members' behavior with a simple Rule of Engagement that is consistently enforced.

The rule requires each team member to provide detailed written answers to the three questions used in the Daily Meeting. The three questions are, first, "What did I do yesterday?" then, "What will I be doing today?" and finally, "What obstacles are preventing my progress?" The email must be sent at least 2 hours preceding the Daily Meeting call.

The rule also requires that when each team member begins their sharing, they must start by reading their written answers, verbatim. The magic is in the read-verbatim-first part of the rule. Doing so allows the other teammates to read what they are hearing and in the process the "eyes train the ears" for the spoken words. This simple practice vastly increases the quality of communication.

The rule must be mandatory for at least three weeks, after which the team should vote on whether to continue for another week or discontinue the practice. Most teams use it for four weeks, but few teams use it for longer than six.

A best practice that supports this structural component is for the organization to fund each team member's investment in a good headset to optimize the ability to hear what is spoken. Remember, pronunciation and vocal clues are very subtle.

Having a structural support that makes hearing and understanding each other vastly easier greatly improves the shared team experience. And that opens the door for truly high performance teams to thrive!

End-of-the-Day Emails

When working with multiple teams, especially virtual ones, it is often hard to remember what each member of each team is currently tackling. It is common to use software that manages requirements and the workflow, but often the data is not updated, or Tasks are unassigned or unavailable to stakeholders outside the team.

An effective practice for Program Managers to overcome these challenges is to complement the Daily Meeting with an end of the day email, summarizing the work progress, problems, or solutions that occurred, and send it to all the teams in the Program. This also serves to prepare members for the next Daily Meeting, anticipate potential questions, and align the teams with the same goals. Given that not all teams may be working in the same time zone, this practice is especially helpful for individuals working outside of the normal business hours of the Program's central location.

Team Photos in the Workspace

Having team member photos on the wall helps team members "see" each other throughout the day. During conference calls or Daily meetings having such visual information posted near the team space motivates members to resist multi-tasking and reduces other distractions by reminding them of the person "behind" the voice.

Using individual photos of all the team members to create a panoramic view of the team is a very beneficial practice that enhances team building and bonding, as shown in *Figure 12.01.* Including extra details other than names, such as home town, role or title, and hobby or favorite quote above or below each picture encourages team members to interact and form stronger relationships.

Figure 12.01 | Team Photos in the Work Place

Word of the Day

Whether a Program has multiple teams from different cultures, or just one team, with members from different backgrounds, it is natural to have varying dialects. If you compare American to British English, you will find many differences. If you compare American to Swedish English, you will find even more!

A way to decrease the language and cultural barriers is to have a Word of the Day (or week, depending on the preference of the team) included on the team wall. This can be a fun exercise where each member gets to select a word (or phrase) on a rotating basis that increases communication comprehension, insight into different backgrounds and, in turn, team bonding!

Information Radiators

Information radiators help teams and Program Managers have a visual overview of the progress and health of each team at any given time. For virtual teams, radiators must be accessible online or in a software program, even if it is something as simple as a working Excel document in a shared folder. The benefit of the radiator is increased if the updated information is always present so the team can give it attention without having to login or open a folder or URL.

Conclusion

Leading Programs working with virtual, remote and distributed teams is complex due to the many challenges and benefits in the varieties of configurations and different staffing strategies. These different strategies generate impacts on deliverables, ceremonies, artifacts, and everyone involved in the Program. Always remember to take into consideration individual perspectives and bring context from the Program level to the team level. This will not only motivate Program Managers to compose the right teams, but also align them with the right Agile practices to enhance team cohesion and give them a higher level purpose.

END NOTES

[1] Tuckman, Bruce W. (1965) 'Developmental Sequence in Small Groups', Psychological Bulletin, 63, 384-399. The article was reprinted in Group Facilitation: A Research and Applications Journal, No. 3, 2001 and is available as a PDF. According to the Tuckman theory of group development, there are four phases: Forming, Storming, Norming, and Performing – Adjourning was added in 1977. For more information on Bruce W. Tuckman and his research into the theory of group dynamics, visit: *https://en.wikipedia.org/wiki/Bruce_Tuckman.*

[2] Covey, Stephen R. *The 7 Habits of Highly Effective People.* Free Press, 1989. Covey (1932 –2012) was an American educator, author, businessman, and keynote speaker.

CHAPTER

13

Estimating & Scope Management

Overview

The target for every project or Program is successful delivery. The path to that successful delivery can vary depending on which approach is used and how well it is executed. Agile, Traditional, and hybrid Frameworks all offer many tools and practices to assist teams in their development process. Programs require the same diligent, focused team efforts as projects, but on a much larger scale, creating the need to purposefully and carefully select the correct approach, or combination of approaches, tailor them appropriately, then leverage the ceremonies, tools, and artifacts to achieve the Vision of the Program.

Agile offers unique solutions to estimating and scope management, not found in Traditional Frameworks, that minimize waste and increase accuracy, while also remaining flexible to the inevitable uncertainty at the project level. Program level estimating and scope management requires much more vigilance due to the increased uncertainty and complexity. This chapter will assist with reconciling how to manage estimating and scope in Programs containing Agile, Traditional, and hybrid projects.

Project vs Program Estimating and Scope Management

Estimating and scope management at the Program level differs from the project level in a few fundamental ways, beginning with the Program Manager's focus. Specifically in the AIF Foundation Paradigm *(Figure 11.01)*, they are further down, starting in the early window of strategic planning. The intent of having the Program Manager here is to not repeat or usurp the efforts Project Managers undertake when planning projects, but rather to support the planning process and provide structure and guidelines for projects to function.

Similarly to a project, the primary input to start the process is establishing a Flexibility Matrix for the Program that is part of the Program Charter. *(See Figure 13.01.)* Agile organizations that have embraced the Project Data Sheet (PDS) to replace the traditional Project Charter should consider using a similarly formatted PDS to replace the Program Charter. The PDS concept is explored in detail in Chapter 3 of *The Agile Almanac – Book 1.* The Flexibility Matrix will determine which Program-level constraints are fixed, negotiable, or flexible, but its application is not a step to lock these choices in for every project within the Program. The matrix helps define how the Program is going to be managed against the same constraints projects work under. If there are trade-offs at the project level, it will alert the Program Manager and Project Manager of the project that they are working against a different set of expectations, allowing them to implement controls and touch-points in the project to address the issues.

	FIXED	NEGOTIABLE	FLEXIBLE
SCOPE	X		
SCHEDULE		X	
COST			X

Figure 13.01 | Program Flexibility Matrix

Every organization differs in how they view, fund, and manage Programs. An organization that commits to a fixed budget at the Program level would have a budget as a fixed constraint, with scope and timeframe fighting for the negotiable and flexible boxes. An organization with a fixed Release schedule would have schedule as the fixed constraint; or if they had a clear Vision for the Product's features, scope would be the fixed constraint.

Understanding the fundamental axiom of "Good, Fast, Cheap: Pick Two" and how an organization measures success on this dynamic is key to setting a Program up to succeed. For the Program Manager, once the Flexibility Matrix is established, the level of effort and controls they put in place for projects within the Program to govern scope, timeline, and budget are relatively simple to understand. Focus should be placed on managing the fixed constraint to keep it within the Program's established guardrails. From there, the attention shifts to managing the negotiable constraint so if any changes need to be made to keep a project in control, the flexible constraint loses most of the time. The negotiable constraint can be impacted if necessary, but the fixed constraint is only affected as a last resort.

At the Program level, Agile estimating and scope management are intertwined. The Program must have a means to strategically estimate their capacity to deliver at the Roadmap and Release level for the Agile projects so they can be properly integrated with any hybrid or Waterfall projects also within the Program scope. Developing this capability is the cornerstone to the Agile Integration Framework and also the starting point to communicate required information to accurately and successfully manage Program schedules, risk, quality, and budget. These will be discussed in greater detail in Chapters 14-17.

Benefits / Challenges

Benefits

Estimating and scope management, done well, make everything else easier to govern at both the Program and project level. Chapter 11 discussed the AIF foundation and defined granularity at the Program level, illustrating the impact of time to estimating accuracy in Figure 11 – 03, and determined the primary risk to be underestimation. Multiple studies have proven that organizations are far more likely to underestimate than overestimate their resource needs. Despite both this fact being well-known and padding estimates to avoid doing so, they still fail to capture the true effort of the endeavor! Mastering a process to effectively and reliably estimate the level of effort needed to deliver the desired scope of a Program will make you a rock star in any organization. And, once mastered, budgeting, risk management, and establishing a Release schedule for a Program become far easier to achieve with reliable precision.

Contains Tools & Practices to Reduce Waste

The remarkable, yet rarely explored power of Agile is the ability to use the Agile tools and practices to deal with uncertainty at the Program level regardless of the Framework or approach used to deliver the project once it is initiated. Program management inherently possesses a high degree of uncertainty and complexity when attempting to estimate the level of effort on a set of Features at the level of a FFC or EWP. Affinity Planning or Planning Poker techniques outlined in Chapter 11 are a rapid path to estimating the level of effort on a future endeavor as ubiquitous and vague as a FFC or EWP. Any attempts to map out a Traditional tool, like a WBS, even if the project will eventually be managed using Waterfall techniques, are often a waste of time and effort. For the wise Program Manager, the gift of Agile multiplies efficiency and improves accuracy, working within the strategic planning efforts when doubt is at its highest and details at their lowest levels.

Even if the Program Manager works in an organization that uses 100% Waterfall to deliver projects, adjusting to the applicable Agile tools and techniques outlined in this almanac, specifically those mentioned in the Agile Integrated Framework chapter, to scope and estimate at the Program level makes perfect sense. Agile excels at coming to a ROM estimate in short order with limited detail. Program Managers live at the edge of strategic planning when attempting to scope and estimate FFCs, as details are in short supply and uncertainty is high.

Minimizes Reactive Responses to Change by Using the Flexibility Matrix

Understanding the landscape the Program will be judged for success is paramount for the Program Manager. The Flexibility Matrix sets the path for the Program and projects that fall underneath it. Securing a definitive ranking for when a constraint should be compromised and difficult decisions need to be made will not only aid the decisions, it will avoid the need to make them at all. If every participant contributing to the Program's success clearly understands the ground rules of the Program, they will know what direction decisions need to flow without active coaching from the Program Manager.

For example, a project team member working within a Program, where schedule is fixed and scope is the most flexible constraint, encounters an issue where a desired, but not mandatory, Feature is consuming a fair bit of time to work through. With a clear understanding of the ground rules, they are far more likely to set it aside and bring up the concern at the Daily Stand-up, recommending halting development and dropping it from scope for the next Release in the interest of the schedule. Because the Program Manager, embracing the AIF Framework, uses information radiators to openly communicate the Program objectives and status, no issue needs to be escalated for consideration at all. Open, candid information radiators, outlining the Program Vision and how each contributor's efforts aid in moving the goals of the Program along, will vastly simplify the Program Manager's job and allow them to remain focused on the strategic Vision instead of working to address escalated issues.

Enables Integration of Projects Using Agile, Traditional, & Hybrid Approaches
This may be a tough concept for some Program Managers to grasp at first, but at the Program level, the methodology used to deliver the project should not guide how the Program Manager works through the defined granularity process described in the AIF to plan from high-level Feature, Function, and Capability (FFC) clusters through defining Epic Work Packages (EWP). If the Program Manager can resist the urge to work with any planning efforts differently until work is bundled into EWPs, then integrating Agile, Traditional, and hybrid approaches at the Program level is infinitely simpler than many scaled Agile Frameworks and Traditional approaches to Program management make it out to be.

Once a Program Manager has achieved forming inbound demands on the Program into EWPs, then discussions can be held with the Product Manager, Product Owner (if known), Project Manager (if known), and other stakeholders about the complexity and uncertainty levels and advantages or disadvantages present in one project delivery Framework over another. This is the magic within the *PMBOK® Guide Sixth Edition's* vision for the future. Select the right Framework for the right work to be done and, do not allow dogmatic devotion to any Framework to stand in the way of delivering Program-level success.

Challenges

People are inherently bad at estimating the level of effort for a given Task in the form of hours, but are quite adept at estimating the relative complexity of one Task against another[1]. Leveraging the practices and tools Agile provides at the User Story level will aid the Program Manager with ROM estimates across the entire spectrum of Agile, Traditional, and hybrid projects, however, learning how to do so is not easy.

New Techniques to Learn

Most often, when an initial project estimate is shown to the Program Manager it is not at the finite level a Project Manager could achieve if Agile techniques were applied. Agile techniques can be employed to reach the level of accuracy and flexibility required for the Program, not just that particular project within. The challenge is gaining competence and trust in the tools. It is a difficult leap of faith, for some, to accept that Agile methods are equally, or more, accurate as Traditional, but require half the time to execute. Spending hours and hours trying to break down the WBS for a future project as far as the Program Manager can, with the vague goals they work with, is no more accurate than a few minutes of discussion with some key SMEs and a deck of Fibonacci cards for a game of Planning Poker. This may seem unbelievable, but it is true!

As at the project level, the mastery task is understanding how to use the deck of cards in Planning Poker or affinity comparisons in Affinity Planning. At the Program level, it may be wise to have some completed, real-world projects laid out across the Fibonacci Sequence or Affinity Grid so there are some solid points of relative comparison for everyone involved to draw from when assessing the complexity and effort required to complete a newly crafted work package.

Getting everyone to understand what level project constitutes a mid-point (usually 8, but can be closer to 13 in some cases and depends on how the organization determines the center point of their Fibonacci deck) of project complexity and cost is a key to grasping the technique at the Program level. Comparing complexity against known, completed projects, either with Affinity Planning or Planning Poker, will yield solid ROM results if there is a common understanding of how the technique works, which takes time and patience. This effort still pales in comparison to attempting to estimate a single project using Traditional estimation techniques at the Program level.

Unless an organization has a firm and deep commitment to Earned Value Management (EVM), once a Project Manager is engaged to initiate and plan a project, Affinity Planning can be applied to any approach used to manage it.

On a well-managed project with clear scope, a firm grasp of the deliverables, and the Tasks and level of effort allowed to dictate the timeline, EVM is a proven technique with a long, storied history of success. Conversely, when a project is planned or managed poorly, there is a sobering history of predicting failure, long before project completion.

Unfortunately, very few organizations truly embrace the power of EVM and instead make a causal, high-level attempt to appear to use EVM to impress sponsors, stakeholders, or other executives. Rather than making a weak attempt at building out a WBS, with nebulous estimates, half-hearted effort, and flawed accuracy, why not use the tools in the AIF to continue planning the projects, improving the chance to accurately estimate with significantly less effort?

"The less effort, the faster and more powerful you will be."
– Bruce Lee

The effort it takes to learn a new practice or toolset may be intimidating, but the value brought to the Program, and organization as a whole, will prove worth it. If the Program team can commit to doing so and using a common toolset and approach for estimating, they will replace a process of lackadaisical efforts and results known to be flawed and inaccurate.

"Success is dependent on effort."
– Sophocles

Blending Approaches Requires Strong Communication

Where does the road fork between Agile, Traditional, and hybrid? There is no one answer to that. Once Pandora's Box has been opened, exposing the organization and project teams to *The Agile Manifesto* and concept of the self-directed team, the Program Manager now must wrestle with team members convinced every project should be Agile and every decision should come from the project team. If an organization opts to dip their toes in somewhere between the opposite poles of pure Agile and pure Traditional, Program Managers will need to work to establish guidelines on when a given approach will be needed. The technique is outlined in the workflow section of this chapter, but communicating and educating the team is a challenge that does not simply go away once planning ceremonies establish the technique that will be used.

Information Radiators for the Program team are a fantastic first step to sharing and inviting input into the decision-making process. The Program

Charter should be simple and openly visible to every stakeholder involved in the Program's success. Decisions, like selecting a Framework, need to be able to pass the "Five Whys" test. If the Program Manager is not prepared to answer five progressive "why?" questions to explain the rationale for selecting a tool or Framework, then they have not done an adequate job of setting the Program up for success.

For organizations amidst an Agile transformation, the organizational landscape becomes even tougher to navigate. The rationale for adopting one Framework or technique over another is fluid and moving further towards Agile and, there are many things the Program Manager needs to juggle. To stay at the pace set by the organization for the transformation, they must:

- Communicate with their PMO leaders to remain informed of any organizational directives
- Work with the Product Manager to establish a selection grid that works for their unique situation
- Communicate the ongoing changes to Product Managers, Product Owners, and team members
- Take all feedback from these resources into account when adjusting the approach

The good news is that if the AIF and mindset are adopted, regardless of how the projects will be managed within the Agile to Traditional spectrum, changes will not need to be communicated about how the Program approaches estimation. Because the techniques do not vary by approach, estimation and scope management become a stable cornerstone, remaining static. The bad news is that regardless of what scaled Framework an organization uses, Agile's approach to scope management is significantly different in nature than Traditional waterfall.

Traditional waterfall attempts to set scope to a finite point when the project is at a high level of uncertainty in planning and place the Project Manager in the position of managing every attempt to change scope as a change request with budgetary implications. Pure Agile would advocate that, in any project or Program with high uncertainty and complexity, scope is the worst constraint to control, and the goal is to deliver the Minimum Viable Feature (MVF) and any additional Features on either a set budget or set timeline.

The communication task for scope management tends to flow more outward to stakeholders than inward to the Project Manager, Product Owner, or Product Team. The stakeholders need to be aware that if an Agile project has a fixed budget or fixed timeframe, the project disbands at the end of that window unless they can make the case, based on the ROI, for the remaining Backlog items. Working within Agile projects does not open a door to scope that cannot be closed. Stakeholders need to be educated and understand that funding or schedule cease at a given date unless they can successfully argue that the remaining Backlog of development items can be of enough benefit that the team should continue work.

Maintaining Flexibility and Direction Simultaneously
Programs, at a fundamental level, will inherently suffer from constant pressure to expand scope because a single project cannot achieve the Program goals. Some Programs will have tactile, clearly achievable goals, but most are more ubiquitous and set up to be a nearly perpetual endeavor, supporting a crucial function of the organization. The challenge for the Program Manager is to embrace expanding scope when it advances the goals set forth in the Program Charter, and recognize and diplomatically resist changes that ultimately do not, even if they touch on the scope of the Program in some way.

Scaled Agile, specifically the AIF, offers a solution to help with this, but it is a challenge because not all organizations recognize the power and flexibility that a continuously engaged Agile Product Team can bring. Scrum aficionados will advocate that once an Agile team has been established and passed the maturity stages of forming, storming, and norming, they are productive by any yardstick applied to measure them. Why disband a team achieving at this level, return them to the resource pool, and assemble different members to form a new Agile Project Team that must work exceptionally hard to get to the same point of productivity? Too often, the problem is simply that Agile is not viewed from a Program management level. From the Agile project perspective, the continuous project team becomes a bit laughable in some instances. A Product Manager, worth their weight in playground sand, can come up with an endless supply of desired Features for a platform or product.

This is where the Agile Integration Framework and Program Manager come into play and the continuously engaged Agile Product Team becomes a powerful tool. The Program Manager can monitor backlogged items at the

EWP-level of granularity and work with stakeholders to determine if that work package is at a higher level of priority than the developed User Stories in the team's Backlog. If the EWP is more important and fits the business case for Agile development, it is inserted as an Epic into the team's Backlog and incorporated into their Release plans moving forward. If the EWP is not more important, it either sits in the Program Backlog or is assigned to another group of resources. Scaling to multiple Agile teams within the Program is easily accomplished if there is a continuous flow of EWPs to occupy their time.

Stepping into the realm of the Agile team creates a new set of hurdles and pitfalls. The Program Manager needs to continually share the purpose of an Agile team, coordinate their efforts with other teams, regardless of the Frameworks being used by each, and provide guidelines for when an EWP is a candidate for work by the Agile team or when it needs to be addressed by a different approach. The first steps are more like leaps to making a team Agile, but if the Program Manager is willing to make the commitment, they will begin leveraging the continuously improving, efficient processes that only an Agile team can deliver!

Program-level Attributes

Roles

There are key roles within Agile Program Management with responsibilities for scope management and estimating. In addition to those, at the Program level there can be roles from a mixed environment, which are more Traditional in nature.

Program Manager

In Agile, Program Managers have ultimate responsibility to deliver the scope of the Program to the stakeholders. They organize the Delivery Team into projects and operations and charter them through delivering the product or service. The Program Manager facilitates the development of a Program Roadmap and Program Release Plan then orchestrates the scope delivery, using them as guides to keep the teams focused on the Feature prioritization and Release schedule contained within.

Program Managers interface with and report to management within the organization to communicate progress toward the goal of delivering the scope as outlined in the Program Charter and reflected in the Program

Roadmap. They are responsible for keeping the Program within scope, within budget, and on schedule. Working with the management team to balance each based on the Program Flexibility Matrix, the Program Manager selects the Framework(s) the delivery team will use to deliver the scope of the Program.

In some organizations, the Framework, or blend of Frameworks, used to execute the Program objectives are dictated to the Program Manager. Some organizations will choose to execute Programs strictly using Agile methodologies and others will choose a hybrid approach. A Program Manager who leverages the project management methodologies to work within their organization increases their ability to scale Agile to the Program level. Ultimately, the team's ability to deliver the scope and subsequent Features, Functions, and Capabilities is dependent on how well the Program Manager guides the delivery teams to meet their objectives, regardless of the Framework and methodologies used.

Product Manager

The Product Manager is integral to the formulation of the solution delivered to the Customer in Agile approaches. This challenging role requires a close connection with the Customer and a strong understanding of their needs so they can clearly articulate the requirements and define the product or service and associated Features. Their close association with the Customer provides a central focal point for Feature delivery feedback to the team that can influence changes to the scope or solutions to stay within it.

The Product Manager continually aligns the scope with the Program Roadmap and Release Plan, prioritizing the Product Backlog to deliver the Features as agreed upon. The Feature requests, in the form of Feature Stories and Epics, are then allocated to each team's Iteration Backlog. Following this approach allows the Product Manager to facilitate the correct Feature Releases per the Release Plan.

When the Program consists of both Agile and Traditional projects, the Product Manager should consider the scope assigned to the Traditional teams to ensure the FFCs they deliver align with a delivery method reminiscent of a Traditional approach. Additionally, the Product Manager should encourage, or better yet mandate, that the Traditional team deliver using Rolling Wave Releases.

Project Manager
The Project Manager, in both Agile and Traditional Frameworks, is responsible for the delivery of the scope of the project. When using Agile, they work with the Product Owner and team to meet the delivery requirements by producing the defined Features in the Program Release Plan. Working with the Program Manager, Product Manager, Product Owner, and their team, they provide ROM estimates during the Highway and Roadmap planning sessions. They also work with their team, as Stories are pulled into each Iteration, to size the work appropriately.

Product Owner
In Agile approaches, the Product Owner works with the Product Manager to represent the Customer. At the project level, the Product Owner represents the Customer's voice in all meetings and communications with the team and other stakeholders. They provide well-formed and clearly defined Users Stories, which the team uses to identify estimates and deliver solutions.

Domain Experts
The Domain Experts are key to the estimation process. Using their knowledge and experience in their area of expertise, they provide a solid basis for accurate estimates, regardless of the Program management methodology used.

Delivery Team
The Agile team is responsible for producing the Features and solutions according to the scope of their project. They size the work in each Iteration and commit to its completion prior to the end of the Iteration.

Other Stakeholders
Depending on the organization and needs of the Program, the following resources could be consulted and engaged when needed to assist with estimating and planning:

- Architecture Owner & Integrator Stakeholders
- Process Owner
- Architecture Owner
- SMEs
- Independent Integrator

Workflow

Scope Management

One of the keys to scaling Agile is successfully managing the scope of the Program. Program scope management begins with the charge provided by the organization, which determines the scope. The Program Charter should lay out the Vision for the Program, any known, anticipated benefits the Program will achieve, and its initial scope. If the scope is set to fixed or flexible in the Flexibility Grid, scope management should become a significant focus for the Program Manager.

Some in the Agile community have the mistaken impression that scope is not a critical aspect to manage as they think they ought to be flexible as the customers' needs change. Whereas it is important to deliver the highest priority FFCs first followed by the next important FFCs, understanding and managing the scope of work is still important, especially at the Macro level. For instance, if the Program is established to deliver a specific product, but ends up delivering a completely unrelated product, the Program is off course. This is the effect known as scope creep.

Scope Creep

Scope Creep is the continually increasing requests for changes to the initially defined Program scope. In Traditional project management, these changes are managed via change control. Agile accepts, and even embraces, the fact that things will change as open communication with the Customer produces requests, altering the scope. With change inevitable, it is important to understand how to address and manage it.

There are several ways scope creep occurs. Some originate at the project level and some at the Program level. A project scope change that cannot be absorbed within the project's reserves should be elevated to the Program level. These types of project changes can result from Customer requests, technical limitations in the development of the FFCs, or other unseen forces impacting the project. Another possible change factor to Program scope is the addition of new projects, known as Epic Work Packages (EPW) in Agile. A Program-level Burn-up chart is an excellent tool to visually depict the ongoing growth of the Program scope. This is shown in *Figure 13.02* where additional scope was added in anticipation of the delivery of the full amount of the prior scope.

Programs can experience some external pressures to scope that must be managed and addressed by the Program Manager as well.

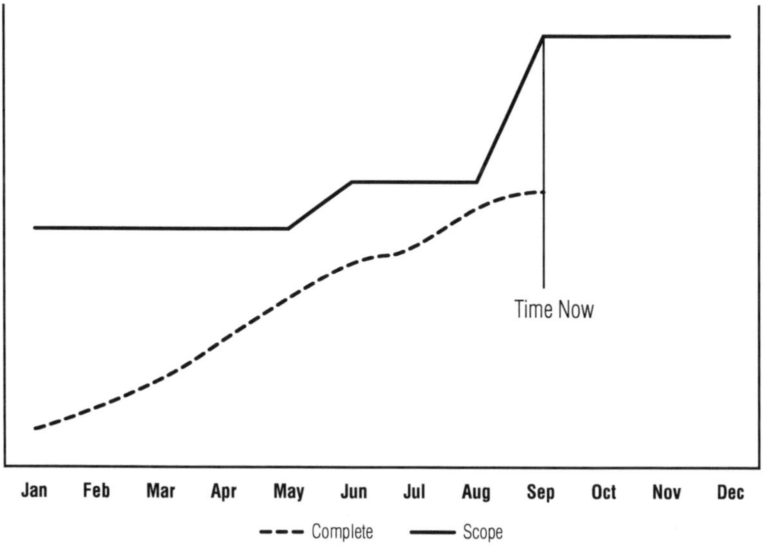

Figure 13.02 | Program Burn Up Chart

Using an example of a Program to improve a company's capabilities within their Human Resources (HR) department, we can quickly see how external forces will attempt to attach other initiatives to the Program scope. An HR Program to develop new software and generate new materials to streamline the hiring process has been assigned to a Program Manager and several teams. Shortly into the development process, the organization makes the decision to also do an Enterprise Resource Planning (ERP) system upgrade. While the ERP may have human resources as a stakeholder, its span is far beyond simply that department and is unlikely to advance the goal of the Program. Therefore, it is an unlikely candidate to include in its scope.

Often, organizations will either not recognize this fact, or flat out ignore it, and add it to the scope, reasoning that there is already a team and Program in place, so surely they can just slip it into the workflow to be managed along with the rest of the projects. This thought process and Program dynamic are significant risks of scope creep found at the Program level.

Another scope creep situation occurs when smaller projects, with no ties to the outcome of a Program, get added anyway. An example of this, again using HR, is if a small project to install a system used for new hire orientation sessions is added without any relation to other projects in Program. Despite having only the HR department as its stakeholder, it is not a predecessor for or reliant on any other projects in the Program, so there is no reason for it to be part of it. This will only increase complexity with no benefit and that is precisely the opposite goal of Agile!

Delivering Scope
Winning the battle against scope creep is an important victory when marching toward the goal of providing increased value to the stakeholders. If the Program Manager can recognize and protect the Program from scope creep, the team will be better equipped to deliver what is expected.

Once protected, the scope can be delivered using good Agile practices, as outlined in previous chapters. In Chapter 11 specifically, the AIF focused on the importance of decomposing the scope into Features, Functions, and Capabilities. When this is accomplished, the teams can focus on the "bite sized" pieces, allowing them to successfully deliver scope.

Estimating
The Program Manager has ultimate responsibility and accountability for delivering the goals of the Program Charter. For estimating and scope management their primary role is to lead the ceremonies establishing the initial scope into Feature, Function, and Capability (FFC) clusters, creating a Customer-Value Logic Network (CVLN) that lays Program deliverables out into a logical Roadmap and Release path that develops into an Execution Logic Network (ELN) comprised of Epic Work Packages (EWP). See Chapter 11 for a thorough discussion how AIF approaches the estimation process.

Methodology Selection
At this level of composition, two forks in the road occur in determining how the Program will be executed. In order to guide the team down the right path, crucial discussions need to happen. These should consider factors such as:

- ***How interlaced the work packages are*** – Is there a clear Stop-Start path of ending one EWP before starting the next, where the work packages should be set up in a single rail of work? How many packages are so interlaced they must be worked simultaneously?
- ***How complex and uncertain the work is in the packages*** – Can a Project Manager and team break the work into Tasks and estimate the effort to complete them? Is so much new knowledge required to achieve the goal there is no easy way to estimate how long it will take to get the work done?

These two dimensions will assist the Program Manager with mapping out the approach and Framework that will set the Program up for success.

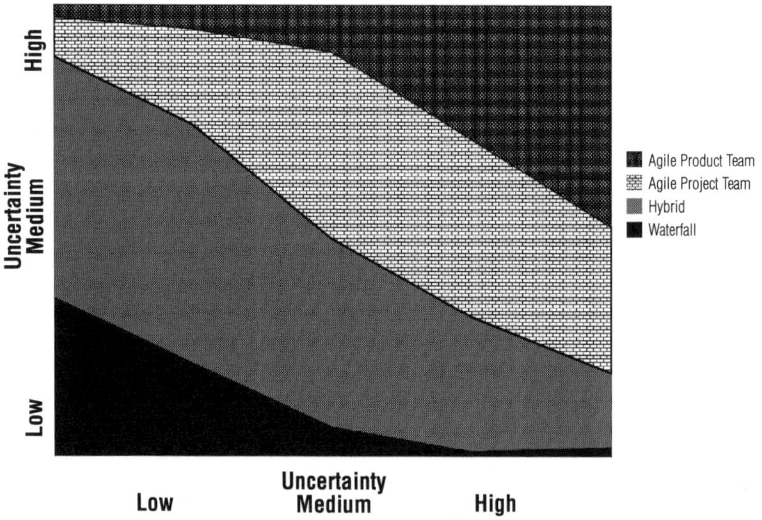

Figure 13.03 | Methodology Select Matrix

The Methodology Selection Matrix in *Figure 13.03* is a sample matrix. Each organization will vary in their approach based on how far along it is with an Agile transformation and if it has embraced and implemented the concept of the Agile product team vs. project team. An organization early in their Agile transformation may have a narrow selection band for hybrid or Agile, with the majority of the grid being occupied by Waterfall (Traditional). An organization mature and experienced in Agile may have little to no area allocated to Waterfall.

An Agile Product Team is continuously engaged, working a dynamically changing Backlog with no set timeline or budgetary constraint to continue. They avoid the penalties of forming, storming, and norming that project teams experience at the beginning of each project. Agile Product Teams are more aligned with delivering the goals of a Program than the narrow focus of a project. Many organizations adopt Agile from a Traditional project management approach and, in doing so, find themselves in a transitional stage where some teams have found their Agile stride, and others are still either storming or have not yet adopted Agile methodologies. These hybrid Programs require the Program Manager to consider the Agile maturity of the delivery team when addressing the estimation and scope delivery processes.

Once a solid strategy of approach to the management and execution of all work packages within the Program is set, they can be grouped into Product Backlogs for Agile projects, Project Backlogs for Agile or hybrid projects, or high-level WBSes for Waterfall projects.

Regardless of the execution method for projects, the influx of new requirements needing integration into the Program management plan is a near-continuous process. Agile processes and techniques are every Program Manager's friend because they can be applied to any method, even if every project will be managed using Traditional methodologies. Virtually no Program sustains the initial scope and closes without changes. Programs and Portfolios are scaled Agile projects, whether or not the Program or Portfolio Manager recognizes it.

Project Managers add meat to the bones the Program Manager puts on the platter ahead of the project planning process. As projects are executed, plans become actual spent resources and achieved scope. When projects close, resources return to the Program Manager's available pool of talent and financial reserves. As this project execution cycle takes place, new items are added to the Program scope and the process begins again.

Ceremonies

These ceremonies are listed out as separate events, but depending on an organization's complexity and size, some can be condensed with phase gates, not progressing until the goal is achieved.

Annual or Semi-Annual Highway Planning

The goal of this ceremony is to validate that all known FFCs have been captured and leave with an updated CVLN. The CVLN categorizes the goals of the Program into major themes and validates that they tie into the Value Stream of the organization. More detail on the CVLN is outlined in Chapter 11 – Agile Integrated Framework.

Quarterly Roadmap Planning

The goal of this ceremony is to convert the CVLN into an ELN comprised of EWPs, which should be estimated at an affinity level. Affinity Planning or Planning Poker are recommended methods to quickly estimate the relative complexity of the project. When defining scope for the EWP, a primary objective should be to outline what is not in scope to set up guardrails for what the EWP is and is not meant to represent. In some ways, these exclusions, rather than attempts to roughly outline scope, will bring more structure and understanding to the goals of the EWP. The Program Manager and Product Manager should review EWPs at this point to determine if the project will be managed using an Agile, hybrid, or Traditional approach. Once EWPs have reached this point, the Project Manager and Product Manager work to prioritize the Backlog of all EWPs not started and select which ones should be assigned to a project for work to begin.

Bi-Monthly Release Planning

Once the Program EWPs are estimated at an affinity level and priorities established, the Program and Product Manager hold a bi-monthly Release planning meeting with the Project Manager and Product Owners to coordinate upcoming Releases. The outcome of these meetings is an update to the Program Release Roadmap, reflecting how all active teams working on projects will coordinate their upcoming work. Affinity Planning and Planning Poker remain effective tools to estimate and coordinate major work packages, if any estimates need to be revisited as part of the discussion.

The primary requirement of this ceremony is to define any integration points requiring delivery at the same time. If they are within the same project team, the Project Manager is responsible for monitoring the delivery of these Features on the Release. If the integration points span across multiple projects, the Program Manager becomes responsible for managing the development and providing additional resources, if needed, to keep the Release on target once it is being executed.

Iteration and Milestone WAG & SWAG

The Iteration and Milestone WAG and Iteration and Milestone SWAG ceremonies are more project-focused, but outcomes of these discussions do cross into the domain of the Program Manager. If they adjust the probability of delivering planned scope for the next Release, the Program Manager will interpret this feedback and take action accordingly. The key difference in roles between the Program and Project Manager in these discussions is the Program Manager works with the Project Manager to arrange for external resources to assist with resolving challenges or exploiting opportunities while the Project Manager oversees the assigned project resources.

If a project is falling behind on delivering scope, the Program Manager can work with the Project Manager to either execute corrective actions by arranging for a swarming or spike Sprint to assist the project team, using contingency resources, or adjust the Release plan to reflect the revised estimates. Swarming Sprints allow the Program Manager to assign skilled resources from the Program resource reserve to pick up and work User Stories to help bring the project back on track. For hybrid and Waterfall projects, the same premise applies with resources jumping into the project and taking on items at the WBS element level to assist in delivering the project, with a focus on Tasks that can be worked in relative isolation from the project team.

A spike Sprint in Agile is a Sprint where exploration and learning are the goals. In the context of bringing a project back on track, the project team, sometimes with the assistance of reserve resources, would halt work on advancing User Stories and use the next Iteration to solve a difficult problem or gain knowledge that will help increase velocity or get past a barrier that requires total focus.

When a project is running ahead of scope, the immediate response from most organizations is to add scope to the team, creating significant issues at the Program level. The dialogue between Program and Project Manager needs to focus around what actions can be taken to exploit the opportunity to benefit the Program. Some key aspects to consider are:

- If a project team takes on a portion of scope for a future Release, can they deliver the original scope Features to production without causing integration or user experience challenges?
- Are any other project teams within the Program struggling that could use some help?
- Does the project have technical debt that can be worked instead of new User Stories?
- Are there refactoring or other technical User Stories in the Backlog that can be pulled forward in the Release plan to further increase velocity moving forward?

Artifacts

Estimation and Scope Management at the Program level uses, updates, and generates a number of artifacts. Program Managers should remember that generating or updating an artifact is not the end of the process, it is the beginning. Communicating formally and socializing the knowledge gained developing the artifact and the final product is key to generating value. In addition to the Flexibility Matrix, Methodology Selection Matrix, and Program Burn-up chart already outlined earlier in the chapter, there are some other artifacts that factor into estimation and scope management.

The Program Charter

Beyond the initial formation of the Program Charter, it can, and should be, updated as the Program matures. The scope and Vision of the Program can frequently change as new problems and FCCs are introduced. If the Program Vision and scope do not account for FCCs actively being worked by the teams, it is time to update the Program Charter.

Organizational Process Assets

Good, old fashioned Organizational Process Assets (OPA) are the artifacts offering the best chance for successful estimating. It is recommended to use the organization's OPA to identify where historical estimation and scope management issues are coming from to ensure they are confronted and managed. Closed projects are the source of relative comparison and evidence of any historical bias with estimation or challenges with scope management. As the Program matures and establishes its own catalog of OPA, these updates will bring more relevance and insight into guiding future planning efforts.

FFC, CVLN, ELN, and EWP Scope Statements and Estimates

The Agile Integration Framework outlines the process that ties together moving from general FFC to a tight EWP scope statement and level of effort estimation. Estimation and Scope Management efforts forge and refine the general FFC Milestones into a EWP that can be picked up by a Project Manager and Product Owner to decompose into a project plan. Navigating and establishing guidelines on how deep the Program and Product Managers dig into details to flush out a EWP so there is enough detail for the Project Managers and Product Owners to run with, but minimal duplication of effort, is crucial to maintaining a clean process with the least waste possible.

Program Roadmaps

Program Roadmaps can visually depict current and backlogged projects within the Program against a Release schedule. It is tempting to try to overload the Roadmap with additional information, but sometimes it is wiser to leave the Roadmap as simple as possible and use other information radiators to share indicators like the type of project management methodology used, the current level of accuracy for the project's estimate, and the names of the Project Manager, Program Manager, and Project Team. All of this information is available in a project's PDS, so leverage that artifact instead.

Figure 13.04 shows a standard Gantt chart. *Figure 13.05* shows how the Defined Granularity process overlays on a Program Roadmap expressed as a Gantt Chart.

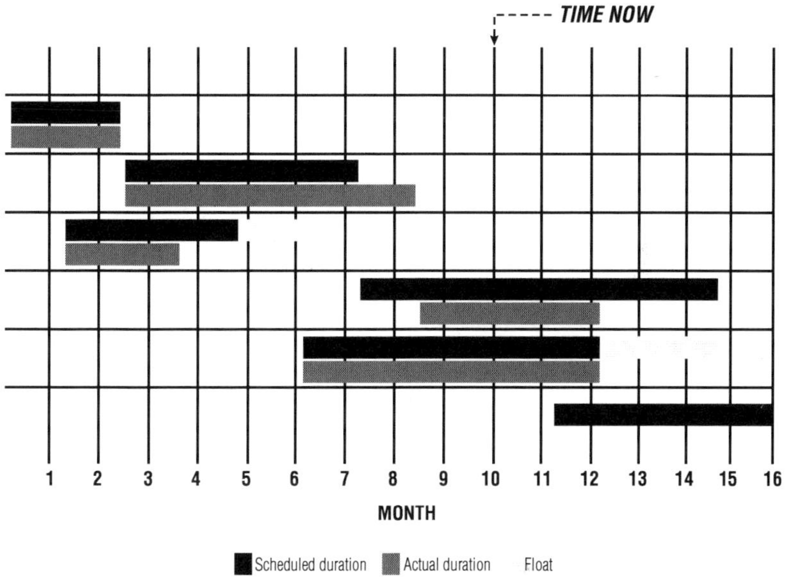

Figure 13.04 | Gantt Chart

Month 12 is time now for the Program so everything before it is complete or overdue and everything beyond it is to be done or ahead of schedule. The projects being actively worked, and those slated to start soon, were high risk or problematic so they got prioritized near the beginning of the Program Roadmap.

Putting the challenges near the beginning allows for more scope refinement and clarification of estimates as granularity increases, and discovery and learning occur. It also allows for some time flexibility, and in a worst case scenario, killing a bad project when it is proven that vital Features will be so expensive that they invalidate the business case's fundamental assumptions for benefits realization.

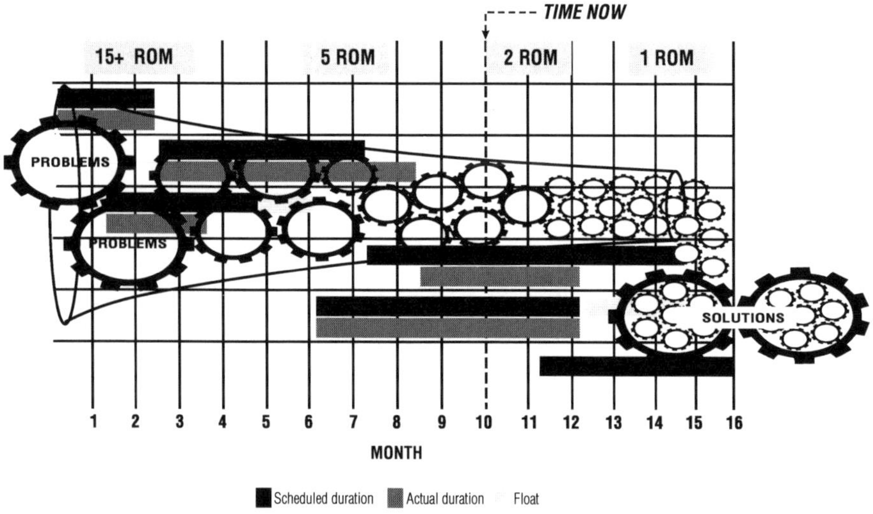

Figure 13.05 | Granularity Overlaying Gantt Chart

The arrows in *Figure 13.06* illustrate how discovery and learning, combined with appropriate granularity, empower the team to operate like Olympic Relay Race competitors, securely passing the baton – from Program Manager and Product Manager to Project Manager and Product Owner – once an EWP has been defined to include a ROM budget. Then, a choice can be made regarding whether the project will be managed using an Agile, Traditional,

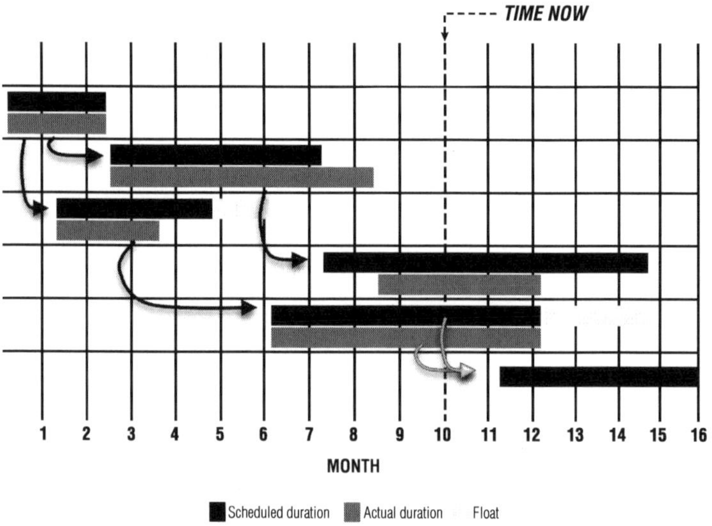

Figure 13.06 | Passing the Relay-Race Baton

or hybrid approach. This passing of the baton allows the Project Manager and Product Owner to work on refining and generating a healthy Backlog of EWPs awaiting resources so the Program remains sustainable.

Using a relay race as the visual, the Program Manager and Product Manager's lap starts with problems and, during their lap, they use the Defined Granularity process to develop EWPs. At the baton exchange, the Project Manager and Product Owner pick up the EWP to manage as a project to deliver to production. When the Program Manager and Product Manager hand off the baton, they go back to the beginning of the track and start the process again.

How to Make It Work Effectively

Estimation and scope management, done right, make everything else downstream easier to manage. Pressure on risks, budget, quality, and schedule presents when estimation fails to capture the true level of effort if an undiscovered component of scope must be completed within the constraints of the project. Setting a Program up to succeed means establishing reserves to address challenges and working with all stakeholders to continually review and improve upon their accuracy.

Establish Contingencies During the Planning Phase
Setting up funding and resource reserves at the Program level and applying those resources to projects to address scope changes or compensate for estimation errors is a good practice. This should occur at the beginning of the Program, as part of the Program Charter, to establish initial funding then be reviewed for spend and projected needs during quarterly Roadmap Planning. The goal of the Program reserve is to allot a contingency percentage of the overall Program resources to address the known, and, more importantly, unknown challenges with estimation. As the Program matures, the contingency needs will reduce, as long as the Program Manager is actively mentoring and coaching the teams, and supporting the Program to improve estimating accuracy.

The actual spend rate on the Program reserves should be reflected in the Program financial reporting updates shared with the team, stakeholders, and PMO on, at least, a quarterly basis. It should also be the input to discussing any funding adjustments during the quarterly Roadmap Planning session. This traceable decrease in the need for contingencies is a significant success factor, feeding into success at the portfolio or PMO level, by relieving those resources from having to, potentially, rescue the Program when it depletes its own. This is achieved when the project-level estimates adequately predict resource needs and can absorb minor setbacks without pulling from the Program reserves.

Use Reviews Effectively

The team and Program reviews, conducted as part of administering the Program, are excellent opportunities to perform sanity checks on scope. The Program Vision should be visible in these ceremonies and all participants should be challenged to validate everything – from an Agile project's potentially shippable User Story to a Waterfall project's upcoming Release – as advancing the Vision and goal of the Program. Making sure that all work effort is aligned with the Program Vision is a simple, natural means to effectively manage its scope.

Use Retrospectives Effectively

Agile Retrospectives are excellent opportunities to review any identified challenges in an open, non-punitive way that challenges the team to work towards improving their accuracy. Make improving estimating time and resource efforts a priority, at all levels of planning, by placing the topic up for discussion during Retrospectives. It will not take long to realize that estimation errors are a frequent root cause of issues encountered in a team's Iteration. A principal goal of Agile is to create a sustainable pace that can continue indefinitely. This only works if the Program, Product, and Project managers, the Product Owners, and teams are providing accurate estimates for their efforts. Helping all stakeholders understand the importance of accurate estimates and empowering them with data to improve their accuracy is the best means to that end.

Eliminate Bias

The goal for any organization is to identify if there is a natural bias within the Program Manager, stakeholder group, or even itself, as a whole, to overwhelmingly over- or under-estimate during planning activities. To determine whether a bias exists, begin using a control chart to track how each resource in the Program is estimating versus delivering on their estimates. At the team level, this would be on a User Story basis. For the Project Manager and Product Owner, this would be at the Iteration and Release level. For the Program and Product Managers, it would be for all estimates back to the FFC through delivery to production. The team is being measured on how well they can predict efforts against Tasks. At the project level, the measurement is the estimates generated by the Product and Project Managers, once the project was handed to them through delivery to production. For the Program and Product Managers, the measurement is from the initial FFC estimate through delivery to production. Each tier of engagement must be measured and their accuracy should be universally available for any stakeholder to review.

The purpose of the control chart is to visually see how frequently an individual is over- or under-estimating the level of effort and how far the estimate fell from actual. Someone that is continually under-estimating is easy to spot with this sort of tool and presenting this data will help them work towards improving their techniques. Control charts are discussed in Chapter 16 in greater detail.

When a bias is identified, the source should be confronted as a topic in Retrospectives, challenging the team to determine the root causes behind it and work towards avoiding it in the future to improve accuracy. The Program Manager should never simply correct the error. Estimates should be openly accessible and a "quick fix" will likely result in distrust and frustration from stakeholders. Not to mention the fact that doing so may solve the problem now, but it will simply occur again the future.

Tools and Practices Recommendations

Baselines

Establish and track baselines for estimates and scope at each layer of decomposition. Program Managers will never learn what estimating phase needs improvement if they are not tracking and documenting how estimates have evolved through the different layers of planning. The Cone of Uncertainty is unavoidable, but the scale of accuracy for estimates can certainly be narrowed if there is a commitment to continuous improvement. Using baselines and control charts will lay out the challenges unique to each organization with estimating level of effort and empower the Program Manager to work the issue with data instead of instincts.

Low-tech, High-touch Rooms

Estimation is a process that lends itself to a low-tech, high-touch approach for success. Companies as technical and enormous as Intel use low-tech, high-touch techniques when mapping out large processes. Plenty of Agile tools include the ability to play Planning Poker online, but the tactile touch of the cards and the face-to-face engagement with other resources infinitely shortens the time needed to come to an accurate estimate compared to an asynchronous exchange in an online platform. If a team is comprised of resources that must work virtually, it is recommended to use the low-touch tool and bridge the communication with video conferencing.

Information Radiators

Information Radiators allow team members to passively pull feedback on the status of Programs, as they do with projects. Publicly displaying artifacts in an open, visual way keeps the Vision, goals, constraints, and progress of the Program at the forefront of stakeholder's thoughts without expending active effort to convey the information. One clear sign of how Agile an organization has become can frequently be measured in how little blank wall space is present around the organization because information radiators are filling all of the available white space in common areas. The following Program-level artifacts, related to estimation and scope management, should be publicly visible to all team members and stakeholders:

- Program Charter
- Program Data Sheet – The same concept as the Project Data Sheet outlined in *The Agile Almanac – Book 1*, but for the Program Vision and goals.
- Program Roadmap
- Burn-up chart
- Flexibility matrix
- Metrics related to estimation or scope management

Conclusion

Agile Program estimation and scope management is a critical success factor for the Program Manager. Acknowledging that estimation is a known challenge, with a heavy bias towards under-estimation, and setting Program activities to address and acknowledge this is the path to success. Continuous feedback and improvement efforts, based on projected versus actual resource utilization, from the Program through the Task level estimates, will narrow the Cone of Uncertainty.

Scope management for the Agile Program Manager, at an initial pass, appears to sound like juggling snakes. The key is for the Program, Product, and

Project Managers and Product Owners to work together to ensure only items advancing the goals in the Program Charter are added to the scope. For an organization early in their Agile transformation, or a mature organization that has chosen to integrate approaches from Agile to Traditional, a Program with flexible scope is a perceived answer to a lot of challenges. Resisting the forces seeking to expand scope when it is not valuable or warranted embracing the ones that follow the path to advancing the goals of the Program is the foothold needed to support an Agile transformation.

END NOTES

[1] Lederer, Albert L., and Prasad, Jayesh. "A Casual Model for Software Cost Estimating Error." *IEEE Transactions of Software Engineering,* vol. 24, no. 2, 1998, pp. 137-148.

[2] Detailed in great length in Chapter 10 of *The Agile Almanac - Book 1.*

CHAPTER

14

Integration Management & Scheduling

Overview

Organizations establish Programs to provide structure to deliver value to the Customer. In this chapter, Agile Program Integration Management (APIM) is explored, which consists of the processes and methods that provide the structure to integrate Program components. A major aspect of Integration Management includes the coordination of Program schedules. Agile Program Management (APM) takes a unique approach to integration and Program scheduling. This chapter will explore this in contrast to Traditional integration management and scheduling.

The key to remaining Agile while scaling up to Programs is understanding that Lean principles can be applied to Traditional methods and supply critical practices and tools to support the project integration needed to execute Programs successfully. Decades of knowledge and experience have constructed important Traditional methods that aid the unification of Program components. This chapter leverages the knowledge from Traditional project management and identifies the practices and tools necessary to scale Program Management while exploiting the benefits of Agile and Lean principles.

In concept, a Traditional Program and Agile Program have many similarities. For instance, when an organization creates a Program, the business goals driving its creation, and the mechanisms used to do so, are similar. Regardless of approach, in the business case creating the Program Charter and, in turn, the Program, the organization identifies the business value that will be delivered, who the stakeholders are, and the strategy that will be used to attain it. When closing a Program, the similarities are also clear. The organization ensures the Program delivered the business value through the pre-defined deliverables and benefits, determines how the resources will be reassigned, and finalizes reporting to provide closure.

Where Traditional and Agile Program Management diverge is in the delivery method, but the ultimate goal is always to deliver business value to the customer. Traditional Program management is heavy in planning, whereas APM uses incremental and iterative Milestone delivery.

Even with the differences in delivery methods, the following is critical for both Traditional and Agile Program management to provide integration across the Program:

- Clearly defined goals communicated to team members
- Cross-project coordination to deliver unified benefits to the customer
- Consistent processes, tools, methods, and procedures
- Cross-team communication and collaboration
- Effective and consistent reporting and feedback loops

In *The Standard for Program Management® – Third Edition, PMI®* identifies that the Program Life Cycle comprises three phases:

- Program Definition
- Program Benefits Delivery
- Program Closure

Leveraging PMI's® lifecycle as a basis, the Agile Program Life Cycle (APLC) includes the same three phases, however, uses Agile methods to deliver value to the customer through Feature-based planning and incremental, iterative Feature-based deliveries. *Figure 14.01* illustrates the APLC and its approach to delivering iterative Releases based on a Program Roadmap, which always includes feedback from the customer, to ensure proper prioritization of the Features.

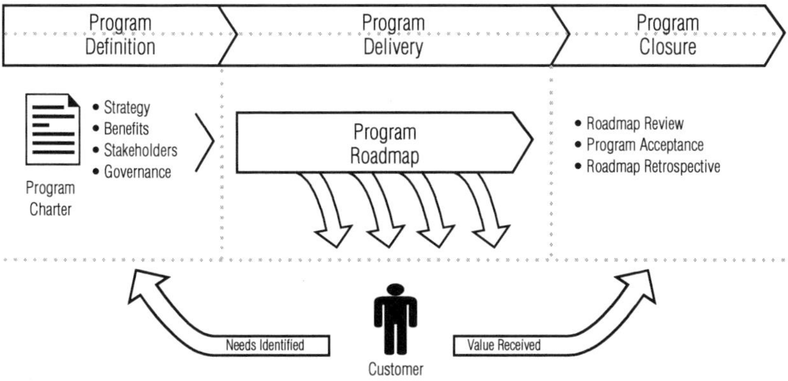

Figure 14.01 | Agile Program Life Cycle (APLC)

This chapter will focus on the processes, tools, methods, and procedures unique to Agile Program Management. Although Agile aspects of the Program Definition and Program Closure phases will be addressed, most attention will be given to the delivery methods in the Program Delivery phase.

Agile Program Delivery Cycle (APDC)

Figure 14.02 illustrates a more detailed view of the Program Delivery phase, referred to as the Agile Program Delivery Cycle (APDC), to more accurately denote the delivery cycle experienced on Agile Programs.

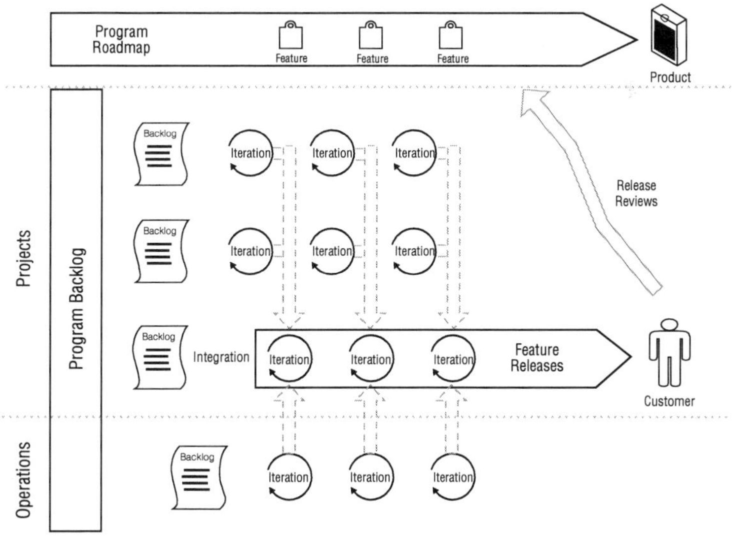

Figure 14.02 | Agile Program Delivery Cycle (APDC)

The APDC can be divided into Projects and Operations. Projects have the mandate to deliver new products, services, or solutions, where Operations typically concentrate on ongoing delivery and support of existing products, services, and solutions. To maintain integration across the Program, projects and operations should share the same Program Backlog, which feeds the individual project and operational Backlogs and, eventually, the Iteration Backlogs. Iterative deliveries are Feature-based and follow the Release plan as defined in the Program Roadmap.

Benefits / Challenges

Benefits

Success comes to a Program when it can deliver a solution to the customer that provides value in a timely manner. Agile methodologies present a unique proposition by advocating the delivery of a Minimal Marketable Product (MMP), which provides value to the customer as quick as possible. Additional functionality is added to the MMP over time to increase its value.

APM's ability to focus on Features to develop the MMP is the key to success. The magic making this possible is centered on Integration Management. The coordination of several teams, working together to deliver integrated Features, using the concepts discussed in the chapter, ultimately drives value to the customer.

Challenges

Most Agile Frameworks were designed to deliver solutions quickly and are very effective at the project level, but fall short when attempting to scale to the Program or Enterprise level. Challenges occur when scaling so additional considerations and practices are required to integrate the projects and operations present in a Program.

Additionally, some in the Agile sphere struggle with being constrained by a schedule, which is typically expected and required in most organizations. Often, the mindset is, "the work is done when it is done…I can't give you a schedule." Aware of this challenge, this chapter will address methods and techniques to dissolve the notion that schedules have no place in Agile, let alone at the Program level.

Program-level Attributes

Roles

Core Program Team

The core Program team consists of team members representing different disciplines and skills, and is typically organized across multiple projects and operational activities. The team works together to deliver business value to the customer as identified in the Program Charter, which can be in the form of a product, service, or other tangible or intangible deliverable. The Agile team is self-organizing and empowered to iterate as they deliver incremental Features per the Program Roadmap. Where possible, team members should be dedicated to a specific project or operations, allowing them to focus without diluting their efforts across multiple projects.

Program Manager

The Program Manager leads the Program and is responsible for delivering the business value defined in the Program Charter. They work with the executive team to identify the Program Roadmap and organizational structure, such as sub-Programs, projects, and operational activities, required to meet the deliverables. The Program Manager coordinates the cross-project Iterations and Feature deliverables to ensure the Program is meeting customer expectations. They also communicate with executives to provide Program progress, usually in the form of reports and other Program metrics.

Product Manager

The Product Manager is responsible for representing the customer and their needs. They manage the Program Backlog to coordinate the cross-project dependencies and ensure the different project teams are delivering the correct Feature needed for each Iteration. They create Themes and Epics, which represent the Features identified in the Program Roadmap, and organize the Program Backlog feeding the Iteration Backlogs.

Product Owner

The Product Owner is responsible for decomposing Themes and Epics into User Stories that can be consumed by the project team during an Iteration. The User Stories should contain the definition, requirements, acceptance criteria, and any collateral required by the team to complete the work within the Iteration.

Program Coordinator

The Program Coordinator assists the Program Manager in coordinating the day-to-day activities, including scheduling and communications, to ensure integration across the Program. They facilitate the gathering of data used to create reports and other metrics.

Workflow

Program Charter

Agile Program Integration Management starts during the Definition phase of a Program. A Program is created because the organization realizes that the customer has a need best fulfilled by initiating a Program. This helps the organization focus on the delivery of a solution to those needs. The Program Charter is crafted by the executive team or sponsor, which provides the Vision and boundaries of the Program and strategic guidance for delivery of the product or solution to the Customer. The Program Charter is the controlling document for the Program and provides the basis for Agile Program Integration Management.

In many aspects, the success of a Program is directly related to how effectively the activities of the Program are orchestrated. Just as the conductor of a symphony provides the leadership for the musicians to play in a coordinated effort to deliver a beautiful piece of art, the Program Manager provides the leadership necessary to coordinate the activities that deliver Value to the Customer. The musical score is the map used by the conductor to guide the musicians, and the Program Charter is the Roadmap used by the Program Manager to lead the Program team.

Feature Based Planning

In 2001, "The Agile Alliance" identified twelve principles behind The Agile Manifesto. The first principle states, "Our highest priority is to satisfy the customer through early and continuous delivery of valuable software." The idea that it is important to deliver early and continuously to the customer is pertinent to all Agile engagements, and not just to the software industry! Feature-based planning allows for the development of a product, service, or solution to be performed in a way that incrementally delivers the most important functionality to the customer as the Minimum Marketable Features (MMFs). Development continues past the MMFs, based on feedback from the customer, who influences which Features are delivered in future Releases.

With the Program Charter firmly in hand, the Program Manager works with the executive team or sponsor, Product Manager, and most importantly, the Customer, to develop the Program Roadmap.

The Program Roadmap is a living document and a graphical representation of Features that will be developed and the order in which they will be released to the customer. The purpose of the Program Roadmap is to identify a plan the team will work toward. This is an important tool, providing the integration glue throughout the Program. All projects and operations will be working on deliverables that align with Features in it. It could be easily argued that only work, directly mapped to the development and support of Features on the Program Roadmap, be performed. In other words, if it is not on the Roadmap, do not do the work.

With regular customer feedback in place, the Program Roadmap can often change. In some cases, the customer might reorganize the delivery order of Features. At other times, a previously desired Feature might become obsolete and be removed from the Program Roadmap. To respond to this uncertainty, Agile Program Management is flexible and ever evolving. For this reason, it is critical to keep the Program Roadmap current and clearly communicated to the team members.

In Traditional Program Management, a plan is developed up front and communicated in the form of a schedule. This schedule is tracked across the Program and communicated with the governing bodies and team members. Management has become accustomed to evaluating the health of a project by tracking the schedule. To successfully scale Agile, it is important to meet management's expectations by providing a schedule so they are able to predict revenue streams based on the Features being delivered.

In Agile, the Release Plan is comparable to the Traditional schedule and can easily be developed from the Program Roadmap. At the basic level, by adding a timeline to the Program Roadmap, a Program Release Plan is established. If a more detailed schedule is preferred by the organization, the Program Roadmap can be decomposed into Features, Functions, and Capabilities (FFCs) to provide a more granular view. It is recommended to only decompose the Release Plan to a level that is trackable. In addition, be prepared to modify it as feedback from the customer drives changes to the Program Roadmap.

Program Backlog

The Program Roadmap provides the Vision at the Feature level, including the order in which the work should be performed. The Product Manager then takes that list of Features and creates the Program Backlog, decomposing the

Features into Themes and Epics, providing detailed definition, and preparing them for consumption by the project and operational teams.

The Product Manager, continually working with the customer, receives feedback regarding the Features delivered and modifies the Program Backlog appropriately to reflect the latest expectation. This causes the Program Backlog to be fluid and continually modified, aligning with the Agile mindset of delivering what is most important to the customer when they need it – even when that need changes.

At the Program level, as the Backlog is modified, the Product and Program Managers work together to update the Roadmap and Release Plan to correctly reflect the latest expectations of the Customer.

Coordinated Iterations

Using the Program Backlog, which feeds the individual project and operations Backlogs, and the Program Roadmap, established with Feature based planning, the Iterations are coordinated toward specific Feature releases. The Product Manager manages much of this synchronization.

The Product Manager populates each of the Iteration Backlogs, works with the Product Owners to coordinate their prioritization, and facilitates the cross-project dependencies in order to ensure the work performed by the teams feeds the delivery of the Features per the Program Roadmap and Release Plan.

Integration Iterations

Where appropriate (especially with software), an Iteration might be required to integrate the functionality produced by individual project and operational teams to ensure seamless functionality as a whole. The integration team receives functionality from the other teams at the end of their Iterations and in a separate Iteration, integrates and performs final testing prior to making available the solution ready for potential release. The integration Iteration considers new functionality coming from the project teams, as well as defect corrections coming from the operations team.

Program Releases

A key aspect of the Agile goal is that the team deliver a potentially shippable solution at the end of each Iteration. This does not mean each Iteration will ship their solution; rather, they will produce a solution, which could be shipped, assuming the customer accepts it. When scaling Agile at the

Program level, it is important to develop solutions that align with the Program Roadmap and Release Plan. The activities and solutions developed by each delivery team are coordinated to culminate in Feature Releases to the customer.

Once again, liken the coordination of Program Releases to a symphony. Similar to the conductor in a symphony harmonizing the members during each song performed, the Program Manager coordinates the activities of the team members within the Iterations to develop a Program Release of the solution. With the Features coordinated and integration in place, Features are released to the customer for review and acceptance.

Operational Support

The operational aspects of a Program are important components and often overlooked. A project has a defined scope with a distinct beginning and end. Anything within the Program, outside of the defined projects, is operational. Operations has an important role to provide the customer by supporting Feature Releases and being a source of direct feedback from the customers to the Product Manager.

With operations being such a key part of the customer experience, it is important to make sure the team is integrated into the Program workflow. To foster the unification of operations and projects within the Program, it is recommended that the Program Backlog feed both the project and operations teams. This allows the Product Manager to direct the work performed by all teams and solidifies the Release process.

Roadmap Review and Acceptance

At the conclusion of the Program, after the delivery phase is complete, but prior to swabbing the deck and buttoning up the hatches, it is important to validate with the customer that the delivery is acceptable. The Program and Product Managers, and probably even the executive team, should hold a Roadmap Review to solicit acceptance from the customer. This review is similar to the Iteration and Program Release reviews, however includes the full scope of the Program.

Roadmap Retrospective

A final Program Retrospective should be held at the close of the Program. This Roadmap Retrospective should include the duration of the Program and its findings will be used to improve other active and future Programs.

This Retrospective can be challenging due to the fact that Programs can execute for several months or more, even years! Agile best practices typically recommend holding Retrospectives at the conclusion of each Iteration. In this case, the Iteration is the length of the Program. For this reason, one approach to the Roadmap Retrospective is to review historical data from the Iteration and other Program Retrospectives held during the delivery phase of the Program.

Ceremonies

Program Release Planning

A Program Release Plan is developed to provide a schedule for the Program Feature Releases. This occurs during a Program Release Planning meeting, led by the Program Manager and includes, at a minimum, the Product Manager. Others should attend, per the Program Manager's request, to provide the input required to facilitate the creation of a well thought out plan.

To create the Program Release Plan, the Features defined in the Program Roadmap are typically evaluated and assigned a Rough Order of Magnitude (ROM) sizing to get an idea of the effort required to deliver the Feature. If necessary, the Features are decomposed into Epics to aid in this process. The ROM is then matched up with the velocity (or anticipated velocity) of the delivery teams who will perform the work to identify how many Iterations will be required to deliver the Feature. The Program Release Plan is then created, based on the number of Iterations to deliver the Features, and should align with the Program Roadmap.

At the onset of the Program, the first Release Planning meeting is held then reconvened on a regular basis or immediately after any Roadmap changes. After the initial meeting, the velocity of the delivery teams begins to provide a clearer view of the validity of the Release Plan, which will continue to evolve as the team evolves. Due to the dynamics of the Agile team and the potentially changing needs of the customer, it is recommended to hold the Release Planning meeting at least every month.

Program Stand-up

Each delivery team should be holding Stand-up meetings to reinforce their commitments to each other. To scale Agile, Program Standups should be held to reinforce cross-project commitments. The Stand-up is a self-organized meeting by the team, facilitated by the Program Manager. It is recommended that all Program team members attend the Stand-up, however, each person does not need to report, rather, each team should be represented and report their commitment to the Program. It is also recommended that the Program Stand-up be held at least once a week.

The purpose of the Program Stand-up is to confirm commitments between team members. It is not a problem-solving meeting. Often during the Stand-up meeting, concerns and impediments are identified. These items should be listed on a whiteboard to be addressed in the Program After Meeting.

Program After Meeting

The Program After Meeting is facilitated by the Program Manager, held immediately after the Program Stand-up, and is intended to address the issues raised during the Stand-up. Program team members, who have input toward the resolution of the issues raised, should remain after the Stand-up to address them. During the meeting, the team works to address the issues. In some cases, the concern can be addressed during the After meeting, while complex issues might require additional actions or meetings to arrive at an acceptable resolution.

Program Feature Reviews

One of the strengths of Agile is the frequent review with the Product Owner and other stakeholders, occurring at the end of each Iteration. This provides a critical feedback loop to the delivery team regarding the work performed and opportunity for acceptance of the Features delivered. At the project level, this occurs at the end of each Iteration.

To scale Agile to the Program level, and for integration purposes, it is important to hold Program Feature Reviews. The Product Manager facilitates these reviews, held upon the completion of a Feature. The purpose of the Feature Review is to review the fully integrated Feature, developed by the delivery teams, with the Product Manager and other stakeholders, and receive acceptance of the Feature and a decision regarding its release per the Program Release Plan.

Program Feature Retrospectives

At the completion of each Feature, the Program Manager assembles the Program Team and holds a Program Feature Retrospective. The purpose of the Retrospective is to reflect on the delivery of the Feature completed. The team evaluates processes and activities required to deliver the Feature, with attention focused on the cross-project and integration aspects. Successes should be celebrated, opportunities for improvements should be identified, and action plans developed to strengthen the team's ability to deliver upcoming Features.

Program Backlog Refinement

The Product Manager is responsible for continually refining the Program Backlog to provide the right level of definition for the Features and Epics within. They work with the customer and other stakeholders to understand the functionality required and document those requirements in the Features and Epic Stories. They then prioritize the Backlog to align with the Program Roadmap and Release Plan, ensuring Features are worked on in the correct order to meet the defined schedule.

The Program Product Manager works with the Product Owners to ensure the teams have enough definition in the Epics and User Stories to perform work, which continually marches toward the delivery of committed Features.

Artifacts

Several key artifacts are needed to for Agile Program Integration and scheduling. Templates and samples, with further discussion, can be found in the Tools and Practices section. Additional artifacts may be needed, so this list should prompt thinking about which ones to add.

1. Program Charter
2. Program Roadmap
3. Program Release Plan
4. Program Dependencies Radiator

How to Make It Work Effectively

Three Levels of Support Required for Scaling

The biggest challenge when scaling Agile Program Management methodologies is coordinating all the activities across the Program in a focused way to deliver an integrated solution to the stakeholders. The responsibility for managing that effort falls squarely on the shoulders of the Program Manager. Failure is certain without support from three specific levels – individual team members, project and operational teams, and the organization.

This section will discuss what is expected from each of these groups to support the successful scaling of Agile across a Program and also what each group needs to meet those expectations.

Individual Team Members

Expected

Each team member must be willing to perform quality work to the best of their ability, engage fully, and work with other team members. They should feel empowered to be creative with their solutions to meet the stakeholders' needs, identify anything impeding their progress, and aid in the resolution of problems.

Need

Individual team members need to be trained in the chosen Agile Framework and associated methodologies, processes, and procedures. To successfully meet expectations, they need to be familiar with and understand the Program Vision and goals. They should have a clear understanding and ongoing visibility of the scope, Program Roadmap, and the associated Features expected at both the Program and Iteration level.

Project and Operational Teams

Expected

The project and operational teams must be self-organizing, willing to commit within and across other teams, and accountable to follow through on what they promised to deliver. As they work through the delivery process, they are expected to collaborate within their own team, and with others, to create viable solutions representative of their commitment. They need to be transparent as they share their progress and identify issues and impediments.

Need

The delivery teams need training, which will allow them to effectively work as a high-functioning Agile team. They also need to have all the right resources available to them to meet their commitments, including members with the skills required.

Organization

Expected

The organization must be committed to delivering solutions via Agile, thus allowing the Lean concepts to take hold and permeate the culture. They need to provide the necessary resources at the Program, project, and operational levels and are expected to formulate and deliver a clear Vision for the Program, as well as its associated scope of work.

Need

All levels of the organization should receive training on the Agile Framework chosen for the Program. This includes training for the executive team and other stakeholders, allowing expectations to be shared across the organization.

Ultimately, the organization needs the Features and solutions delivered as documented in the Program Roadmap and Release Plan. Patience and support at the executive level will run thin and eventually wane if the Program does not deliver the business value in the timeframe expected.

Considerations for Hybrid in a Traditional / Agile Mixed Environment

The focus of this chapter has purposely leaned toward a Program organization entirely operating on Lean principals, using Agile Project Management methodologies. Some organizations will opt to have a hybrid Agile / Waterfall approach within the Program. When this occurs, there are some special considerations to the principals covered in this chapter that should be addressed.

With Agile methodologies becoming an ever-increasing influence in the world of project management, it is not that uncommon for an organization that has been using Traditional project management methodologies to step into the world of Agile by introducing an Agile project team or two into a Traditionally run Program. As the Lean principals begin to prove themselves, additional Agile teams can be added, and eventually, an organization might choose to have a total Agile Program. In this case the principals discussed in this chapter hold true.

This section will discuss the specific condition where the Program is managed by Agile principals, but the organization has opted to have a team or two deliver via Traditional methodologies.

Rolling Wave

When people think of a Waterfall approach to project management they typically think of deliveries at the end of the project. However, the concept of Rolling Wave Releases has been in the PMBOK® Guide for quite some time. With this in mind, Traditional projects, executing in an Agile Program, can fit quite nicely if a rolling release schedule is aligned with the Release Plan. The scope of the work on a non-Agile project can be aligned to deliver in a Rolling Wave, such that the most important scope is delivered in the first wave and the next important delivered in following Releases.

Agile Principals

Just as APM can learn from decades of project management experience, so, too, can Traditional projects learn from Agile methodologies. Many Waterfall projects have benefitted by holding Daily Stand-up meetings to facilitate collaboration between team members. When Traditional projects begin to adapt Lean thinking, communications within the team members, customers, and other stakeholders can improve. Wasted processes can be trimmed to include only value-added activities. And in general, a different thought process ensues.

This does not mean that the project has to switch from a Waterfall approach to Agile, rather, it can simply adopt the Lean principals that will increase efficiencies within the Waterfall approach.

The Program Manager should train the Project Manager and project team members on Agile methodologies and encourage adopting a hybrid approach as much as possible. Even if the methodologies are not fully embraced, the Traditional project team will benefit from the knowledge on how the Agile delivery teams in the Program work, and from there, the communications will improve, producing more integrated delivery.

Team Collaboration

One of the great benefits resulting from many of the ceremonies in APM is the increased transparency with all stakeholders – from customer to team member to management. This increased transparency results in greater collaboration with everyone involved. Although Traditional planning and delivery cycles differ from Agile, they should still be involved in all ceremonies, increasing collaboration throughout the Program. A Traditionally managed project within the Program should not be excluded because it will hinder learning and integration.

Tools & Practices Recommendations

The following tools were referenced in Chapter 3, but are also relevant to integration and scheduling. These tools are also available for download at GR8PM.com.

- Program Charter – *Figures 3.05 and 3.06*
- Program Roadmap – *Figure 3.07*
- Program Release Plan (Program Schedule) – *Figure 3.10*
- Cross Program Dependencies Radiator – *Figure 3.13*

Conclusion

Agile Program Integration Management is an important aspect of the Lean mindset and critical to successfully scaling Agile at the Program level. A coordinated approach to integrating scope throughout the Program begins with a clear Program Charter from which the Program Roadmap and Release Plan are developed. Using the Roadmap, the Program Manager and Product Manager guide the teams to delivering coordinated Releases, which provide the most important value to the stakeholders, when they need it. As a result, the customer receives solutions that address their needs…then comes back for more!

CHAPTER

15

Risk Management

Overview

This chapter explores different thoughts, perspectives, tools, and techniques of Agile Program Risk Management (APRM). It begins by discussing a fundamental and Traditional risk management approach and moves into variations used by Agile Program teams. The specific APRM approach a team will use is based on each Program team's needs and unique circumstances. This chapter explores several variations of risk management practices designed to decrease threats to and increase opportunities for achieving an Agile Program's objectives.

The PMBOK® Guide defines risk as an uncertain event or condition that, if it occurs, has a positive or negative effect on one or more project objectives. This definition can be applied to projects, Programs, and portfolios managed using both Traditional and Agile methodologies. The steps, tools, techniques, timing, organizational risk tolerance, and terminology vary based on size and methodology.

The PMBOK® Guide provides a prescribed process for risk management. Conversely, the Scrum Alliance does not have a formal prescription for management of risk. There are various methods that can be used, and Scrum teams select the method of risk management that best suits their unique team needs. This chapter defines a process for risk identification and management, explores various benefits and challenges, and discusses Program-level attributes within the Framework of an Agile Program. It will also walk through the processes, tools, and techniques that improve early identification, classification, and actionable steps of risk management.

What is Program Risk Management?

The PMBOK® Guide states, "Program Risk Management includes the process of conducting risk management planning, identification, analysis, response planning and controlling risk on a project. The objectives of project risk management are to increase the likelihood and impact of positive events, and decrease the likelihood and impact of negative events in the project."

Traditional Program risk management often begins with the documentation of a Risk Plan, a working agreement on how the team will operate when risk arises. This artifact is documented in the initiation stage of a Program and can be used, regardless of methodology, as a guide to how the team manages risk throughout the project. This ensures the team knows, and agrees, on the processes and artifacts that will be used to do so.

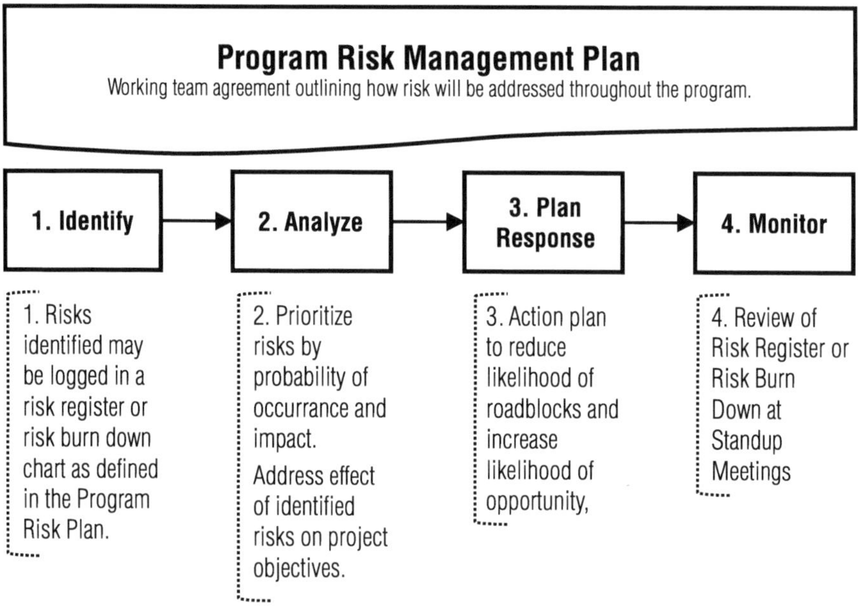

Figure 15.01 | Program Risk Management Plan

Risks are identified at the beginning and throughout Programs. Once identified, they are analyzed to determine priority by considering the potential impact on the Program goals. There are various artifacts and tools that teams may use to qualify and quantify risks. An Action Plan, otherwise known as Risk Response, is generated by the team to increase opportunity and reduce of threats to Program objectives. *Figure 15.01* outlines the Risk Management Process.

Key Differences of Agile vs. Traditional Program Risk Management

The timing of when risks are identified and analyzed, and action planning takes place, may vary between Traditional and Agile Programs. Since Agile performs work in incremental, iterative phases, the sense of urgency regarding risk management is heightened to ensure successful risk mitigation.

Timing of Risk Identification in Agile Program Risk Management
The Agile risk management Cycle is significantly shorter in duration than the Traditional approach. Note that the risk cycle in *Figure 15.02* has a total duration of two months.

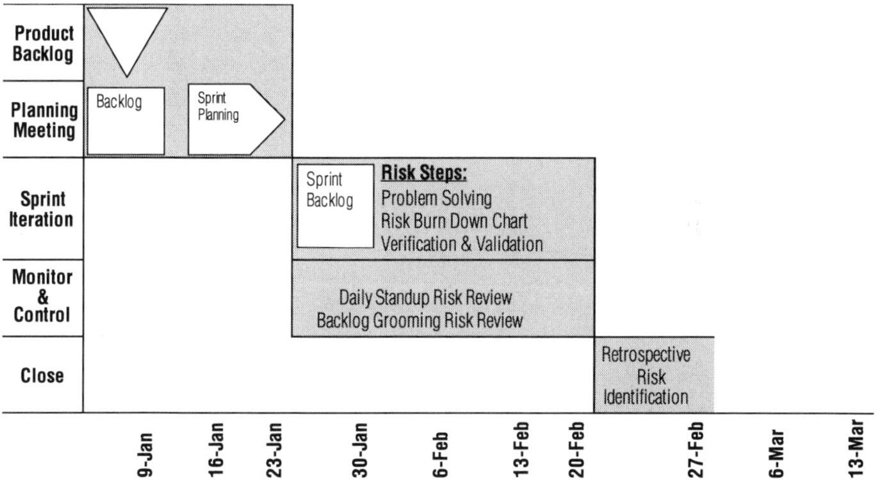

Figure 15.02 | Agile Risk Management Over Time

The Agile deliverables within this timeframe are likely much smaller in scope than in the Traditional scope shown in *Figure 15.03*. In Agile, risks may be short-term (current Iteration) or longer-term (multiple Iteration / Release) risk, and the mechanism for mitigating may be different based on this factor.

Risks identified are to be mitigated within the Iteration as soon as possible. *Figure 15.02* is representative of an Agile Program with projects working in short Iterations. Within Initiation, as the Product Owner grooms the Product Backlog, risk identification and analysis is conducted to ensure the Backlog is adjusted to reduce threats and increase opportunity.

Timing of Risk Identification in Traditional Risk Management

Risk management in a Traditional Program is outlined in *Figure 15.03,* which shows risk planning over the course of several months. This occurs prior to the beginning of execution, giving the team a significant amount of time to identify, analyze, and determine action plans for risk. Also notice that planning continues as the team moves into the execution phase while they monitor the risks identified to determine if the action plans require execution.

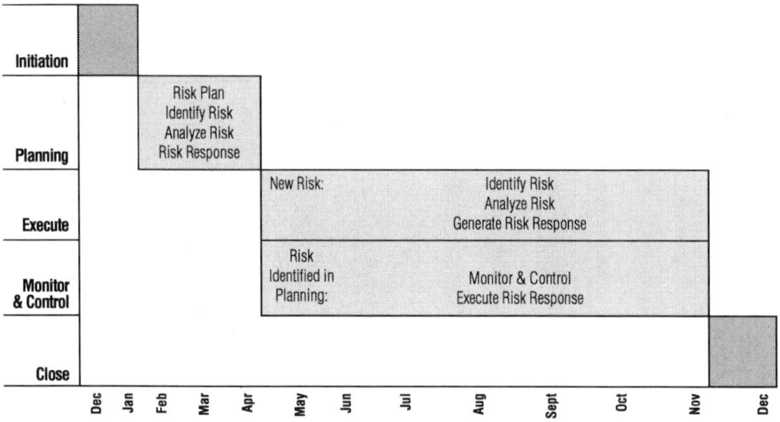

Figure 15.03 | Traditional Risk Management Cycle

Once a Traditional project team begins the execution phase, new risks may be identified and analyzed, and a response action plan documented.

Monitoring Program Risk

Risks to an Iteration in an Agile Program are monitored and discussed, using a Risk Burn-down chart, at the Stand-up meetings *(shown in Figure 15.04).* The team then determines if actionable steps are needed to mitigate a threat or maximize an opportunity. An unusual characteristic of a Risk Burn-down Chart, when compared to other Burn-down charts, is the stair-step nature of the line as it decreases over time. This helps assess the true possible impact because risks either exist or not. They exist if they have not been addressed yet, or they don't exist because they failed to materialize or were solved when they did occur.

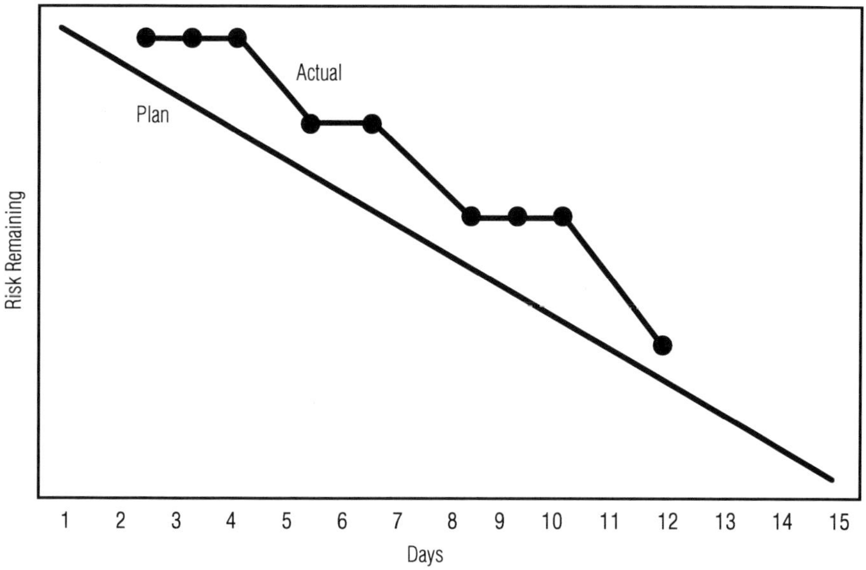

Figure 15.04 | Agile Risk Management Over Time

A Risk Burn-down Chart may also be used during Retrospective meetings to heighten the project team's awareness of risk. Review of the Risk Burn-down often sparks discussion with the Product Owner around re-prioritizing work in order to address risks as soon as possible. This is especially critical for the cross-team dependencies in Programs.

The Risk Burn-down used at the project-level can also feed a Program-level Total Risk (Stacked Bar) Radiator that will be covered in the Tools and Practices section.

The following story will help clarify the different risk management cadence for Agile approaches.

Cupcakes, Cookies and Chloe's Birthday: Agile in Everyday Life

Chloe is having a birthday party, and her mother, Celeste, is planning it. If they were using an Agile approach, this is what it would look like:

Chloe (Customer) tells Celeste (Program Manager) that she wants 2 types of cookies and 3 types of cupcakes, each with different frosting, for her party. Celeste tells her that whatever she chooses needs to be done by noon on Saturday or they can't take them to the park for the party. Chloe says what she wants, from most important to least (Prioritized Backlog),:

Project 1: Cupcakes

- Chocolate with vanilla frosting
- Vanilla with chocolate frosting
- Banana with peanut butter frosting

Project 2: Cookies

- Sugar
- Chocolate Chip

They agree on the priorities and the delivery deadline (Program Vision and Iteration Goals), and Celeste moves on to planning Chloe's party. Because there are two different projects, both relying on Celeste to manage them in a coordinated way to provide a benefit they could not achieve without the other, they are a Program, by definition.

Celeste plans to use the two ovens in her kitchen, and asks two friends to assist her. Together, they review the recipes and make a grocery list (planning session). While compiling the list of ingredients, one friend, Beth, suggests substitutions, in the event that the store does not have an item in stock (risk management). The risk identified by Beth is an important one because it could impact speed to market, quality, or both. If Celeste were not able to find all the ingredients at one store, she would have to travel to another store to get them or proceed without the missing ingredients, sacrificing the flavor (quality) of the cupcakes or cookies (deliverables). This is an Agile approach to risk management because the friends (cross-functional team) identified and analyzed the risk, developed an action plan, and did so in a self-directing manner.

Since all ingredients were acquired without issue, the friends (the team) get to the baking activities (development). Each cookie recipe calls for a different baking temperature – chocolate chip at 350° and sugar at 375°. Knowing Chloe prefers sugar cookies, Beth wants to cook them first. But again, the collocated Agile team uses osmotic communication to decide that it makes more sense, given the temperature requirements, to bake the chocolate chip cookies first then raise the temperature for the sugar cookies. Being a good Program Manager, Celeste discusses the change and reasoning behind it with Chloe (feedback loop), and Chloe agrees to the revised baking schedule, accepting the risk to the chocolate chip development goal.

Next, Celeste consults with her team preparing the cupcakes, and they decide that rather than baking all the cupcakes at once, letting them cool, and frosting them, finishing Chloe's favorites first, so she is sure to have them ready for the party (iterative delivery of the MMF), is the best plan. Sara, who is preparing the frostings, manages them so they will be completed in the same order as the cupcakes (inter-project coordination and communication). Celeste then sets the timer and takes it with her while she organizes and packs the party decorations (external resource coordination).

By using Agile methods and executing the baking in Iterations prioritized by the Customer, the development team is able to provide the highest priority Features first. By discussing impediments to the original agreement (Vision and Goals) with the Customer, the team is able to deliver the products as agreed and avoid several risks:

Risk #1: Burning the Chocolate Chip Cookies
Baking the chocolate chip cookies first avoided the risk of burning them due to a residual higher temperature in the oven.

Risk #2: Cupcake Delays or Quality Issues
Baking the favorite flavor cupcakes first mitigated the risk of disappointing Chloe if the most important cupcakes had not been finished in time for the party. Taking the timer along (to stay aware of the cadence and interim deadlines) while the decorations were arranged also reduced the risk of not hearing the timer and burning the chocolate cupcakes.

If Traditional methods had been used, the cupcake batter would have all been mixed and baked at the same time. Then, if the risks had been realized, all three cupcakes could have been burnt because the timer was not heard, they may have run out of time to frost all of the cupcakes due spending the time spent mixing all 3 batches of batter at once, or the chocolate chip cookies could have been burnt due to the higher oven temperature being misjudged.

Not only did the friends mitigate the risks, they also streamlined the process by self-directing Tasks – mix the cupcake batter, prepare the cookies, make the frostings – and doing these in incremental steps. Each team member managed a specific Task and Feature deliverable, creating more awareness of the risks associated with them while also optimizing the whole by focusing on the Program goal – the party – rather than the individual projects – the baked goods.

Benefits and Challenges

Benefits

Constant Feedback Available

Agile project teams deliver potentially shippable products within a previously agreed upon period of time. Due to the short duration of Iterations, 1-4 weeks, and the consistent involvement of the Product Owner, the probability of risks greatly decreases. Having the Product Owner available for review and feedback as the deliverable is being built has great benefit to risk reduction.

Incremental Approach

The incremental approach provides teams with a higher level of focus on the details. Due to the focus on a lower volume of deliverables within the iteration, the team has the distinct ability to improve quality of delivery. This includes early identification and mitigation or avoidance of risk. The Iterative approach also allows teams to quickly correct course to address risks as they arise.

Planning and Commitments

Prior to the start, the team agrees upon the Features, Functions and Capabilities that will be delivered within the Iteration. At this point the team and Product Owner enter into a reciprocal agreement, stating that the delivery team will complete each FFC selected for the Iteration and, in return, the Product Owner will not change the deliverable expectation for that Iteration. This is beneficial as it decreases the risk of changes that could lead to delays in delivery or reduction in quality produced.

Agile teams are able to navigate risks and embrace opportunities as they arise. Teams that use the tools and methods discussed in this chapter are more likely to identify and address risk early, increasing the probability of mitigation of threats and taking positive risk opportunities. Having a risk information radiator, register, Burn-down chart, or other risk management tools increases the awareness and communication around risks.

Challenges

Cross-project Dependencies
During planning there is opportunity to uncover Program and cross-project dependency risks. When multiple teams are working together toward one objective in an Agile Program there are User Stories that have inter-dependencies across teams. This increases the complexity of fulfilling the objective. Cross-project dependency risks surface within the Iteration Planning meeting and Daily Program Stand-up meetings. These types of risks are a challenge to the Agile Program team to work through to mitigate. Being prepared and leveraging the Agile Program risk management tools helps teams be successful in working through these challenges.

Pace of Delivery
Agile Programs are comprised of multiple teams working toward a common end goal. The iterative approach increases the delivery of potentially shippable products. Although the team is focused on smaller deliverables, the increased pace of Agile Programs challenges the team to ensure risks are identified as early as possible. Due to the fast pace and complexity that comes with Agile Programs, risks may go unnoticed and soon become issues.

Organizational Recognition and Support of Risk Management Process
Researching and selecting the best risk management approach, and gaining organizational support for taking the time to identify and manage risks in an Agile Program may be challenging.

As previously discussed, the idea of risk management while using an Agile methodology may not be a focus for some organizations. A challenge faced by Program Managers is gaining organizational buy-in to the risk management process, which requires time and has a cost associated with the hours spent assessing risk that some companies perceive as unnecessary. Having a risk management plan, and making a conscious effort to agree upon and plan the approach, prior to starting work benefits the team. When they do and the first risk comes up, the team will know how to manage it and will not spend significant time, under pressure, determining how to address it mid-Iteration. This, itself, is a risk!

One approach to managing risk, particularly risks that are small or of little consequence, is to simply not manage it. This allows risks to come to fruition as an issue, roadblock, or impediment. Teams using this approach resolve the issue within the Iteration if it arises. Impediments they cannot resolve are added to the Risk Backlog. As Rick Morris shared, "Our teams take a native approach to management of risk, when a predetermined number of story points are missed within an Iteration, these are documented and the reason is captured for later review. At the end of the iteration the team determines the story point variance, Actual vs Estimated. The story point variance and reason are determined and documented. This provides a record of risks."

An Agile Approach to Risk Management

Approaching risk management from an Agile perspective can yield unexpected benefits. One insurance company discovered this firsthand on a significant Program that was spending too much effort on risk management for only a modest return.

The carrier was challenged to find a simple mechanism to aggregate risk at the Program level in order to provide a comprehensive risk profile to key stakeholders. Although Traditional methods were adequate, a full-time resource was required in the PMO to review projects and deliver a complete risk picture. This was not sustainable for the entire length of the multi-year effort.

At the recommendation of a strategic partner, the company decided to attempt using Agile.

Individual risks from each project were then given a ranking – similar to the T-shirt size method. This was a quick and easy method to determine the relative risk across multiple projects.

The Risk Analyst in the Program Office assembled all the prioritized risks and was able to ascertain the most important – as ranked by the individual teams (who were the closest to it). This became the Risk Backlog. It was easily communicated to stakeholders and could be reviewed as needed by the Program Manager and Product Manager. (The Product Manager held the role of overall Product Owner for the Program.)

The risks were addressed in this priority order – to be mitigated, transferred, or accepted. The Risk Analyst collaborated with project teams as needed to better understand the risk for proper triage and remediation. As is common with Agile practices, this continued until the Product Manager was satisfied with the overall risk profile.

As new risks were identified, the same process was followed to update the Backlog. The Product Manager would periodically review it and determine if more risks should be actively mitigated.

The following benefits were achieved with this new Agile approach:

- Centralized risk management at the Program-level without significant overhead.
- Reduction in the necessity of a full-time Risk Analyst. Eventually the role was reduced to part-time and the individual able to assist with other Program Office responsibilities – notably dependency management.
- Highly satisfied and informed stakeholders. By utilizing the Product Manager for Backlog management, the business was directly involved and informed of the current state of risk in the Program. The groomed Backlog also became an easy to understand information radiator.
- More effective risk mitigation. This was accomplished through the partnership of the Risk Analyst, Product Manager, and individual project teams.

The Agile risk management approach at the Program-level was more efficient, led to stronger collaboration between the Program Office and projects, and fostered more effective communication of key Program indicators.

Todd R Jones, Sr. Project Manager -PMP, CSM, PMI-ACP
Westfield Insurance, (Wadsworth , Ohio)

Program-level Attributes

Roles

Program Manager

Program risks, with potential impacts to the delivery of agreed upon Features, budget, or schedule are the responsibility of the Program Manager. Additionally, this role is responsible for ensuring cross-team risks are identified, analyzed, mitigated, and communicated to key executive stakeholders.

Risk Analyst

This role provides support to the Program Manager in identifying, mitigating, and managing risk. The Risk Analyst is a PMO function responsible for aggregating project risk into the Risk Register to determine the overall profile of the Program. They help mitigate and manage risks that have been escalated to the Program and, in Agile environments, would also attend ceremonies to listen for new risks or reductions for current ones.

Program Coordinator

The Program Coordinator is responsible for documenting risks within the Program Risk Register, and following up on actions relative to mitigation.

Product Owner

The Product Owner generates and manages the Product Backlog and is involved in risk ranking of product Features within it.

Scrum Master

Risk identification within the Iteration, analysis, and mitigation are key to successful Program execution. If a risk Burn-down chart is leveraged by the team, the Scrum Master facilitates review of risks and roadblocks at Daily Stand-up meetings. They also update any parts of the process in Retrospectives and facilitate separate risk discovery meetings.

Scrum Team

The Scrum team is responsible for communication of risks, problem solving, and actively working to reduce risk or optimize opportunities within the Iteration, or over several Iterations.

Workflow

Define the Risk Management Plan

A Program risk management plan is a document generated, prior to initiation, by the Program Risk Analyst, with inputs from the team. This ensures the teams are aware, knowledgeable, and in agreement on how the Program will identify, monitor, and mitigate risk. Some Programs opt to do this within the team working agreement. Regardless of the method or tool used, the key is to ensure the team understands the agreed upon approach to risk management prior to beginning work on an Iteration.

There are several variations of Agile Program risk management. The formal Risk Plan or a variation of this artifact is used to document the agreed upon approach. Gaining team and stakeholder buy-in early on is crucial. Clear communication is best finalized prior to the team having an impediment to manage.

Regardless of the document type used, there are four key steps to APRM.

1. Identify Risks

The identification of risk occurs throughout the Program and can occur in any of the ceremonies. Risks can be subdivided into two categories – known unknowns and unknown unknowns. Although all risks are 'unknown', there is a level of predictability that drives the categories.

Known – Unknowns have a higher degree of predictability, and therefore, can be more readily identified and managed. These risks are routinely documented on the Risk Register with planned responses, mitigation strategies, and calculated contingency. A few examples:

- Schedule slippage due to a supplier missing a deadline
- Quality issues due to a faulty measurement or tolerance level
- Cost overruns due to striking workers requiring higher than planned pay

Unknown – Unknowns cannot be known, discovered, or documented during risk identification. Contingency for these risks is general, non-specific, and often exempted from the Program by governance standards or upper management direction. Some examples include:

- Unpredicted weather events
- Unforeseen shortage of resources
- Impacts of acquisitions and mergers

Nonetheless, a protocol for notifying and escalating Unknown – Unknowns, when they do arise, can be defined and agreed upon.

Risks are described using a cause-effect relationship. A sound format could be: Given that *<description of cause>*, there is a risk that *<description of effect>*.

Given that a *supplier will be utilizing a new manufacturing technique for our materials,* there is a risk that:

- *materials may be delivered later than planned.*
- *materials may not meet our quality expectations (outside of tolerance).*
- *materials may be delivered earlier than planned and/or may exceed our quality expectations.*

Notice that the last situation is an example of a positive risk event, where the Program benefits from its realization. Although rare, this can occur.

Another format for risk description is the If/Then/Impact format.

- IF *a supplier utilizes a new manufacturing technique for our materials* THEN *the materials are at risk for delayed delivery,* potentially impacting the overall Program *delivery schedule and cost.*

Risk Probability is the likelihood of occurrence and degree of potential for a risk to become reality. A common method of ranking this is a simple High-Medium-Low. Where a greater degree of differentiation is needed, Very High and Very Low can be added.

Risk Impact refers to the significance of the effect the risk will have on the Program if it occurs. Again, a common method of ranking is High-Medium-Low, and Very High and Very Low can be added for a more granular measurement. Risk impact is generally qualified in terms of cost and schedule, and in certain situations, quality. The specifics should be documented in the Impact Description along with the triggering event, and an indicator that the risk is about to become a reality.

The Risk Magnitude is a calculation that can be used to compare the relative importance of a risk relative to other risks. Assuming the scale High-Medium-Low has been assigned values of 3 for high, 2 for Medium, and 1 for Low, and that the same scale applies to both Probability and Impact, a simple calculation of Probability Score x Impact Score = Magnitude Score yields values that can be used to compare various risk by their magnitude.

2. Analyze Risk

Once risks are identified and documented they are prioritized by their Magnitude Score. An assessment is conducted to determine options for handling the effect of the risk on the Program objectives.

Teams can run into risks that require research time to determine the approach or solution. The PO will consider risks that are significant and allow planning so they can be reduced as early as possible. A team may spend time working specifically on solving a technical issue in a risk-based spike.

3. Plan Response

An action plan to reduce the likelihood of roadblocks and increase the likelihood of opportunities is discussed, documented, and implemented. In some cases, a risk response may be to defer a Story committed to the Iteration to a subsequent Iteration. In other cases, a new Story may need to be written to address research into the risk and solution planning. Risk response planning takes place outside of the ceremonies, as a single conversation, and can be tracked by adding a research Story to the Backlog. If the risk is complicated, additional stakeholders and escalation plans, documented in the overall risk management plan, may need to be activated.

Agile risk responses mirror those found in Traditional risk management, namely Accept (Ignore, Inspect, Insure), Mitigate, and Prevent.

4. Monitor

Once the Iteration is in progress the teams identify and discuss impediments at Daily Stand-up meetings. The various options for tracking risk are the Risk Register, Risk Burn-down chart, and Risk Backlog. Each will be described in the Tools and Practices Recommendations section.

Any combination of the approaches can be used to monitor risk, dependent upon the circumstances and, in some cases, standards and governance requirements. As actions are taken a record is made, which becomes an artifact for future reference.

Ceremonies

Product Backlog Grooming / Creation of a Risk-Adjusted Product Backlog

In preparation for Iteration work to begin the Product Backlog Grooming ceremony takes place. The Product Owner guides the teams through the Product Backlog review, adjusting it based on risk. A risk-adjusted Backlog takes into consideration regulatory and compliance work, and other critical risk areas required of the Program.

In the financial services and healthcare industries there are a number of regulations that teams need to take into consideration prior to making changes to customer facing information. For example, there are regulatory and compliance reasons to ensure that banking transactions are monitored for fraudulent activity. Delivery of this type of monitoring may be required prior to delivery of any related customer facing activity.

In software development this might mean talking to the PO to delay a Story until another team has completed the required compliance work to minimize the risk of regulatory penalties or rework.

Iteration Planning

In the Iteration planning meeting teams review work to determine a risk-based approach for execution and negotiate with the PO to move Stories up in priority. Higher Story Points may be assigned to User Stories that are more complex to ensure enough time to work. If a team wants to have success and reduce risk related to building a challenging Feature, they take that into consideration when planning and estimating Story Points.

During Iteration planning there is the opportunity to uncover Program and cross-project dependency risks. If Project Team A has a User Story that cannot start prior to Project Team B completing a particular Task or Activity, there is potential risk that if Project Team B does not complete the work in the Iteration, Project Team A will also be impacted by the change of scope.

Daily Stand-up Meetings

After the Product Backlog is groomed, the Iteration Planning meeting has taken place, and development is underway, teams identify new risks in the Daily Stand-up meeting. Detailed problem solving and defining next steps occur outside of the Daily Stand-up in Working Group or Problem Solving meetings.

Retrospective

During the Retrospective meeting risks may be discussed using information from the Risk Register, Risk Burn-down chart, or Risk Board in order to look for process improvements that will help the team avoid or mitigate similar risks in the future.

Artifacts

There are several key artifacts needed to manage risk in an Program. They are listed below. Additional artifacts may be needed and this list should prompt thinking about which ones to add. Samples, with some discussion points, can be found in the Tools and Practices section. These, other templates, and samples can also be downloaded at GR8PM.com.

1. Risk Management Plan
2. Risk Register
3. Risk Burn-down Chart
4. Risk Board
5. Risk Magnitude Score *(Figure 15.05)*

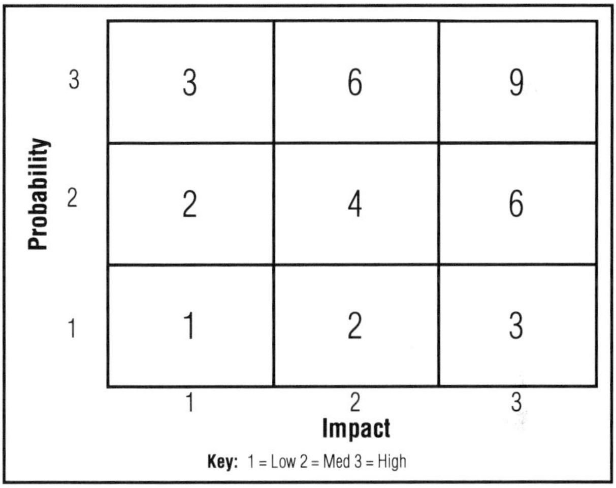

Figure 15.05 | Risk Magnitude Score

Figure 15.05 shows another way to visually represent the Magnitude of Risk by plotting it on a 3x3 matrix and indicating the relative scores. One advantage of showing stakeholders the Risk Magnitude Score is it can then be followed with the additional presentation of colors (usually Red, Yellow, Green) and recommended response categories. *(See Figure 15.06.)*

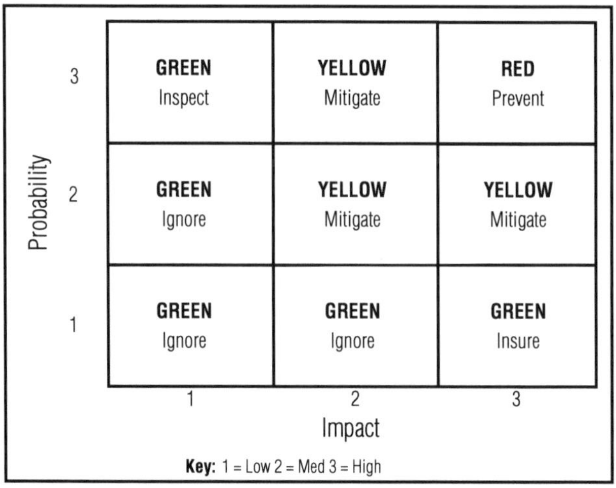

Figure 15.06 | Risk Magnitude Score with colors and response categories

How to Make it Work Effectively

Stakeholder Agreement

Having stakeholder agreement on the approach the Program will take for managing risk is key. Doing so keeps the teams' and stakeholders' expectations synchronized regarding what will happen when a risk becomes reality. Skipping this step has the potential to be detrimental to the success of the Program. Engage stakeholders, who may later be needed to assist in supporting action plans, using the Risk Management Plan. This mitigates the risk of having a lack of support for action later.

The responsibility for leading the meeting and influencing the stakeholders to get involved early so that they save a lot of grief later falls on the shoulders of the Program Manager. When the Program Manage fails to do this they are perceived as weak and "making excuses" when problems must be managed later. Conversely, they are perceived as strong and "having valid reasons" as issues arise if they have done this well.

Constant Customer Feedback

Having the Customer and Product Owner fully engaged in the Program is one of the most effective ways to mitigate risks. Given the increased complexity that accompanies a Program, increased risk is unavoidable. Therefore, it must be managed, and customer feedback is a critical part of that process.

Risks with higher complexity, probability, and severity are to be expected in Programs due to the number of teams and complexity of the deliverables. Having a Product Owner, with full decision-making capabilities, embedded in the team is key to successful mitigation of complex risks as they arise.

Many proponents of Agile will attempt to justify limited risk management, incorrectly citing the absence of explicit direction to do risk management in The Agile Manifesto as the reason. A truly customer-focused team will utilize proper risk management as a means to increase velocity by minimizing or eliminating the effects of risk as efficiently as possible.

Utilize the Tools and Artifacts Effectively
Agile risk management offers many different artifacts and tools to help identify, monitor, and mitigate risks. Leverage them to keep the team aware of the risks and prepared to face them, should they become realities. The Tools and Practices section will dive deeper into these items.

Tools and Practices Recommendations

Risk Management Plan

Typically written in the planning phase of a project, the risk management plan is a document outlining the risk management approach and includes the artifacts, and communication and escalation path. Documenting and reviewing this at the team level sets the expectation for how the team will manage risk. The risk plan generates awareness and clarity around risk prior to encountering it.

Risk Board

A Risk Board is a form of information radiator used to track the status of risk or impediments and is similar to a Kanban Board. Using sticky notes, the risks or impediments are written, and the board sectioned into columns that signify status – new, in progress, and mitigated. The stickies are placed on the board and moved across the categories as the risk status changes. This provides the team with a highly visible tool for tracking risk status.

Risk Register

The Risk Register is a listing of each risk encountered throughout the project, its description, and impact. Organizations have various methods for storing this information, such as spreadsheets or project portfolio management software.

Key data points housed in the Risk Register are:

- **Numbering** – Allows the team to easily communicate and refer to the risk by its identification number
- **Date** – Indicates the date the risk was identified and logged
- **Owner** – Resource responsible for driving risk to closure
- **Description** – Detailed description of the risk
- **Trigger** – Description of activity or occurrence that would trigger the risk to become an issue
- **Probability** – Defines the probability of risk occurrence through the assignment of low, medium or high.
- **Impact** – Defines the impact in terms of low, medium or high
- **Mitigation Strategy** – Defines strategy in terms of: Mitigate, Defer, Transfer or Accept
- **Mitigation Plan** – detailed steps to implement the mitigation strategy
- **Status** – Open / Closed
- **Comments / Notes** – updated with the last date a status change was made, initials of the resource who made it, and a note about what the change was

Computer Associates Project Portfolio Manager (CA PPM) is a project portfolio management tool with a robust Risk Register component. The tool provides Program Managers with various categories of risk, and the ability to enter risk ratings. This data then becomes available for dashboards and reporting.

Total Risk (Stacked Bar) Radiator

As mentioned earlier, a Risk Burn-down chart is a common tool at the project level and can be used as input for the Program's Total Risk (Stacked Bar) Radiator as seen in *Figure 15.07.*

The example shows bars for risks posed by schedule Flow impediments, specification breakdown mistakes, scope creep, personnel issues, and productivity obstacles. In the real world, the Program Manager, with advice from select team members, would define the appropriate categories. The group would then discuss how those categories would be defined in terms of project-level governance. Some might be mandatory for all teams while others might be subject to a team's discretion, perhaps guided by triggers or threshold values.

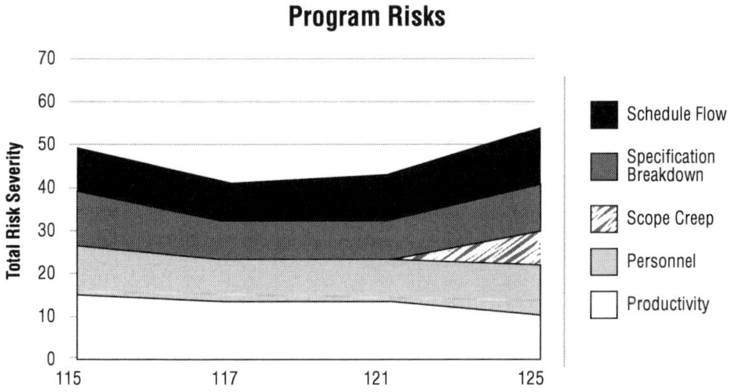

Figure 15.07 | Total Risk (Stacked Bar) Radiator

Discussing risk daily to maintain awareness, and take action as needed, reduces the severity of problems and leverages any opportunities.

Conclusion

This chapter has covered the most common Agile Program risk management practices. The tools provided to identify, analyze, and manage risk will be of great value to many Program Managers. For more information, tools, and tips on Agile Program risk management please join the GR8PM Tribe at GR8PM.com.

CHAPTER 16

Quality Management

Overview

This chapter will explore Lean Quality Management practices and tools to both prepare Program Managers already using the techniques and artifacts within Agile for the next level, and introduce them to those who are just beginning their journey, encouraging the next step in the learning process. With a healthy understanding of the practices and metrics used, effective quality management will fuel Program improvement.

Project vs Program Quality Management

It should be no surprise that there are questions about quality management at the Program management level. The third, and most recent, edition of PMI's *The Standard for Program Management®* devoted less than two and a half pages to the subject matter. In the simplest terms, project-level quality management focuses to deliver a product that is "fit for purpose." The Project Manager identifies the measurements to assure the project delivers the stated purpose and goals of the project.

Program quality management mirrors the shift in focus found in other project endeavors. While its fundamental goal is to deliver a Program "fit for purpose," the main difference is that the assessment and governing processes change from tactical to strategic. Programs have a longer shelf life with different, more complex challenges to measure. Some key areas of concern are:

Monitoring Limited Resources

Monitoring the limited resources (financial, technical, and physical) allocated to the Program and verifying they are directed towards the projects within the Program bringing the greatest value is an important, yet challenging, aspect. Solid, reliable metrics are needed to understand both the relative costs and benefits for each project.

Effective Program Managers will 'kill' or halt a project not delivering great value and redirect those resources towards a project that is. Ending or halting a project is not necessarily a failure on anyone's part. A Program Manager must maximize the organization's investment in the Program. Sticking with a project solely because of sunk costs invested thus far puts the Program at risk for failure and is a quick path to unemployment for the Program Manager and project team. Halting a failing project and reassigning those resources to one delivering results is one of the ways Program Managers and Product Managers bring value to the organization. If the project is struggling but critical to the success of the Program, another option to consider is using resources from Program reserves to rescue the project (discussed in more detail in previous chapters).

Monitoring Conditions for Risks

It is important to monitor organizational and market conditions influencing global risks that will trigger a risk response at the Program level. A Program focusing on app development for a specific phone is globally impacted if there is a dramatic change in market share for that platform. A Program, requiring large quantities of a raw material, must have controls that monitor the commodity markets and risk response plans on how it might exploit a drop in prices or manage a significant increase.

Coordinating Releases

To coordinate the deliverables of different project and product teams sharing a common Release date, Program Managers need to know how each project is faring against their Release plans so if adjustments are required, they can be determined well in advance.

Identifying Recommended Practices

Agile Frameworks bring an environment of rapid learning and discovery within the Agile team. The Program Manager should be looking at teams exceeding the norm on their quality metrics, working with them to identify how they are performing ahead of expectations, and sharing that found knowledge with all project teams within the Program.

Benefits and Challenges

Benefits

Agile Integration Framework (AIF) Program Quality Management is the engine that drives continuous improvement efforts within a Program. Studying both good and bad outliers on the project teams within a Program will identify reasons for unplanned variances and help narrow the Cone of Uncertainty. *(Refer back to Figure 11.04.)* Time is not the element that narrows the Cone of Uncertainty to the point of a released product. Tools, techniques, and sweat equity do. Applied appropriately, quality management is a tool that can narrow the Cone of Uncertainty by identifying and managing variances before the product is released to the customer.

Identifies Better Practices

Not all variance is bad. Teams exceeding their metric targets are likely discovering some recommended practices that could be applied in other areas across the Program, and potentially the enterprise. Done correctly, Program quality management should definitively answer the question "Why are we tracking this stuff?" Metrics without action are useless. Mature Agile project teams will abandon tasks they view as unnecessary overhead if they do not see action on them. Without action, the validity of metrics deteriorates rapidly. Use Lean thinking to continually analyze the value of the metrics and plan to adapt and make the appropriate changes based on input from project teams.

Provides Accurate, Tactile Data to Drive Improvement Efforts

Reliable metrics, for Program Managers, are priceless. Knowing exactly how much a project is over budget or how many User Stories a team is behind on delivering for their planned Release is vital. Accurate, tactile data allows the Program Manager to spot processes falling out of acceptable norms early enough that the project team can implement corrective actions to bring the project back into acceptable ranges without expending Program-level reserves.

An information radiator, like a metric dashboard, that outlines a handful of key Program metrics and is visible to all stakeholders reinforces the Program Vision and how success will be measured. For instance, a smartphone application's dashboard would include metrics like Net Promotor Scores(NPS) for customer satisfaction and employee satisfaction, the number of downloads the app has had over the last 30 days, and escaped defects observed by customers. That dashboard illustrates that customer and employee satisfaction, quality, and sales are the measures of success for the Program.

Demonstrates Program Value Visually and Factually
A Program with solid metrics and visible information radiators will not struggle to demonstrate value to the organization. Metrics bring traceability that can show what value has been delivered with the resources invested in the Program and what Features can reliably be expected on the near horizon. Metrics that can trace the Program's efforts to employee engagement, customer satisfaction, customer retention, cost management, or revenue increases confirm the value the Program brings to the organization beyond the tactical goals of implementing or improving a given product or workflow.

Challenges

Managing a Program that contains a blend of Agile, Traditional, and hybrid projects presents some unique challenges. Normalizing metrics at the Program level requires some effort. Setting up controls across all project teams to guarantee they are populating uniform and consistent values that calculate metrics is no easy task. If different teams use the same terms, but with different meanings implied to each, the metrics will be inaccurate at best. AIF addresses the broad spectrum of Programs using Agile to Waterfall methodologies, which will require some time and effort, but is a crucial step.

Not All Metrics Are Equally Valuable for Every Project Within a Program
Sometimes a project that falls within a Program needs to be excluded from a given metric because it will skew the distributions or paint a false impression of Program success. In an environment spanning Agile, hybrid, and Waterfall projects, it is unlikely all projects can feed the same groups of metrics and provide a true measure of success. Understanding the constraints that are fixed and those that are flexible will help capture accurate metrics.

Agile projects tend to create a challenge in a mixed environment. In Waterfall, the general focus is clearly defining the scope of the project and reporting against quality, timeline, and budget. With Agile, typically, either budget or timeline is fixed. This means, even within a Program of pure Agile projects, the need to split metrics into subgroups to avoid misrepresentations could arise. Taking the approach of "all projects feed all metrics" is a recipe for unreliable results, incorrect assumptions, and faulty decisions. If a project needs to be excluded from certain metrics, this does not mean it is excluded from the Program. In these cases, that project is simply not tracked at the Program level for the given metric, or it is split into sub-groupings under the Program. It is important to document any projects excluded from a given set of metrics so it is transparent and known to all stakeholders. Some options Agile provides on how to group projects within a Program include:

- Using T-Shirt Sizes to define the project by scope, budget, delivery date, etc.
- Grouping by the fixed constraint found in the project Charter's flexibility matrix[1].
- Grouping by project type.

Migrating to Metrics of Relative Comparisons May Be Required
Another challenge with Program-level quality management is developing and selecting metrics that are relative comparisons, which makes assessing different types of projects easier. For instance, Cost Variance (CV) may not be a good metric because a $100million project that is $1million over budget compared against a $1million project that is $1million over budget should not be viewed or acted upon equally by the Program Manager. Using Cost Performance Index (CPI) instead normalizes the values so they can be better compared for variances. The same example would net a CPI of 0.99 and 0.5, making it easier for the Program Manager to identify the project that requires attention and corrective action.

Another factor to consider when selecting metrics for relative comparisons and determining if they apply across all projects is scope size. Programs can suffer from scope creep when projects are unnecessarily added. These projects can be either small in nature or enormous endeavors, and impact metrics significantly. Including small projects in a Program will create tighter tolerances because they should experience less variance, making the other projects appear out of control. Massive projects can impact metrics by dwarfing the variances seen within the rest of the Program, making them hard to identify and correct.

No Easy Answer to "What Metrics Should be Tracked?"
Selecting the right metrics to drive process improvement is an endeavor that will vary by industry, organization, and Program. Some questions that need to be answered before selecting metrics are:

- What are the market forces dominating the organization's industry?
- What are the organization's known capabilities and opportunities to improve?
- What are the upper and lower control limits for the metric?
- What is the action plan if a project falls out of those control limits?
- Are Define, Measure, Analyze, Improve, and Control (DMAIC) or Plan-Do-Check-Act (PDCA) processes in place to monitor those action plans and validate the corrective actions have achieved the desired improvements?
- Does every stakeholder feeding data into the calculation of that metric understand why the metric is being captured, what is being done with that information, and how it is relevant to Program success?

Time-Based Metrics Ethics

Time-based metrics are a challenge at all levels of project, Program, and portfolio management. Agile methodologies frequently advocate the use of Story Points because the Agile practitioner accepts that, as a species, humans are not capable of providing accurate estimates in the form of time, but are quite adept at sorting a group of tasks by complexity[2]. Agile also answers the challenge of normalizing a time metric, using Story Points across teams, by analyzing the actual hours spent against the aggregate Story Points completed within a Sprint. Program Managers can then use these results to convert into hours per Story Point.

For organizations looking at actual hours, most do not have the capabilities to track time down to the User Story or WBS element. If they do track down to this level, they rely upon the individual contributor to document this on their own, splitting their time across their assigned Tasks. Even with the most ethical humans tracking their efforts manually, this remains a flawed approach, and trust in metrics based on individuals documenting their own time should be viewed with a critical eye.

Elapsed time is another method organizations use to work around the challenge of time-based metrics. This eliminates the potential for manipulation, at the employee level, by splitting time between multiple open, assigned Tasks. The criteria is simple enough to understand – User Story/Task start and end dates. The challenge with this approach is it will not address any process improvements that are narrower than a day in elapsed time. Holidays, vacations, illness, mandatory meetings, and other demands away from the project are likely to skew results as well.

All time-based metrics need to be evaluated for attempts to manipulate the measurements. Most time-based metrics can be worked like a geometry problem. A team member bent on gaming the system already knows the answer to the question in the form of estimates, they simply need to write out a proof justifying it when they log their time. If someone is always 100% accurate at estimated vs. actual time, there is a problem meriting additional review. If an Agile team has a constant velocity, it usually means they are sandbagging and can do more work. Program Managers need to look at distributions of time-based metrics in two passes. The first is evaluating the outliers. The second is evaluating those continuously at near perfection.

Program-level Attributes

Roles

Beyond the Program Manager, Product Owner, and other Agile Integrated Framework roles outlined in Chapter 11, there are no additional roles for Program management to address quality. Quality is a shared responsibility across all project team members, stakeholders, the Project Manager, and the Program Manager. The quality management systems should be transparent and accessible to all stakeholders vested in Program success.

Workflow

Quality is a continuous process, not a daily, weekly, or monthly endeavor. The Program Manager and Product Manager work together to define the metrics that will be used to monitor the projects within the Program.

As a project is added to the Program, the Program Manager and Product Manager work with the Project Manager and team to discuss the quality expectations, metrics being tracked, upper and lower control limits on those metrics, and response plans for when a metric breaches them.

Throughout the project's lifecycle the Program Manager and Product Manager not only monitor its metrics, they regularly inspect and communicate with the team to validate quality is a focus beyond the limited metrics being captured. This prompts discussions around quality assurance and testing methodologies to minimize escaped defects.

Ceremonies

If metrics remain within upper and lower control limits and there are no known issues, there are no unique ceremonies for quality management. When a metric falls outside of the control limits, the response plan will serve as a guide for what ceremonies need to take place. At a minimum, there should be a meeting between Program Manager, Product Manager, Project Manager, and Product Owner to discuss the contributing factors that led to the metric falling out of control limits, and to determine if there are any exceptional circumstances that would exclude the project from executing the response plan. If the response plan needs to be executed, the group discusses any additional resources needed to do so, and where the funds will come from.

During every project and Program ceremony, from the daily Scrum through Roadmap planning sessions, quality should be a potential topic for discussion. A sign of organizational maturity and successful adoption of the AIF for quality management is seeing daily Scrum notes tying identified impediments to an impact on the Program's metrics. If a Program Manager sees impediments like, "Jerry is not able to get clarity on acceptance criteria for User Story 23. This is a Feature we think will delight customers so it will potentially impact the Net Promoter Score (NPS) if it is released to production in the current state," then it is time to celebrate! This indicates that the team has grasped why metrics are tracked and how their daily activities influence them.

Artifacts

Artifacts will vary by project and Program. Some suggested artifacts for the Program Manager to maintain include:

1. Program Metrics
2. Documentation and reasoning of any projects excluded from a Program metric
3. Upper and lower control limits for each metric and the response plan
4. Information radiators
5. Any of the tools outlined in the "Tools and Practices Recommendations" section of this chapter that apply to the Program.

How to Make It Work

Transforming metrics from abstract numbers in a dashboard to action requires attention and focus from everyone working on delivering the Program. Transparency is vital so project team members understand how the metrics apply to Program success.

Be Continuously Engaged

Effective Program Managers are continuously engaged with the Project Managers and project teams. Communicating the goals of the Program and how each project contributes and delivers to those goals is crucial. Nobody working within the Program should question their role and the importance of what they are doing.

Select Metrics That Are Easy to Understand & Trace Directly to Daily Activities

Metrics should seamlessly flow between organizational, departmental, portfolio, Program, project, and individual goals. The best metrics have a clear purpose and application within the organization. Reliable, actionable metrics start with communicating to everyone what each is, how each person's performance and data gathering efforts populate it, why it is important, what the upper and lower control limits are, and what corrective actions will be taken if it reaches one of those limits.

Normalize Reporting Windows for All Project Teams Within the Program

While the projects under the Program may have varying methodologies, the cadence that Program metrics are captured and reported must be normalized across the Program. Not standardizing the reporting window for metrics across the Program can introduce false results. For instance, if Agile Project A reports metrics at the end of weekly Sprints and Traditional Project B reports at the end of each fiscal quarter, multiple issues will present for the Program Manager. Project A will naturally have greater variance because the measurement window is weekly; any event that cuts the availability of the project team for a day or more during the Sprint will cause a significant drop in productivity for that week (holidays, sick days, etc.).

Unfortunately, there is no suggested reporting window across all metrics, but setting it to the same cadence for the organization will increase accuracy.

Tools and Practices Recommendations

The seven basic tools for quality improvement can be traced back to Kaoru Ishikawa and his work developing quality circles[3].

Ishikawa Diagram

Ishikawa is most famous for the Ishikawa Diagram, better known as a Fishbone Diagram in western cultures *(sample shown in Figure 16.01)*. For Program Managers, the purpose of the tool remains unchanged, but the focus shifts to looking at root causes within the Program. An excellent technique in the AIF is to use an Ishikawa Diagram to track impediments across all projects. This will help identify themes and areas where the same impediment is restricting progress across multiple projects. These impediments are a likely sign of a process flaw that should be addressed beyond issue resolution at the project level, using Value Stream Mapping or another, appropriate quality improvement technique.

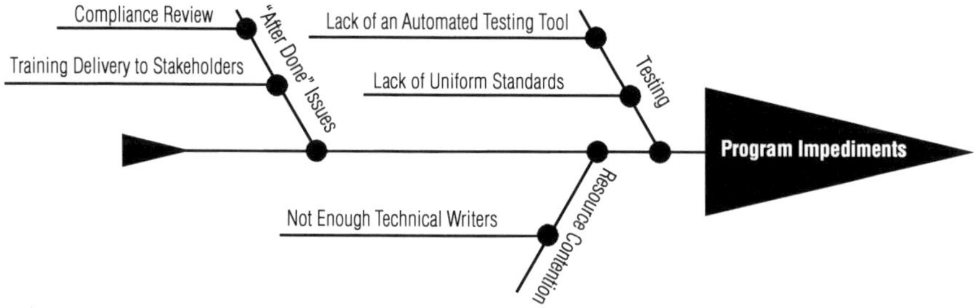

Figure 16.01 | Ishikawa Diagram

Check Sheets

Check sheets should remain at the project level and not be condensed or merged at the Program level. Merging these data sources will obscure patterns easiest to identify and manage at the project level. The Program Manager should review all check sheets to identify any common patterns and work to determine the causes or practices that created the data – good or bad. *(See Figure 16.02.)*

Histograms

Histograms show the distribution of numerical data points, as shown in *Figure 16.03.* Unless the metric can be normalized across multiple projects using relative values, like ratios or percentages, keep histograms at the project level. Even with relative values, the varying scales between individual projects

Tracking Scrum Board Status by Day

Check Sheet - Items In Each Scrum Board Lane - Sprint #4

	Release Backlog	Selected	Build	Unit Test	Integrated Test	Done
Monday	238	35	4	0	0	0
Tuesday	238	30	6	0	3	0
Wednesday	240	25	5	4	5	0
Thursday	240	20	3	6	2	8
Friday	240	17	2	4	4	12
Monday	240	12	1	4	8	14
Tuesday	250	5	2	4	7	21
Wednesday	250	0	0	4	8	27
Thursday	250	0	0	0	5	34
Friday	255	0	0	0	2	37

Figure 16.02 | Check Sheet

can still skew results. A critical eye is needed to evaluate the distributions and a measure of restraint should be applied before making any sweeping conclusions about the relative health of one project against another from just what the histogram shows.

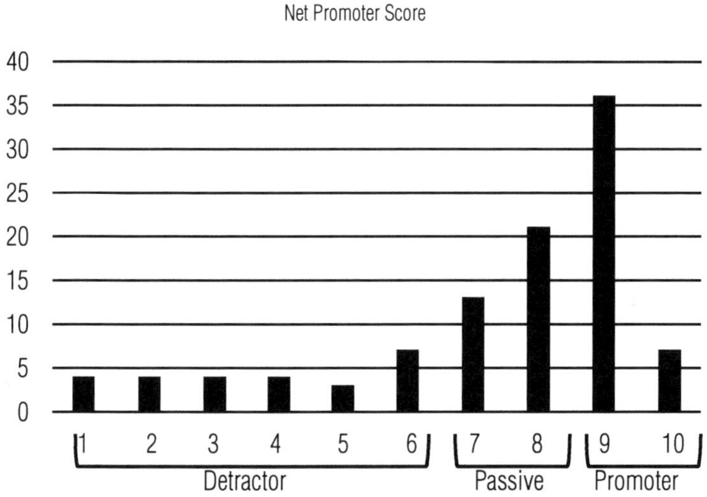

Figure 16.03 | Histogram

Histograms are excellent visual guides to measure the maturity and adherence of the process for the metric being evaluated. Histograms should spur questions such as:

- How tight is the distribution? A tight distribution will show very little relative variances between the captured measurements with little or no values captured in the upper and lower limits of the chart. A wide distribution will spill outside of the established limits of the histogram and not accurately depict the true distribution of measurements.

  - If too tight, are measurements granular enough?
  - If too wide, are measurements too detailed?

- What values and projects are outside of three standard deviations? Standard deviation is an expression of the level of variation in a sample of data. In a normal distribution of data, one standard deviation is around 68% of the captured measurements, two standard deviations is around 95% of the captured measurements, and three standard deviations is around 99.7% of the captured measurement. Any measurement that falls outside of three standard deviations is an extreme variation from the norm and should be evaluated.

  - Has root cause analysis been conducted?

- Is the distribution beginning to normalize over time? A normalized distribution will begin to resemble the iconic bell curve. Few distributions ever perfectly resemble a bell curve, so the evaluation is more of a relative comparison than trying to meet an ideal that may not be achievable with the best possible efforts.

Control Charts

Control Charts graphically map measurements over time against an acceptable range of metric values at upper and lower control limits. Like check sheets, control charts should remain at the project level so the patterns and stability of the process being measured can be evaluated accurately for each project. *(See Figure 16.04.)*

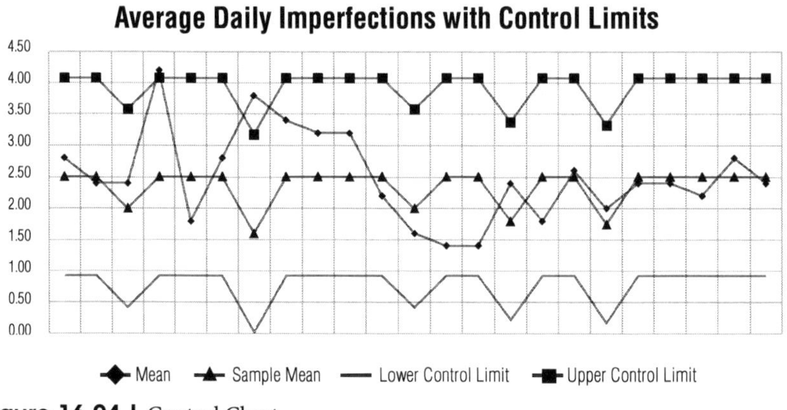

Figure 16.04 | Control Chart

Pareto Diagram

The Pareto Diagram may be the best quality tool for the Program Manager. Data can be fed from control charts or check sheets when a data point falls out of the acceptable control limits for a given metric. Because the criteria can vary between projects, the Pareto Diagram focuses on process failures or impediments and why the issue occurred. Each outlier is categorized down to a root cause, and the Pareto Diagram shows the frequency of the issues. *(See Figure 16.05.)*

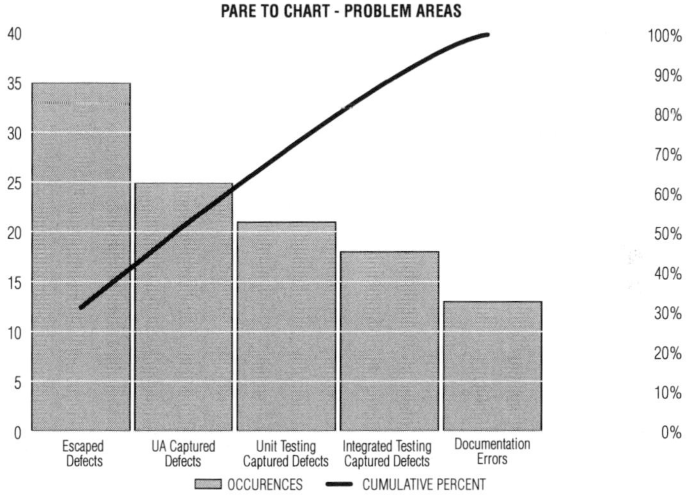

Figure 16.05 | Pareto Chart

The AIF Program Manager focuses on challenges with the most occurrences first. The Pareto Diagram is a good visual tool to engage stakeholders and show the impact a process challenge is having on projects in a Program.

Scatter Diagrams

Scatter Diagrams are a niche quality tool *(Figure 16.06).* If there are two sets of numerical metrics being captured, a scatter diagram can show if there is a relationship between one value and another. Even if there is a relationship, it is important to remember that correlation does not equal causation. Two metrics may have a strong relationship, but the cause of variation may be a third variable not currently captured or another metric altogether.

For instance, a project has substantially more escaped defects when testing hours fall below 8 hours/team member/week. The natural assumption would

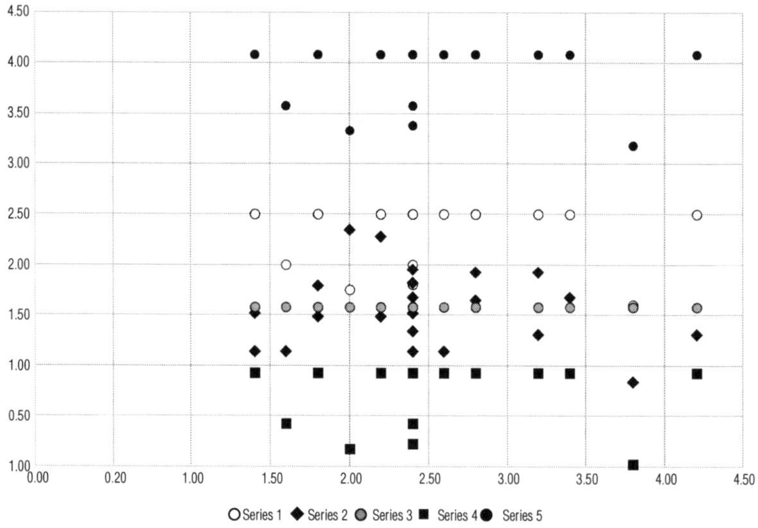

Figure 16.06 | Scatter Chart

be to make sure that project always tests more than 8 hours/team member/ week. Thus, the Program Manager instructs all the Project Managers to ensure this occurs. Everyone complies, yet defects still escape at the same rate as before. Further analysis shows that the metric dropped when a senior programmer, excellent at testing, was on vacation. Therefore, the appropriate corrective action would have been to task the Project Manager and senior programmer with coaching and training the rest of the project team on better testing techniques. Metrics can show a variance exists, but inspection and analysis is still required to determine a root cause and correct response to address the issue.

"When is it appropriate to expand corrective actions out to all projects in a Program?" is the quality challenge for Programs, in a nutshell. This is one of the great advantages of an Agile approach to project management. Before making a unilateral change, task one of the Agile teams with trying out a corrective action or recommended practice, and determine if the action delivers the anticipated benefits. The commitment to change, at the Agile project team level, is the next Iteration, and a mature Agile team can test a hypothesis in the span of an Iteration or two. AIF Program Managers should leverage this flexibility and learning culture before making any unilateral assumptions about how to correct a quality issue or improve an existing practice.

Stratification Charts

Stratification Charts permit the Program Manager to place multiple data points in the same grid from different sources to identify patterns in the results *(Figure 16.07.)* For an AIF Program Manager, stratification charts help to validate the metric captured, by testing early results across multiple projects to see if it can be used to compare and if it is a good predictor of project success.

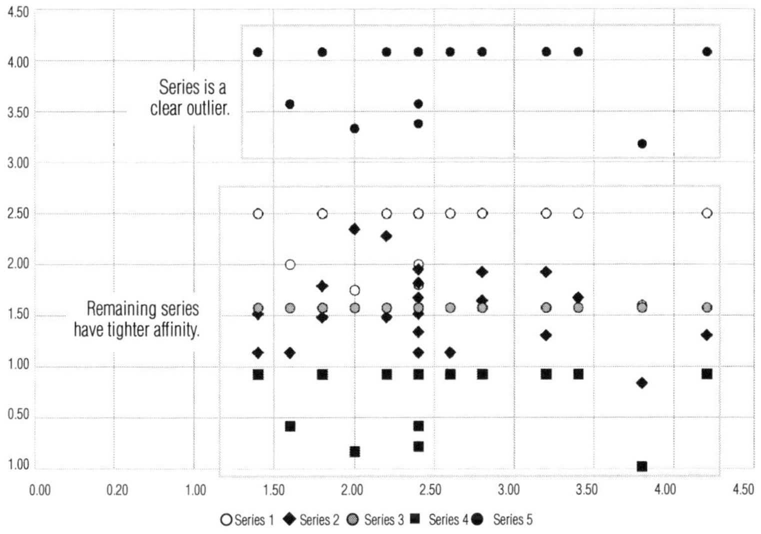

Figure 16.07 | Stratification Chart

Each source should be set up to show as a different color or shape on the chart so patterns can be easily traced and identified. When reviewing the stratification chart, the ultimate goal is to see overlapping data points between projects in the Program, but the realistic evaluation should be if the results lie within a reasonable range where variances can be fairly compared. For instance, if one project is wildly out of range from the rest of the projects in a Program, it is wise to exclude that project from reports on that metric if that project is perceived to be in control. If a project is perceived as out of control, it should be an outlier on the stratification chart. Exclusion decisions should follow the "Five Whys" process.

As noted earlier, including a significant outlier will skew results and cloud executive stakeholders' visibility to seeing variances on the other projects because the scale of that project will dwarf the other projects in the Program.

Any exclusions should be documented, using Program artifacts, in the interest of full transparency. All focus with a Program steering committee will narrow down to that project for that metric because of the visual cues being displayed.

Cumulative Flow Diagram (CFD)

Cumulative Flow Diagrams are a good visual aid for the AIF Program Manager. The data points tracked in a CFD, for the AIF Program Manager, transition to the Agile Release level, but the intent remains the same. In Agile projects, the elements that stratify the CFD are at the User Story level and typically track as completion states of Done, testing, development, and Backlog[4].

At the AIF Program level, the CFD tracks the states of production – WIP (Work In Progress), and Backlog. Building a CFD that crosses from Agile to Waterfall is a challenge, but not impossible. The Program-level CFD shows the cumulative accomplishments the Program has achieved by delivering projects to production, identifying the WIP so it can be managed, and showing the active Backlog of work. Use the following guidelines as a starting point and adjust so the Program CFD suits the intended purpose.

Waterfall Projects – Track at the project level.

- Backlog
    - Track a Waterfall project as Backlog if it is a known request that is unfunded/awaiting project team resources through Initiating
- WIP
    - The project is Planning/Executing/Monitoring and Controlling
- Production
    - The project is Closed

Agile/Hybrid Projects – Track at the Release level if there are clear Releases in the project plan. If there is one Release to production, track it as a Waterfall project regardless of the techniques used to get there.

- Backlog
    - Future funded/scheduled Releases
- WIP
    - Current Release

- Production
  - Releases in production

Agile Product Teams – Track at the Release level. A continuously engaged product team should be recognized at the Program level for their ongoing accomplishments of delivering content to production.

- Backlog
  - Future planned Releases – A rule of thumb would be to count Releases of no more than a calendar year out in the future.
- WIP
  - Current Release
- Production
  - Releases in production

Once the Program CFD is constructed, the same ideals apply as they do at the project level[4]. Lead time and cycle time are measured at the project or Release level rather than User Story. The velocity of the teams' ability to deliver completed Releases and projects to production is visually evident in *Figure 16.08.*

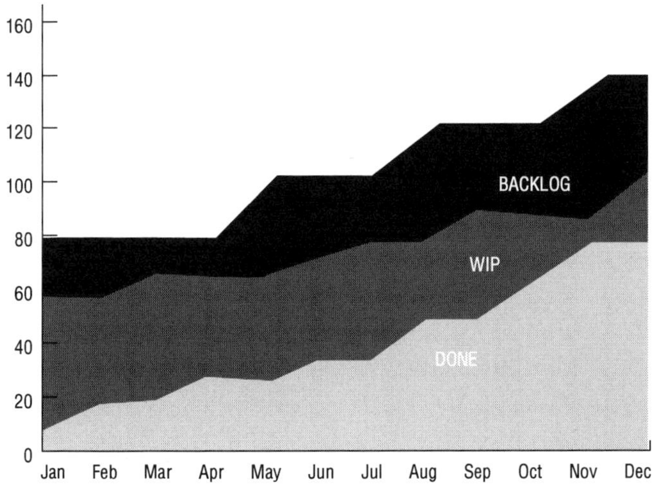

Figure 16.08 | Cumulative Flow Diagram

Flexibility Matrix

The Flexibility Matrix is a vital piece of information to know and understand when managing quality at the Program level. A project with a fixed budget should always have a CPI of 1. A project with a fixed timeline should always have a Schedule Performance Index (SPI) of 1. At all costs, avoid the trap of tracking a fixed constraint, then declaring the project a success and pulling some flawed lesson learned as a general practice for all projects. Grouping projects by the fixed constraint and eliminating metrics, that will be skewed as a result, is a solid recommended practice.

Grouping Projects by Type or Size

Grouping projects by size or type within a Program to establish quality expectations and capture accurate measurements is a wise approach compared to using the same metrics and expectations across an entire program. Lumping all endeavors within a Program and measuring them all against the same standards of accountability is not realistically achievable or a fair measure of each component's successful contribution to the Vision of the Program. The Program Vision should be the guiding principal in selecting the metrics for Program success, and how a given endeavor contributes to that Vision should guide the Program Manager's decisions with grouping projects together and selecting the Program metrics that best match the efforts of that group.

A functional Program, appropriately scoped and managed by the Program Manager and Product Owner, may include an endeavor, too small to be considered a standalone project, that is managed within the Program because it achieves a deliverable crucial to success. A Program can also include an omnibus endeavor, so large it becomes known to the organization simply by a generic label, such as "The Building" or "The Project". Embracing and permitting these differences in expectations faces reality, allows focus to be applied where it is most important by project, and avoids undue pressure on Project Managers to meet a metric goal that is unachievable due to the nature of their project.

Programs may include endeavors that have internal stakeholders as the end user of the system and others with customers using the product under development. Products consumed by a customer should be viewed and measured differently from a product that is only digested and consumed within the organization. For example, a company with a smartphone application for internal use and another application that is customer facing that generates revenue should not be grouped together to track in-app purchases as a measure of success against both applications. One will always fail, and the other will always look like it is winning, even though it is the only competitor.

Grouping decisions and metrics selections, for those endeavors within a Program, vary by organization, but could be by verticals within the organization, software development versus implementing a commercial product, or T-shirt sizing by budget/scope/level of effort. Scaling metrics accordingly to groups broken into different categories furthers the value of the detail captured and avoids skewed data.

Conclusion

The advent and explosive improvement of project, Program, and portfolio management information systems for both Agile and Waterfall projects create a significant problem. The maturity of these systems has achieved a point where they can track more metrics than any organization can hope to truly monitor and act upon. A dangerous trap is to become enamored with the tools instead of the process. Too many metrics are just as damaging as none!

A devotion to metrics, as the sole source of quality measurement, is a recipe for disaster. A good Program Manager will use Management by Walking Around (MBWA), as much as the metrics, and quality reports project teams are providing to assess how teams are performing and identify quality issues. Metrics capture a negligible sample of the work and outcomes project teams deliver.

Some thought leaders advocate that an Agile organization should track as few as just four metrics[5]. If an organization is just starting out with Agile or quality management, then four metrics are plenty to work with. Start small, prove the value of quality management, and expand from there!

Select metrics in a space that points to processes that clearly need improvement or are vital to the success of the Program. Avoid focusing on a single dimension of Program success and instead work across the dimensions of customer engagement, cost management, team growth and maturity, and Agile process maturity. The selected metrics should be a driving force for continuous improvement. As the Program improves, the upper and lower control limits for the metrics need to shift to avoid complacency.

The following table references Releases in some of the metrics. For a Waterfall project or project with a single Release, the metric can be applied to the project-level. These metrics are a massive subset of the current lexicon, but they apply equally well to Agile, hybrid, and Waterfall projects and can be a strong foundation to work towards process improvement. A full listing of potential metrics is available, along with other artifact examples, at GR8PM.com.

NAME	CALCULATION	DESCRIPTION	USE
CUSTOMER ENGAGEMENT			
Cost Per Acquisition (CPA) – Cost to acquire a new customer	The total sales and marketing costs per month / new customers per month	The total sales and marketing budget includes operating costs (like salary, bonus, utilities, and rent)	The metric identifies what it costs the organization to win over a new customer. The higher the CPA, the more crucial it is for the organization to win and secure customer loyalty.
Customer Satisfaction	Net Promoter Score (NPS). Surveys are given on a 10 point scale for the question, "How likely are you to recommend the product or service to a friend?" Promoter = 9-10 Passives = 7-8 Detractors = 1-6 NPS=((promoters – detractors)/total respondents) X 100	The scores will range from -100 to 100. A positive score is good and a negative score is bad.	Net promoter measures the relationship between delighted customers (promoters) against ambivalent or dissatisfied customers (detractors) that are likely to look elsewhere in the near future. Many organizations have a follow-up process that reaches out to any detractors directly to understand why they are not satisfied with the product.

NAME	CALCULATION	DESCRIPTION	USE
Customer Retention	(New Customers – Lost Customers)/All Customers	Is the organization growing the customer base or shrinking?	A negative % on this metric is a warning sign that recent Releases are not meeting customer needs. Is the organization addressing the customer's pain points they have sought your help with addressing?
COST MANAGEMENT			
Cost Performance Index (CPI)	CPI = Earned Value/ Actual Cost	This is a standard EVM calculation.	Greater than 1 is good. Less than 1 is bad.
Cost Per Release	The total cost the project team has incurred to deliver the Release to production.	This should include salaries, technology, and operating expenses like telco, utilities, and rent.	Is the value being delivered in the Release worth the cost? This is a core question to measure the value of the project within the Program.
Unexpected Expense Per Release	The sum of unplanned expenses incurred during the release.	Total unplanned expenses incurred during the release.	This metric helps to identify if planning process can accurately predict future development costs.

NAME	CALCULATION	DESCRIPTION	USE
TEAM GROWTH AND MATURITY			
Attrition	Lost Team Members/ Total Team Members	A lost team member is any member on a project that left the team for any reason other than a planned departure by the Project Manager. Internal transfers, retirement, resignations, and separations should all be counted.	This metric measures how much turnover is taking place within the teams and the Program as a whole.
Cross-functional Team Maturity	Total Skills/Team Members	Total skills can be calculated in a few different ways and will vary by organization. The general rule is to count each unique skill each team member has that contributes to the project's success.	This measure is intended to gauge the maturity of the team and how much they have embraced the cross-functional team model. The minimum threshold to count a skill as an attained skill and the granularity of the skills being tracked are important decisions.
Employee Satisfaction	The NPS for customer satisfaction applied to the question "How likely are you to recommend working here to a friend/ relative?"	Scores range from -100 to 100. Positive numbers are good. Negative numbers are bad.	Truly engaged team members are vested in the project's success and feel their contributions and suggestions are valued.

NAME	CALCULATION	DESCRIPTION	USE
AGILE PROCESS MATURITY			
Cycle Time	Average unit of time used / work item produced	Essentially, how long it takes from the start of developing a work item until it is finished.	While Agile has guard rails that aid in improving and measuring Cycle Time, a Waterfall project with a network diagram and WBS should also be able to calculate the Cycle Time to complete each WBS element in the project plan.
Escaped Defects Per Release	The number of bugs reported by customers.	Lower is clearly better.	This metric measures the maturity of the team's testing and QA processes. It also is a strong candidate to correlate with customer satisfaction.
"Done" to Production Release	The time gap between an item marked as Done and released to production.	This metric measures the amount of work that falls outside of the project team's control. Lowering this metric is essential to delivering completed work to production.	For a Waterfall project, it goes back to the WBS. When was the WBS element completed and how long did the project take to go to production? Do this to a Waterfall project to show the value of the MVR to skeptics by identifying the MVR and showing the organization the delay in delivering the MVR so the full scope can be achieved.

END NOTES

[1] More information on the flexibility matrix can be found in Chapter 13 of this book and Chapter 3 in *The Agile Almanac - Book 1.*

[2] Lederer, Albert L., and Prasad, Jayesh. "A Casual Model for Software Cost Estimating Error." *IEEE Transactions of Software Engineering,* vol. 24, no. 2, 1998, pp. 137-148.

[3] For more information on the seven basic tools, please visit the American Society for Quality for an overview of the tools and purpose. *http://asq.org/learn-about-quality/seven-basic-quality-tools/overview/overview.html.*

[4] For more detail on CFDs, please reference Chapter 7 of *The Agile Almanac - Book 1*

[5] *https://www.agileconnection.com/article/4-balanced-metrics-tracking-agile-teams?page=0%2C0*

CHAPTER

17

Budget Management

Overview

This chapter explores different thoughts, perspectives, tools, and methods used to manage Agile Program budgets. An overview of Agile Program budget management approaches, commonly used to measure the health of a Program based on forecast, actuals, and work produced, is presented. Several methods are explored to bring awareness to a variety of management approaches to Agile Program Budgets. The chapter will discuss the benefits of managing budgets with an Agile Program methodology. Enterprise- and Program-level challenges faced by Agile Program Managers are also outlined, with recommended approaches to avoiding them. Several tools, methods, examples, and artifacts are provided within the chapter and also at GR8PM.com to assist Program Managers in continued success.

Earned Value Management

Earned Value Management (EVM) is a set of tools and techniques developed and defined by the Department of Defense of the United States of America. Within *The PMBOK® Guide,* there is coverage of Earned Value Analysis (EVA) and a discussion of how the various variables and indexes created by EVM calculations can be used to control the cost of projects and Programs. Earned Value Management requires a disciplined approach from both a Program and Executive management perspective.

The PMBOK® Guide states that, "Earned value management (EVM) is a methodology that combines scope, schedule, and resource measurements to assess project performance and progress." It integrates the scope, cost, and schedule baselines, to form the performance measurement baseline, which provides data to assess and measure project performance and progress. This technique, requiring the formation of an integrated baseline against which performance can be measured for the duration of the project, can be applied to projects and Programs in any industry.

Agile Earned Value Management (A-EVM) is similar to Traditional EVM in that the work is still broken down and estimated, and the cost estimate planned over time, however, the work breakdown is at the Roadmap and Iteration levels, opposed to the Traditional WBS and schedule.

Complexity increases in Agile Programs due to the challenging deliverables, number of teams required to execute, and cost of execution. Agile Program Earned Value Management (AP-EVM) expands the foundation of Agile Earned Value Management through the addition of tools and techniques to manage the larger scale and increased uncertainty.

Lean Budgets

Lean Budgets, and SAFe Budget Management also, introduce a different perspective on Program and Portfolio funding. Traditional and Agile projects and Programs are funded at the project or program level, based on set scope and expected value added to the organization.

"Lean Budgets is a set of practices that minimize overhead by funding and empowering Value Streams rather than projects, while maintaining financial and fitness-for-use governance. This is achieved through objective evaluation of working systems, prudent management of Epic investments, and dynamic budget adjustments."[1]

Agile Program Incremental Cost Management

Agile Program Incremental Cost Management (ICM) uses the Resource and Release Plans in combination with enterprise cost reports to measure the cost of an Iteration. This method of measurement compares forecast to actual cost and provides the Program Manager with an indication of the incremental cost. This is a useful practice when Agile teams charging to a project are 100% dedicated to it.

This chapter will reference the use of EVM, Agile EVM, Agile Program EVM and SAFe Budget management. The method used to manage any Program is dependent upon each Program's unique circumstance. A good practice is to take time within Initiation to determine the best approach. Often, it is determined by the PMO that then provides the Program Managers with the methodology and expected artifacts. In that instance, the step of determining budget management approach is eliminated.

Benefits / Challenges

Benefits

Expands on EVM

Program-level A-EVM expands upon the Earned Value model and provides Program Managers a tool-kit to measure scope, schedule, cost, and the ability to understand and communicate the status of each area through budget analysis. When all of the data is available and used properly, A-EVM is a great tool for quantification of status.

SAFe - Lean Budgets Funding Model

The Lean Budget funding model supports the agility of a Program by empowering the team with decision-making authority. Funding is approved at the Feature level, which gives teams the ability to select Epics and Stories without having to revisit with the PMO or approval committee should scope change. This approach increases speed-to-market and improves the teams' sense of ownership of the Product.

Agile Program Incremental Cost Management

The ability of this metric to report at this granular of a level improves Product Owner and team decision-making abilities by including the incremental cost of a Feature or function.

Challenges

Organizations adopting Agile often implement the delivery methodology, but continue to fund efforts using a Traditional model. This section will discuss some challenges with this funding approach and alternatives that, depending on the organization's appetite for change, could be more beneficial.

Loss of Pre-Defined Scope

APM moves away from a key Traditional approach of locking in scope prior to execution, and allows teams the agility to select the most appropriate scope, given Product Owner priority and technical synergy or constraint. With the loss of pre-defined scope, full adherence to A-EVM becomes challenging for Program Managers and analysts as the scope baseline becomes fluid. This is an unfamiliar approach for many so it requires the Program Manager to communicate the process, practices, and tools clearly and ensure team members fully understand them. Adjusting to any change can be difficult, but once the A-EVM methodology is fully adopted, teams will soon see that the benefits far outweigh the challenges that occurred during transition. Like they say, "The proof is in the pudding!"

Shared Funding Models
Project teams often have little to no input regarding the funding model and Framework used to manage Agile Program Budgets. Depending on the maturity of the organization's Agile adoption, Programs may use the same funding model as the Traditional projects. This presents a challenge to the Agile teams' ability to quickly adjust scope without the use of a potentially lengthy change control process. Upfront discussion with decisions makers about this challenge will help as scope change begins to occur. The Lean Budget or SAFe approach to funding Value Streams and empowering Program teams to make decisions regarding functions for delivery is one way Agile addresses this challenge.

Program-level Attributes

The AIF paradigm is designed to ease the transition from current Framework thoughts to the future of Agile Program Management. This evolution includes the current thinking about Agile Program budget management, and outlines how budgeting with Traditional and Agile planning is extremely similar, with minor variances to support the differences in delivery methodologies.

The Agile Almanac - Book 1 outlines the steps in EVM and A-EVM, showing parallels and differences between Traditional and Agile budget management at a detailed workflow level. With the increased complexity of Programs, the parallels further evolve to increase stability in Program budgets. The evolution of attributes includes the addition of AP-EVM and Lean Budgets - SAFe, shown in *Figure 17.01,* outlining each approach and the appropriate steps to each methodology taken after the ROM funding is established.

EVM	A-EVM	AP-EVM	AIF BUDGETS	LEAN BUDGETS SAFe
Project Funding Approval	Program Funding Approval	• ROM Estimate • NPV/ Break even analysis • Strategic Value definition • Approval of Funding	Portfolio or Program Level Approved Funding	Portfolio Level Approved Operating Budget (Investment Spend)
Define project scope	Create Roadmap/ Release plans	Product Roadmap Release Plans	Fracture Program Scope into Feature, Function and Capability (FFC) *(See Figure 11-13)*	Fund Value Streams
Assemble Team	Assemble Team	Assemble Teams	Assign initial team	Empower Value Streams with content authority
Decompose Work	Document Stories	Document Stories	• Decomposition to Defined FFC Milestones • Creation of Customer Value Logic Network (CVLN) • Epic Work Package (EWP) Definition with sizing	
Outline Project Schedule	Define Release Iterations	• Identify cross-team dependencies. • Define Program Release Iterations	Affinity Estimation Technique	Provide Objective Evidence of fitness for purpose.
Estimate Work Package Budgets	Estimate Story / Feature Budgets	Estimate Story / Feature Budgets	Analysis of ELN using Critical Path Analysis to determine timebox schedule	Approve Epic Level initiatives
Specify Time Phased Budgets	Specify Iteration Budgets	Specify Program Iteration Budgets	• Resource allocation based on schedule • Specify Program Budget	Exercise Fiscal Governance with Dynamic Budgeting

Figure 17.01 – Attributes of Various Program Budget Management Options

Roles

Portfolio Manager

The Portfolio Manager is responsible for the collection and reporting of all Program and project Planned and Actual cost, and the total view and understanding into the cost and value of all Projects and Programs within the Portfolio.

Program Manager

In addition to the responsibilities previously outlined in several other chapters, the Program Manager manages the Program budget and potential impacts to delivery of agreed upon functions, budget or schedule, and communicates updates to key executive stakeholders.

Program Analyst

The Program Analyst performs analysis of forecast and actual data to determine variance. Additional responsibilities include identification of reason for variance and communication of all budget analysis and reporting to Project Managers and Program Managers.

Program Product Owner

Generating the Product Roadmap and reviewing monthly budget variance reporting for awareness and understanding are two aspects of the Program Product Owner role. Details regarding change requests for additional features, functions, or capabilities are also part of their responsibilities, should the methodology used require change requests for scope changes.

Workflow

This next section will explore the process of determining and monitoring the Agile Program Budget throughout the Program duration.

Initiate

In this phase, ideas for new solutions or enhancements to existing products are generated. They must have perceived value and align to organizational strategy. Each idea is assessed for the Rough Order of Magnitude (ROM) estimated cost and NPV (Net Present Value) or break-even analysis.

Funding is approved for projects that align to the enterprise strategy and have perceived value to the organization. Once ROM funding is available, the scope or Roadmap is defined, teams are assembled, work is broken down and estimated, and the duration for delivery determined.

Plan

With approved funding, the Product Owner generates the Program Product Roadmap or FFC breakout. The Roadmap is a path for the Features to be delivered by the Program. The Release Plan is also generated in this phase.

Once these are in place, the next step is to build the baseline Program budget. Key lead resources are assigned to breaking down the work into FFCs, as discussed in AIF chapter. The teams decompose work to more granular levels, allowing them to work with Epic Work Packages (EWP) that are easily consumed and estimated. This was outlined in *Figure 11.14.*

These inputs enable the Program Manager and Program Analyst to produce the Resource Plan, which indicates resource requirements, equating to cost over time. Dependent on the number of fully allocated resources to the Program team, this estimate, shown over each timebox, may be consistent from Iteration to Iteration. It is important to identify areas of potential increase in cost due to inter-dependency on human or non-human resources. A good understanding of these provides the Program Manager and Program Analyst with more information to increase the accuracy of the forecast.

With the Program Product Roadmap, FFCs, and Release plan in place, the teams are able to move into Estimation, which is done at a detailed level in the Sprint Planning meeting for each Sprint. The Program Analyst, with input from the team, Project Manager, and Program Manager, generates the budget. As the team works through Sprint Planning, and Iterations are complete, the confidence level of the Program budget increases.

Estimation

The Iteration Release or Program schedule is also defined at a high level and, together with the overall Program budget estimates, provides the Program Analyst enough data to produce the Program Iteration budget.

Using the Affinity Estimation technique for high level EWP sizing, later refined using Planning Poker, the teams prepare to pick up Stories for completion of work. Assigning Story Points to each User Story to determine ROM velocity gives an indication of the Value planned for delivery within each Iteration. The number of resources allocated to each team and their rate provides an Iteration cost, which the Program Manager uses as a guide to measure expected cost over time (forecast) to actual cost over time throughout the duration of the Program. With the inputs of Story estimation, team size, and velocity, a Feature Release budget can be determined for each project then rolled up to the Program level. The focus on a coordinated Definition of Done and Program Release Cycle is a primary responsibility of the Program leadership team.

These budgets should be re-assessed every few Iterations as ROM estimates will improve in accuracy as the work becomes better understood and more defined.

At the single-team project level, *Figure 17.02* shows an example of the interrelationship between Team cost, Velocity and Iteration cost and value, if all planned Stories are completed. For programs this example can be extended to show Iteration cost and value for multiple teams.

Team 1:	Story ID:	Story Points:	Iteration 1:
• 8 Resources • 32 Production hours / week • \$95 per hour labor rate	1	1	• Velocity = 30 (Story Points) • Cost of Iteration = \$48,640 (8 x 32 x \$95 x 2 weeks) • Value (of 30 Story Points) = \$48,640
	1	1	
	1	1	

Figure 17.02 | Cost and Value of 2-Week Iteration

Funding Approval

After the estimation process, the budget is more refined and has a lower degree of variability than when initially approved. The Program Manager is responsible for presentation of the updated estimate to the organization's designated funding committee for formal review and approval. Items of consideration at the executive level are to determine if the Program deliverables remain in line with the strategic goals of the enterprise. Programs are reviewed to ensure they still meet the NPV or break-even analysis. The organization's funding committee will take these, and other items, into consideration when approving or pausing efforts. This checkpoint ensures the Program continues to align with the enterprise Vision.

Iterate, Monitor and Control

The Program Manager and Program Analyst compare the expected cost to the actual cost on a weekly or monthly basis, depending on the enterprise standards. The Agile Program Budget Forecast and Expected Value and Actuals, once made available, are analyzed by the Program Analyst to determine trends indicating success, risks, or issues throughout the Program.

The A-EVM tool-kit provides the Program Analyst with a number of formulas to determine the Schedule and Cost Performance. In addition to Planned Value, Earned Value, and Actual Cost, the Schedule Performance Index (SPI) and Cost Performance Index (CPI) are used to determine if schedule and cost are on track throughout the duration of the Program. As stated earlier, the original ROM Epic/Theme estimates will have a variance. Continued monitoring and adoption of the team estimates are essential, and must be regularly communicated to executives and the PMO.

Change Request

The budget change request process is leveraged when there is a change in expected cost that exceeds the contingency threshold. The contingency threshold is commonly +/- 10% of the overall budget, and differs based on the organization and Program circumstances. Cost changes may come as a result of a better understanding of the solution or additional scope items being added. The latter is based on the funding model, and the agility of adding scope is arguable. In organizations funding Agile Programs similarly to Traditional, they include the requirement of traceability to agreed upon scope within the funding approval process. A requested change is documented in both a change request document and the Change Request Log. This request is presented to Program stakeholders for approval, the outcome documented, along with reasoning for the decision, and the teams proceed accordingly.

An example process flow for obtaining Agile Program budget funding can be found in *Figure 17.03.*

Ceremonies

Program Daily Stand-up Meeting

The Program Daily Stand-up meeting is a forum for project leaders to gather and share information regarding individual projects. Teams select from various tools for tracking risks and roadblocks that arise. These artifacts – Risk Board, Risk Burndown, Roadblock Board, and Issues Log – were discussed in Chapter 15.

Backlog Grooming

When working in an organization that requires scope alignment to funding, one potential outcome of Backlog grooming may be additional Epics, Themes, or User Stories. These may require a funding change request prior to moving forward with grooming, however, not when Lean Budgeting practices are in place.

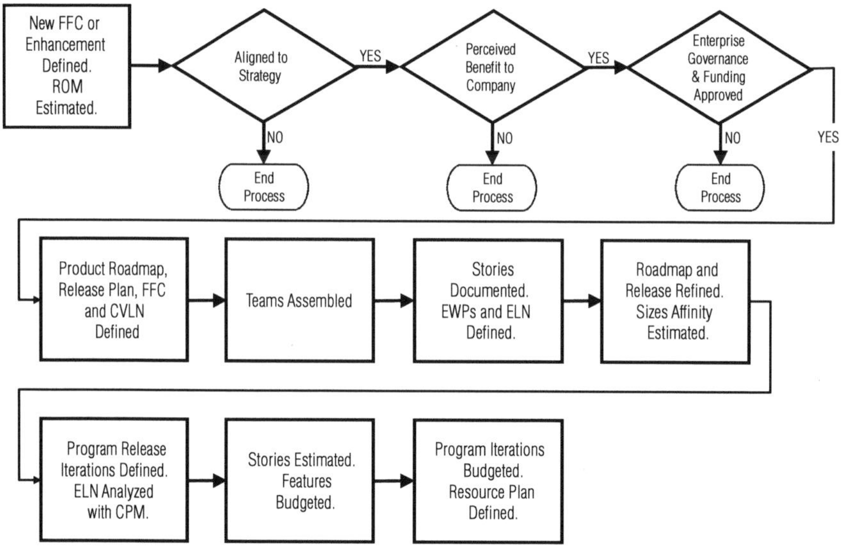

Figure 17.03 | Agile Program Process Flow

Artifacts

The key artifacts needed to manage an Agile Program are listed below. This section includes a description of them while the Tools and Practices Recommendations section provides more detail. You can also find templates and samples for download at GR8PM.com.

1. Initial Funding Request / Approval
2. Agile Program Resource Cost Plan
3. Agile Program Budget
4. Change Request
5. Change Control Log

How To Make It Work Effectively

To this point, the process by which Agile Program initial budgets are defined and approved have been reviewed. A few key components for tracking an Agile Program Budget using A-EVM are:

- Planned Value (PV)
- Earned Value (EV)

- Actual Cost (AC)
- Schedule Variance
- Schedule Index
- Cost Variance
- Cost Index

A good practice for scaling these tools and formulas is to have the Program Analyst evaluate these calculations at both the project and aggregated Program level. Having budgets for each project or team estimated and documented enables the Agile Program Budget PV, EV, AC, SV, SI, CV, CI to be calculated. *Figure 17.03* defines the terms discussed and scales their definitions to the Program level.

TERM	EVM DEFINITION	A-EVM DEFINITION	AP-EVM DEFINITION
Planned Value (PV)	The budgeted cost of work planned for a specific time period.	The budgeted cost of work planned for a single-team Iteration.	The budgeted cost of work planned for a single Iteration across multiple teams, working toward a common end deliverable.
Earned Value (EV)	The budgeted cost of work completed during a specific time period.	The budgeted cost of work completed during an Iteration.	The budgeted cost of work completed for a single Iteration across multiple teams, working toward a common end deliverable.
Actual Cost (AC)	The actual cost of work completed during a specific time period.	The actual cost of work completed during an Iteration.	The actual cost of work completed for a single Iteration across multiple teams working toward a common end deliverable.

Figure 17.03: Scaling A-EVM Terms to AP-EVM Terms

Figure 17.04 is an example of a budget plan for 4 teams over 3 Iterations, inclusive of their size, rates, and velocity; all crucial to tracking the health of the Agile Program Budget on a regular cadence.

The calculation of human resources (aka, man hours) is the number of hours multiplied by the rate of the resource. Physical resources, such as hardware, software, and fixed bid agreements, are measured by the invoices paid within a given time period. Actuals are made available to Program Managers on a Weekly or Monthly basis, and are used to measure Planned versus Actual

		RELEASE 1		
		Iteration 1 (2 Weeks)	Iteration 2 (2 Weeks)	Iteration 3 (2 Weeks)
TEAM 1	Velocity	40	40	40
8 resources	Planned Cost	$ 48,640	$ 48,640	$ 48,640
$95/HR	Actual Cost			
32 hr weeks	Value Delivered			
TEAM 2	Velocity	30	30	30
6 resources	Planned Cost	$ 36,480	$ 36,480	$ 36,480
$95/HR	Actual Cost			
32 hr weeks	Value Delivered			
TEAM 3	Velocity	60	60	60
12 resources	Planned Cost	$ 72,960	$ 72,960	$ 72,960
$95/HR	Actual Cost			
32 hr weeks	Value Delivered			
Team 4	Velocity	50	50	50
9 resources	Planned Cost	$ 14,976	$ 14,976	$ 14,976
$26/HR	Actual Cost			
32 hr weeks	Value Delivered			
External Program Costs	Velocity Planned Cost Actual Cost Value Delivered	$ 20,000	$ 15,400	$ 24,000
TOTAL	Velocity			
	Planned Cost	$ 193,056	$ 188,456	$ 197,056
	Actual Cost			
	Value Delivered	$ -	$ -	$ -

Figure 17.04 | Budget Plan *(4 Teams; 3 Iterations)*

cost. It is also a common practice, due to frequent requests from Project and Program Managers, for the analyst to provide details on Committed spending. Depending on the Program environment, the Committed spending, which is money that is contractually obligated and therefore a sunk cost in the event of a scope change or Feature cancellation, may be divided between normal and long-lead items.

If all work planned – no more, no less – for an Iteration is completed, the Earned and Planned Values will be the same. If more worked than Planned is completed, the Earned Value will be higher. Similarly, if less work than Planned occurs, the Earned Value will be lower.

Tools and Practices Recommendations

EVM Tool Kit

The following list of formulas provides a Program Analyst or Program Manager with the calculations to measure the Agile Program Budget. The formulas are the same at the project and Program level.[2]

Formula	Equation
Schedule Variance (SV)	SV = EV-PV
Schedule Index (SI)	SI = EV/PV
Cost Variance (CV)	CV = EV-PV
Cost Index (CI)	CI = EV/PV

A negative value for Schedule or Cost Variance, or a value less than 1 for Schedule or Cost Index, is an indication that the Program is behind schedule or over budget.

Software Tools

Agile Program budget management may be simplified through the use of tools. Computerized tools provide Program Managers with an easy-to-use source for forecast and actual cost comparisons. Typically, the tool is configured so resource allocation can be managed by a designated Resource Manager. The resources are usually given access to the estimates used for tracking Task time, and can adjust them directly in the system. That way, if additional time is needed, they increase the hours and it is reflected in the reporting being used to manage the Program. Likewise, if the resource completes an activity in less hours than estimated, they supply that data and the reporting reflects it. Queries and reports provide Program Managers with the ability to manage many areas of Program data within a single tool.

Among computerized tools, we appreciate the team level integration of CA Agile with CA PPM that lets the system be configured to automatically generate Capital and Expense costs that are correlated to Story Points. This feature allows companies to adhere to financial reporting rules with increased ease, and at a much lower overhead cost for collecting and reporting.

This topic is given deep-dive coverage in Appendix B – Advanced Toolsets.

Conclusion

This chapter has covered the most common Agile Program budget management practices. The tools provided to identify, analyze, and manage budgets will be of great value to many Program Managers. For more information, tools, and tips, please join the GR8PM Tribe at GR8PM.com.

END NOTES

[1] SAFe, Lean Budgets 4.5

[2] Terms and Formulas are from the Department of Defense of the United States of America.

PART FOUR

APPENDICES

APPENDIX

A

Academic Resources

Academic Overview

The intent of this Appendix is to provide an instructional aide for the Professor to navigate through the Agile Almanac Field Guide for Extending Agile into Programs. It should be noted that this is a Desk Reference and Field Guide; not a textbook; although this book would provide an accurate, informative, instructional guide for the student while learning Agile Methodologies and extending Agile into the Program environment. This Agile Almanac Appendix, designed for the Professor, highlights teachable moments where the student should be particularly attentive, as they represent areas that are important in both the academic and professional environments.

Appendix A contains these sections for each chapter:

- **Chapter Vision** – The goal of the chapter.
- **Student Learning Objectives** – The proposed outcome for the reader.
- **Chapter Highlights** – Concepts, benefits, challenges, "how-to," artifacts, practices, roles, ceremonies, and any other element critical to execution of the Agile approach discussed.
- **Key Terms** – Vocabulary, language, a terms used in the chapter (included, b not limited to).

- **Discussion Questions** – Topics for Professors and Students to use to engage in furthering the comprehension of the material within the chapter.
- **Exercises** – Activities and research suggestions for Professors and Students to use in expanding on and applying the content in their situation.
- **Additional Related Resources** – Sources to expand on the concepts within the chapter.

The Agile Almanac – Book 2 is broken down into 3 parts:

- **Part One** – Introduction
- **Part Two** – Frameworks
- **Part Three** – Applied Scaled Agile

The student should become familiar with all three to set the foundation for understanding the inter-relationships between Project, Program, and Portfolio Management. The student will most likely relate to the practical discussion of Agile Myths, Misconceptions, and Anti-Patterns discussed in Part One.

A succinct evaluation of the existing and emerging Frameworks, such as SoS, Kanban, DevOps, SAFe, DA, LeSS, and *PMBOK® Guide Sixth Edition,* is contained in Part Two. The introduction of the Agile Integration Framework (AIF), which provides a revolutionary approach to scaling Agile across enterprises in private, public, and non-profit domains, is also in Part Two.

In Part Three, the student learns how to maneuver in environments complicated by multiple teams and virtual/remote resources, and explores the need for robust estimating, scheduling, and scope and integration management. In addition, the students will become immersed in the challenges of risk, quality, and budget management.

I. PART ONE - INTRODUCTION

Chapter 01 - Critical Foundation

Chapter Vision

The vision of this chapter is to unveil the hidden force that has fostered the undeniable success and broad adoption and acceptance of Agile. The same force has moved beyond the current body of knowledge published in Scrum-aligned circles. This chapter demonstrates that there is something quantifiably different between Scrum and the many variants that have come forth since the Agile Manifesto was published in 2001, and the approaches that preceded Scrum.

It sets the stage for learning about a scaled Agile organizational model that empowers and enables teams and individuals to be their best while also optimizing the throughput of the whole enterprise, detailed in the remaining parts of the book.

Student Learning Objectives

Students who successfully complete this chapter will demonstrate the following specific objectives:

- Explore the marketplace forces that govern Agile.
- Analyze and differentiate between Agile and Scaled Agile.
- Acquire a paradigm or perspective for measuring and discriminating between the various Frameworks' strengths and weakness in a variety of enterprise settings.

Chapter Highlights

- Technology as an enabler of chaotic expectations
- The impact of technology as forecasted by Intel co-founder Gordon Moore
- The critical foundation for stakeholders, executives, technical development professionals, as well as students, to use a common lexicon to speak with one another in understandable terms
- Scaling Agile, as an extension of Lean Principles, using integrative thinking at the overlapping intersection of the *PMBOK® Guide,* the Big 5, and Traditional business schools.

- Project Management as an antidote to chaotic expectations
- Scrum as an antidote to Chaotic Expectations
- The 'Big 5' Agile Frameworks are part of the solution; none, alone, are the solution.

Key Terms

- Moore's Law
- Cone of Uncertainty
- *PMBOK®*
- RAD
- RUP
- Spiral
- *Agile Manifesto*
- ROM
- Transistors per Integrated Circuit (IC)
- ARPANET
- Standish Group *Chaos Report*
- Lean Principles
- Test-Driven Development (TDD)
- PMI Agile Certified Practitioner (PMI-ACP®)
- Scrum Framework
- 'Big 5' Agile Frameworks
- Generally Accepted Accounting Principles (GAAP)
- Defined Granularity

Discussion Questions

1. What is Moore's law, why is it important, and how does this impact Agile Project Management?
2. What is the 'Cone of Uncertainty'? Why is it relevant to project management?
3. Describe what is referred to as the 'Big 5' Agile Frameworks?
4. What is unique about the *PMBOK® Guide Sixth Edition?* Why is this significant?

Exercises

1. Take a 'Trip to the Web' and find out more information about the Standish Group's *Chaos Reports.* Although full reports are only

obtained via purchase, there are numerous articles that contain interviews and discussions of the findings. Briefly discuss the Report(s) and one or two points that you find of interest; include why you selected the specific discussion point?

Additional Related Resources

- Chapter endnotes provide useful source information so this book can be used as both a *Desk Reference and Field Guide.*

Chapter 02 - Agile Myths, Misconceptions, & Anti-Patterns

Chapter Vision

The vision for this chapter is for it to be a resource for change agents getting resistance from senior management and naysayers as they attempt to get buy-in to do an Agile transformation or adoption. For each dysfunction presented, there is enough guidance to avoid or correct it if it is seen in their organization. For each myth listed, facts and data are provided to help persuade colleagues and overcome institutional ignorance.

Student Learning Objectives

Students who successfully complete this chapter will demonstrate the following specific objectives:

- Critique Agile myths, and misconceptions, and analyze the fact-based arguments
- Explore the Anti-patterns framed in a role-based examination of common dysfunctions

Chapter Highlights

- Common myths, misconceptions, and anti-patterns plaguing serious Agile practitioners
- Information and fact-based arguments to assist in becoming effective change agents to overcome potential resistance that is based on myths, misconceptions, and anti-patterns
- A role-based examination of common dysfunctions, such as with the Product Owner and Scrum Master

- Myths and misconceptions specific to a scaled Agile environment
- 'Red flags' signaling the need for Agile Coaches
- Dysfunctional behaviors such as extending the timebox, and ineffective Daily Stand-ups
- Leadership dysfunctions and the Program Manager's responsibility for cultivating leadership on the application of Lean-Agile principles
- Myths including: Agile is Only for Software', 'Too Many Meetings', 'Agile is an *All or Nothing*', 'Agile Projects are Difficult to Budget' or 'Budgeting is Difficult Because there is no End', and more
- As Agile Scales... So Do the Myths- myths related to scalability, distributed teams, and the integration of Agile and non-Agile teams

Key Terms

- Anti-Patterns
- Product Owner
- Scrum Master
- "Diffusion of responsibility"
- Cone of Uncertainty
- Fibonacci sequence
- Minimum Viable Product (MVP)
- Rational Unified Process (RUP)
- *Agile Manifesto*

Discussion Questions

1. When implementing Agile within your organization should you strive for 'Pure' Agile? Why or why not?
2. Why is the selection of a Product Owner critical to the success of a project? How would you select a Product Owner for your organization's strategic projects?

Exercises

1. There are many reasons that an organization may want to engage an Agile Coach. Identify and discuss what you consider to be the top three reasons.
2. Take a 'Trip to the Web' and find out more about the Fibonacci sequence. What is it, and how is it applied to Story Points?

3. Take a 'Trip to the Web' and learn more about W. Edwards Deming and Lean Manufacturing.
4. Select a myth and relate it to a situation familiar to you; your support should be 'busting the myth'.
5. Consider several questions when implementing your own flavor of Agile; discuss how these questions provide guidance when evaluating your organization's approach to Agile.
6. Discuss the "red flags" concept used by Agile Coaches to assess an organization.

Additional Related Resources

- The Scrum Guide, Page 8 Link: *http://www.scrumguides.org/docs/scrumguide/v2016/2016-Scrum-Guide-US.pdf.*
- *Agile Almanac – Book 1* covers the Product Owner role in detail.
- *The State of Scrum* reports – Link: *https://www.scrumalliance.org/why-scrum/state-of-scrum-report/2016-state-of-scrum.*
- The Scrum Guide, Page 8 – Link: *http://www.scrumguides.org/docs/scrumguide/v2016/2016-Scrum-Guide-US.pdf*
- VersionOne *State of Agile Report* for 2017 lists the top five benefits seen by organizations who adopted Agile. Link: *https://explore.versionone.com/state-of-Agile/versionone-11th-annual-state-of-Agile-report-2*

Chapter 03 - Agile Program Management

Chapter Vision

This chapter focuses on the shift to Lean Thinking, and collaboration and adaption, over Traditional command-and-control thinking. Additionally, it provides important environmental considerations for roles, configuration, and artifacts, and setting up the proper feedback loops for continuous improvement cycles across the Program.

Student Learning Objectives

Students who successfully complete this chapter will demonstrate the following specific objectives:

- Analyze and differentiate the mindset of Agile Program management and Traditional Program management
- Rationalize and explain the cultural and organizational changes related to setting the organization up for optimal Agile performance

Chapter Highlights

- Understanding the inter-relationships between Project and Program.
- Things to consider, avoid or watch closely when scaling Agile
- When APM is needed to supplement existing Agile Frameworks, such as Scrum, eXtreme Programming (XP), or Kanban
- Agile Program Activities
- The concept of True North
- Lean principles for Agile
- Benefits and Challenges of APM
- Environmental considerations for implementing feedback loops, optimizing the whole, and delivering a product "fit for purpose"
- Program-level focus on integration and reducing waste, using specified artifacts, tools, ceremonies, and practices
- Communicating Agile to management
- Roles within APM
- Value Stream Mapping from inception to delivery
- Programs and Agile governance structures
- Agile Coaching and how to properly vet an Agile Coach
- Supporting an environment of safety
- Breaking down organization silos and impediments interfering with delivering fast
- Continuous improvement efforts and the right behaviors needed to deliver quality products and services
- Flexibility, Feedback Loops, and Adaption
- Cross-project and team coordination.

- The cultural and organizational changes necessary to set the organization up for optimal Agile performance

Key Terms

- Program
- Scrum
- Kanban
- Lean Principles
- Minimal Viable Outcomes (MVO)
- Minimal Marketable Features (MMF)
- Roadmap
- Backlog
- Release
- Iteration
- True North
- Rolling Wave Planning
- Progressive Elaboration
- Continuous Improvement (Kaizen)
- Core Program Team: Program Manager, Program Product Owner, Program Coordinator, Program Specialist, Agile Change/Transition Manager, Communication Specialist, Program Coach
- Ceremonies: Daily Stand-up, Executive Roadshows, Agile Governance, Impediment and Escalation Forums
- Artifacts
- Servant Leadership
- Improvement Kata
- Community of Practice (CoP)
- Center of Excellence (CoE)
- Environment of Safety
- Agile coaching

Discussion Questions

1. Why is strategic-level planning important, and how does this support a culture that is supportive of Agile Program Management?
2. Under what conditions would an over-arching Program benefit the organization versus selecting a Framework and implementing a basic process to report status and risk?

3. What are the key elements to consider when developing an Agile Program? Why are these elements important?
4. What strategy would you follow when building your core team? Study the roles of the project team members, comment on roles that are new to you.
5. Describe how an Agile PMO can provide continuous improvement guidance to projects and Programs. Why is it vital that the PMO and Program Manager develop a partnership?
6. Ceremonies such as Daily Stand-up meetings at the project level are familiar to Agile practitioners; however, what ceremonies should occur at the Agile Program level? What is the ceremony's purpose?
7. What is meant by 'Personal Safety'? How does this benefit the Agile project team and the organization?

Exercises

1. Take a 'Trip to the Web' to determine what is meant by 'Optimize the Whole', and how is this related to Program management?
2. Take a 'Trip to the Web' to search on 'High Trust Culture' and determine how this could help or hinder team performance. Support your response.
3. Compare the management styles of 'Servant Leadership' and 'Power-Oriented leadership'.

Additional Related Resources

- *Managing for Happiness: Games, Tools, Practices to Motivate Any Team,* by Jurgen Appelo, has an excellent tool called the Celebration Grid. For more information, visit *https://management30.com/practice/.*
- Read about the Agile mindset from author and Agile Coach Susan McIntosh at *https://www.infoq.com/articles/what-Agile-mindset.*
- *Lean Software Development: An Agile Toolkit,* by Mary and Tom Poppendeick
- *Lean Enterprise: How High Performance Organizations Innovate at Scale,* by Barry OReilly, Jez Humble,and Joanne Molesky
- Trust building – see: *The Decision to Trust, How Leaders Create High-Trust Organizations,* by Robert F. Hurley

II. PART TWO - FRAMEWORKS

Chapter 04 - Scrum of Scrums (SoS)

Chapter Vision

This chapter provides the knowledge and tools needed to scale Scrum, using Scrum of Scrums (SoS). Since Scrum of Scrums is basically Scrum, this chapter spends time detailing the differences between ceremonies at the single-team and Program level, and provides a discussion of how to scale the Product Owner and Scrum Master roles.

Student Learning Objectives

Students who successfully complete this chapter will demonstrate the following specific objectives:

- Analyze and articulate the difference between single-team Scrum and multi-team Scrum (Scrum of Scrums)
- Analyze the pros and cons of the lack of a built-in budgeting or resource planning mechanism in the Scrum of Scrums Framework, and evaluate the effect on a familiar organization
- Articulate the key obstacles to overcome when scaling the Product Owner and Scrum Master roles, and identify methods for decomposing the obstacles in each role
- Understand general norms regarding the number of teams both Product Owners and Scrum Masters can support
- Support the statement: "Just like in single-team Scrum, in Scrum of Scrums, Scrum itself cannot be customized."
- Understand why ensuring all teams have the same Sprint length and are synchronized is important

Chapter Highlights

- A history of both single-team Scrum and Scrum of Scrums, with a brief refresher on single-team Scrum, which is an essential foundation for success with SoS
- Communities of Practice (CoP) used to foster cross-team learning and provide a way for teams to share ideas, successes, and failures
- Lines of Communication constraint and calculation when scaling Agile

- The lack of a built-in mechanism for budgeting and enterprise resource planning
- The introduction of several new roles, including the Chief Scrum Master, Chief Architect, Product Manager, and Chief Product Owner
- New ceremonies associated with the multiple team approach, which include the Scrum of Scrums, Meta Scrum, Integrated Sprint Demo, Integrated Program Retrospective, and Backlog Refinement
- How to establish and run Communities of Practice to speed the inter-team idea transfer rate
- The primary artifacts of SoS – completed work and necessary documentation – and descriptions
- A structure for teams to discuss and manage dependencies and bottleneck
- Big Room Sprint Planning, conducted with as many teams physically in the same room as possible to foster osmotic communication
- Developing a plan for managing cross-team dependencies

Key Terms

- Team (Sprint) Backlogs
- Product Backlog
- Daily Scrum
- SoS Meeting
- "Meta Scrum" (or Management Scrum)
- Communities of Practice
- Chief Product Owner
- Chief Scrum Master
- Chief Architect
- Agile Coaches
- Big Room Sprint Planning
- Big Visible Information Radiators
- Synchronizing Multiple Teams

Discussion Questions

1. What roles are important to the Scrum process? Describe each role and the value they add to the team.

2. What is 'Big Room Sprint Planning'? Discuss who participates, the activities during the planning session, and the anticipated results.
3. What happens if there are blockers raised at the SoS that cannot be solved during that meeting?
4. What is meant by 'Done'? Do all teams need to share the same Definition of Done? Why, or why not?
5. You may have heard another name for Scrum of Scrums that is just starting to be used. What is the new name? In your opinion, is this a better name? Why, or why not?
6. What factors are used to determine if a SoS team maintains a Backlog? Discuss how the decision is made.
7. What are some technology solutions that can be used when working with distributed or virtual teams?
8. Why does SoS use Retrospectives at both the team and the Program level?
9. Why is it important for teams to integrate all their work and test it as a unit in the Integrated Sprint Demo?
10. Why is working software (or other deliverables) the most important deliverable?

Exercises

1. To implement SoS in your organization, discuss which metrics you would select and why you choose them. Likewise, provide rationale for excluding any.
2. Discuss the SoS Ceremonies by identifying each ceremony, its purpose, the key participants, and specific tools used.
3. Discuss why the following is true: Just like in Single-team Scrum, in Scrum of Scrums, Scrum itself cannot be customized. There are opportunities for Program Managers to customize budgeting and resource planning components of SoS, but Scrum, itself, cannot be changed or customized.
4. SoS features three levels of meetings for specific purposes. Identify each meeting, the intended audience, and purpose. Include why these meetings add value.

5. Explain what is meant by 'Osmotic Communication'. In your own words, discuss how this helps to reduce risk and speed development.
6. Discuss the general norms relating to the number of teams both Product Owners and Scrum Masters can support.
7. Explain why it is important that all teams in a Program have the same Sprint length and are synchronized.

Additional Related Resources

- Single-team Scrum is discussed in detail in Chapter 4 of the *Agile Almanac – Book 1*
- Sutherland, Jeff. *Agile Can Scale: Inventing and Reinventing Scrum in Five Companies.* Cutter IT Journal, Dec. 2001, vol. 14, no. 12. Link: *https://www.researchgate.net/publication/290823579_Agile_Can_Scale_Inventing_and_Reinventing_SCRUM_in_Five_Companies*
- *11th Annual State of Agile Development Report.* VersionOne. Link: http://stateofAgile.versionone.com.
- Cohn, Mike. "Advice on Conducting the Scrum of Scrums Meeting", Scrum Alliance. 7 May 2007. Link: *https://www.scrumalliance.org/community/articles/2007/may/advice-on-conducting-the-scrum-of-scrums-meeting*
- Appendix B of this book

Chapter 05 - Kanban

Chapter Vision

Kanban is such a powerful tool that can be used by any organization to increase workflow efficiency, and, in turn, productivity. This chapter is intended to provide the knowledge and tools to successfully implement and scale Kanban to the Program level.

Student Learning Objectives

Students who successfully complete this chapter will demonstrate the following specific objectives:

- Analyze Kanban's core concepts and practices compared to other Lean Frameworks

- Articulate the steps in holding a successful Kaizen event
- Explain the theory and use of Kanban Cards

Chapter Highlights

- The adaptation from Lean manufacturing system concepts used in the Toyota Production System (TPS)
- Work pulled into the workflow as the result of a customer or team member's request to provide a solution for a problem, or work from a preceding process step
- Work In Progress (WIP), which optimizes the team's ability to consistently deliver results by focusing on one task at a time to deliver the Minimal Marketable Feature (MMF) sooner
- Two core Kanban practices, 'Implement Feedback Loops' and 'Improve collaboratively, evolve experimentally'
- Project Kanban boards, evolving as the workflow becomes more efficient, and the recommended steps in documenting the workflow and process
- Project Planning meeting and Retrospectives
- Utilizing the 'Plan-Do-Check-Act' (PDCA) cycle to support continuous improvement
- Leveraging Kaizen events to focus on a troubled portion of the workflow to gain efficiencies

Key Terms

- Kanban
- Work In Progress (WIP)
- Minimal Marketable Feature (MMF)
- Throughput
- Cycle Time
- Card Status
- Minimal Marketable Feature (MMF)
- Kanban Cards
- Kanban Board
- Cumulative Flow Diagrams (CFD)
- Flow Efficiency
- Unique Phase Task Chart
- Project Planning Meeting

- Plan-Do-Check-Act' (PDCA) cycle
- Kaizen events

Discussion Questions

1. What are the core concepts of Kanban?
2. What are the core practices of Kanban?
3. Is there an advantage to focusing on one task over multi-tasking? Support your response.
4. Although Kanban does not have established roles, what affect does Kanban have on existing roles?

Exercises

1. Take a 'Trip to the Web' to research how TPS influenced Kanban. Report your findings.
2. Take a 'Trip to the Web' and search for the term MMF (Minimal Marketable Feature), discuss what this term means, and why it is important to the project and the customer.
3. Explain how Kanban can improve any workflow.
4. Discuss why Kanban is easy to implement.

Additional Related Resources

- Chapter 7 in Book One of The Agile Almanac does a deep dive into single-team Kanban, along with a step-by-step approach to creating a Kanban Board.

Chapter 06 - DevOps

Chapter Vision

This chapter explains the many components of DevOps, and presents a candid view of the benefits and risks of both adopting and not adopting these practices. It provides guidance on how to approach a DevOps transformation and implementation, and outlines the first steps in planning and evaluating what an organization DevOps initiative would encompass.

Student Learning Objectives

Students who successfully complete this chapter will demonstrate the following specific objectives:

- Examine and describe, in broad terms: DevOps, Continuous Delivery, and Continuous Integration
- Recall the history of what is defined in this chapter as DevOps and identify seminal works by the founding fathers of DevOps
- Comprehend, at a high-level, the complexity of adopting the interlocking set of practices that is DevOps, and implementing them in one's organization
- Explain the value of an Agile Coach or a DevOps Coach
- Evaluate the constellation of tools available, describe their role in DevOps, and prepare a cost-benefit analysis for budget discussions with executive management

Chapter Highlights

- A history of the genesis of DevOps and a brief survey of the foundational literature in the area
- The technical terms and complexities involved in a DevOps implementation, and a discussion of why many, but not all, are usually implemented, and in some cases, not appropriate
- Fundamentals of a DevOps organization, such as continuous improvement, transparency, and continuous integration of all organizational units that encompass customer request to customer delivery of that request
- Technical practices and the associated popular tools
- The concept of a "DevOps Toolchain"
- The significant cultural change necessary to adopt a DevOps mindset, and why it is frequently the most difficult part of a DevOps transformation
- An analysis of some of the myths and misconceptions surrounding DevOps
- Value Stream Mapping, along with establishing a delivery (deployment) pipeline and creating a plan to establish awareness across the organization
- High performance characteristics, leadership transformation dimensions required, metrics associated with technical performance indicators, and achieving business goals with DevOps

- The benefits and challenges of DevOps
- The maturity of DevOps as an emerging Framework
- The essence of 'Shift Left', which builds in quality through disciplined practices and automation at earlier stages throughout the process
- The cost of not testing
- A few emerging roles being defined by DevOps practitioners
- The Principles of Measure and a table that lists metrics to consider, along with warning signs that can be observed, and their typical meanings and required actions
- Components and techniques related to building quality in, building a Delivery Pipeline, Feature Toggling, Trunk Based Development (TBD), and Test Driven Development (TDD)
- Configuration Management

Key Terms

- DevOps
- Rational Unified Process (RUP)
- Iterative Development
- Clean Code
- Refactoring
- Pair Programming
- Continuous Delivery
- Continuous Integration
- Version Control
- Trunk Based Development (TBD)
- Test Driven Development (TDD) and Automated TDD
- Behavior Driven Development (BDD)
- Build Quality In
- Loosely Coupled Services
- Shift Left Thinking
- Roadshow
- Systems Thinking

Discussion Questions

1. What are five leadership characteristics that help drive performance?

2. What does the TRACE acronym stand for with respect to principles of measurement?
3. What is the cost of not testing?
4. Why can't you implement DevOps all at once?
5. Why does training have to continue even after the DevOps implementation?
6. Why is automated testing so expensive to implement? What makes it worth it (or not)?
7. Discuss the critical success factors that must be considered when adopting a DevOps initiative? Under what conditions is DevOps a strong and workable solution for the organization?

Exercises

1. Take a 'Trip to the Web' to browse the 2017 State of DevOps report. Discuss two important findings of the report.
2. Discuss the evolution of DevOps in a short paper, be sure to include research and references for information from the Web.
3. Create a short outline for a presentation to executive management soliciting their approval to fund and implement DevOps in your organization.
    - What is the reason you want to implement DevOps?
    - What will it mean to the executives? Why do they care?
    - How will you justify the costs?
    - Are there any non-monetary expenses and opportunity costs that come with the implementation?
    - How long will you tell them it will take?
4. One of the challenges noted was the steep learning curve. Discuss why this is the case and what skills need to be developed.
5. Review Rafferty and Griffin's 2004 Transformational Leadership in the chapter, the 2017 State of DevOps Report, or 'Take a trip to the Web'. Discuss the five dimensions of this model and how the dimensions relate to DevOps.

Additional Related Resources

- The "DevOps Toolchain"
- State of DevOps report, released in late June of 2017 https://puppet.com/resources/whitepaper/state-of-devops-report
- Behr, Gene, Behr, Kim. The Phoenix Project. 2011.

Chapter 07 - Scaled Agile Framework (SAFe)

Chapter Vision

The vision for this chapter is to guide a journey to understanding SAFe and the intricacies of its Framework, which features four distinctive configurations that provide a unique model for each organization's implementation of SAFe. In addition, this chapter analyzes and explains how the Program level Kanban flow is crucial to delivering work in SAFe's 10-week timebox, staffed with cross-functional groups of teams.

Student Learning Objectives

Students who successfully complete this chapter will demonstrate the following specific objectives:

- Critique and validate the philosophy of SAFe's Core Values and Principles to those guided by the Lean-Agile mindset
- Analyze and compare SAFe's benefits and challenges to other Agile Frameworks
- Examine and distinguish the roles, artifacts, and tools unique to SAFe

Chapter Highlights

- Lean-oriented approach that aligns development with the enterprise's strategic focus
- The concept of an "Agile Release Train (ART)" to improve throughput
- SAFe's Core Values and Principles guided by the Lean-Agile mindset
- Benefits and Challenges of SAFe
- A longer timebox (10-Weeks), designed to deliver larger Features, focuses on Roadmaps, which improves forecasts and future demand capacity models

- Four levels of implementation
- Program level Kanban flow
- The Scrum Master time commitment to the project
- The Agile community debate that SAFe is too prescriptive to qualify as an Agile Framework
- Consistent review of metrics and dashboards to see progress over the commitment at the PI Planning event
- Utilizing the Program Kanban Board, PI Burn-down chart, and Cumulative Flow Diagram
- System Demos showcasing the Product or Features to those interested in seeing the Value
- ART Sync meetings

Key Terms

- SAFe House of Lean
- Program Increment (PI)
- Agile Release Train (ART)
- Roadmap
- Weighted Shortest Job First (WSJF)
- Program Kanban Board
- DevOps

Discussion Questions

1. What is the PI Planning Event, and why is it an important ceremony?
2. Despite some debate, what makes SAFe an Agile Framework?

Exercises

1. Select a SAFe artifact that you would like to learn more about and take a 'Trip to the Web' to research it. Discuss your findings in your own words (in 300-500 words). Be sure to list your references.
2. Compare and contrast the Core Values and principles associated with SAFe and one of the other 'Big 5' Agile Frameworks.
3. SAFe Framework consists of four distinct levels of implementation. Briefly discuss and differentiate each level.

Additional Related Resources

- Schwaber, Ken. *"unSAFe at any speed." https://kenschwaber.wordpress.com/2013/08/06/unsafe-at-any-speed.*

Chapter 08 - Disciplined Agile (DA)

Chapter Vision

This chapter speaks to Agile leaders, making a decision on employing Agile beyond initial team level and evaluating the usefulness of various scaling methodologies, to learn about Disciplined Agile (DA), which provides process tailoring guidance on the integration of development, operations, and other support to deliver effective IT, while coexisting with SAFe, LeSS, and CMMI. This chapter provides distilled information from a practitioner's perspective intended to support an understanding of this transformative Framework and provide references for a deeper dive.

Student Learning Objectives

Students who successfully complete this chapter will demonstrate the following specific objectives:

- Identify and distinguish Disciplined Agile characteristics
- Explain the strengths, and clarify tradeoffs of Disciplined Agile
- Evaluate when Disciplined Agile could be used in an organization

Chapter Highlights

- Insight from Scott Ambler on why you should choose Disciplined Agile (DA)
- Going beyond SAFe, and evolving to adapt to new Agile and Lean strategies
- DA's strength in its governance and process goals
- Blending Waterfall for an easy transition to Agile
- Phases and milestones, with checks for viability and sufficient functionality
- Process Framework and Process levels – Disciplined Agile Delivery, Disciplined DevOps, Disciplined Agile IT, and Disciplined Agile Enterprise

- Process goals that support IT solution delivery and each of the DA Framework categories
- Twenty-two goals within the topics Inception, Construction, Transition, and Ongoing
- Principles such as delight customers, build a team around motivated individuals with a supportive environment, pragmatism, content counts, choice is good, optimize flow, and Enterprise awareness
- Factors including geographical distribution, team size, compliance requirements, and several others
- Detailed lifecycles to choose from – Agile/basic, Lean/Advanced, Continuous Delivery: Agile, Continuous Delivery: Lean, and Exploratory (Lean Startup)
- The benefits and challenges of DA
- Goal-Driven approach
- The adoption rate compared to that of SAFe and the growing training/knowledge base
- Lack of prescriptiveness, due to the large number of options
- The primary roles defined in DA: Stakeholder, Product Owner, Architecture Owner, Team Lead, Team Member, and Program Manager. As the project scales to Program-level, the secondary roles defined in DA: Specialist, Independent Tester, Domain Expert, Technical Expert, and Integrator.
- Tailoring the lifecycle selection based on the needs of the organization
- The Process Tailoring Workshop – offers 4 lifecycles, 22 goals, and hundreds of options – addresses issues such as roles, lifecycle selection, practices/strategies, Definition of Done, and agreement on tools

Key Terms

- Disciplined Agile Delivery (DAD)
- Disciplined DevOps
- Disciplined Agile IT (DAIT)
- Disciplined Agile Enterprise (DAE)
- Specialist
- Independent Tester

- Domain Expert
- Technical Expert
- Integrator
- Process Tailoring Workshop
- Agile/Basic lifecycle
- Lean/Advanced lifecycle
- Continuous Delivery: Agile lifecycle
- Continuous Delivery: Lean lifecycle
- Exploratory (Lean Startup)

Discussion Questions

1. What are the distinguishing characteristics of Disciplined Agile (DA)?
2. How is DA different from the other Agile Frameworks?
3. When could DA be used in an organization and what would that entail?

Exercises

1. Take a 'Trip to the Web' and visit the Disciplined Agile Consortium and read the case studies.
2. Identify the four DA lifecycles and discuss what criteria you would use to select the most appropriate one.
3. Discuss the purpose of the Process Tailoring Workshop, who should attend, and the anticipated results.
4. Perform a SWOT analysis on DA by identifying the strengths, weaknesses, opportunities, and threats.

Additional Related Resources

- The Disciplined Agile Consortium - Link: *https://disciplinedAgileconsortium.org*

Chapter 09 - Large Scale Scrum (LeSS)

Chapter Vision

When considering LeSS or LeSS Huge for your organization, management, outside of the IT department, will have to go much more hands-off with the people, and much more hands-on with improving the environment for productive work. LeSS requires the organization, as a whole, to have an understanding and commitment to Lean principles, and this chapter describes the implementation process.

Student Learning Objectives

Students who successfully complete this chapter will demonstrate the following specific objectives:

- Identify and distinguish LeSS and LeSS Huge characteristics
- Analyze and explain why LeSS is difficult to implement
- Evaluate when LeSS and LeSS Huge could be used in an organization

Chapter Highlights

- How LeSS began
- 10 core principles, based on years of testing, governed by a minimal Framework of rules
- The extra role of Area Product Owner
- The benefits and challenges of LeSS
- Sprint Planning split into two parts to coordinate the Product Backlog Items
- The Daily Scrum coordination for extra and frequent communication among teams, using tools specific for this purpose
- The need for both an overall Product Backlog Refinement (PBR) and a single-team PBR
- Five communication paths, described as Relationships, of the Product Owner
- Combined teams into a single Sprint, on one Feature or Product, at the same time, with the same goal
- The workflow from the Initial PBR, Sprint Planning, Daily Scrum, Coordination and Integration, Overall PBR, to Sprint Review and Retrospectives (Team and Overall)
- Why LeSS is difficult to implement
- Three principles guiding implementation – Deep and Narrow over Broad and Shallow, Top-Down and Bottom-Up, and Use Volunteering
- The 'Definition of Done'

- The transformation possibilities of the team in an organization
- A discussion with Craig Larman and Bas Vodde, the founders of LeSS

Key Terms

- LeSS Huge
- Overall Product Backlog Refinement (PBR)
- Organizational Improvement Backlog (OIB)
- Area Product Owner (APO)

Discussion Questions

1. Describe the role of Product Owner in LeSS. How does the role differ from other Agile methodologies?
2. How is the term 'Team' used in LeSS? Discuss the difference between the Traditional roles, and the use in LeSS.
3. What is role of the Scrum Master in LeSS, and how does this differ from single-team Scrum?
4. The 'Area Product Owner' is a new role in LeSS Huge. Why is this role needed? What functions does the role perform? Do you think this new role adds value? Why, or why not?
5. Describe the difference between LeSS and LeSS Huge. What are some of the challenges associated with LeSS Huge compared to those of LeSS?
6. What is the role of the Project Manager in LeSS?
7. Why is the Definition of Done important?

Exercises

1. LeSS's rules are simple and the Framework is small; however, the author has stated that 'LeSS is not just something an organization picks up and starts with next Tuesday. Analyze and explain why LeSS is difficult to implement.
2. Discuss the 10 principles of LeSS.

Additional Related Resources

- LeSS website: http://less.works

Chapter 10 - *PMBOK® Guide Sixth Edition*

Chapter Vision

This chapter provides insights to help foster practical, useful dialogue within the community by explaining and exploring the vocabulary and principles that will underpin integrating customer value and enterprise growth – the ultimate goal of scaling Agile.

This chapter will also highlight how the release of the *PMBOK® Guide Sixth Edition* is strangely Agile for the typically bureaucratic PMI organization because it is being released before reaching a more robust level of maturity. It will show that filling the 'maturity gap' sets the stage for useful, powerful discussions among professional practitioners.

Student Learning Objectives

Students who successfully complete this chapter will demonstrate the following specific objectives:

- Explore the Key Concepts, Trends and Emerging Practices, Tailoring Considerations, and Approaches in Agile, Iterative, and Adaptive Environments sections of Knowledge Areas
- Compare and contrast the Traditional Work Breakdown Structure (WBS) and the Agile Feature Breakdown Structure (FBS)
- Analyze and compare the Agile lifecycle with the lifecycle described in the PMBOK® Guide Sixth Edition.

Chapter Highlights

- How to differentiate between Project and Product Scope and the importance of doing so
- Raises awareness that Program management and scaled Agile are more process oriented, while project management and Agile are more product oriented
- A brief history on the evolution of the PMBOK® Guide
- Changes in the Sixth Edition – Three new processes, movement of existing activities within the same knowledge area, and the renaming of some processes for ease of understanding and better alignment
- The four new elements of each Knowledge Areas in the Sixth Edition: Key Concepts, Trends and Emerging Practices, Tailoring

Considerations, and Approaches in Agile, Iterative, and Adaptive Environments

- The integration of Agile into PMI's broadly known and accepted lexicon available to Program Managers
- The role of the Program Managers as a change agent
- The logic supporting Agile practices, including Affinity Estimating and Planning Poker
- The risk of installing heavy-weight processes that disable Agile advantages, and fostering a 'Wait and See' attitude
- The risk of budgeting and scheduling imbalance, where a misalignment in the level of granularity applied to planning versus budgeting can create confusion and waste.
- The expansion of the Traditional approach to include Waterfall, Iterative, Adaptive, Agile, and Hybrid development approaches
- The shift away from command-and-control structure to a more collaborative approach
- A review of the areas where the PMBOK® Guide incorrectly or inaccurately refers to Agile practices, processes, or techniques.
- The two Adaptive patterns – Sequential Iteration-Based Phases and Continuous Overlapping Phases – which includes the workflow in a Kanban system
- Compares the Scheduling component of Agile and Traditional
- Compares the Roadmap to Rough Order of Magnitude (ROM); Release Plan to ROM's Budgetary level; and Iteration Plan to Budgetary or Definitive levels
- The comparison to Rolling Wave Planning in Traditional to the Iterative scheduling of work items from the Backlog in Agile
- The vital role that ceremonies play in Program-wide communication
- Discussions, generated from any inaccuracies within the PMBOK® Guide Sixth Edition, becoming great educational launch pads, bringing the opportunity to either teach other colleagues or learn from them
- The dynamics of change as a project evolves, based on the voice-of-the-customer

- A review of the PMBOK® Guide Sixth Edition's Appendix
- Low-cost, light-weight estimation methods
- Why the use of hybrid approaches should not be ignored
- Highlights several tools and practices – Osmotic Communication, Low-Tech/High-Touch, and the unrelenting Focus on Customer Satisfaction

Key Terms

- Earned Value Management (EVM)
- Affinity Estimating
- Planning Poker
- Sequential Iteration-Based Phases
- Continuous Overlapping Phases
- Work Breakdown Structure (WBS)
- Agile Feature Breakdown Structure (FBS)
- Roadmap
- Rough Order of Magnitude (ROM)

Discussion Questions

1. How has the role of the Project Manager evolved in the PMBOK® Guide Sixth Edition?
2. Why is it important that governance cultivate an open, engaged environment?
3. Why is it important to achieve significant levels of stakeholder engagement and participation?
4. What are the differences between Project and Product Scope?
5. Debate the pros and cons of the change in Knowledge Area titles in relationship to the prior version of the PMBOK® Guide; specifically, the change from 'Project Time' to 'Project Schedule', and the removal of the 'Human' from 'Resource' Management. Do you think the change better represents the Knowledge Area or would you have changed the title to a different name? Support your response. Would you recommend changes to other Knowledge Areas?

Exercises

1. Prepare an argument that presents how, as a Program manager, you would convince management to use Affinity estimating and Planning Poker.

2. Compare the Iterative scheduling of work items from the Backlog in Agile to the Rolling Wave planning in Traditional.

Additional Related Resources

- PMBOK® Guide Sixth Edition
- The Standard for Project Management®

Chapter 11 - Agile Integration Framework (AIF)

Chapter Vision

This chapter starts with the perspective that scaling Agile often requires major organizational change to be successful. Further, getting all the key stakeholders to explore, accept, implement, and embrace the changes required by scaled Agile has a much higher probability of success if important principles, methods, processes, and practices can be shown as a mere evolution of beliefs they already hold as true.

The foundational principle of the AIF, that this chapter introduces, is that the many decades of developing advanced business school models and strategies, appropriately combined with five decades of developing the PMBOK® Guide and the Standards for Program and Portfolio Management, while leveraging the distinct improvements of Agile drawn from Lean principles provides the most robust, most reliable, and most flexible approach for scaling Agile. That is true, in large part, because the AIF reduces stakeholder resistance by making the perceived risk of change dramatically lower.

This chapter hopes to describe the AIF and provide a thorough understanding of its implementation so it can be a Rosetta stone for Program Managers, providing a cogent, flexible Framework that works in any setting and has a common lexicon to make it understandable for stakeholders, executives, and technical development professionals alike.

Student Learning Objectives

Students who successfully complete this chapter will demonstrate the following specific objectives:

- Examine and distinguish the differences between Agile Integration Framework and other Agile Frameworks
- Identify key differences between Agile Integration Framework and Traditional Project Management
- Explain the evolution to Agile Integration Framework
- Articulate the Agile Integration Framework workflow

Chapter Highlights

- AIF at the overlapping intersection of the Agile Frameworks, the PMBOK® Guides and its related standards, and strategic business models
- Defined Granularity to document the Program purpose, properly size the initiative, and define scaled time-horizons for planning, executing, and reporting
- The leverage of PMI standards and vocabulary
- Insight into planning, executing, and reporting on Programs using Scaled Agile
- Iterative development anchored by customer involvement to define business value
- DevOps metrics and measurements combined with insights from PMBOK® Guide to improve stakeholder understanding and acceptance
- Proven options for budgeting and advanced scheduling
- How to combine granularity for decision-making
- Planning-by-design
- 'Be effective first and efficient second'
- The balance between optimizing the whole and sub-optimizing the teams
- Four-Dimensional communication
- Gartner's hierarchy of People, Processes, Data, and Technology
- Roles, Workflows, Ceremonies, and Artifacts within AIF
- The empirical approach of transparency, inspection, and adaptation

- Agile levels of granularity – Product, Theme, Epic, Story, and Task
- Introduces the Customer-Value Logic Network (CVLN) and how to create it
- Introduces the Execution Logic Network (ELN) and how to construct it
- Affinity Estimating
- Critical Path Analysis/Critical Path Method (CPM)
- Defined-granularity schedules
- Progressively elaborated budgets
- Ceremonies with the AIF – Annual and Semi- Annual Freeway Planning, Quarterly Release Planning, Iteration & Milestone WAG and SWAG, Iteration Point Review (IPR), and Monthly Program Steering Meeting.
- Knowing constraints and defining the symptoms to identify risk and triggering events that underpin professional responsiveness
- The resistance to proper testing

Key Terms

- Work Decomposition Structure (WDS)
- Customer-Value Logic Network (CVLN)
- Epic Work Packages (EWP)
- Execution Logic Network (ELN)
- Osmotic Communication

Discussion Questions

1. What biases do you think Traditional Project Managers have regarding Agile Project methodologies and vice versa?
2. What best-known project management practices are integrated into AIF? How does this increase AIF's credibility?
3. Why is AIF considered the Rosetta stone?
4. What are the principles underpinning the AIF?
5. What is meant by Four-Dimensional Communication?

6. What is the role of the Independent Integrator?
7. What is the Customer-Value Logic Network (CVLN), and why is it important?
8. What are AIF's strengths?
9. What is the purpose of the Annual Freeway Planning? How does that differ from the Semi-Annual Roadway Planning and the Quarterly Release Planning?

Exercises

1. Discuss when the Execution Logic Network (ELN) is used, and its purpose. Include why it is important to keep the Network organized.
2. Describe AIF's Work Decomposition Structure. Include ROM in your description.
3. Describe the Critical Path Method and discuss what needs to be accomplished before the CPM can be determined in the context of AIF.
4. Demonstrate your knowledge of the Cone of Uncertainty regarding estimating accuracy by preparing a discussion to enlighten stakeholders.
5. Describe Affinity Estimating
6. Prepare an argument that you would use to convince management that Proper Testing is a good business decision.

III. PART THREE - APPLIED SCALED AGILE

Chapter 12 - Virtual, Distributed & Multi-Team Environments

Chapter Vision

This chapter explores the complexity in Programs working with multiple teams, and at least one using Agile methodologies. In this chapter, different formats, such as collocated and remote teams, and how staffing strategies generate impacts on deliverables, ceremonies, artifacts, and teams are discussed. It is mainly focused to provide insight for Program Managers, but is also a good source of information for Project Managers, Product Managers, and IT leaders, in general.

Student Learning Objectives

Students who successfully complete this chapter will demonstrate the following specific objectives:

- Investigate group dynamics in a remote team environments
- Appraise tools and practices to improve communication among diverse, remote Program teams

Chapter Highlights

- Differences, benefits, and challenges associated with collocated and remote teams, working on inter-dependent tasks to achieve a common goal
- Creating a social connection that builds trust and collaboration
- Complex problem solving and collaboration when implementing solutions
- Qualitative challenges associated with launching and sustaining effective virtual teams, such as language, trust, and behavioral norms amplified by distance
- The advantages of offshore and nearshore teams within a Program
- "Eyes Train Ears" technique to improve verbal communication
- Trade-offs and strategies associated with staffing virtual teams, including quality assurance, and staff retention/attrition
- Pair representation
- The challenges of creating durable communication
- Mitigating the risks of shared dependencies inherent with virtual teams
- Integrating 'communication by design' into all workflows
- Guidelines for Cross-Team planning
- Creating 'living documentation' to reduce future risks and increase tribal knowledge
- Meeting norms should not be assumed as 'common sense'
- How to protect time to minimize disruption for the individuals staffing those teams through the use of Golden or Core Hours

- Team Photos in the Workspace and "Word of the Day" to decrease the language and cultural barrier

Key Terms

- Functional Point Analysis (FPA)
- DevOps
- Acceptance Tests Driven-Development (ATDD)
- Behavior Driven-Development (BDD)
- Core Hours
- Eyes Train Ears
- Pair representation
- Meeting Norms
- Fractional Team Member

Discussion Questions

1. What are the advantages and disadvantages of working within the twenty-four-hour work cycle? Under what circumstance would you recommend this work cycle?
2. What is the difference between offshore and nearshore? Include advantages and disadvantages for each.
3. What considerations are needed when the team has a fractional member? When the entire team is composed of fractional members?
4. Discuss the technique 'Eyes Train the Ears', when is this technique used and explain how the technique improves communication.
5. What is the 'Team Photos in the Workspace'? What can be posted? What is the benefit? Have you had the opportunity to try this technique?

Exercises

1. Take a 'Trip to the Web' to discover more about Tuckman's stages of group development. Discuss what you have learned. Do you recognize these stages in teams that you were, or are, a member of?
2. Take a 'Trip to the Web' to learn more about code as living documentation through Acceptance Tests Driven-Development (ATDD) or Behavior Driven-Development (BDD). Write a short paper (less than two pages) discussing ATDD and/or BDD and provide your opinion on using code as living documentation.

3. Create a 'team agreement' that you would recommend to your team. Consider remote members and include a Meeting Norms section.

Chapter 13 - Estimating & Scope Management

Chapter Vision

The vision for this chapter is to assist the reader with reconciling how to deal with estimating and scope with a Program that contains Agile, hybrid, and Waterfall projects, and to understand how the Program Manager role differs from the Project Manager role in relation to estimation and scope management.

Student Learning Objectives

Students who successfully complete this chapter will demonstrate the following specific objectives:

- Explore estimating techniques at the Program level that can be used regardless of the project methodology
- Analyze the role of the Program Manager and compare to the role of the Project Manager
- Explain how Planning Poker or Affinity Planning can yield solid ROM results

Chapter Highlights

- The use of the Flexibility Matrix to classify Program-level constraints – fixed, negotiable, flexible – in the areas of scope, schedule, and cost
- The fundamental axiom of "Good, Fast, Cheap: Pick Two"
- Managing the fixed constraint to keep it within the Program's guardrails
- Methods to strategically estimate the capacity to deliver at the Roadmap and Release level, regardless of the methodology – the cornerstone of the Agile Integration Framework
- Defined Granularity at the Program level to illustrate the impact of time to estimating accuracy
- Tools and practices to deal with Program uncertainty, regardless of the Framework used to deliver the project once it is initiated

- Using Agile tools and techniques to scope and provide a ROM estimate
- Defining Epic Work Packages (EWP)
- Affinity Planning, as an alternative to Earned Value Management (EVM)
- Suggestions on where the Project Manager should focus to deliver the MVFs since Agile and Traditional approaches vary significantly
- Maintaining flexibility and direction, simultaneously
- Monitoring the backlogged work at the EWP-level of granularity, as discussed in the AIF
- Roles and their application to the estimation process – Program Manager, Project Manager, Product Owner, Domain Experts, Delivery Team, and possibly Architecture Owner, Integrator stakeholders, Independent Integrator(s), and Process Owner.
- Addressing scope creep
- Decomposing the scope into Features, Functions, and Capabilities
- Determining how the Program will be executed, interlaced the work packages are, and complex and uncertain the work is within them
- Planning ceremonies, including Annual or Semi-Annual Highway, Quarterly Roadmap, and Bi-Monthly Release Planning
- Organizational Process Assets (OPAs) used to identify potential estimate and scope management bias and challenges
- Managing the downstream process of risk, budget, quality, and schedule
- Establishing contingencies during the planning process
- Eliminating bias from estimates
- Creating baselines for estimates and scope at each layer of decomposition
- Low-Tech, High-Touch approach

Key Terms

- Methodology Selection Matrix
- Feature, Function, and Capability (FFC)
- Epic Work Packages (EWP)

- Customer-Value Logic Network (CVLN)
- Execution Logic Network (ELN)
- Flexibility Matrix
- Fibonacci cards
- Planning Poker
- Affinity Planning
- Information Radiators
- Swarming/Spike Sprint
- Organizational Process Assets (OPA)
- Low-Tech, High-Touch Rooms

Discussion Questions

1. What is the purpose of the Flexibility Matrix, and how is it used?
2. What is Planning Poker, and why is it a viable estimating option?
3. What are Fibonacci cards, and how are they used in the estimating process?
4. Describe the Affinity planning concept, and why would you use this process?
5. How does a Program Manager select the Program methodology?
6. How are new requirements handled at the Program level?
7. What is a 'Low-Tech, High-Touch' Room? Provide examples of how this is used.
8. What is a Swarming Sprint?

Exercises

1. In groups, simulate a Planning Poker session on a familiar topic. Evaluate the results. What lessons were learned? Try Planning Poker on a different project and evaluate those results.
2. An alternate Planning Poker topic, applicable to anyone in any industry: Provide a list of 10 -15 animals from an ant to an elephant. Sort the anima from the smallest to largest using Planning Poker.
3. To introduce students to Agile and Planning Poker, start with a simple task like estimating how we would score mowing the grass. The lesson here is, until the requirements are well understood, the accuracy of any estimate is in question because of faulty assumptions.

Other Academic Resources

- Lederer, Albert L., and Prasad, Jayesh. "A Casual Model for Software Cost Estimating Error." *IEEE Transactions of Software Engineering,* vol. 24, no. 2, 1998, pp. 137-148.

Chapter 14 - Scheduling & Integration Management

Chapter Vision

This chapter discusses concepts, methods, and techniques to integrate all delivery work, starting with the Program Charter, to build a Program Roadmap and Release Plan for guiding the delivery team to meet the Programs objectives. It aims to help the understanding of what is necessary to deliver value to the stakeholders through Agile Program Integration Management.

Student Learning Objectives

Students who successfully complete this chapter will demonstrate the following specific objectives:

- Examine and compare the three phases of the Program Lifecycle to the Agile Program Lifecycle
- Analyze the ceremonies of Agile methodologies that can be adapted to a hybrid environment
- Examine the role of Agile Program Scheduling and Integration Management

Chapter Highlights

- Blends the knowledge and experience of Traditional project management with the benefits of Agile and Lean principles
- Identifies areas in which the initiation of a Traditional Program and an Agile Program are similar and how they differ in the delivery method
- Three phases of the Program Lifecycle – Program Definition, Program Delivery and Program Closure
- Agile Program Life Cycle's (APLC) approach to delivering iterative Releases based on a Program Roadmap with continual delivery and feedback from the customer

- The benefits and challenges of Integration Management
- Delivery of a Minimal Marketable Product (MMP)
- Practitioners struggling with being 'constrained' by a schedule
- Roles, such as Core Program Team and Program Manager, Product Manager, Product Owner, and Product Coordinator
- Product Definition Phase
- Feature Based Planning
- Decomposing the Program Backlog into Themes and Epics for the Project and operational teams
- The operational aspects of a Program
- Program closure
- Ceremonies pertaining to Scheduling and Integration - Program Daily Stand-up meeting, Program After Meeting, Program Feature Review, Program Feature Retrospective, and Program Backlog Refinement
- Review of the Program Charter, Program Roadmap, Program Release Plan, and Program
- Dependencies Radiator
- Program Manager's three levels of support: the individual team members, project and operations teams, and the organization
- The needs and expectations of each role
- Workflow discussion of Programs adopting a Hybrid approach for the projects within the Program
- Rolling Wave delivery alignment with the Agile Release Plan

Key Terms

- Agile Program Management (APM)
- Agile Program Integration Management (APIM)
- Agile Program Life Cycle (APLC)
- Agile Program Delivery Cycle (APDC)
- Minimal Marketable Product (MMP)
- Core Program Team
- Integration Team
- Program Roadmap

- Program Release Plan
- Rough Order of Magnitude (ROM)
- Program Dependencies Radiator

Discussion Questions

1. Describe the three phases of the Agile Program Life cycle. What events occur in each and why is this important to the delivery of a Program?
2. Discuss what is meant by Minimal Marketable Product (MMP). Why is this important? How does Integration Management enable this benefit?

Exercises

1. Analyze the ceremonies of Agile methodologies and recommend those that can be adapted to a hybrid environment.
2. Describe the Program Dependencies Radiator and how it is used by the teams.

Additional Related Resources

- *The Standard for Program Management® – Third Edition*, the Project Management Institute (PMI)

Chapter 15 - Agile Program Risk Management

Chapter Vision

This chapter outlines the differences and similarities between Traditional and Agile Program Risk Management, and strives to offer a clear understanding of Agile Risk Management process by providing the knowledge and tools needed to successfully identify and manage risk within Agile Programs.

Student Learning Objectives

Students who successfully complete this chapter will demonstrate the following specific objectives:

- Analyze and distinguish the characteristics of Traditional Program Risk management and Agile Program Risk Management

- Examine and describe the methods for tracking risks using the Risk Register, Risk Burndown, and Risk Board
- Demonstrate understanding by explaining the Risk Cause-Effect relationship, Risk Probability or likelihood of occurrence, Risk Impact, and calculating a Risk Magnitude Score.

Chapter Highlights

- The objectives of project and Program risk management
- Key differences of Agile vs. Traditional Program risk management
- Managing risk using a Risk Burn-down chart, Risk Register, Total Risk (Stacked Bar) chart, Risk Management Plan, Risk Board, Risk Backlog, and several ceremonies.
- Utilizing proper risk management as a means to increase velocity
- Engaging stakeholders in risk planning
- Identifying known unknowns and unknown unknowns
- Analyzing and ranking risk impacts using the Magnitude Score
- Monitoring risk to identify and discuss new or evolving impediments
- Planning risk responses - Accept (Ignore, Inspect, Insure), Mitigate, and Prevent
- Defining the Risk Management Plan
- Four key steps to APRM – Identify, Analyze, Plan, Monitor
- The roles within a Program team required to successfully implement and manage Agile Program Risk Management
- Real-world example, in grey box form, of Agile Program Risk Management

Key Terms

- Agile Program Risk Management
- Risk Plan
- Risk Burn-down chart
- Risk Information Radiator
- Risk Register
- Reciprocal Agreement
- Story Point Variance

- Risk Board
- Risk Magnitude Score
- Risk Response
- Known-unknowns and Unknown-unknowns

Discussion Questions

1. What is the purpose of the Risk Burn-down chart? Identify the ceremonies that utilize this tool and how the tool is used to mitigate threats or maximize opportunities.
2. How does the Reciprocal Agreement reduce risk?
3. Under what conditions does a risk-based spike occur?
4. What are known-unknowns and unknown-unknowns?

Exercises

1. Take a 'Trip to the Web' to research what is meant by a 'Story Point' and 'Story Point Variance'? What does the planned verses actual metric reveal?
2. Take a 'Trip to the Web' and visit GR8PM.com; review the list of Templates and examples available for download. Select one and describe the Template, why you chose it, and how you would use the template in a future (or could have used in a past) project.
3. Describe the Risk Plan, include when the plan is developed in your discussion; add your own experiences with risk planning.
4. Agile risk responses mirror those found in traditional Risk Management: Mitigate, Accept, Defer, Monitor, transfer. Define and provide an example of each of the risk responses.

Chapter 16 - Quality Management

Chapter Vision

This chapter appeals to all levels of quality management experience. For those experienced, it goes beyond basic quality management by highlighting techniques on how to apply the tools; and for those beginning, it provides descriptions and details to obtain enough information to entice the desire to perform further research.

Student Learning Objectives

Students who successfully complete this chapter will demonstrate the following specific objectives:

- Analyze and differentiate quality improvement tools that can be applied to the project level verses the Program level
- Evaluate quality improvement tools and analyze how the tools could be implemented in a familiar environment

Chapter Highlights

- Acting on what is reflected in reports, dashboards, or metrics, to bring the process back into control
- Examines the corrective actions and continuous improvement initiatives
- Metrics without action are useless
- Using scorecards and dashboards to reflect the project status
- Monitoring the limited resources (financial, technical, and physical) allocated to the Program
- Monitoring organizational and market conditions influencing global risks that will trigger a risk response at the Program level
- Coordinating Releases
- Identifying recommended practices
- Demonstrating Program Value visually and factually
- Migrating to metrics of relative comparisons
- Using Cost Performance Index (CPI)
- The workflow of quality management, including roles and ceremonies
- Setting upper and lower control limits within metrics
- Normalizing reporting

Key Terms

- Check Sheets
- Pareto Diagram
- Ishikawa/Cause & Effect Diagram
- Control Charts
- Histogram
- Scatter Diagram
- Flow Charts
- Cumulative Flow Diagrams
- Stratification Charts
- Flexibility Matrix
- Cost Performance Index (CPI)
- Schedule Performance Index (SPI)
- Define, Measure, Analyze, Improve, and Control (DMAIC)
- Net Promotor Scores (NPS)
- "Fit for purpose"

Discussion Questions

1. What is the purpose and benefit of quality management?
2. One of the unique challenges of managing quality at the Program level is the normalization of metrics in a mixed project management environment. This chapter offered several alternatives. Which alternative(s) would you select and why? Are there any alternatives that you would avoid, why?
3. Time-based metrics have several inherent challenges that undermine the integrity of the metric. Discuss these challenges, triggers, and potential solutions. What techniques can a Program Manager employ to validate the authenticity of the time-based metric?
4. Which quality tools should be applied to the project level verses the Program level? Support your response.

Exercises

1. Take a 'Trip to the Web' and research past winners of the Baldrige Award and/or the Deming Prize in an industry that is familiar to you. Select a winner and identify 10 quality approaches that the organization showcased in their award application. Which quality approaches are currently visible in your organization? Which quality approaches would you consider recommending to your organization?

2. There are seven basic tools for quality improvement that can be traced back to Kaoru Ishikawa and his work developing quality circles. Take a 'Trip to the Web' to explore the tools.
3. A well-known quality diagram is Ishikawa's Fishbone diagram. Discuss the purpose of this diagram and how it is used at the Program level.

Additional Related Resources

- The ASQ Website Link: *http://www.asq.org*
- The Deming Institute Link: *https://www.deming.org*
- Baldrige Performance Excellence Program and Baldrige Award Link: *www.nist.gov/baldrige*
- Chartered Quality Institute (CQI) Link: *https://www.quality.org*
- Mean/Average vs. Median clarification Link: *https://www2.census.gov/Programs-surveys/cps/tables/time-series/historical-income-households/h06ar.xls*
- *Agile Almanac – Book 1:* "Another source for identifying the benefits of emergent design is quantifying the value of moving from quality control (QC) to quality assurance (QA) How valuable is it to prevent defects not merely catch them?" (pg. 96)

Chapter 17 - Budget Management

Chapter Vision

This chapter appeals to anyone managing and reporting on Agile Program Budget Health within an Agile Program and strives to offer various tools, examples, and methods for measuring and controlling Agile Program Costs. This chapter provides the knowledge and tools needed to successfully identify and manage an Agile Program Budget.

Student Learning Objectives

Students who successfully complete this chapter will demonstrate the following specific objectives:

- Analyze and describe the Program Budget process
- Explore tools and methods used to manage Agile Program Budgets
- Examine the role of the Program Analyst

Chapter Highlights

- Overview of Agile Program Budget Management
- Introduces Agile Project Earned Value Management (A-EVM)
- References the Agile Integrated Framework's Progressive Elaborate Budgets
- Determining estimates, schedules, and resource allocation to the project using Affinity Estimation and Planning Poker
- Discusses the Agile Program Incremental Cost Management (ICM)
- Funding Value Streams using the Lean Budget –SAFe approach
- The process of determining and monitoring the Agile Budgct
- Using estimates and velocity in financial analysis
- Funding Approval process
- Measuring and reporting on budget health
- The change request process and its associated documents
- The ceremonies related to the Agile Program Budget Management – Daily Scrum, Backlog grooming

Key Terms

- Earned Value Management (EVM)
- Agile Project Earned Value Management (A-EVM)
- Agile Program Incremental Cost Management (ICM)
- Rough Order of Magnitude (ROM)
- Net Present Value (NPV)
- Planned Value (PV)
- Earned Value (EV)
- Actual Cost (AC)
- Schedule Variance (SV)
- Schedule Index (SI)
- Cost Variance (CV)
- Cost Index (CI)
- Initial Funding Request and Approval
- Resource Cost Plan
- Change Request
- Change Control Log
- Lean Budgets – SAFe

Discussion Questions

1. What is Agile Program Earned Value Management (A-EVM -Program)? How does it differ from A-EVM? EVM?
2. What are some of the benefits and challenges of Agile Program Budget Management?
3. What is Lean Budgets -SAFe Budget Management?
4. What is meant by Velocity in financial analysis?
5. What are the differences between AIF and other EVM methodologies?
6. What tools are in the A-EVM Program Tool Kit and how are they used?

Exercises

1. Discuss the process flow for obtaining Agile Program Budget funding. Discuss decision points and each of the steps in the process.
2. Explore Appendix B – Advanced Toolset or take a 'Trip to the Web' and explore CA Agile software. Discuss the benefits of using the software or other advanced Program Budget Management tools.

APPENDIX

B

Advanced Toolset

"Begin with the end in mind."

– Habit 2 in *Seven Habits of Highly Effective People*, by Stephen Covey.

For organizations and Program Managers making the strategic decision to use Agile to gain competitive advantage by producing customer delight, and do it faster, better, and cheaper, the fact that there is a direct correlation between scaled Agile complexity and chaos must not be ignored. Using Agile to generate and deploy powerful responses, based on keen insights, requires a robust linkage between the many-fold increase in technological capabilities and the non-linear increase in customer communication that opens the gateway for success.

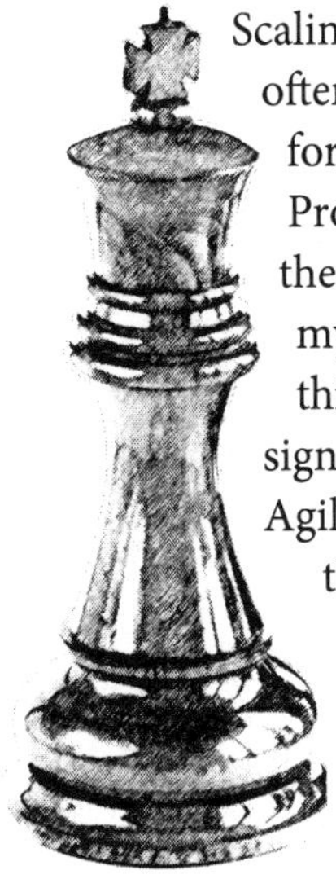

Scaling Agile means entering the realm where discovery and learning often lead to non-linear increases in the opportunity to plot a path for progress to reliable solutions and systems development. For Programs or Portfolios where scaled Agile brings the most value, the environment demands expert support systems to manage the myriad of decisions occurring in the Cone of Uncertainty. Making things even more crazy, Programs or Portfolios that have strategic significance must thrive in an environment where Traditional and Agile approaches require the embrace of a "both and" model of thinking. An "either or" model is simply untenable!

With that understanding, and in keeping with the vision of Book 2 of the Agile Almanac, this chapter on Advanced Tools will give professionals a resource that is useful in the real-world, where there is no possibility of "prescriptive outcomes" like those proposed in canned presentations, using pristine data and unlimited resources. Life is messy, and this chapter will show how to best prepare for success amid the very real, very challenging elements of Agile Programs or Portfolios.

Successfully leading in such a challenging environment demands that Executives, Program, and Portfolio Managers have access to content unlocking the critical principles and techniques that facilitate success. That content needs to be explained with serious depth, and not be more of the abundance of shallow clichés espoused for simpler project environments.

To fulfill that objective, this chapter will discuss the tools of the trade with a tight focus on the differentiators. The differentiators that will make success probable despite the complex, chaotic challenges that must be overcome. For the sake of argument, most Agile and project management tools can create Tasks, organize resources, structure Programs, and some even have simple portfolio management capabilities. ***This chapter is not a discussion of the basics.*** Rather, it will move beyond the current approach of typical IT departments, just purchasing tools, and explain and demonstrate the next level of thinking required to assess, purchase, and configure software tools that can flex, scale, and drive Program and Portfolio success. It will also show how to reduce the cost and burden of recording key data for the teams, and improve the quality of dashboards and reporting for significant stakeholders.

By now you may be saying, "Please tell me, right now, what is the best software currently on the market, in your opinion?"

Sadly, when building an effective and efficient IT organization, far too often it mirrors the adage, "The cobbler's kids have no shoes." Many organizations do not budget or create strategic plans for the IT organization until it is too late. Agile and Traditional Project Management, and even other methodologies such as Six Sigma, Total Quality Management, and ISO, have been born out of the need for efficiencies. These efficiencies all stem from wanting to improve processes and decision making based on better understanding the capabilities of the organization. It is important to understand that, no matter how efficient an Agile transformation is, there is still one fundamental issue that plagues almost every company: ***there are more projects than people!***

This issue stems from decisions being based on what the organization can spend, instead of what the organization can reasonably accomplish. A robust strategy, sensibly deployed, will crush the competition, regardless of whether that competition is after taxpayer funding or consumer dollars. But to understand what the organization's resources can achieve, the concept of portfolio management must be married to the strategy, and Program-level resource management must provide timely, reliable feedback so the strategy can be continuously improved. Applying the Lean principle of continuous improvement so that the strategy is unrelentingly sharpened and focused will provide unparalleled success.

Returning to the question, you may now be screaming, "Yes! But what is the best software tool currently on the market for doing that?"

The answer is the tool that can meet the standard just described. It must recognize that many organizations – perhaps even yours – are struggling with having the data necessary to refine the strategy, and make the decisions needed to execute effectively. It must provide a coherent, cohesive understanding of where the data will come from, be able to effectively maintain the data, and produce a realization of what data is missing. Otherwise, the battle is lost before it even begins, leaving organizations in a constant state of overloading their most precious and loyal resources, thereby setting the organization up for strategic failure. As Stephen Covey points out, "You must begin with the end in mind!" Install and configure a toolset that can integrate the strategy and budget decisions with the execution and day-to-day tasks needed to fulfill it, and you will have the best software available...for you!

Current Landscape of IT

While the landscape of the modern IT department continues to change rapidly, the core of operations has largely remained the same. Technology has enabled the IT department to move at a faster pace, however, this still does not mean that resource constraints do not exist. For example, several years ago, virtualized servers did not exist. A project would have to wait for a server to be ordered, built, tested, and placed on a raised floor before an application could be installed, which often took weeks on a project schedule. In today's virtualized world, a new server can be deployed in a matter of hours. This fast forward world has the potential to create unrealistic expectations in the modern consumer's mind. Even with many advances, there are still a few principal areas of the IT department with distinct needs.

Support – The support team normally uses a help desk tool that creates tickets and tracks issues that arise from a user. This can be anything from password resets to large system wide outages. Tickets can be originated from a call center or a self-service portal. Some tickets are transactional and take less than a minute to resolve, while other tickets wind up being an entire project. Popular tools for these types of systems include CA Service Management, HEAT, ServiceNow, and Remedy.

Development –Application development teams require a tool that takes inputs from projects, or the support help desk system, then applies the proper workflow. In an Agile world, outputs can be distributed to a Product Owner, who transforms them into User Stories, Use Cases, and Tasks so they can be appropriately estimated, planned, pulled, and completed. Popular tools for achieving this include CA Agile Central (formerly known as Rally), Jira, and Version One.

Finance – Many organizations require a financial tool of record to keep employee salary, cost information, and budgets. Popular tools for this purpose include SAP, PeopleSoft, and other Enterprise Resource Planning (ERP) systems.

Project – Every large organization tracks project information at some level. If no centralized system exists, then there are spreadsheets, databases, or other mechanisms to keep track of current approved projects, their status, and key information about project deliverables. Often, a project management system will house data in a consolidated format. Popular tools in this genre are CA Project and Portfolio Management (CA PPM), PlanView, Microsoft Project, and Project Server.

Strategic Plan – Most organizations have a strategic plan defining the organization's plan for future growth. Unfortunately, they often lack a direct alignment to the projects and information driving the success, or failure, of the plan.

For each of these core areas, the IT department usually goes after specific issues without a clear understanding of the larger picture and the integration needed for success. They also make decisions based on the current maturity of the organization, which leads to the purchase of tools that do not integrate or anticipate the future. For example, the development department will be in the initial stages of their Agile transformation and pick a freeware tool that meets an individual team's need, but has limited integration capability, thereby stranding the help desk and project management departments unless they duplicate data entry and reporting. Any efficiency gains the software was supposed to deliver are depleted by the inability to exchange information across departments. As more Agile teams and other departments make uncoordinated decisions, more and more technical debt is created.

In the case of a project management tool, a common mistake is to choose a less robust product, assuming functionality the company does not currently need is functionality it will never need, or that it can be added at a later time, somehow saving money. For example, the company might choose Workfront as its solution because they think they are not mature enough to use CA PPM, even though they could have CA PPM for the same cost. Sadly, as the company matures, they outgrow the functionality of Workfront, so they begin to bridge the functionality shortfall by building extracts through API's to provide additional functionality and reporting. After two years, they realize that they have built seven Web Apps and a variety of spreadsheets and reports to supply functionality that was already built into CA PPM. Depression sets in when they discover the internal cost to develop and maintain those additional apps, and the lost productivity of duplicate entry costs as much as $250,000 per year. When the costs to implement a new system, re-train staff, transfer data, and resume operations is factored in, the cost of the initial defective decision could approach eight times the cost of purchasing the right one in the beginning.

The mistaken assumption made by the IT department is that of the organization, only 30% will be Agile, only 15% will use the help desk tool, or only 20% will be impacted by the project management tool. However, at some point, the IT department must realize that organizational growth will force the silos of information to be broken down so investment decisions regarding tool purchases must not reinforce the silo mentality, they must anticipate the innovative growth that is coming.

By now you know our answer to the question, "What is the best software on the market?"

CA Project and Portfolio Management with CA Agile Central

After a thorough analysis, the tool that gives an organization the greatest adaptability for success is CA PPM with CA Agile Central. It efficiently handles where you are now, and smoothly transforms as you grow your way into the future.

In Chapter 1, you heard that the Vision of this book was to be a Rosetta stone for Program Managers, Project Management Office (PMO) directors, and business unit leaders. CA PPM is already a true Rosetta stone because it has a long history as one of the most adaptable and configurable tools on the market.

One of its most under-appreciated features is now gaining recognition, thanks to the rise of Agile. It is what is known as Non-Project Investment Objects or NPIO's. To demonstrate the power of CA PPM, we will focus on two NPIO's – Other Work and Applications. These two objects are powerful because of their ability to allocate resources to a portion of time without needing a detailed project schedule. That means they adapt to both Iteration-based Agile approaches, like Scrum, and continuous-flow Agile approaches, like Kanban, intuitively. In addition, when timesheets are used, allocations can be adjusted over time to more accurately reflect the true cost relationship of each resource to the work being performed.

Recall that at the beginning of this chapter we said, "This chapter is not a discussion of the basics." Whether you choose CA PPM and CA Agile Central, or some other tool as your solution, be prepared to ask sharp-edged questions when they are being evaluated by seriously understanding the program management needs in Traditional, Agile, and even more importantly, Hybrid environments, using both approaches. This is not basic so expect it to be technical and deep. (You might want a fresh cup of coffee before you proceed!)

Challenge: There are more projects than people.

This challenge boils down to the sharp-edged question, "How does the system help us know what percentage of resources are available to complete projects that roll up to Programs and drive enterprise success?" The answer is wrapped up in how allocations are used for planning purposes.

The allocation of a resource removes the percentage of time (or hours) from the pool available for strategic projects, leaving the remaining time available in a clear format.

Using the Application object, resources can be allocated against products the same way to reduce the overall amount of time available to perform projects. In the Agile world, this allows for the allocation against product portfolios. Here is where the real magic comes in. Through integrations and the open

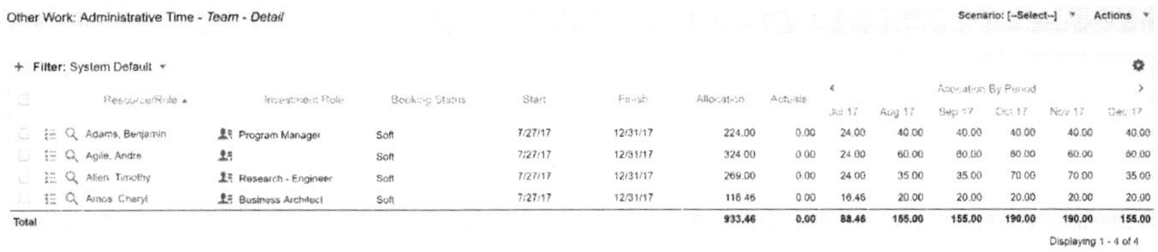

Other Work: Administrative Time - *Team* - *Detail*

Scenario: [--Select--] Actions

Filter: System Default

Resource/Role	Investment Role	Booking Status	Start	Finish	Allocation	Actuals	Jul 17	Aug 17	Sep 17	Oct 17	Nov 17	Dec 17
							Allocation By Period					
Adams, Benjamin	Program Manager	Soft	7/27/17	12/31/17	224.00	0.00	24.00	40.00	40.00	40.00	40.00	40.00
Agile, Andre		Soft	7/27/17	12/31/17	324.00	0.00	24.00	60.00	60.00	60.00	60.00	60.00
Allen, Timothy	Research - Engineer	Soft	7/27/17	12/31/17	269.00	0.00	24.00	35.00	35.00	70.00	70.00	35.00
Amos, Cheryl	Business Architect	Soft	7/27/17	12/31/17	116.46	0.00	16.46	20.00	20.00	20.00	20.00	20.00
Total					**933.46**	**0.00**	**88.46**	**155.00**	**155.00**	**190.00**	**190.00**	**155.00**

Displaying 1 - 4 of 4

Fig B.01 | Resource Allocation

infrastructure, CA PPM allows the native recording of work to occur in the system of choice then be pulled into the proper object to marry allocation versus actuals. This creates the ability to get true cost by product.

For example, if your Agile team is working in CA Agile Central while developing support and project items, the time spent should go to two objects. In most organizations, the team member, who is the resource, must remember to code their timesheet with the appropriate support and project items at the end of the day or week. Human nature, being what it is, means that it is true magic when it gets done correctly, or promptly.

Figure B.01 | Agile Program Magic

The longer the resource waits to record their time, the less accurate it becomes. Also, the more granular the time tracking needs to be, for regulatory or contract compliance, or organizational governance, the more complexity is created in the timesheet, driving probability of non-compliance up instead of down.

Or consider the example of an organization that wants to understand how much it costs to support their top 20 applications across the support, training, bug fix, and enhancements domains. The common data source to track and analyze that is timesheets. An object is created for each application and then a category for each type of time entry. Depending on the week, the resource could have as many as 10 or 15 categories on the timesheet to try to classify time. Each level of complexity further reduces the likelihood of accuracy of reporting, and creates the potential for "time-dumping." However, if the time can be tracked natively in the system of record as tasks are completed then pulled into a system generated timesheet, accuracy improves and the categories for tracking become convenient instead of painful. That means in an Agile environment, a developer selects a Task, completes it, and then marks that it took four hours to complete. From there, the system logic has the Task already coded as a bug fix, and, based on that code, automatically feed the resource's timesheet with all of the reporting needed to support the organization. The resource simply completes their activities in a native work environment, and, at the end of the week, fills in the gaps for administrative time and meetings to complete the timesheet. Everything else was captured and recorded, real-time, as part of the day-to-day activity by the system. The same is true for every day-to-day activity in the support, training, and enhancements domains.

Challenge: Developers are using Story Points and not tracking time or allocations.

This challenge boils down to the sharp-edged question, "How does the system deal with developers who are using Story Points and not tracking time while Finance (or the Regulators) require GAAP compliant capitalization and expenses (or other standards-based compliance reporting)?"

Organizations, historically, have had difficulty demonstrating compliance with time tracking in a system of record. There are organizations that are very good at time tracking while others believe time tracking is not worthwhile (in part because it feels impossible). Regardless, at some point, an organization needs to understand the cost of development efforts to create products and analyze profitability. CA PPM's ability to integrate and allocate, again, becomes the Rosetta stone.

CA PPM allows developers to stay in the Agile tool and work with Story Points. The non-Agile resources can stay in PPM and allocate their work and time using percentages applied to NPIOs. CA PPM then runs a routine that translates that data, and creates a cost model that works with the finance application to create a line item cost per application to understand the total effort and cost per application. While the explanation seems simplified (and it is for the sake of this chapter) the outcome is that CA PPM can work with native applications to create capitalized and expense calculations per application that quantifies total product cost without compliance or audit challenges, based on resources improperly filling out timesheets. (This one of the big reasons CA PPM with CA Agile Central surpasses anything on the market today.)

Consider now, the benefits such a system provides to the stakeholders in the following roles.

Resource Managers: Resource Managers can view capacity and demand by resource or role. Each manager can choose to view data by week, month, quarter, year, or combination of time periods. Each manager can evaluate the data by percentage of full time equivalent or hours. They can add data, such as their allocations, as well, and can then see their allocations compared against what a Project Manager schedules and what a resource tracks, creating a true 360-degree view of resource utilization. This allows for the ability to lobby for a work-life balance, and utilize data to drive discussions for headcount and deadlines. Data is entered and consumed in spreadsheet type interfaces where maintenance can take as little as ten to fifteen minutes per week.

Program and Project Managers: Project Managers can build their projects from templates or import past projects. Once in the system, the PM can then work process by process or project by project. The system thereby supports accountability for the appropriate resource. During status meetings, this eliminates arguments about who is in arrears. A typical status meeting consists of reviewing information that occurred in the past, which requires the Project Manager to spend valuable time updating all of the documentation and sending it to the team so they can be prepared for the meeting. With CA PPM, the issues, risks, and tasks are owned by the team members. Those items are updated in real time as they complete tasks. The status report is a real-time, living artifact, automatically updated and accessed throughout the week. It transforms the status meeting into a forum where the key items are updated and issues resolved, increasing productivity so that the entire team can be focused forward instead of arguing about the past. This is a great benefit for everyone driven by automating the collection and improving the fidelity of the data.

Executives: Executives gain real-time access to a single source of the truth. Instead of massive reports, PowerPoints, and long meetings, they get consolidated dashboards and drillable reports that answer whatever "the next question on the Executive's mind" auto-magically. CA PPM rolls up reporting against strategic objectives in order to support better funding decisions and ensure that projects are being selected based on what the organization can accomplish instead of just on what it can spend.

These benefits, for all the various roles, happen because one core piece of the CA PPM system, critical to its success, is the understanding that no organization approaches their information consumption or projects the same way as another. Therefore, configurability is a core competence of the CA PPM platform. The ability for every organization to configure CA PPM for themselves is really what pushes it over the top. Each organization has its own language and terminology. The ease with which CA PPM accommodates that language to enable the user's experience, without compromising upgrade paths or requiring multiple databases, is the best in the industry.

It is because of this "best in the industry" status that we are using the CA PPM and CA Agile Central integration as the baseline for discussion. You can use it to measure the viability of the various other options you may be considering.

Integration of CA PPM and CA Agile Central

CA acquired Rally Software in July 2015 and rebranded the product to CA Agile Central. This integration has further solidified the CA suite as a best-of-breed solution. There are three main areas in which this integration is improving the abilities of teams.

Project Management

Many organizations struggle to decide what level is appropriate to track time and allocate resources. This is most common in billable and IT organizations that have a high volume of tasks. For instance, a services organization needs to track assignments, deliverables, billable work, and administrative activities. Many of the project plans can exceed 800- or 1,000-line items. Many of these are customer focused while some, like product launch, are fixed and reportable. Invariably, in the middle of the plan, there is a 10-week stretch that produces the customer deliverables and creates the greatest amount of "churn" within the schedule. Instead of trying to manage and schedule a critical path for these 450 tasks, the Project Manager can use CA Agile Central. They create one task for each major customer deliverable on the project plan. This task then creates a feature in CA Agile Central with two time keeping tasks, billable and administrative. The project team then breaks down the customer deliverable, estimates the activities, pulls the activities, and records completion (i.e., actual time), and progress gets reported in CA Agile Central. CA Agile Central reports who worked on the deliverable, the number of billable and administrative hours, and total progress at the deliverable-level back to CA PPM, freeing the team from that burden. The team generates the level of detail appropriate to produce the deliverable, and the Project Manager only has to manage the critical path to the level of detail required. Both get the relevant details with the least amount of burden and, each group gets the level of information that they need, creating greater productivity and less churn.

Agile Teams

As in the example above, Features can be sent over to CA Agile Central from CA PPM. Those Features or projects are then taken over by the Agile teams and worked in the Agile format within CA Agile Central. Features can be broken down into User Stories and Tasks, estimates given, Sprints planned, work pulled and completed. While all of this is occurring, information is constantly being rolled back up to the Feature level and synchronized back to CA PPM so every stakeholder is kept aware of the progress. This allows all teams to work in their native applications and communicate appropriately.

Multiple Agile methodologies are supported in CA Agile Central. As in the example provided earlier, flexibility and allowing the teams' autonomy and control in decomposing the Stories and Tasks, without needlessly increasing the work required to do so, becomes key to effective and efficient progress. Prior to the purchase of CA Agile Central, CA PPM would have two projects per year to represent the major Releases. Each project would have roughly 40 Tasks representing the time tracking deliverables around the Features being delivered per Release. Now that CA PPM utilizes CA Agile Central and Agile methodologies, there are 10 Tasks representing the marketable Features, with three template time tracking Tasks. In CA Agile Central, the team collaboration and User Stories created would have taken perhaps 2,000 – 3,000 items on a project schedule. The integration between CA PPM and CA Agile Central allows Agile teams to be more descriptive, highly collaborative, and more productive in the creation of the Features without creating an unruly project schedule. Each stakeholder receives the appropriate and desired amount of data, as necessary.

Integrated Time Sheet

The CA PPM timesheet is embedded into CA Agile Central. For team members using CA Agile Central, and for the organizations time tracking, the team members never have to leave the application. This is a fast and convenient way to ensure there is no duplicate entry. Templates can be created to automatically add categories of time per Feature or line item created in CA Agile Central. These categories can represent details such as Research, Development, and Bug-Fixes. They also can be as simple as Capital and Expense, or Billable and Non-Billable. This gives flexibility to the organization to track time at a detailed and consistent level, without over-burdening teams or making the process overly complex, a type of Lean waste.

CA Agile Central versus Best of Breed

Best-of-breed tool combinations are only as good as their weakest component. CA Agile Central was created to be a best-choice, best-practice system for teams and delivery groups leveraging Agile principles and practices to deliver better solutions faster and with higher quality.

As with most Agile project management tools out there, CA Agile Central gives teams and organizations visibility into their prioritized Backlog, allowing them to plan Sprints, manage workflow, populate information radiators, and provide feedback on how well the system is working.

Where CA Agile Central shines is when Agile is practiced at scale, which inevitably must happen if you are growing and succeeding. Remember that, even organizations that develop and maintain their systems with just 10 people, when they grow, Agile will need to scale. As Agile scales, it becomes vital to ensure that work remains aligned to strategy, and that each team can autonomously make good decisions. Good decisions occur when teams see how their work ties to the bigger picture. That is where Agile Central shines. With the ability to model teams and organizational structure to create a defined hierarchy above the User Story level, rollups occur that provide true, actionable status, while teams retain autonomous control of their Working Agreements and development approach. Product and Program Managers can see the whole, and everyone can collaborate on the small pivots, leading to better software. Conversely, the big pivots in investment are managed in CA PPM without aggravating the teams.

CA Agile Central was purpose-built from Day One to support an Agile way of working, and the product has evolved along with the industry's understanding of how to do enterprise-scale Agile effectively.

Other Important Questions You Should Ask

While it is a well-considered opinion that CA PPM and CA Agile Central are the best tools on the market, when exploring the purchase of tools, you must see beyond the sales cycle and demonstrations, and determine for your organization what the best choice will be in the long run.

When pursuing the purchase, remember most vendors know the strengths and weaknesses of their tools and their competitors' tools. In the demonstrations, they are experts at laying landmines for each other to ensure their tool looks the most impressive. That approach seldom serves your needs or best interest. Don't become a victim of industry practice. Arm yourself by preparing questions that get to the truth.

Here are some questions you may want to ask before making such an important purchase decision:

- Is everything you showed me today part of a single platform or database purchase?
- Can we add our own objects, attributes, forms, or views to the application?
- If we add our own items to the application, does that require simple configuration or complex customization? (Then provide an example or two, and ask them to demonstrate your choices, not theirs!)
- When we add such items ourselves, does it require an added license feature and your services to do it? If yes, what is the cost (of, Administrator licenses, for example)?
- How many applications or ways can we integrate with the software? XML? API? Open Database Structures?
- Can you import and export data? Is it a simple, flexible interface or a difficult, complex one? (Then provide an example or two, and ask them to demonstrate your choices, not theirs!)
- What happens to our data if we leave this application at the end of the contract?

- Are their data accelerators that come with the application (i.e., additional reports, views, etc.?)
- When was the last overhaul (major upgraded feature improvement release) of this application?
- When we pay for support of the application, does that mean future upgrades are included?
- In the last 10 years, were customers ever charged for an upgrade, even if they paid for support?
- How many developers are working on innovating this application?

Conclusion

The final reason that CA PPM and CA Agile Central are the best solution choice is the speed of implementation. Whether your organization is strong in Agile, Traditional, or neither, each product can be phased in through a SaaS purchase model. The organization can choose the direction of implementation and begin with the end in mind.

Whether the organization wants to start with the Agile transformation first, only implement resource management, bring project management maturity in at a later date, complete integrations all at once or one at a time, all of these decisions are supported and operate at the organization's discretion. There is not one way, and only one way, to implement the tools, and it allows the organization to use Lean and Agile principles as they desire in the implementation. For all of these reasons, it is our opinion that this is the best software currently on the market.

PART FIVE

ABOUT THE AUTHORS & RESOURCES

DEDICATIONS
&
ACKNOWLEDGEMENTS

Dedications & Acknowledgements

John Stenbeck

It seems silly to me that a few brief words could possibly convey a heartfelt thanks to the people who have enriched my life with their kindness in so many ways. Nonetheless, I know their generous hearts will allow them to hear how deeply I love them by way of this small gesture.

To the co-authors of this book, who started out as a cohort of 19 but finished with the dedicated, insightful team of 11. You have in every way made this book possible. Along the way you have challenged, dared and pressed me and each other to rise to the potential of this moment in the history of the evolution of Lean, Agile and the project management profession. Your individual insights have been astonishing, your collective wisdom astounding, and your care for one another, and me as your accidental leader, humbling. Everyone should be so blessed, at least once in their life, to receive what all of you have given me.

JT, Lindsey, Grayson, and Hensley, and Michael and Olivia, you inspire me every day as you move into the future, embracing it with the expectation of giving and receiving abundantly, and without limitation or condition. Jamie, cherished daughter-of-my-heart, you continue to impress me with the courage and daring you demonstrate by loving everyone around you, setting a standard for me to admire and seek. Someday, may I do as well as each of you already do. Thank you all!

My amazing, long-time Cursillo brothers, and newly found St. Mary's Men's Group brothers; thank for always cheering me on while lovingly admonishing me to be the man God is calling me to be, please keep praying for me and know that I love you all!

Joe Montalbano

To my wife Julie, the love of my life, and successful author and editor in her own right; thank you for enduring my long periods of absence while I wrote this, and for everything else. And thank you to my mother, for having high expectations, patience, and teaching me never to give up.

Diane Brady

All accomplishments and personal successes can be traced to my life partner, Norman, who sustains and supports me. He is my rock. The reward for all my hard work is never-ending adventures with Norman and our four-legged side-kick, Lulu, an English Bull Terrier. This might involve "being one with nature" off the beaten path in the RV, visiting an antique car show, or plinking in a farmer's field! With every adventure, I am renewed and ready to tackle the next challenge. Thank you, Norman, for making everything possible.

Mark Phillipy

Words, alone, cannot express my appreciation and love for my family. They have always been there for me, not only during the writing of this book, but throughout my project management career that led to this point. To my bride, Monica; thank you for your unending love and supporting my wild dreams. To each of my kids, Stacha, Shane, Melanie, Shaunae, Kalie, Ryan, Kiara, and Chad; thank you for your love. I truly love and admire each of you. Thanks also to my parents, Lawrence & Evelyn, for teaching me that I can do anything I put my mind to.

James Sperry

I would not be in project management without the mentorship of my father. He introduced me to it at a young age, and I grew up doing construction projects with him. He was an incredible teacher and a natural servant leader. The # 1 thing he taught me was, do a good job the first time and have fun while you're doing it. I strive to emulate those qualities in my life. Thanks, Dad.

I'd like to thank my children, James and Samantha, for inspiring me to be the best man I can be, and to thank my wife, Christine, for supporting and loving me. I would also like to thank all the team members I have worked with in the past, both volunteering and in business. All of you have imparted a small piece of your style into my practice. Big high-fives to everybody!

Steven M. McGee, Sr.

My wife, Loretta, daughter, Macauley, and son, Mike, have steadied me. I thank John Stenbeck for the opportunity to participate in this project, and Scott Ambler for giving his time. Our co-authors are fantastic! I thank God for the blessings!

My passion is for demystifying democracy. I teach advocacy skills with RESULTS.Org, and am working with other global volunteers to create the political will to end poverty!

Michael Williams

Let me first thank John Stenbeck for his belief in my capabilities as well as giving me a couple of, not so subtle, nudges that this will be good for me in the long run.

Speaking of long runs, I would like to thank my wife, Saundra, for her perseverance through any number of questionable projects I have thrown myself into, including the current one of trying to be an author. Just knowing she is there supporting anything I put my heart into brings abundant joy to my life.

Guilherme Motta

I dedicate this work to my current, previous, and future colleagues and employers. It is a result of a collective effort towards deliberate practice and continuous learning. Most of the knowledge brought into this book was based on real life experiences that were only possible because of the different contexts, countries, and organizations that I've had the chance to be part of. Thanks to my family and friends for all the support.

I would also like to thank John Stenbeck for the wonderful opportunity and experience that was being part of this book. To all the other co-authors, a big thanks for collaborating on this diverse, distributed, and rewarding initiative.

Doug Martin

I want to thank my wife, Susan, for her unending support and understanding. She is, in every way, my better half in all things.

Special thanks to my PMO teammates and leaders at Carilion Clinic for their support, especially Leo Stiltner. Leo put me on the path to project management years ago, and I have not looked back.

Nichole Tubiolo

Thank you to my daughter, Abigail. Your energy and curiosity inspire me daily. Your patience and understanding throughout this process is greatly appreciated. Thank you, to my family and friends, for your support and encouragement through my career.

Thank you to the many teams I have had the opportunity to work with over the years. Every project brings something new, and I have had extreme fortune in being able to work with extraordinary individuals over the course of my career.

A special thanks to the coaches and members at Crossfit Williamsville, being a part of this family provides me with the ability to AMRAP life, without which this would not have been possible.

Diane McCann

I would like to express my deepest gratitude to John Stenbeck and the chapter co-authors, who diligently shared their expertise and encouragement that enabled me to complete the Academic Resource Appendix. Furthermore, I would like to express a heartfelt thanks to my husband, Paul, and to my children Gwyndolyn, Gail, and James, along with his bride, Claire, who make everyday a Mother's Day! I would like to acknowledge my granddaughter, Saige Sierra, and encourage her to continue following her dreams and reaching for the stars. In addition, I thank my brother-in-law, Dennis, and my Uncle Carl for their enthusiasm and genuine interest; and to all family members and friends that have inquired about my progress and provided words of encouragement.

Finally, I would like to dedicate the Academic Resource Appendix in memory of my father, William N. Pannabecker, my mother, Anna May Pannabecker, and my sister, Linda Flickinger, who had always been supportive.

Rick A. Morris

Thank you to everyone who has been a part of my successes and failures. My wife, Stephanie, continues to inspire me to chase my dreams with passion. My daughter, Ramsey, always challenges me to be a better person. My son, Remo, makes me want to create a legacy for his name. Thank you to my business partner, Cary Blaes, who has stuck with me through thick and thin throughout my career. To Mike Stephens, best man at my wedding, and now, back at my side to help build a legacy for our families. Thank you to several of my favorite people on the speaking circuit who continue to inspire and collaborate with me, including Traci Duez and John Stenbeck; you both mean the world to me. To my late father, Dudley; may you always look down and be proud of what I have become.

ABOUT THE AUTHORS

About the Authors

You can reach any of the authors by emailing Authors@GR8PM.com and specifying who you'd like to reply. Providing a brief bit of background or the question also helps.

John Stenbeck, PMP, PMI-ACP, CSM, CSP

John is the Founder of GR8PM, Inc. (pronounced "Great PM"). John is a two-time Amazon #1 Best Selling author. His Project Management and Leadership books have achieved almost $2 million in sales. He has been a guest on VoiceAmerica talk radio, Fox News, Good Morning America, the Today Show, and the Oprah Winfrey Show. John has been featured on the front page of the *Los Angeles Times* and the *San Diego Union.*

John is a sought-after Keynote speaker because he enables technical professionals to become powerfully productive leaders. He recently recorded 71 video lectures for Villanova University's online certificate and degree programs and has taught numerous public and corporate on-site programs to over 10,000 participants. John helps technical professionals master project management and leadership skills, dramatically improving their contribution to enterprise results.

A partial list of John's clients includes: Booz Allen Hamilton, Inc. - Defense Information Technologies Group, Boy Scouts of America, City of Spokane, County of Spokane, County of Orange, CA, Greater Spokane Inc., Guinness Bass Import Company, Hewlett-Packard Company, Lucent Technologies, Nike Corp., Oracle Corp., Qualcomm, Inc., U.S. Army - Space and Terrestrial Communications Directorate, U.S.D.A. - National Finance Center, and Visa - Smart Cards.

John is certified by PMI as a Project Management Professional (PMP®) and an Agile Certified Practitioner (PMI-ACP®). He also holds Certified Scrum Master (CSM) and Certified Scrum Professional (CSP) designations from the Scrum Alliance, and an ITIL v3 Foundations certification.

Joe Montalbano, MBA, PMP, PMI-ACP, SASM, CSM

Joe has over 20 years of software development, integration, testing, maintenance, and operations experience. He has full-SDLC experience in enterprise, consulting, and startup environments where he has succeeded in roles such as Developer, Lead Developer, Solution Architect, Project Manager, Director of Software Development, Consultant, and Scrum Master.

Joe has spent the last 10 years developing and maintaining large financial and insurance applications at Zurich North America first, as a Senior Software Architect, and currently, as a Senior Application Development Manager.

He has successfully led Agile transformations and managed dozens of software development efforts using multiple onshore, offshore, distributed, and virtual development teams. Joe also has hands-on skills throughout the Microsoft technology stack.

In addition to his work at Zurich, Joe's clients include Battelle, Prometric, RDA Corporation, and several small, high-technology startups. Joe is a member of the PMI Baltimore Chapter, Scaled Agile Community, Scrum Alliance, and Agile Alliance.

Joe is certified by PMI as a Project Management Professional (PMP®) and Agile Certified Practitioner (PMI-ACP®); by Scaled Agile, Inc. as a SAFe Advanced Scrum Master (SASM), SAFe Agilist (SA), and SAFe Product Owner/Product Manager (POPM); designated by the Scrum Alliance as a Certified Scrum Master (CSM) and Certified Scrum Produce Owner (CSPO); and by Scrum.org as a Professional Scrum Master I & II (PSMI & PSMII), Professional Scrum Product Owner I (PSPOI), and Professional Scrum Developer (PSD). He also holds an ITIL v3 Foundation certification.

Joe has an MBA, with a focus in Information Technology, from Johns Hopkins University.

Diane Brady, PMP, PMP-ACP, CSM

Diane is an accomplished Agile mentor and instructor. She is also founder of ProALT Consulting, LLC., a coaching and consulting firm in the Pacific

Northwest. Her focus is on Lean and Agile coaching, training, and facilitation techniques for team development and engagement.

During her 19 years of management and consulting work in the Information Technology industry, she has provided expertise as a methodologist specializing in planning, analysis, systems integration, change management and deployment readiness. Her significant experience in Lean and Agile has been leveraged to help clients transform and improve their current systems. She has provided leadership in software implementation, development lifecycles, business process workflow, ERP system replacement and mergers, and has been instrumental in defining the best practices for the companies she has served.

In addition, she works directly with professionals to balance their professional and personal goals so they can lead rewarding and fulfilling lives.

A few of the organizations Diane has had the privilege to serve are Avalara, Glasstech, Hydro Resources, Nike, and Microsoft Corporation. She is currently an instructor for the PMI-ACP® Certification and is Past President of the PMI Portland Chapter. Diane is certified by PMI as a Project Management Professional (PMP®), and an Agile Certified Practitioner (PMI-ACP®). She also holds a Yellow Belt in Lean Leadership from the Liker Leadership Institute, is certified in Principles of Lean Thinking, and is a Certified ScrumMaster (CSM).

Mark Phillipy, PMP, PMI-ACP, CSM

Mark is the Founder of AmpVal, and known online as The Sensible Project Manager. Mark shares his knowledge and experiences about project management through his blogs at SensiblePM.com. He is also the host of The Sensible Project Manager Podcast.

Mark has been a Project Manager for 17+ years, leading teams using both Traditional and Agile project management methodologies. Much of his project management career has been in the IT arena, with a wide variety of projects including software development, system integration, hardware deployments, and IT construction. As Director of Project Management, he introduced Agile project management to two separate companies.

Beginning his career at The Boeing Company, he discovered his leadership capabilities, which led to his project management career at a variety of companies, including Getronics, Ambassadors, Nike, Avista, and Regency Blue Shield. He is currently the Director of Project Management and IT at Tedder Industries.

Mark is a member of PMI and has served as the Vice-President of Programs at the Inland Northwest PMI Chapter in Spokane, Washington. Mark has presented at the PMI Global Congress, and enjoys speaking at his local chapter and other organizations on a wide range of project management topics.

Mark is certified by PMI as a Project Management Professional (PMP®) and an Agile Certified Practitioner (PMI-ACP®). He also holds the Certified Scrum Master (CSM) designation from the Scrum Alliance. Mark graduated from Brigham Young University with a Bachelor of Science in Design Engineering Technology.

James Sperry, PMP, PMI-ACP, CSM, CSP, SPC4

James has considerable experience working with organizations in both Traditional and Agile project management models to increase their time to deliver, and focus on capacity and demand signals coming from good reporting and visualization. There is not one right way to work. The team will show their right way to deliver.

Companies he has worked with include Hewlett Packard, Hewlett Packard Enterprise, DXC Technology, Sony Electronics, & BusinessOnline.

James is a Past VP of Communications of the PMI – San Diego Chapter where he also served as the Annual Conference Co-Chair, PMP® and PMI-ACP® Instructor, and Professional Development course administrator, Webmaster, and Ambassador.

James is certified by PMI as a Project Management Professional (PMP®) and an Agile Certified Practitioner (PMI-ACP®). He also holds Certified Scrum Master (CSM) and Certified Scrum Professional (CSP) designations from the Scrum Alliance. He holds SAFe Program Consultant 4 (SPC4) and Scaled Agilest (SA) from Scaled Agile Framework.

James graduated from San Diego State University with Bachelor of Arts and Sciences in Communication.

Steven M. McGee Sr, PMP, PMI-ACP, CSP, SPC4, CSM, CDA, CHC, ITP, PAHM, ITIL

Steve is the Agile Practice Lead at Blue Cross Blue Shield of Louisiana.

Steven is a retired United States Air Force Officer where he served as a Communications / Computer Systems Engineer. He is a regular speaker at local universities and PMI chapters and conferences on the topic of Agile.

Steven is a successful technology leader with extensive experience in project management, enterprise data and systems development, and information technology service management. He has led multiple software development projects, from concept to deployment, with onshore and offshore teams, for both a departmental and global client base. Hc has worked through the evolution of Waterfall, spiral, iterative/incremental, timeboxed, and Agile project delivery methods, and managed large, highly-critical Data, Communications, and Air Traffic Control Centers. Steven has led several PMOs in Quality, Knowledge, and Risk Management, with Project Planning and Scheduling teams.

In addition to the Department of Defense, Steven has worked for MITRE, SAIC, Bearingpoint, SEA, AES, Space and Naval Warfare (SPAWAR) Information Technology Center, and Blue Cross Blue Shield of Louisiana.

He is a member of PMI , and the Scrum Alliance, Agile Alliance, Discipline Agile Consortium, and Scaled Agile Community. Steven also leads the Louisiana chapter of an international volunteer advocacy group, RESULTS, that lobbies for policies that will end poverty, both global and domestic.

Steven is certified by PMI as a Project Management Professional (PMP®) and an Agile Certified Practitioner (PMI-ACP®); designated as a Certified Scrum Master (CSM) and Certified Scrum Professional (CSP) by the Scrum Alliance; is a Scaled Agile Program Consultant (SPC4); a certified Disciplined Agilist (CDA); and holds an ITIL v3 Foundations certification. He is a Professional in the Academy of Healthcare Management(PAHM), and Certified Healthcare Consultant (CHC).

Steven graduated from Troy State University with a Bachelor of Science in Computer Science, and received a Graduate Certificate in Software Engineering from Central Michigan University.

Michael Williams, PMP, PMI-ACP

Michael is currently a senior consultant who helps companies integrate Project and Portfolio Management software into their workflow. He enjoys process modeling and training people in a PMO to find their own efficiencies. Over the past ten years, Michael has worked as a Project Manager, mainly in the utility and energy sector, where he managed both infrastructure and software projects using Agile methods.

Michael studied electrical engineering, music composition, and philosophy before settling down into a career in IT management. This led to consulting work, helping companies manage IT costs while still participating in the online, connected economy. It was during this time that he discovered and embraced project management as his next career choice.

Michael is a member of PMI and the local PMI Inland Northwest Chapter, where he volunteers diligently to avoid being nominated to the board. He is certified by PMI as a Project Management Professional (PMP®) and an Agile Certified Practitioner (PMI-ACP®), and holds many technical certifications outside of the project management sphere.

Guilherme Motta, CSM, CSP, SAFe SA, PSM I, ISQTB-CTFL

Guilherme, known as "Motta" to his friends, currently works as Technology Coordinator at Globo.com and Lecturer for the Post-Graduate degree in Agile Software Development at UniRitter Laureate Universities.

Guilherme has been working with Agile adoptions and transformations since before Agile Coach was a title. With a technical background, working towards building and creating better environments for individuals and teams to operate and grow, while promoting experiments based on previous experiences with Lean and software engineering practices.

Motta has helped companies structure and execute Agile transformation plans from the strategic level all the way to implementing them with individuals and teams. He studies, practices, and shares experiences in management and software development. He has worked with companies in retail, media, energy, and finance.

Currently, he is serving as Vice-President at Agile Alliance Brazil, volunteer organizer at Agile Brazil Conference, volunteer coordinator at The Developer's Conference, and a member of GUMA-RS, the local user group dedicated to discussing Agile Methods.

Motta is certified as a Certified Scrum Master (CSM) and Certified Scrum Professional (CSP) by the Scrum Alliance, PSM I by Scrum.org, and Certified Tester Foundation Level (CTFL) by International Software Testing Qualifications Board (ISTQB®). Motta graduated from Pontifícia Universidade Católica do Rio Grande do Sul with a Bachelor of Science in Information Systems and has an MBA from Fundação Getúlio Vargas (FGV) in Strategic IT Management.

Doug Martin, PMP, PMI-ACP, CSM, CSP, M.P.M.

Doug is a Project Manager for Carilion Clinic. At Carilion, he leads an enterprise project management Community of Practice and an Agile/Scrum Community of Practice. Doug has led enterprise-level projects for over ten years, spanning technical, administrative, and clinical systems implementations.

Doug is a member of the PMI Southwest Virginia Chapter. He is certified by PMI as a Project Management Professional (PMP®) and an Agile Certified Practitioner (PMI-ACP®). He also holds Certified Scrum Master (CSM) and Certified Scrum Professional (CSP) designations from the Scrum Alliance.

Doug graduated from American Graduate University with a Masters Degree in Project Management.

Nichole Tubiolo, PMP, PMI-ACP, CSM

Nichole is a Project Manager for M&T Bank in Buffalo NY, leading a digital banking Program team with a focus on mobile application development. She has led enterprise level projects for over eight years, spanning back-end upgrades to customer facing applications. Nichole is a freelance writer, trainer, and Agile coach in her spare time.

Nichole previously held the Director of Community Outreach position and is currently a member of the PMI Buffalo, NY Chapter. During her time as Director of Community Outreach, Nichole was responsible for running a Project Management for Non-profits Program to train, mentor, and design an e-toolbox of forms and templates on best practices in western New York charitable organizations. Nichole is a member of the Buffalo Junior League, a philanthropic organization committed to volunteerism, developing the potential of women, and improving the community through effective action and leadership.

Nichole is a certified by PMI as a Project Management Professional (PMP®) and Agile Certified Practitioner (PMI-ACP®). She also holds Certified Scrum Master (CSM) designation from the Scrum Alliance.

Nichole graduated from Empire State College with a Bachelor of Arts in Business Administration and Economics.

Diane McCann, Ph.D., MBA, PMP, PMI-ACP

Diane is an IT Integration Manager at Brenntag North America, Inc., and prior Director of Information Technology at Exide Technologies.

In addition, Diane is a Visiting Professor teaching courses in Project Management, e-Commerce, and Information Technology. A partial list of College and Universities includes: DeSales University (MBA Program), DeVry University, Penn State - Berks Campus, Albright College, and Cedar Crest College.

She is a member of the PMI Keystone, PA Chapter, past Director of Professional Development, and speaker coordinator for the Chapter's Professional Development Days.

Diane is certified by PMI as a Project Management Professional (PMP®) and an Agile Certified Practitioner (PMI-ACP®). Her Six Sigma Green Belt – Quality Assurance certification is from the University of Michigan College of Engineering.

Diane earned her Ph.D. in Applied Management & Decision Sciences with specialization in Information Systems Management at Walden University, Minneapolis, MN (Degree Conferred August 2013). Her dissertation title is, 'Managing Changes in Project Scope: The Role of the Project Constraints'. Diane earned her M.B.A. in Management and E-Commerce at DeSales University, Allentown, PA, and her B.S. in Business Administration, at Albright College, Reading, PA.

Rick A. Morris, PMP, CSM, M.P.M., OPM3, MCITP, MCTS, MCSE, TQM, ATM-S, ITIL

Rick A. Morris, PMP, is a Certified Scrum Agile Master, Human Behavior Consultant, best-selling author, mentor, and evangelist for project management. Rick is an accomplished project manager and public speaker. His appetite for knowledge and passion for the profession makes him an internationally sought-after speaker, delivering keynote presentations for large conferences and PMI events around the world.

He holds PMP® (Project Management Professional), MPM (Masters of Project Management), Scrum Agile Master, OPM3, Six Sigma Green Belt, MCITP, MCTS, MCSE, TQM, ATM-S, ITIL, and ISO certifications, and is an Executive Director for the John Maxwell Team. Rick is the Owner of R2 Consulting, LLC, and has worked for organizations such as GE, Xerox, and CA. He has consulted to numerous clients in a wide variety of industries, including financial services, entertainment, construction, non-profit, hospitality, pharmaceutical, retail, and manufacturing. Rick has over 100 implementations of Project and Portfolio Management systems.

He has authored three books; The Everything Project Management Book, 2nd Edition, Project Management That Works!, and Stop Playing Games!. His latest book, No Day But Today!, is an Amazon #1 best seller. Rick also appears weekly on his live radio show, "The Work/Life Balance", on the Voice America Business Network Fridays at 5 PM EST. Rick is no stranger to being center stage in front of large groups of people. At age 11, he was a Walt Disney World Performer in their seasonal shows. In high school, he worked at MGM Studios on various projects including the New Mickey Mouse Club.

Taking the experience of his youth and blending it with the knowledge he attained throughout his career, Rick has been able to inspire and mentor many Project Managers. His blend of real world experience and down to earth delivery style makes his passion for the profession contagious.

ABOUT THE PRODUCTION TEAM

About the Editor

Lauren Seybert Mix, President, LM Editing Co., has a unique background that makes her a gifted editor of technically sophisticated books. She works on selected projects where she feels her background can provide more than just spelling and grammar checks. The manuscripts she edits involve collaborations where her value as a neutral and independent expert adds to the competence of the author, assisting in the struggle to find the clearest, most accessible way to create maximum knowledge transfer for the reader.

A sample of texts Lauren has edited includes:

John G. Stenbeck's

Agile Almanac – Book 1

Agile Almanac – Book 2

PMI Agile Certified Practitioner (ACP®) Exam Preparation

Agile Almanac: Desk Reference and PM Field Guide

Agile Government Contracting

Rick A. Morris's

No Day But Today

Brian Rabon's

Scrum For the Rest of Us

In addition to editing, Lauren has over a decade of experience in the Oil and Gas, Energy, and Chemical industries in various roles, including Technical

Project Manager, Director of Business Development, and Senior Project Coordinator. Over the past 8 years she has mainly consulted with clients in Energy, assisting them with capital project financial analysis, maintenance trending and root-cause analysis, and budget and execution process streamlining. She regularly consults with Dominion Resources Services, carrying out statistical analysis of performance at 3 generating facilities, which is used to guide decisions when planning major outages. She has been a member of the Project Management Institute (PMI) since 2011.

A sample of clients Lauren has worked with includes: Dominion Resources Services (formally Dominion Power), Duke Energy, Fuel Cell Energy, DuPont Chemical, Valero, and Colonial Pipeline.

In her "spare" time, she enjoys caring for and playing with her 27 animals on her farm in New England.

Lauren's husband, Patrick, and daughter, Mallory, complete her.

Lauren Mix, Owner/President
LM Editing
(615) 815-7021
LMix7712@gmail.com

LM Editing

About the Graphic Designer

Over the last 25 years, Tamara Parsons, owner of KenType, has taken the natural gift of "an eye for graphics" and developed it into an unparalleled level of expertise in graphic design and print production.

Starting as a typographer in the printing industry, she applied passion and discipline to achieve mastery of the critical disciplines of type-setting, layout and the entire printing process. Again and again she impressed clients with unexpected insights in the production of logos, branding and identity packages, advertisements, and brochures. Time after time Tamara delivered high-impact customer value with "clean and clear" messages powerfully delivered.

As the KenType client list grew Tamara remained restless, driven to achieve constantly more for her clients. The result has been extensions of service lines as clients requested help with newsletters, books and more. And all of that effort on behalf of her clients has been rewarded by consistent, organic growth based on client referrals.

It was one of those referrals that brought Tamara and John Stenbeck together for his first book. Finding that they were both driven by a desire to constantly deliver amazing world-class results, an alliance rooted in mutual respect and trust was formed. With Tamara's unique skills both in graphic design, and as an organized multitasking maven, the Agile Almanac – Book 1 was both an Amazon #1 Best Seller and critically acclaimed. The current project, the Agile Almanac – Book 2, is forecast to exceed all previous books in her collaboration with John Stenbeck and his team of co-authors.

John has been quick to refer Tamara to his clients, saying her work burnishes his reputation! In fact, it was his idea – insistence really! – that this tribute be included in the Agile Almanac. He invites you to contact KenType and experience how much better your results could be!

Kensington Type & Graphics
(619) 281-1520 | tami@kentype.com

About the Illustrators and Photo Retouch Artist

We are grateful for the help and support of our illustrators and photo retouch artist. Please feel free to reach out to them.

Inkolla Graphics

Gian Luca Rigliano
Graphic Brilliance delivered with elegance, simplicity, passion and creativity (Bologna, Italy)

Facebook Page: inkolla graphic

https://www.flickr.com/photos/artgian-gianluca

Krikus Strip

Illustrator / Graphic Artist (Serbia)

www.fiverr.com/krikys

www.behance.net/krikusstri3d9f

Daniel Skarda

Photo Retouch Artist / Photographer / Graphic Designer (California, USA)

www.behance.net/danielskarda

GLOSSARY

Glossary

Acceptance Tests Driven-Development (ATDD) – Involves team members with different perspectives (customer, development, testing) collaborating to write acceptance tests in advance of implementing that corresponding functionality.

Actual Cost – For a program, project, or sub-project, or Roadmap, Release or Iteration, the total cost of all elements of development, up to a certain date, spent on the finished or in-progress work items.

Affinity Estimating – Compares work items to each other to assess their relative size.

Governance Meetings – Facilitate the Core Program Team need to have regular check-in meetings, typically weekly at the beginning of the Program, to review inter-project dependencies, risks, impediments, and development activities in order to confirm proper synchronization across the Program.

Agile Product Team – Continuously engaged, working a dynamically changing Backlog with no set timeline or budgetary constraint to continue.

Program Charter – Clearly and concisely articulate the over-arching strategic vision of the Program and details its Vision and boundaries.

Agile Program Earned Value Management (A-EVM Program) – Expands the foundation of Agile Earned Value Management through the addition of tools and techniques that manage the increased size and complexity of Agile Programs.

Incremental Cost Management (ICM) – Measures the forecasted spend to the actual cost over time to determine variance at a stated increment.

Agile Program Management – Advances the enterprise towards a state of competitive dominance known as perfection by creating an environment where every project, and every team, understands how its work aligns with True North and finds itself motivated to continually strive towards attaining it.

Agile Program Risk Management –The process of conducting risk management planning, identification, analysis, response planning, and controlling risk on Program.

Program Scorecard – Addresses how to optimize the whole organizational process from "Ideation" to delivery of "Customer Delight."

Agile Earned Value Management (A-EVM) – The Agile version of Earned Value Management (EVM).

Agile Project Management (APM) –Organizational cultures aligned with the values and principles of the Agile Manifesto using iterative, incremental approaches to develop and deliver value in products or services.

Agile Release Train (ART) – A set of cross-functional Agile teams that focus on Feature and Capability completion in a 10 week, 5 Sprint timebox.

Agile Stakeholder Management – Educating stakeholders about how an Agile Framework is different and what it involves, and how Lean principles interrelate.

Agile/Basic (Scrum-based) – A lifecycle of Disciplined Agile. An extension of Scrum with elements of the Rational Unified Process.

Annual Freeway Planning – When stakeholders, with a vested interest in strategic success, formalize the budgetary and resource commitments, creating the Freeways that connect and support the Roadmaps.

Application Lifecycle Management (ALM) – A term commonly used for addressing the end-to-end development process, which must be tailored to the project and organizational context.

Architecture Owner – Owns architecture decisions and is responsible for solution design.

ART Syncs – Stand-up style meetings where the Scrum Masters and Product Owners walk through the Program Kanban board to review the current WIP, groom future Features and Capabilities, and discuss any dependencies and impediments that may stop the ART from meeting its committed objectives.

Automated Tests – Test cases that run without human intervention and makes sure system code produces the expected output.

Backlog – A prioritized list of capabilities, features, and Stories to be completed during the Release or Iteration. See Product Backlog, Release Backlog, and Iteration Backlog.

Backlog Refinement – The process that prioritizes and clarifies Backlog items as they move from the long-term edge of the time horizon into a time horizon that is more near-term. Also referred to as Backlog Grooming.

Barely Sufficient – The practice of only doing the minimum necessary to delivery everything required and nothing that is not required. It is the balance point between insufficient and gold plating.

Behavior Driven-Development (BDD) – a synthesis and refinement of practices stemming from Test Driven Development (TDD) and Acceptance Test Driven Development (ATDD); embraces a broader view of requirements, from the user perspective, towards a desired outcome. Usually expressed in a Domain-specific language (DSL) very close to English, reducing the barriers for non-technical professionals to be able to read, understand, and run contexts and fixtures that represent user behaviors.

Big Room Planning – Sprint Planning with as many of the teams physically in the same room as possible to foster osmotic communication.

Build – A software development term that refers to a process in which source code files are converted into a final product and able to run on a computer.

Burn-down Chart – A chart with time indicated on the x-axis and showing the work remaining, based on the results of the team's daily meeting, compared to the baseline plan on the y-axis.

Burn-up Chart – A chart with time indicated on the x-axis and showing the work completed compared to the baseline plan for the project or release on the y-axis.

Capabilities – Logical groups of Features. Features, in turn, can be conceptualized as logical groups of User Stories; Epics, the largest group of functionality, and be conceptualized as logical groups of capabilities.

Card Status Radiator – Records and reports total card counts and percentages for the Total Kanban Cards on the Kanban Board; Total / Percentage of cards in the Backlog, Total / Percentage of In-Progress cards, Total / Percentage of Blocked cards, Total / Percent of Done cards.

Celebration Grid – Used to facilitate a session where team members examine practices and tools, look at failures as well as successes, and celebrate those failures that led to improved understanding and learning. Developed by Jurgen Appelo.

Centers of Excellence (CoE) – Groups with management support and direction, and one or more members collecting data, evaluating results, and framing up best practices.

Check Sheets – A document used to collect data in real-time; called a check sheet because it frequently uses tick marks or checks on the form to tally measures.

Chief Architect – Coordinate all the architects and unify technology decisions for an entire product; responsible for making technical decisions that affect all teams.

Chief Product Owner – Responsible for coordinating decisions and ensuring that communication happens so appropriate visibility is created.

Chief Scrum Master – Coordinates planning, manages cross-team dependencies, manages and track risks, and resolves or escalates blockers that have not been resolved at the team level.

Coach – Supports coachee(s) in reaching Agile/Lean skills and the culture and mindset required for the Agile transformation by providing training, advice, and guidance.

Communities of Practices (CoP) – An informal group of like-minded members that come together to share their experiences, learnings, and best practices around interdependent practices.

Configuration Management – Maintaining a robust version control system so that systems can be recovered quickly and reliably.

Continuous Delivery (CD) – The defined, repeatable, reliable process for releasing products.

Continuous Delivery: Agile – A lifecycle of Disciplined Agile. A Scrum-based strategy where the team releases into production every Sprint.

Continuous Delivery: Lean – A lifecycle of Disciplined Agile. Frequent continuous deliveries supported by DevOps practices.

Continuous Improvement – Incremental or disruptive changes to the design of the delivery process that increase efficiency, effectiveness and flexibility.

Continuous Integration – Emphasizes merging all developers' work to a shared repository several times a day.

Continuous Overlapping Phases – Applies the process groups continuously throughout the lifecycle to aggressively refine and improve both development and planning; the workflow continuously pulls work items from a prioritized Backlog.

Continuous Testing – Executing the automated test cases, at various stages of the build pipeline, to get the feedback as early as possible.

Control Charts – Graphically map measurements over time against an acceptable range of metric values at upper and lower control limits.

Core Program Team – Responsible for successful delivery of the Program; focus is cross-project collaboration and coordination.

Critical Path Method (CPM) – A tool, developed in the 1950's, for analyzing project schedules using an algorithm applied to interdependent activities.

Cross-functional Teams – A team of people, each with different functional expertise, working on a project and typically operating as a self-directing unit for decision-making.

Cumulative Flow Diagrams (CFD) – A graphical tool that shows work in progress, for a given time period and a given project, and can be used to reduce risk by identifying and correcting a workload imbalance creating a more effective and sustainable pace.

Customer-Value Logic Network (CVLN) – Categorizes the goals of the Program into major themes and validates that they tie into the Value Stream of the organization.

Cycle Time – A measure of process throughput, which is the time it takes work items to flow through the process, expressed as the average unit of time used per work item produced. See also Lead Time.

Daily Stand-up for Core Program Team – A Stand-up at the Program level; typically includes representatives from each project team reporting on progress and receiving information applicable to all teams.

Defined Granularity –The appropriate time boundaries for applying Rolling Wave decomposition to the requirements whether they are Epics and User Stories or Work Packages and Activities.

Delivery Pipeline –Models the continuous integration and release management process necessary to build, test, and deploy; Consists of various stages of the delivery process.

Development Team – A cross-functional group, in Scrum, that creates solutions by analyzing, designing, developing, testing, and implementing deliverables. It is assumed that it has all the needed skills, is highly trusted and self-managing.

Development to deployment – Cycle time from receiving a customer request to successfully deploying into production metric.

DevOps – A set of practices enterprises employ to plan, develop, test, and deploy working software or hardware into a production environment.

DevOps Toolchain – The constellation of tools deployed in a DevOps organization.

Disciplined Agile Delivery (DAD) – Part, and the foundation, of the Disciplined Agile Process Framework; addresses IT solution delivery as a whole to include an Agile lifecycle based on Scrum, a Lean lifecycle based on Kanban, and a lifecycle for continuous delivery.

Disciplined Agile Enterprise (DAE) – Part of the Disciplined Agile Process Framework; able to anticipate and respond swiftly to changes in the marketplace through an organizational culture and structure that facilitates change within the context of the situation that it faces.

Disciplined Agile IT (DAIT) – Part of the Disciplined Agile Process Framework; takes Agile and Lean strategies beyond development and balances enterprise architecture, data management, and portfolio management as well as IT governance.

Disciplined DevOps – Part of the Disciplined Agile Process Framework; combines and streamlines elements of security, data management, development, release management, IT operations, and business operations into a fluid cohesive whole.

DMAIC – The acronym for Define, Measure, Analyze, Improve, and Control.

Dot Voting – See Prioritize with Dots

Earned Value Management (EVM) – A program management technique integrating scope, schedule, and resource consumption information in order to measure project performance against planned cost metrics.

Enablers – Stories that set up the architectural runway for the teams.

Enterprise Resource Planning (ERP) – The practice reconciling the future plans of an organization with the ability of their employees to deliver on the future plans. In multi-team environments this can be surprisingly complicated.

Epic – A high-level Story expressing a feature or function to be developed, that is typically decomposed into smaller Stories as planning progresses. It fits into the commonly used Agile taxonomy of Theme, Epic, Story, and Task.

Epic Work Packages (EWPs) – The constituent elements of Feature, Function, Capability Milestones, produced by fracturing the FFC Milestones into smaller parts for planning and estimating purposes.

Escalation Plan – A set of transparent guidelines that can be actively worked by the project managers seeking guidance from the Program Manager. See also Impediment Plan.

Escaped defects – Any product deficiency that was not detected by testing and quality assurance processes and therefore escaped remediation before the product was delivered to the customer.

Execution Logic Network (ELN) – Determines how to maximize efficiencies.

Exploration Days – Teams suggest ideas for experiments and set aside time to develop the new ideas.

Exploratory (Lean Startup-based) – A lifecycle of Disciplined Agile; uses rapid build, deploy, and feedback cycles tested in the market; based on Lean Startup.

eXtreme Programming (XP) – A software engineering programmer-centric framework appling engineering techniques and practices with extreme rigor to create higher quality of software and support more responsiveness to customer needs.

Features – A function, requirement or component of the system being developed that provides value to the customer, and typically described in a Story.

Feature Toggle – A technique that allows for system behavior modification without changing or rolling-back packaged code; used as a safe technique to deploy or release un-finished features at production along with finished features and can hide whether they are "on" or "off" at runtime.

Fibonacci Sequence (Series) – A non-linear number series derived from the sum of two previous numbers and expressed in the equation Fn = Fn-1 + Fn-2. See also Planning Poker.

Fishbone Diagrams – See Ishikawa Diagram.

Fist of Five – A validation process used by the team to demonstrate individual support for a particular decision by holding up a hand and displaying fingers representing agreement; five fingers means I strongly agree, three means I can support it, and one means I am very concerned and opposed.

Fit for Purpose – A term used to describe a deliverable good enough to do the job it was designed to do.

Five Whys – A technique for determining the root cause of a failure or problem. Teams ask Why multiple times until they've reached the root cause.

Flexibility Matrix – A tool that communicates how to handle unavoidable tradeoffs via a grid showing the relative importance of constraints such as scope, schedule, cost, and quality by defining them as fixed, firm, or flexible; only one constraint may be fixed.

Float – The time difference between when an activity that is not on the critical path is scheduled for completion and the latest allowable time it can be completed without negatively impacting the finish of the Program.

Flow – The concept that the development and delivery of continuous value to customers is a process, similar to throughput in Lean manufacturing.

Flow Efficiency – Measures the actual work time spent against total elapse time from start to finish.

Frameworks – Context specific foundations created to support particular industries or activities.

Freeway Plan – An enterprise-level strategic plan that is updated on an annual or semi-annual basis in order to guide planning that flows down to CVLN and ELN planning as part of quarterly Roadmap planning and bi-monthly Release planning thereby organizing and harnessing enterprise-wide efforts to deliver the designated strategy.

Function Point Analysis (FPA) – An approach that defines a "unit of measurement" to express the amount of business a functionality in an information system provided in the perspective of a user.

Low-Tech, High-Touch – An approach that uses sticky notes, contact paper, and other paper-based tools to map out complex endeavors during the planning phase of determining a solution. The approach grants flexibility and drives interaction from participation in ways that a technology-driven process would not. Once the process or solution is solidified and accepted by the participants, it can be transferred to an electronic medium.

Histograms – Show the distribution of numerical data points.

Idea Transfer Rate – A measure of the processing bandwidth needed by a team simultaneously exploring and investigating multiple, often opposing possibilities in search of a synthesized solution that contains elements that improve each other in previously unconsidered ways.

Impediment and Escalation Forums – A set of transparent guidelines that can be actively worked by the Project Managers seeking guidance from the Program Manager. See also Escalation Plan.

Impediment Backlog – A prioritized list of obstacles that interfere with efficiently completing work.

Improvement Backlog – Used to record items teams identify that they can improve for future Sprints in their Sprint Retrospective and Integrated Program Retrospective.

Improvement Kata – A management approach that entails repeating a routine of establishing challenging target conditions, working through obstacles, learning from what is encountered, adjusting and meeting the targets, again and again.

Inception phase – An optional initial Iteration preceding the first standard development Iteration, where activities like acquiring needed technology, procuring team work space, or defining the product vision are done; precede and follow standard development Iterations, respectively, but typically do not include new development work. Also known as Iteration or Sprint 0, Hardening Iteration.

Independent Integrator - Specializes in providing and configuring the platform; works with the Project Team, under the watchful eye of the Program Manager and contracting authority, to ensure the system is ready and will not cause lag time for integration and product release; may be one or more people who assemble the subcomponents and subsystems into the overall solution and are responsible for constructing a cohesive solution that expresses an entire system, or a major portion of it, being released into production.

Inspect and Adapt – The ART comes together to assess its accomplishments and conduct a structured root cause analysis workshop of any problems it encountered.

Integrated Program Retrospective – Provides continuous process improvement opportunities to identify and expose issues, impediments, and areas for improvement across the Program.

Integrated Sprint Demo – The primary method for the team to show its work to the business and user communities and for the Product Owner to solicit feedback.

Integration Point Review (IPR) – Interfaces the Traditional Milestones and the Agile Iterations together for stakeholders to see and respond to solution deliverables and provide actionable-insight on the outcome; follows the Quarterly Release planning ceremony.

Integration Points – The points in a project or program plan where development by different teams are assembled into interim or final subassemblies that can be tested and/or demonstrated to show progress towards a defined goal. The various teams may be using the same or different development approaches so integration points create transparency into the actual alignment of teams progress compared to the planned level of progress.

Internal Rate of Return (IRR) – Measures of profitability of Features delivered that make it easy for executives and Program Managers to compare project performance and make funding decisions. See also Return on Investment (ROI).

Ishikawa Diagrams – Cause-and-effect diagrams created by Kaoru Ishikawa in 1968 commonly used to identify potential factors causing errors and imperfect output. The causes are typically grouped by categories, such as people, methods, machines, materials, measurements, and environment.

Iteration – A single cycle of development with a fixed-length that is not varied during the Release. Commonly the length is fixed at one to four weeks. It is the basic operational process used in Agile to deliver desired results in small increments. The standard Iteration typically delivers new development work that has been subjected to full quality assurance and user acceptance testing. It is begins with the Iteration Planning meeting and concludes with a Review meeting for interested stakeholders and a Retrospective meeting for the team. In Scrum it is called a Sprint.

Iteration-Based Phases – A sequence of Iterations utilizing a cadence of predictable, timeboxes to aid scheduling and the application of relevant project management processes.

ITTOs – Abbreviation for Inputs, Tools, Techniques, and Outputs.

Kaizen – Refers to incremental, continuous improvement of a process and originates in Lean Manufacturing.

Kaizen Events – A timeboxed event where key stakeholders, who understand the troubled Workflow, gather together to identify the process inefficiencies.

Kanban – A Lean manufacturing control or signaling system where needed inputs are produced based on actual usage being pulled by work centers. It can be contrasted with inputs being produced into inventories based forecasted usage and demand scheduling assumptions. It has been adapted to Agile project management as a framework for continuous-flow product development without strict iteration lengths.

Kanban Board – A physical board or virtual table showing a collection of Stories or Tasks represented by cards that are pulled through the development system within the boundaries of the scheduling process. They are often used to manage limits on work-in-process (WIP) and thereby increase development throughput.

Knowledge Workers – Persons who combine various forms of structured and unstructured data and use creative thinking to solve mostly non-routine problems.

Lead Time – A measure of elapsed time between "ideation and customer receipt." It is expressed as the unit of time between when the work item is made available for development and when it is delivered. See also Cycle Time.

Lean Budgets -SAFe Budget Management – A set of practices that minimize overhead by funding and empowering Value Streams rather than projects, while maintaining financial and fitness-for-use governance.

Lines of Communication – Refers to how many different two-person conversations are possible; formula of n(n-1)/2 can be used to calculate the number.

MBWA – Acronym for Management by Walking Around.

Mean Time To Recovery (MTTR) – Metric that measures the time it takes the team to recover from failure.

Meta Scrum Meeting –Meeting held weekly to resolve any escalated issues, review the Product Roadmap, make funding decisions, and set the direction for going forward and is attended by senior management and stakeholders. Also referred to as Management Scrum.

Milestone – A Traditional term that allows process checks for inception and transition.

Minimal Marketable Feature (MMF) – The smallest set of features that provide the level of functionality required to fulfill customer expectations

Minimal Viable Outcomes (MVO) – A derivation of the concept of a minimum viable product (MVP). Both MVO and MVP indicate a product with 'barely sufficient' array of features that minimize cost and risk will demonstrating the ability to satisfy customers while providing access to feedback that guides future product development. Typically and MVO or MVP can be decomposed into Minimal Marketable Features (MMF) that can be sued to guide and govern development.

Net Present Value of Features Delivered – A measure of the current value of the future cash streams expected to be realized by Features delivered.

New customers obtained – A measure of the number of new customers that have been, or are expected to be, secured by development of the completed Features.

Non-value Added – A Lean term for any work that does not add value as defined by the customer, which is a type of waste and slows the delivery of business value.

Optimize the Whole – A guiding Lean principle; analyzes the Value Stream back from the future, keeping the Program goal and Vision ahead of individual Features.

Pair Programming – A practice used in eXtreme Programming (XP) where two programmers work together, typically on one computer. The first programmer types in code while the second programmer reviews each line of code as it is written. The first programmer is called the driver. The second programmer is called the observer or navigator. They switch roles frequently

Pareto Analysis – An analysis used to find the most impactful issues affecting the team.

Pareto Diagram – A bar chart that aids determining which problem should be worked first to improve a process. The problem with the greatest percentage of impact on quality is worked first. Once the changes are implemented, data is gathered and analyzed again and a new leading cause of quality problems are identified and addressed.

Personal Safety – Occurs when team members feel support during the unavoidable productive tension and respectful disagreements that accompany developing solutions.

Phase Chart – A tool that describes each phase (in high-level components) in the workflow, which group or role has activities in each phase, the desired outcome of each phase, the deliverables expected each phase, typical time for each phase.

Phase Task Chart – Consists of the repeatable Tasks (or Stories) that should be included in each phase of the PDLC.

PI – Acronym for Program Increment.

PI Objectives – The culmination of the PI Planning Event.

PI Planning Event – A two-day planning meeting where the business expresses the Business Context, Solution Intent, and Architectural Vision for the proposed Features.

Plan-Do-Check-Act (PDCA) Cycle – The planning cycle taught by W. Edwards Deming as central to Lean manufacturing.

Planned vs. Actual Story Points – A metric to track the accuracy of Sprint Planning and estimating.

Planning Poker – A consensus-based estimating technique commonly used by Agile teams that employs a simplified Delphi technique approach to estimate the relative size of Stories. A Fibonacci sequence is commonly used to establish the range of numbers applied.

Portfolio Management – Practices and techniques for making decisions about investment choices to align them with organizational objectives so that resource allocations balance risk and desired performance.

Prioritize with Dots – A tool used by the Team to prioritize lists so they can focus on the top ideas, issues, or opportunities. Voting with dots is not intended to be scientific. It is used after activities to generate insights as a tool to narrow a list of choices.

Process Goal Diagram – Combines the notation standard for graphing with the strong Disciplined Agile approach and can be used in tailoring a process to assure effective and efficient use of IT in enabling organization goals.

Process Tailoring Workshop – Where the team reviews the process goals and decides how they intend to work.

Product Backlog – A prioritized collection of short descriptions of features, functions and capabilities included in the solution being developed. It is similar to the specification list used in Traditional project management.

Product Backlog Items (PBIs) – Lists of items identified as targets for process improvement from Sprint Retrospectives.

Product Development Lifecycle (PDLC) – Documents the repeatable workflow using four phases - Envision - Product Development - Product Launch - Post Launch.

Product Family – A high-level diagram that presents a major process, service, or large function.

Product Manager – Has overall ownership of the Product Vision and Roadmap; work closely with sales, marketing, finance, and executives to constantly ensure their Product Vision and Roadmap are in line with corporate strategy; manage dependencies and communications with outside departments, attend trade shows, and stay up-to-date with market trends and competition.

Product Owner – Primarily responsible for making decisions about product functionality, acceptance criteria, and assigning business value to Product Backlog items; answer questions from the Development Team, solicit feedback from users, and act as the voice of the customer; responsible to the business for ensuring that the team is always working on the items with the highest value.

Product Roadmap – An artifact that shows the strategic development path a product is intended to follow, including what specific features it will contain, in broad strokes, at given future release points.

Product Team Gatherings - Integrate the assessments from the Product Review Meetings with the Roadmap, Program Backlog, Epic Work Packages (EWPs), and even significant User Stories from individual projects to create a "compiled" view of the Program as a unified body of work.

Program – A group of related projects managed in a coordinated way to obtain benefits and control not available from managing them individually.

Program Coordinator – Manages day-to-day budget tracking, progress reporting, and Backlog synchronization as directed by the Program Manager.

Program Dependencies Radiator – Displays inter-project or inter-team dependencies that are expected to have significant impact on the Program should they fail to be executed in the right sequence or at the right time.

Program Executive Status Report – Presents the tightly focused, high-level status information executives tend to prefer.

Program Manager – Manages the overall Program budget, has authority to make budgetary decisions, hires and manages the Core Team resources, sets and manages high-level Program Vision and expectations, reports Program status at the executive and leadership levels, creates the Program Charter, Roadmap, and Backlog, and is responsible for delivering the Program outcome successfully.

Program Risks Radiator – A graph that includes data from multiple teams and uses an Agile risk game approach for risk identification and assessment; inspired by Mike Griffith's presentation at the 2006 Agile Conference.

Program Roadmap – A simple, at a glance, one-page radiator of all Program components.

Program Specialist – Manages specific program elements, such as cross-program architecture, cross-program engineering and quality practices, or feature driven components, as directed by the Program Manager.

Program Steering Meeting – Presented jointly by the Program and Product Managers to review every in-flight project, validate their alignment to the strategic goals of the Program.

Progressive Elaboration – The Agile process of refining the product vision so that the high priority features are developed and the waste of developing unneeded or low priority features is avoided.

Quarterly Release Planning – Sessions that deliver results as ELNs focused on driving program efficiencies.

RACI – An acronym for responsible, accountable, consult, and inform as used in a responsibility assignment matrix (RAM).

Rational Unified Process – A software development process defined by Rational, a division of IBM. The process has four distinct phases with business modeling, analysis and design, implementation, testing, and deployment. The phases are Inception, Elaboration, Construction and Transition.

Readiness Workbook – A preparation artifact that aggregates all the pertinent information needed to run a successful PI Planning Event.

Refactoring – The process where a programming tool makes changes to the code that do not modify its functionality, but improve attributes like readability, simplicity, and extensibility, and also improve compliance with architecture or object model standards.

Release – A logical, deployable set of product functionality developed over the course of multiple iterations. Releases may be defined as internal, incremental or final. A final release indicates it is ready for deployment to customers and end users.

Release Train Engineer – Facilitates Program Ceremonies, including Pre- and Post-PI Planning, PI Planning Event, Scrum of Scrums, Program Council, and PO Synchronization; tracks and escalates impediments affecting the ART delivery; coach Program leaders, Scrum Masters, Product Owners, and Agile Teams on the Lean-Agile practices and mindset; monitors PI execution and reports against the metrics in the information radiators. A role in SAFe.

Retained customers – A measurement of the estimated number of customers who have not left because a completed Feature was developed.

Risk – An uncertain event or condition that, if it occurs, has a positive or negative effect on one or more project objectives.

Risk Plan – A working agreement of how the team will operate when risk arises.

Risk Response – Another phrase for Risk Plan.

Roadmap – A planning tool used to align Agile's short development cycles with a desired future business result. They are equivalent to a Traditional portfolio plan.

Rolling Wave Planning – The process of planning projects where multiple passes (i.e., waves) decompose the work required with increasing levels of detail. Work in the near term has been subjected to more iterations of refinement so they include greater detail, whereas work in the future has lower granularity because it has gone through less decomposition.

ROM – Rough Order of Magnitude

SAFe House of Lean – describes the Lean focus in the Lean-Agile mindset; a set of six constructs describing the frames, actions, and behaviors of SAFe teams.

Scatter Diagrams – A chart that shows the relationship between two quantitative variables to determine if there is a correlation between the captured values; a quick checkpoint to determine if there is a relationship between two captured metrics.

Schedule Baseline – The total number of planned iterations multiplied by iteration length.

Scope Creep – The continually increasing requests for changes to the initially defined Program scope.

Scrum – A project management framework developed by Jeff Sutherland and Ken Schwaber that uses an iterative and incremental process to produce a potentially shippable set of functionality during the iteration.

Scrum of Scrums (SoS) – a highly customizable, lightweight proto-framework for scaling Scrum

Scrum of Scrum of Scrums (SoSoS) – Scales the SoS meeting when the lines of communication grows past nine; includes representatives from SoS meetings.

Scrum of Scrums Meeting – focuses on removing cross-team blockers and managing dependencies.

Scrum Team – A group in Scrum that has three members – Product Owner, Scrum Master and Development Team.

Semi-Annual Roadmap Planning – Where choices that drive effectiveness are integrated with those that maximize efficiencies.

Sequential Iteration-Based Phases – Projects are delivered with a sequence of Iterations utilizing a cadence of predictable timeboxes to aid scheduling and the application of relevant project management processes.

Servant Leadership – A philosophy that emphasizes awareness, listening, and persuasion as the path to creating value.

Seven Fundamental Principles in DAD – Delight Customers, Be Awesome, Pragmatism, Context Counts, Choice is Good, Optimize Workflow, and Enterprise Awareness.

Shift Left – Doing things earlier in the process.

Software Development Context Framework (SDCF) – Provides a situation dependent strategy for organizing people, process, and tools for a software-based solution delivery team.

Spike – A short experiment or Task carried out to gain knowledge so that estimating and planning can be based on data instead of purely hypothetical assumptions, and where the result is typically intended to be discarded. The goal of a spike is to solve a difficult technical problem or to learn enough to posit how to solve it.

Sprint Retrospective Meeting – A process-centric meeting where the Team identifies how it can improve its development process.

Story – A tool, device or technique used to capture a description of important functionality considered valuable to the customer or user of the solution being developed. Can be a Feature Story or User Story depending on the level of detail it includes.

Stratification Charts – A chart that pulls in data collection points from different sources to determine if there are patterns or relationships between those sources.

SWAG – Abbreviation for Scientific Wild Ass Guess (WAG).

System Architect – Develops and communicates the high-level architecture of the System so that the team can have an accurate Vision during development.

System Demo – Shows the progress of the integrated team work to the stakeholders.

System Team – A special team in the ART dynamic; works directly on the ART as a collaborator, bringing multiple teams' work together to form the system.

Tech stack – The set of languages, Frameworks, software, subsystems, modules, or components needed to create a complete platform or solution; applications are often said to "run on" or "run on top of" the resulting platform.

Test Driven Development (TDD) – A process where the tests are written before any code is written. The test is run before any code is written and, of course, it fails. The developers then code and test until the test passes.

Throughput – The number of cards completed during a specific timeframe.

Timebox – Work periods used to manage product development cycles in Agile project management. Examples include Iterations that are fixed-length timeboxes and Releases and Roadmaps that are variable-length timeboxes.

Toyota Production System (TPS) – The widely respected process that organizes manufacturing, logistics, and relationships with suppliers and customers at Toyota and emphasizes improving the value and flow product delivery by eliminating waste.

True North – A Lean term originating from the Toyota Production System (TPS) describing the ideal that will create the most customer value and therefore the highest level of organizational success.

Trunk Based Development (TBD) – A branching strategy where all code is committed to a single branch, referred to as the trunk, with developers making frequent check-ins.

T-Shirt Sizes – An estimation method used by Agile teams, usually on larger Product Backlog items; sizes are XS, S, M, L, XL.

User Experience (UX) – Refers to user emotions and attitudes when using a particular product, system, or service; includes the practical, experiential, affective, meaningful, and valuable aspects of human–computer interaction and product ownership.

Value Stream – The flow of materials and information required to deliver a product or service that the customer values.

Value Stream Mapping – A Lean manufacturing process developed to improve the production flow that delivers value to the customer by analyzing, and potentially redesigning how raw materials are turned into finished goods so the process delivers more value without sacrificing future opportunities.

Velocity – The number of Story points that a team is able to achieve within the defined Iteration version control.

Vision – A high-level statement of what need the product will fill and who its consumers will be.

WAG – Abbreviation for Wild Ass Guess.

Weighted Shortest Job First (WSJF) – A process to prioritize the Program work items using a calculation to identify the highest priority work.

Whole System Thinking – The concept that not only is the software that is being built a system, but the organization building it is also a system. Systems Thinking seeks to optimize the whole system, not just some sub-components.

WIP Limit – A tool for managing development bottlenecks by aligning the amount of WIP to the system's capacity, thereby creating planning options, accelerating throughput, and clarifying focus with transparency throughout the production cycle.

Work Decomposition Structure (WDS) – Senior leaders define the composition and priorities of the Portfolio and organizational governance guides the process of defining product deliverables.

Workflow Efficiency – A process used to gauge efficiencies in the development process - usually Work Not Started -WIP - Work Complete.

Work-in-Progress (WIP) – A Lean manufacturing concept developed to manage unfinished items in the production because, by definition, they produce no value until they are finished. In Agile, the WIP concept is used in Kanban-type continuous-flow development environments.

INDEX

Agile Almanac - Book 2 Index